NATO

— AND THE —

UN

NATO

— AND THE —

UN

A Peculiar Relationship

Lawrence S. Kaplan

University of Missouri Press
Columbia and London

Copyright © 2010 by
The Curators of the University of Missouri
University of Missouri Press, Columbia, Missouri 65201
Printed and bound in the United States of America
All rights reserved
5 4 3 2 1   14 13 12 11 10

Library of Congress Cataloging-in-Publication Data

Kaplan, Lawrence S.
  NATO and the UN : a peculiar relationship / Lawrence S. Kaplan.
     p. cm.
  Includes bibliographical references and index.
  ISBN 978–0–8262–1883–4 (cloth edition : alk. paper)
  ISBN 978–0–8262–1895–7 (pbk. : alk. paper)
  1. North Atlantic Treaty Organization. 2. United Nations. 3. World politics—1945–1989. 4.
World politics—1989– I. Title.
  JZ5930.K36 2010
  341.23—dc22

                                                                        2009040743

∞™ This paper meets the requirements of the
American National Standard for Permanence of Paper
for Printed Library Materials, Z39.48, 1984.

Designer: Stephanie Foley
Typesetter: FoleyDesign
Printer and binder: Integrated Book Technology, Inc.
Typeface: Adobe Garamond

to Jan

CONTENTS

ACKNOWLEDGMENTS

Robert H. Ferrell, whose friendship I have cherished for sixty years, introduced me to Beverly Jarrett, director and editor-in-chief of the University of Missouri Press, in the summer of 2006. He urged me to work with her on this project. Her enthusiasm required little urging on my part, and I enjoyed her support until her unexpected retirement in 2008. Clair Willcox took over the assignment and, along with project editor John Brenner, has seen the manuscript through to completion. I am grateful for their support, and to Bob in bringing me to the Press in the first place. In the course of research and writing I am indebted to those scholars whom I mention in the introduction, and most particularly to Ryan Hendrickson, who read and commented on a number of the chapters; to Alan Henrikson, whose pioneer studies of NATO and the UN were an inspiration for me; to Gary Ostrower, the leading American historian of the UN; and to David Yost, whose special expertise in this subject was of great help. From Brussels, prominent NATO officials Jamie Shea and Diego A. Ruiz Palmer responded to basic questions I had about NATO's relations with the UN. And a special note of thanks goes to W. Bruce Weinrod, defense advisor, U.S. Mission to NATO, for informing me about the UN-NATO declaration of September 23, 2008.

I am happy to acknowledge the continued cooperation of Georgetown's documents librarian Kristina Bobé, whose familiarity with the documents facilitated my studies. Her colleagues at the reference desk, especially Mary Bowen and Maura Seale, responded with unfailing good cheer to my many importunities. Steve Rearden, Stanley Bober, and Morris Honick offered advice and support at all times. And finally, I dedicate this book to my wife, Janice, whose patience I have tried too many times over the years.

LIST OF ABBREVIATIONS

ACTWARN	activation warning
AFSOUTH	Allied Forces, Southern Europe
ANC	Armée Nationale Congolaise (originally Africanization of the Force Publique)
CIA	Central Intelligence Agency
CJTF	Combined Joint Task Forces
CSCE	Committee for Security and Cooperation in Europe
DPC	Defense Planning Committee
DPO	Department of Peacekeeping Operations
DRV	Democratic Republic of Vietnam (North Vietnam)
EC	European Community
EEC	European Economic Community
EU	European Union
EUFOR	European Union Forces
FO	British Foreign Office
FRUS	*Foreign Relations of the United States*
GVN	Government of the Republic of Vietnam (South Vietnam)
IFOR	Implementation Force
IPTF	UN International Police Task Force
ISAF	International Security Assistance Force
JNA	Yugoslav People's Army
KFOR	Allied Occupation Force in Kosovo
KLA	Kosovo Liberation Army (radical)
LDK	Democratic League of Kosovo (moderate)
MSC	Military Staff Committee
NAC	North Atlantic Council
NACC	North Atlantic Cooperation Council
NARA	National Archives and Records Administration, College Park, Maryland

NLF	National Liberation Front (the Vietcong)
NSC	National Security Council
ONUC	Opérations des Nations Unies au Congo
OSCE	Organization of Security and Cooperation in Europe
PRO	Public Record Office, Kew, England
RPR	Rassemblement Pour la République
SACEUR	Supreme Allied Commander, Europe
SALT II	Strategic Arms Limitation Talks
SCUA	Suez Canal Users Association
SFOR	Stabilization Force
SHAPE	Supreme Headquarters Allied Powers, Europe
SPRSKA	Serb Republika Sprska
SR	Senate resolution
SS	*Schutzstaffel,* a unit of Nazi intelligence forces, initially Hitler's bodyguard
TNA	The National Archives, Kew, England
UNAMA	UN Assistance Mission in Afghanistan
UNAMI	UN Assistance Mission in Iraq
UNEF	United Nations Emergency Force
UNHCR	UN High Commissioner for Refugees
UNMIBH	UN Mission in Bosnia and Herzegovina
UNMIK	UN Interim Administration Mission in Kosovo
UNPROFOR	United Nations Protective Force
UNSC	UN Security Council
UNSCR	UN Security Council Resolution
USSR	Union of Soviet Socialist Republics
WEU	Western European Union
WMDs	weapons of mass destruction
WU	Western Union

NATO

— AND THE —

UN

INTRODUCTION

Nature of the Relationship

There is no more contentious subject in the history of the North Atlantic Treaty Organization (NATO) than its relationship with the United Nations (UN). Granted, NATO's efforts were devoted primarily to coping with the Soviet empire and communist expansion during the Cold War. Involvement with the UN was not the focus of NATO's or the United States' attention in those years. Although the UN inevitably was present at NATO's creation in 1949, over the next forty years for the most part NATO went its own way. When their paths did cross, it was rarely an amicable connection. The UN repeatedly asserted its ultimate authority over an indifferent or often hostile NATO. Yet at critical moments in the Cold War, the UN served as an arena for NATO partners to work out their differences, as in the Suez crisis in 1956, and NATO served as an enforcer in support of UN peacekeepers, as in the Congo civil war in the early 1960s.

When the Soviet empire imploded in 1991 there was a dramatic change in the relationship, which brought the two organizations closer together. Sometimes in harmony but often in discord, they collaborated in efforts to manage global crises in unstable environments. As NATO enlarged its scope in the 1990s, it needed the UN to give legitimacy to its activities even as it chafed against the claims of the world organization. Internal frictions within NATO frequently inhibited its efforts to function independently of the UN, as in the Balkans Wars of that decade, and in the unilateral actions of the United States in the twenty-first century.

The war against Iraq since 2003 and the ongoing war against the Taliban in Afghanistan since 2001 have tested NATO's ability to collaborate with the UN in the management of crises. In Iraq both organizations initially played minor roles as a consequence of the U.S. decision to overthrow Saddam Hussein. Yet as Iraq descended into chaos, both the UN and NATO agreed to provide modest support for reconstruction of the country, and the United States retreated from its unilateral stance. More prominent was the presence of both organizations alongside the United States in the war against the Taliban forces in Afghanistan that generated terrorist actions against the West. Here too the unilateral U.S. control

1

of operations in 2001 yielded to the UN, legitimizing NATO and U.S. efforts to defeat common adversaries. While questions of ultimate authority have not been settled, NATO is no longer simply a regional organization (as the UN has periodically proclaimed), and the UN is no longer an irrelevance (as NATO has identified it in the past). A symbiotic relationship between the two organizations prevails at this time (2009) in such a critical area as Afghanistan.

From the very beginnings of the Atlantic alliance the United Nations occupied a prominent place in NATO's perception of its role in the world. The initial inspiration for the transatlantic alliance itself was the product of the UN's difficulties in fulfilling its obligation to provide the security its framers had anticipated. The Soviet Union's repeated use of the veto in the UN Security Council, where unanimity among the victors in World War II was written into the UN Charter, frustrated the Western powers. The division between East and West had been evident since the Yalta agreements in 1945, and it was only through the veto that the Soviet Union as a seeming permanent minority in the organization could find its voice. The three votes in the General Assembly held by the Union of Soviet Socialist Republics (USSR), the Ukraine, and Belorussia, combined with the few East European countries within the Soviet orbit, were vastly outnumbered by those UN members in the Western camp. While the United States had only one vote in the General Assembly, this was by choice; there was no need in 1945 to accept the three seats allotted in the Yalta agreements.

The North Atlantic Treaty Organization was created in order to circumvent the veto power of the Soviet Union, with the expectation that its creation would invigorate the world organization. NATO was intended to protect its members within the provenance of the charter but outside the veto challenge of the communist adversary. When the USSR—along with many American supporters of the UN—judged the alliance to be a threat to the integrity of the UN, the Truman administration was forced to spend time and energy to defend its assertion of the treaty's compatibility with the charter. The case was argued in the UN's General Assembly in April 1949 where the Soviet bloc pilloried the West for subverting the charter. Just as vigorously, U.S. opponents of the alliance at hearings before the U.S. Senate Foreign Relations Committee later in the month condemned the treaty as a return to the discredited balance-of-power politics that had led to World War II. So, less than a month after the signing of the North Atlantic Treaty, the alliance was embroiled in conflict both at the UN and in the U.S. Senate. Such was the inauspicious beginning of a long relationship between NATO and the UN.

The uneasy entanglement of NATO with the UN persisted throughout the Cold War, and beyond. The problems that arose in the Cold War years were not always a confrontation between the terms of the treaty and those of the charter. The enlarging United Nations grew threefold in those years, with new members drawn primarily from nations from what was to be called the Third World, Asia and Africa.

Many resented the power of the Atlantic allies, and particularly the power of its senior partner, the United States. NATO's communist opponent exploited the new nations' grievances against former colonial masters and included the United States as the heir, if not the sponsor, of European imperialism.

The NATO alliance fought back, with the UN General Assembly serving as an arena for counterattacks against Soviet calumnies. At one time or another, often at the same time, both antagonists used the UN to advance their respective agendas. The question of the relationship between NATO and the UN was further muddled when the UN was the scene not only for displaying Soviet-American and Warsaw Pact–NATO rivalries but also for divisions within NATO itself. The Soviets invariably leaped into the fray to enlarge whatever differences existed among the Western allies.

The end of the Cold War, however, did not push either NATO or the UN into the background. New crises developed immediately, even if they lacked the magnitude of those during the Cold War. The result was a new prominence for NATO, as the only organization with impressive military capabilities, and for the UN, as a forum where actions could be taken without the constant threat of automatic vetoes hanging over the proceedings. In the eighteen years since the communist empire collapsed, the UN has played a more significant and often a more positive role in NATO's history. Still, there continued underlying tensions between the two organizations—and within NATO itself—that focused on positions taken by the United States.

The Historiographical Challenge

While there have been numerous articles and essays connecting NATO with the UN, there has been no book-length monograph covering the span of two generations from 1949 to the present. This study is an effort to fill this gap. The subject has been on my mind for a generation. In 1969 I wrote a brief essay, "The United States, the NATO Treaty, and the UN," in the May 1969 issue of the *NATO Letter* (the predecessor of the *NATO Review*). I have drawn on this article for Chapter 1. A generation later, for a conference in Germany on NATO's first fifty years, I wrote a survey of NATO's relations with the UN in the journal *Contemporary European History*. I am using the same title for this larger study.[1] When teaching at the University of Leuven as a Fulbright lecturer in 1964, I examined the origins of the Congo crisis in an article "The United States, NATO, and the Congo Crisis of 1969." This article is incorporated into Chapter 3.[2]

In the early years of both organizations, political scientists Francis O. Wilcox of Johns Hopkins University and Lincoln Bloomfield of MIT attempted to show the basic compatibility not only between NATO and the UN but also between them and U.S. foreign policy.[3] These scholars saw the two organizations as partners seeking to maintain peace in a volatile world. The Cold War's long tenure seemed to have discouraged efforts to rationalize the relationship, and the paucity of literature in this area attests to the pessimism of that era. A rare example of an analysis of NATO-UN connections in those years was by Irish diplomat Conor Cruise O'Brien who was recounting his own experiences as a mediator in a war involving Western European powers, the Soviet Union, and the new state of Congo.[4] Memoirs of UN officials did mention NATO but only peripherally in those years.

The post–Cold War era afforded opportunities for journalists and policy-makers as well as political scientists and historians to look specifically at NATO-UN relations during the Gulf War of 1991 and the Balkan Wars of 1995 and 1999. Important examples are by Mats Berdal, Dick Leurdijk, Mark A. Bucknam, and Tim Ripley.[5] It is noteworthy that these able studies are all narrowly defined, dealing with special cases without generalizing about the long-term significance of the relationship between the two organizations. An exception is an insightful essay, "NATO and the UN: Toward a Nonallergic Relationship," by Alan K. Henrikson, who found enough elements in their common history to feel optimistic about their future. Henrikson continued to find a positive outcome in the NATO-UN relationship during the Kosovo crisis in 1999.[6]

Gustav Schmidt made an effort to highlight the UN role in his monumental edited three-volume *History of NATO: The First Fifty Years.* Two important chapters in the UN segment of Volume 1 were by Hall Gardner and Jack Granatstein. Gardner's essay focused on contemporary issues, not those of the past, and Granatstein's chapter is essentially an introductory sketch. Granatstein, a leading Canadian scholar, expressed the perceptions of most analysts (with the prominent exception of Henrikson) when he observed that until the 1990s "NATO and the UN, while not wholly separate and certainly not wholly equal, were different organizations, each operating in its own sphere, not ordinarily congruent nor in opposition."[7] He was correct, of course. They are two separate organizations, but before as well as after the end of the Cold War there was an increasing overlap between the UN's essential function of peacekeeping and NATO's concentration on defense against Soviet aggression in Europe and later on managing military crises on a global scale.

David S. Yost has provided a new assessment of NATO-UN relations in his survey "NATO and International Organizations."[8] He gave pride of place to NATO over the European Union (EU) and the Organization for Security and Cooperation in Europe (OSCE). Ryan C. Hendrickson and Kent J. Kille have produced the most recent examination of the subject in addressing the interaction of the secretaries-general of NATO and the UN, particularly in the Kosovo crisis of 1999. Their paper, "Leadership at the United Nations and NATO: A Comparative Analysis of Conflict Engagement by the Secretaries-General," was delivered at the annual meeting of the International Studies Association in New York City, February 15–18, 2009, and is worthy of publication in a major journal.

This study has a different point of view and a different objective. It will document the many interactions between NATO and the UN in their interconnected history. I propose to build the manuscript around the major flashpoints where either NATO clashed with the UN leadership, or the United States and the Soviet Union confronted each other directly, or fissures within the Atlantic alliance were dramatized in UN sessions at the Security Council or the General Assembly.

There are ample source materials for this project. Key documents include official records of the UN General Assembly, which are published. The records of the UN Security Council in the Dag Hammarskjöld Library in New York are available online. The annual volumes of the *Yearbook of the United Nations* contain the major documents, as well as commentaries on resolutions of the Security Council and General Assembly. NATO communiqués are purposely elliptical but are useful for illuminating connections with the UN. The *Foreign Relations* series of the U.S. State Department covers volumes dealing specifically with NATO and the UN, while congressional hearings in the House and Senate along with the *Congressional Record* offer a legislative perspective on the many issues in this project.

Similar government documents of other NATO members are also important for this project. Newspapers of record, such as the *New York Times, Times* (London), and *Le Monde,* carry articles and editorial commentaries pertinent to this study. Other primary materials will be found in unpublished files, such as those in the National Archives in College Park, Maryland, and its counterparts in Britain, France, and Germany. Memoirs and diaries of major figures in the UN, NATO, and national foreign offices are available in abundance. I have used oral histories of key actors and correspondence with officials on critical questions. Much of the secondary literature—either in articles or book-length monographs touching on the links between NATO and the UN—is marginal, but some of these sources may supply interesting insights.

The relationship between the two organizations has changed over the course of two generations. The distant connections of the Cold War years are permanently gone. What remains constant from the beginning is the UN presence as the scene where NATO problems were on display, from Suez in 1956 to Afghanistan in 1980, to Iraq and Afghanistan again in the twenty-first century. That NATO could be an instrument serving the common goals was also demonstrated in the Bosnian crises of the 1990s. Crisis management has been a source of conflict between NATO and the UN in the past, but it has also served as an incentive for collaboration. How this peculiar but persistent relationship has functioned since 1949 is the subject of this book.

1

Treaty versus Charter, 1949

The Setting

Like the League of Nations Covenant, the United Nations Charter rested on the assumption that its purpose was to create a new world order. The UN's goal in a sense was less ambitious; it had no illusions about banishing warfare in the future. But like its ill-fated predecessor, the UN was based on a putative consensus among the great powers that would assure the collective security of all its members. There was even Article 47, which established a Military Staff Committee (MSC) that would help the UN Security Council maintain order in the postwar world. Although the presence of the United States and the Soviet Union in the creation of the UN gave the new organization a greater chance for success than the failed League of Nations in 1919, the developing Cold War after 1945 seemed to make the UN as much a failure as the league had been.

What differentiated the UN from the league in the Cold War world was the initiative of the United States and its Western partners to enable the new organization to fulfill its goal of preventing future wars and settling international disputes by peaceful means. The Western powers were fearful of the rising communist threat that could not be contained within the UN. The veto powers invested in the great powers, the victors of World War II, gave the Soviet Union the instrument to frustrate the will of the vast majority of members. To avoid the veto, the United States and its allies devised an alliance, which, they asserted, conformed to the letter and spirit of the charter yet would allow the collective defense of its members without the interference of the Soviet adversary.

Was compatibility between treaty and charter possible? It required an exercise in casuistry to fit the two documents together—and an element of hypocrisy. The United States no more than its rival had any intention of giving up its veto power, or of allowing the smaller nations to remove the constitutional authority of Congress to declare war. This had been the critical factor in the Senate's defeat

6

of membership in the League of Nations a generation before. Nor were the Joint Chiefs of Staff interested in utilizing the MSC beyond its use in decolonizing activities. The U.S. military had no expectation of enlisting the MSC against a major power.[1] The veto power in this context was appreciated as much in the Pentagon as in the Kremlin.

There was still another dimension to the veto issue, namely, the Soviet recognition that its voice would not be heard in a Western-dominated General Assembly, or even in the Security Council where the other members would be in the Western European or Latin America camps, hostile to Soviet interests. The Soviets could count only on the three votes in the General Assembly that it had been granted in the Yalta agreements and three from Communist Poland, Czechoslovakia, and (less reliably) Yugoslavia. It is understandable that the communist nations would regard any deviation from the understandings of 1945 as a subversion of the UN. Without the veto power, the Soviet Union, like the United States, would not have accepted the charter.

But in the eyes of the West the veto became the symbol of Soviet obstructionism, and even more, as an instrument of advancing communism worldwide. Frustration over Soviet policies in Iran, Greece, and Germany joined with a recognition that the UN was an insufficient bulwark against Soviet-led communism. Worry over its weakness in the face of external and internal communist agitation had accounted for the efforts of British foreign minister Ernest Bevin and French foreign minister Georges Bidault to induce the United States to ally with West Europeans in defending them from communist aggression. The British and the French hoped to lure the United States into the Brussels Pact in 1948. Although they failed in this instance, they inspired a bipartisan excitement in the administration and in the Senate where such diplomatists as John D. Hickerson and Theodore A. Achilles and such Republican statesmen as John Foster Dulles pushed a hesitant State Department into supporting an alliance in which the Brussels Pact would be subsumed under a larger Atlantic alliance.[2] The key issue for them was not harmony between a projected treaty and the UN Charter but, rather, the immediate need to throw the cloak of American protection over the defenseless Western Europeans. In 1948 the West remembered the fate of Czechoslovakia when the democratic government of Eduard Benes was overthrown and its foreign minister, Jan Masaryk, died by suicide or murder.

Secret conversations in the Pentagon in March, shortly after the conclusion of the Brussels Pact, resulted in a decision (not made public) that an Atlantic security pact, in which the United States would be a participant, was the only way to prevent a communist takeover of vulnerable European states and to deter a Soviet invasion. Irregardless of whether those scenarios were realistic, U.S. policymakers in the spring and summer of 1948 prepared to abandon a tradition of nonentanglement that was almost 150 years old. Much of the planning and all of the negotiations in this period were conducted in secret. The public was made aware of what the administration was producing only gradually, late in the negotiating process.

The Vandenberg Influence

Given the sense of urgency that pervaded the scene in Washington, it was surprising that over a year had to pass before the North Atlantic Treaty was signed. The cautious leadership of Secretary of State George C. Marshall and Undersecretary of State Robert A. Lovett was one of the factors delaying immediate action. Both men wanted to go slowly. They were keeping their eyes on reactions in the Senate to such a radical departure from tradition. The incipient panic accompanying the Prague coup in February 1948 and Soviet pressure on Norway for a nonaggression pact in March had subsided later in the spring. The new National Security Council, it was hoped, might satisfy the Brussels Pact powers with NSC 9, a report offering military support without opening the Pandora's box of U.S. membership in the Western Union.[3] The offer was not sufficient to allay the Europeans' fears. They wanted more.

While the Truman administration understood the reasons for Western Europe's insecurity and had recognized that some sort of security pact was necessary, the perceived political realities slowed its reaction. The isolationists dominating Congress before World War II had dwindled to a small but articulate band in the Senate. Led by Robert A. Taft of Ohio they had lost much of their influence, but what little was left still had to be reckoned with. They were resolutely opposed to any entangling alliance with any European country. The Joint Chiefs of Staff were nervous about overextending U.S. commitments and were particularly wary of giving military aid at their expense when the military budgets for all the services were strained by a $15 billion ceiling. But the military would fall into line if the civilian leaders required their compliance.

Neither the isolationist remnant nor the military's caveats posed serious obstacles to the development of a military alliance with Western Europe. The major problem lay with the advocates of the United Nations who feared that an Atlantic security pact would undermine the new direction the nation had taken since World War II. Many of these advocates were converts from isolationism who conveyed the enthusiasm of true believers in the virtue of internationalism. For them World War II had left the message that withdrawal from the responsibilities of a great power had accelerated the path to war. If the errors of the past were not to be repeated, then the alliances seeking a balance of power must be removed from the international scene. The UN was the instrument to achieve a new world order, and

American power should be used to further this cause. While the friends of the UN shared the frustrations of the supporters of an Atlantic military pact in decrying Soviet abuses of the veto in the UN Security Council, they wanted to counter the Soviets without doing damage to the world organization. Only if the pact clearly stated its conformity with the UN Charter would this formidable lobby find the pact acceptable.

The most influential friend of the UN in the Senate was Arthur H. Vandenberg of Michigan, Republican chairman of the Foreign Relations Committee in the Eightieth Congress. A passionate internationalist since Pearl Harbor, he had been equally passionate as an isolationist when he was a presidential candidate in 1940. Vandenberg looked the part of a senator, a big man with an even bigger ego who required appropriate attention from legislators at all times. Undersecretary of State Lovett was appropriately deferential, stopping by regularly at Vandenberg's suite at the Wardman Park Hotel for a drink and conversation. The senator regarded himself as one of the authors of the UN Charter's Article 51 when he served on the U.S. delegation at the San Francisco conference in 1945. But George Kennan was bemused by the senator's preening over his actions and professed "not to understand the rationale for the elaborate deference paid to him at that time in the State Department." Dean Acheson did know the reason, even if he disliked participating in the courtship of the senator when he served under Marshall in 1947 or as secretary of state in 1949.[4] His towering ego notwithstanding, Vandenberg was the key to the Senate's acceptance of an Atlantic pact, a fact that Acheson fully understood.

Vandenberg's commitment to the world organization did not preclude his backing a transatlantic alliance. Article 51 involved the inherent right of individual and collective self-defense in the event of an attack and was the cornerstone of the U.S. commitment to Western Europe. The article had its origins in the U.S. requirement that the Monroe Doctrine and the Americas in general be able to protect hemispheric defense. The article's absence from the league covenant was one of the reasons for the Senate's rejection of the League of Nations in 1919. Vandenberg embraced the article. He was not comfortable with a resolution prepared by conservative colleagues demanding the rewriting of the UN Charter as a way of preventing further Soviet abuse of the veto. He pigeonholed the resolution in the Foreign Relations Committee. If the resolution removed the veto only in case of armed aggression but kept all other charter provisions for settling international disputes, it would place the UN in the position of allowing "others to tell us when we must go to war."[5] Vandenberg agreed with the State Department that the defense of Europe was a vital interest of the United States, and that a military response to aggression could not be ruled out.

Despite his appreciation of the plight of Europe, Vandenberg wanted to take the sting out of a military approach to an Atlantic alliance. In this regard he was close to the isolationist wing of the Republican Party, which labeled the projected pact an old-fashioned alliance. Unlike the isolationists, however, he was concerned with creating the perception that no American obligation to the Western union and other potential European allies would violate the terms of the charter. He was determined to see that any resolution emerging from the Foreign Relations Committee would give prominence to its conformity with the charter.[6]

The equation of the treaty with a traditional military alliance remained a sensitive subject to Vandenberg. A year later, in responding to a letter from a pacifist history professor, he insisted that "he too would disapprove a military alliance in the historic pattern. But in my humble opinion the North Atlantic Pact is *fundamentally* of an entirely different character. It is a *peace* Pact. It is written scrupulously within the structure of the United Nations Charter and is directly authorized by the U.N. charter."[7] In Vandenberg's eyes, neither he nor the American public could accept a commitment that would undo the change in America's outlook on the world symbolized by the UN.

Undersecretary Lovett, in charge of the State Department during Secretary Marshall's absence in Bogota and now a convert to the Hickerson and Achilles approach to American involvement in an Atlantic alliance, accepted Vandenberg's demand that the United States declare clearly the linkage between the projected treaty and the UN Charter. The result was the Vandenberg Resolution (S.239) of June 11, 1948, which paved the way for the Washington exploratory talks in the summer of that year. The logjam was broken, and the UN Charter became a very visible part of both the Vandenberg Resolution and the North Atlantic Treaty. Of the six paragraphs in the Vandenberg Resolution, four emphasized the role of the UN, and these were not incidental references. They began with the Senate's reaffirming "the policy of the United States to achieve international peace and security through the United Nations, so that armed force shall not be used except in the common interest, and that the President be advised of the sense of the Senate that this Government, by constitutional process, should particularly pursue the following objectives within the United Nations Charter." The resolution concluded with the recommendation that there be "if necessary, after adequate effort toward strengthening the United Nations, review of the Charter at an appropriate time by a general conference called under Article 109 or by the General Assembly." Under this rubric there should be no question about the legitimacy of whatever treaty should follow with Europe.[8]

Appropriately, this has come down in history as "the Vandenberg Resolution" and was so dubbed from the day of its passage. Achilles insisted that the senator did his bipartisan best to label it as simply a resolution from the Foreign Relations Committee. But modesty does not fit the Vandenberg persona, no matter how sincere he may have been in disclaiming credit. Achilles added, "He could not have been displeased when the press and everyone else preferred to call it by his name."[9]

Signing the Treaty

If the language of the Vandenberg Resolution in June 1948 strained too hard to fit the planned Atlantic pact into the UN Charter, the ambassadors from the five Brussels Pact countries, meeting with their American and Canadian counterparts in Washington less than a month later, strained to avoid the issue as long as possible. The framers at the negotiating sessions assumed that the treaty would support, not undermine, the charter by strengthening the defense capabilities of its members. Article 51 with its inherent right of self-defense was a proof of compatibility with the charter. As Bevin noted complacently in a message to the State Department in May 1948, based on Article 51 "it is clear that the ultimate conclusion of some world wide system can only be rendered practicable if a way is prepared by a defence arrangement in the North Atlantic area."[10]

In the course of their deliberations the ambassadors and the working group both assumed the involvement not only of Article 51 but also of Articles 52–54 dealing with NATO as a regional organization. Canada and the Netherlands even added Article 56 to the list of the charter's articles that the allies should embrace. This article involved cooperation for economic, cultural, and spiritual purposes. Canada's Lester Pearson, undersecretary of state for external affairs, expressed a long-standing Canadian concern when he wished that any new pact move beyond purely military fields into positive cooperation in other areas. At that same session of the Washington exploratory talks, the Netherlands ambassador E. N. Van Kleffens expanded on Pearson's point, believing that "the North Atlantic community was too good to be limited merely to material welfare and military security, in that it rested on a community of certain basic conceptions of the highest moral order."[11]

The possibility of conflict between the language of the treaty and the terms of the charter did not even surface in these sessions. It sufficed that the first major draft emerging from the exploratory talks, the White Paper in September 1948, finessed the issue by noting simply that its articles would place the treaty "within the framework of the United Nations Charter" as well as "demonstrate the determination of the parties fully to meet their obligations under the Charter."[12] Linkage would pose no problem, according to the December report of the ambassadors' working group. The treaty presumably would be placed under the rubric of Chapter 8, identifying the alliance as a regional organization. However, Articles 53 and 54, the pertinent models in the charter's Chapter 8, required that regional organizations report to the UN Security Council where their operations would be subject to Soviet scrutiny and their decisions subject to a Soviet veto. This would be an intolerable prospect, although the allies did not deal with this dilemma in 1948.[13]

The question of compatibility could not be evaded in 1949. The allies finally met it head-on in the sixteenth meeting of the Ambassadors' Committee less than a month before the treaty was signed. Secretary of State Acheson went to the heart of the matter: To admit that the North Atlantic Treaty was not a regional arrangement would ensure "endless confusion." Why bother with any mention of Articles 53 and 54? He urged concentration on Article 51 in Chapter 7, which would be the only article cited in the text of the treaty. The treaty's implementation required no Security Council authorization and involved a right that existed before the creation of the United Nations. As for the articles under the rubric of regional organization, Acheson suggested that the framers simply assume that the treaty created a regional arrangement. He noted that "Chapter VIII talked about arrangements which were less than universal; when a group of states smaller than the total membership of the United Nations undertook to do anything, that was called a regional arrangement." In this context the North Atlantic Treaty would be included automatically. The allies could report an armed attack to the UN Security Council and would ask the council to take action. And if the council would not or could not, then the allies themselves would do so under Article 51.[14]

The final version of the treaty reprised the language of the Vandenberg Resolution, if not its spirit. In addition to the preamble, four of the fourteen articles referred to the charter by name, and the treaty's Article 7 piously respected the primary responsibility of the Security Council for the maintenance of international peace and security. Acheson seemingly had solved the problem of compatibility, and the NATO partners appeared satisfied with the lip service to the charter.

Although the legal hairs Acheson had split to show the treaty's conformity with the charter persuaded allies preoccupied with more pressing elements in the pact, the treaty's defenders in the Truman administration could not be as complacent about the links. They knew that opponents in the Senate and the press were lurking in the background waiting to locate chinks in the document. They also awaited reactions within the UN itself where they assumed the Soviets would be waiting for the right moment to attack. Their uncertainties contrasted sharply with the relaxed attitudes of their allies toward the UN Charter.

President Truman's pledge of continued support of the UN "in all respects" appeared as deeply felt as the pledge in the treaty's Article 5 to defend Europe. In his letter to Congress transmitting a report on the participation of the United States in UN activities in 1948, Truman blamed the indiscriminate use of the veto power for his (and the nation's) disappointment in the UN as a security organization. Alluding to the Soviet Union, he noted that "the Charter is a guide to action. While this is so for all members, it is particularly so for those enjoying the right of veto. . . . During 1948 we have continued to recognize these Charter obligations as restrictions upon our conduct. We will continue to recognize them. And we have a right to expect other members of the United Nations to act similarly."

Because of the behavior of the Soviets (and only because of it), the United States and its allies have taken supplemental measures in the form of the North Atlantic Treaty to seek the security the UN has not been able to provide. But this situation has arisen "not because the United States has not put forth real efforts to develop the United Nations to its full stature." This message was an appeal to the U.S. public rather than to the NATO allies, not only to approve the rationalizations for the treaty but also to show that it was framed in support of the UN. The tone of Truman's statement betrays his sensitivity to America's relations with the UN and seems an almost desperate plea for understanding that NATO was not designed to be a substitute for or to evade the obligations of the UN Charter.[15]

It was not only a problem of the literal application of the treaty's articles to the requirements of the charter's that worried the Truman administration. It was the opening given by the treaty to those who recoiled at a militant—rather than pacific—approach to international problems. Secretary of State Acheson tried to divert attention from this aspect of the alliance in his report on U.S. participation in the UN for 1948. He emphasized the leadership taken by the United States in focusing on political issues such as a future government of Palestine and the independence of Korea as well as the more mundane but still important act of extending a 65 million–dollar interest-free loan for construction of the UN's headquarters.[16]

The Treaty at the UN

The U.S. officials responsible for the ratification of the new treaty had some justification for their worries. Within the United States, objections were raised not only by the usual sources (the surviving isolationists from the right and Soviet sympathizers from the left) but also from leading Protestant ministers whose statement declared that the Atlantic pact "means the continuance of the Cold War in a divided world." Twenty-two ministers and theologians from estimable institutions such as Harvard Divinity School and the Union Theological Seminary declared that it was time to take action against such provocative measures as NATO, "instead of supinely underwriting national policy."[17] These were voices that would be heard again before the United States ratified the treaty.

Within the international community two key leaders in the UN, Secretary-General Trygve Lie and president of the General Assembly Australian Herbert Evatt, were skeptical about NATO's claims of conformity with the UN. Not that either of them was in sympathy with the Soviet Union or with communist ideology. Lie, a prominent Norwegian statesman, had been foreign minister with the Norwegian government in London during World War II, chairman of the commission drafting the Security Council charter, and head of the Norwegian delegation at the first meeting of the UN General Assembly. Acceptable to both Western and communist blocs, he became secretary-general in 1946. His concern was to protect the integrity of the UN when he warned, two days before the signing of the treaty, that "no regional arrangement can ever be a satisfactory substitute for the United Nations." In his introduction to the annual report in July, he reiterated his belief that "there can be no security that excludes any of the Great Powers." He claimed in one of his memoirs that he "favored the North Atlantic Treaty Organization and other measures to strengthen the West, but not at the cost of allowing the United Nations to wither on the vine." He despaired of a lasting peace in the world "if alliances were regarded as a path to genuine collective security."[18]

Like Trygve Lie, Herbert Evatt had been foreign minister during World War II. And like Lie he was a strong backer of the United Nations, as delegate to the San Francisco Conference. His was an articulate voice speaking for the smaller nations, and he positioned himself as an opponent of the veto power. It was from this perspective that he spoke as president of the UN General Assembly in 1949. Evatt's belief in the primacy of the UN colored an important address he delivered on April 5 before the General Assembly, including ten foreign ministers who had signed the North Atlantic Treaty the day before. Without identifying the treaty as a problem for the UN, he made the point, "It is impossible to ignore the fact that great difficulties have arisen in the last few years." He insisted that it was "crystal clear that these difficulties have not been caused by the United Nations. . . . The fact is that nearly all the difficulties of the United Nations have been caused by one factor: great power disagreement outside the United Nations and completely independent of the United Nations." He went on to remind his listeners that "world-wide security, and surely that is our goal[,] can only be found in a world-wide organization."[19]

There was no doubt about Evatt's targeting NATO in his speech. His criticism was sharper than Lie's. Yet it was not the internationalists who caused the NATO advocates distress. It was the anticipated attack from the Soviet adversary that they assumed would burst forth at the UN meeting in the following week. There seemed to have been enough signals in advance of the General Assembly session that the Soviets would strike hard at the West's new alliance. Kremlin pressure on Norway to reject an Atlantic pact had been evident in January 1949, and the harsh dismissal of that country's promise not to permit military bases on its territory indicated a hard line toward the projected alliance even if in this instance the United States was not the direct target.[20]

The Soviet charges of violations of the UN Charter picked up steam as the allies concluded their negotiations. The Soviet press printed the full text of the treaty on March 29, 1949, in order to expose the hollowness of its claim of harmony with the UN Charter. And on March 31, just five days before the official signing, the

Soviets issued a formal protest against the twelve allies. It mocked the treaty's claim to be a regional agreement under Article 52 in light of the location of its members "in both hemispheres of the globe." Moreover, "Article 5 of the North Atlantic Treaty envisages the application of armed forces by parties to the Treaty without any authority whatsoever from the Security Council. Thus even if the North Atlantic Treaty were considered a regional agreement, Article 5 of this Treaty is incompatible with the UNO Charter."[21] It appeared that the Kremlin was preparing to zero in on the weaknesses of the treaty.

In preparation for the Soviet onslaught at the General Assembly, the staff of the U.S. delegation produced a position paper on March 30, suggesting ways of coping with its polemics. First, the United States should not oppose placing the issue of the treaty's compatibility with the charter on the agenda; rather, it should accept the challenge and then, if at all possible, immediately send it into committee for discussion without prior debate in the plenary session. The U.S. delegation should "content itself with a moderate and straightforward exposition in general terms of the true meaning of the Pact within the framework of the Charter." If the Soviet delegates become excessively abusive, then turn tables on them by emphasizing how the Soviet abuse of the veto has paralyzed the UN Security Council. They were to dwell also on the contrast between the constructive role played by Western democracies with the repressive behavior of the Soviets toward their satellites.[22]

This sound advice notwithstanding, the U.S. delegation became increasingly nervous as the opening of the third session of the General Assembly drew near. There was some division over whether the United States should be in a reactive position, responding to Soviet polemics about the threat of the treaty to the UN with the line that the repeated exercise of the veto by the Soviets made it necessary to find other means under the charter to safeguard the security of the West. This was the position of Warren R. Austin, chairman of the U.S. delegation. Others on the delegation preferred that the United States take the initiative in explaining and justifying the treaty instead of waiting for a Soviet denunciation. Why not use, as Benjamin V. Cohen recommended, the platform of the General Assembly to explain to the world just how the treaty supported rather than subverted its obligations under the UN Charter? The decision, however, was made to keep the issue out of the General Assembly unless the Soviets introduced it.[23]

State Department fears about a violent Soviet response to the treaty were excessive at this time. With all their bombast against the transatlantic alliance, the Soviets' reaction was only verbal after the treaty was signed. No aggressive action followed, either against the Scandinavian allies or against the United States. Reasons for the mild Soviet response may be found in the extensive peace campaign that Moscow had mounted in the midst of the West's final negotiations on the treaty. It would hardly serve the Kremlin's campaign if the Soviets went beyond oral complaints against the Western allies. Their stake in the winter and spring of 1949 was in showing a peaceful face, with the West being pictured as the enemy of the UN. A Soviet-inspired Cultural and Scientific Confederation for World Peace convened at the Waldorf-Astoria Hotel in New York City on March 25–27, 1949, to alert America and the world to dangers of a new war that the United States was creating. Elsewhere, peace conferences were held in Bucharest, Tokyo, Mexico City, Paris, and Moscow. The Soviet press exploited comments from American sources—editorials in the *Chicago Tribune,* a resolution from the Society of Friends, and pronouncements from Henry Wallace's Progressive Party, for example—to depict the alliance as provocative and the United States as an enemy of the UN.[24]

In this environment communist incitements to civil strife and new threats of intervention in Western Europe had to yield to the image of the Soviet Union as the defender of the UN Charter. Even the State Department's position paper recognized the presence of the "peace offensive," although the paper characterized it as a vehicle to intimidate UN members. The Joint Intelligence Committee of the U.S. Embassy in Moscow concluded on April 1, 1949, however, that the Soviet Union "will not resort to direct military action against the West in the near future and counts on a period of several years of peace."[25]

Nor was there a polemical outburst when the General Assembly convened on April 5. The Soviets' delay in pressuring an attack against the NATO powers may have reflected their sense of isolation in the assembly. The only votes the delegation could count on were from the three within the Soviet Union and the few other communist nations, Poland, Czechoslovakia, and Yugoslavia. Not a word was heard against the treaty from the Middle Eastern or African members, conscious though they were of the prominence of colonial powers among the signatories of the North Atlantic Treaty. The first issue before the General Assembly in that session was to complete arrangements on the future of Italian colonies, a subject left over from the 1948 meetings. When the Soviet delegates tried to present themselves to Africans as the enemies of colonialism, particularly over the disposition of Italy's former African colonies, they could not erase memories of their recent approval of Italian claims on the same very territories, presumably to bolster the Italian Communist party. Their confused behavior over Italy's African empire spoiled the image they were seeking to polish in the UN.

A more serious embarrassment for the Soviet bloc was the question of the veto. It was not just the NATO allies who had become frustrated over the Soviet use of that instrument. The smaller nations, as Evatt had observed, were never satisfied with the special powers the victors of World War II had awarded themselves. The smaller nations' anger could have fallen as heavily on the Western allies as on their communist adversary. In November 1947 the General Assembly adopted a resolution referring the question of voting procedure to an interim committee for a report. The committee submitted its report on July 15, 1948, to the assembly where the report was referred ultimately to the Ad Hoc Political Committee. Out of these discussions, representatives of the United States, Britain, France, and China introduced a draft resolution asking the General Assembly to recommend to the Security Council that, on issues deemed procedural, "the permanent members of the Council . . . might forbear to exercise the veto." Australia offered an amendment to the joint resolution, asking that the permanent members of the Security Council forbear from exercising the power of veto except in cases arising under Chapter 7 of the UN Charter (concerning enforcement measures). The Australian amendment failed because it went too far in infringing on the prerogatives of the five great powers.[26]

Both drafts were unacceptable to the Soviets. Rejecting the authors' assertions that they made their proposal in order to strengthen the authority of the Security Council and of the UN as a whole, the three Soviet representatives along with Poland and Yugoslavia complained that the draft's real aim was to revise the charter under the guise of procedural changes. The communists identified the principle of unanimity among the five permanent members as a cornerstone of the UN, and only unanimity on their part could guarantee international peace. For them the proposal of the four other permanent members was just a sly way of ending the veto power.[27]

When Argentina submitted an amendment for the General Assembly to convene a "General Conference of the United Nations," the United States and USSR did come together to oppose this draft resolution. Actually, with his proposal the Argentine delegate won favor with many smaller powers. The delegate stated that smaller nations had agreed to put their fate in the hands of the great powers on the condition that the latter would work together. This did not happen. It was not so much the veto itself as it was disagreement among the great powers that had failed to meet the conditions. So if the principle of unanimity stood in the way of achieving the objectives of the charter, then a general conference should seek solutions to the impasse. The negative vote on the Argentine proposal was arguably influenced by the concern that any attempt to abolish the veto would wreck the UN, or so the opponents claimed. Neither antagonist in the Cold War would permit such an abridgment of its powers.[28]

Given the Soviet Union's minority status in the General Assembly, it should have come as no surprise that the Soviets would introduce the North Atlantic Treaty into the proceedings as a way of diverting attention from the assembly's displeasure with their stance on Italian colonies and particularly on the veto. Attacking the West's draft resolution would underscore the incompatibility of the treaty with the charter and remind the world that their own resolution would strengthen the UN. The treaty would be a vehicle for the Soviets to keep the United States on the defensive in the assembly.

Led by the USSR's deputy foreign minister, Andrei Gromyko, the Soviet delegation charged on April 13, 1949, that the treaty was simply a device to wreck the UN by forming an aggressive bloc that would lead to a new world war. "The USSR," Gromyko asserted, "deemed it necessary to draw the attention of the General Assembly to the aggressive policy of the ruling circles in the United States and United Kingdom. . . . The North Atlantic group of countries was being set up as an instrument to enforce United States and United Kingdom domination over other countries and peoples." Gromyko invoked familiar charges of the West's isolating the Soviet Union, much as the West had done in collaboration with "Hitlerite Germany." Gromyko added that the British and the French in particular were violating obligations to the Soviet Union in the Anglo-Soviet Treaty of 1942 and the Franco-Soviet Treaty of 1944. It should be obvious to the General Assembly that the West's draft resolution seeking "forbearance" on the part of the permanent members of the Security Council in the exercise of the veto was part of the plot to attack both the Soviet Union and the UN, while all the USSR wanted was to underscore its support of the charter.[29]

There was no doubt that Gromyko had disregarded the agenda in launching his assault against the United States. The debate should have been confined to the veto power. The U.S. delegates were taken by surprise by the lack of any formal notice on the part of the Soviet delegation. But should they have been surprised? The Soviets needed an excuse to move to an offensive position, and the Atlantic pact was just the instrument for this. Over the next few days, the Soviets had assistance from the Polish and Czech delegates in directing attention from their own abuse of the veto to accusations that NATO would be nothing more than a refinement of the Dunkirk and Brussels pacts in preparing for war against the communist nations. Why else would the United States consider providing military assistance to its allies if it were not for "receiving in return air bases and vital staging areas for the offensive."[30]

In focusing on the military aspects of the alliance, Gromyko and his colleagues were giving sinister significance to U.S. military aid to future allies, an issue that bothered supporters of the Atlantic alliance, for different reasons. American supporters of the UN feared that linkage to military aid might compromise the peaceful intentions of the treaty. But the U.S. delegation need not have been alarmed by Soviet attempts to arouse world opinion over arms aid. Neither Gromyko nor his Czech or Polish allies intended to rest their case primarily upon the treaty's impact on the Cold War. They looked backward instead to World War II in order to emphasize the injustice of the Anglo-Americans creating a concert against a former partner in the war against Nazi Germany. Ten years before, the West had tried to isolate the Soviet Union in concert with the Nazis, and the new alliance under American leadership was repeating this error.[31]

To Americans, the communists' points were out of focus and seemed to have little in common with the issues of the day. Why should the USSR introduce such subjects as the sufferings of World War II and the dangers of a Nazi revival when there were so many contemporary problems in which the United States would appear to be more vulnerable to criticism? The answer to this query lay in the realistic appraisal that the Soviet Union and its small band of allies made of their position in the UN. Only by recalling to the world the communist role in the liberation of Europe would they have a possibility of undoing the treaty. A legalistic approach pointing out specific breaches between treaty and charter would not move the majority in the UN General Assembly. Nor would an attack exclusively on the aggressive intentions of the NATO allies do anything to serve the Soviets. Too many members were angry over Soviet obstructionism in the UN to castigate the United States and its partners over the legality of the treaty. The thirty vetoes cast by Soviet delegates in less than four years provided the reason for the assembly's investigation of ways to limit the abuse of this power.

If Ambassador Austin was really surprised at the Soviet effort to change the subject, he recovered sufficiently to point out that the Soviets should accept the will of the majority in the UN and agree to voluntary moderation in the use of the veto. Austin then warned that "if a permanent member attempts to destroy through force the political independence of his neighbor . . . the responsibility for the violation cannot be avoided or obscured through the casting of a negative vote when the victim takes the aggression before the Security Council." Gladwyn Jebb, head of the British delegation, observed that while Austin had "a considerable capacity for indignation . . . he was a little old-fashioned both in his oratory and his outlook and therefore was not entirely suitable to represent the USA."[32] Jebb's colleague Hector McNeil spoke contemptuously of Gromyko's introduction of the North Atlantic Treaty into a debate on the veto, "in spite of the fact that it was not on the agenda." McNeil wanted to

> remind the Soviet Union delegation and the other delegations which supported its view on the North Atlantic Treaty . . . that they could request the inclusion of the question in the agenda of the General Assembly in accordance with the established procedure. He doubted, however, that the USSR delegation would follow such a procedure. He expected, on the contrary, that it would prefer to make repeated attacks on the North Atlantic Treaty every time it should find itself in a political tight corner.

McNeil dismissed the Soviet case by noting the differences between the military agreements the USSR had concluded with its satellites and the free association of the Atlantic countries.[33]

At the end of the day, the failure of the Soviets to place the United States on the defensive was manifested by the defeat of its draft resolution by a vote of six in favor and forty against. The six comprised the communist bloc—USSR, Ukrainian SSR, Byelorussian SSR, Poland, Czechoslovakia, and Yugoslavia. By contrast the draft resolution approved by the Ad Hoc Political Committee was adopted by votes of forty-three to six.[34] While the practical results of the votes were slight, they were sufficient to puncture any illusions the Soviet Union might have had about the credibility of its pose as the champion of the charter. The repeated abuse of the veto alone would have spoiled that picture. The mounting resentment against Soviet behavior undoubtedly accounted for the majority's tolerance of the North Atlantic Treaty's putative infractions of the UN Charter's obligations. For the balance of this session the Soviets ignored the treaty. The defense of their veto power was more important than a continued attack against the NATO allies. It was this power alone in the Security Council that was a brake against what they considered the automatic majority in the UN General Assembly.

The Treaty and the U.S. Senate

Although the North Atlantic Treaty emerged from the UN debates unscarred, the vulnerabilities the Soviet bloc was unable to expose did not go unnoticed by critics in the U.S. Senate and by the American public at large. From April 27 intermittently to May 18, 1949, the Senate Committee on Foreign Relations listened to ninety-six witnesses air their views about the treaty. Of this number fifty spoke in opposition. It was a bold move on the part of the administration to give a platform to public and private witnesses ranging over the entire ideological spectrum, many of whom would assail the pact as a violation of the basic traditions of American foreign policy. The administration invited the most hostile Republican senators, Forrest C. Donnell of Missouri and Arthur V. Watkins of Utah, to the hearings, even though they were not members of the Foreign Relations Committee. The result was a full-scale attack on the treaty on more counts than the Soviet could muster—its rejection of an isolationist tradition that stretched back to the termination of the Franco-American alliance in 1800, its obvious violation of the Monroe Doctrine, its embrace of an alliance system that Americans had always condemned, and its flouting of the UN Charter. No one spoke more passionately against the treaty than Curtis P. Nettels, a distinguished professor of colonial history at Cornell University. In his opinion, by joining the Atlantic alliance the United States would "abandon the historic policies of the Nation and substitute therefore a new policy utterly alien to our traditions. We are asked to forsake the unbroken practice of 149 years—the practice of abstaining from peacetime military alliances."[35]

None of these obstacles fazed Acheson, who seemed to welcome the challenge. Acheson, with his Guardsman's mustache, looked every bit the part of an aristocrat who, in the words of Robert Donovan, "would have looked as much at home at 10 Downing Street as in Foggy Bottom."[36] Son of an Episcopal bishop, a product of Yale and Harvard Law School, Acheson displayed an air of arrogant authority that was bound to antagonize most congressmen even if they were disposed to agree with his arguments. Instead of avoiding elements in the North Atlantic Treaty that did not fit American traditions, Secretary Acheson made a point of showing how the treaty accorded with the spirit as well as the letter of isolationism. He put the emotionally charged words of George Washington, Thomas Jefferson, and James Monroe into the service of a new American foreign policy. He proclaimed an elastic interpretation of the Monroe Doctrine, citing the recently signed Inter-American Treaty of Reciprocal Assistance, signed at Rio de Janeiro in 1947, as the multilateralization of the isolationist doctrine. And if the Rio Pact constituted no break with the past, it followed that the Atlantic Pact was just a variation of the Rio Pact. Substantially the same language was used in both documents. Both spoke of fulfilling democratic ideas, both pledged loyalty to the UN Charter, and both contained clauses providing response to armed attack. It was Senator Tom Connally, chairman of the Foreign Relations Committee in the Eighty-first Congress, who stated specifically, "The treaty which the Committee on Foreign Relations now presents for favorable Senate action is but the logical extension of the principle of the Monroe Doctrine to the North Atlantic area."[37]

Acheson's lofty manner allowed him to get away with including Western Europe within the boundaries of the Monroe Doctrine. Given current advances in technology, for all practical purposes the Atlantic Ocean in the twentieth century was only a little wider than the Caribbean Sea had been in the nineteenth century. If American values could be extended to Latin America in 1823 without violating the tradition of isolationism, it seemed reasonable they could cross the Atlantic in 1949 when the world had shrunk to a fraction of its earlier size. The difference between the hemispheres still existed, but it was no longer the Atlantic Ocean but an Iron Curtain that separated America from the Old World. As for the United Nations, Acheson proclaimed that "the treaty is wholly consistent with the Charter and designed to strengthen the system of international law of which the Charter is the basis. It will give security and confidence to the signatory nations, whose common institutions and moral and ethical beliefs draw them naturally together. . . . The added security of nations does not threaten or weaken any other nation or portion of the world."[38]

Ambassador Austin shared these sentiments but lacked enough of Acheson's brio to make an effective case for the treaty's harmony with the charter. His trouble was less with the literal relationship between the two documents than with the images that could be summoned by opponents of the treaty. These centered on the military character of the alliance, which appeared to be contrary to the spirit of the charter, particularly the military assistance the United States intended to supply to the allies. This was a connection the State Department had worried about at the meeting of the General Assembly. The veto question (on which the

United States was on the popular side from the perspective of most of the UN members) prevented the Soviets from doing much with the alliance as a belligerent instrument of American imperialism, but within the United States, this was a very sensitive issue. Typical of the reaction of many UN supporters was that of Mrs. Clifford A. Bender, an active member of the Women's Division of Christian Service of the Methodist Church. "History indicates," she asserted, "that the most that can be achieved by military alliances is a temporary balance of power, while they eventually give rise to increasing insecurity and a menacing armaments race, ending in war."[39]

Austin tried homespun language to exorcise the notion that the treaty created an alliance of the kind associated with the European balance-of-power policies. A new order has replaced the balance-of-power system, and the North Atlantic Treaty is an example of the change. He noted:

> I have been asked whether the North Atlantic Treaty is not the resumption of the practice of setting up a power equilibrium. . . . My answer is "No." The ancient theory of balance of power lost its potential utility through the voluntary association of states, on the basis of sovereign equality and universality. The old veteran, balance of power, was given a blue discharge when the United Nations was formed. The undertaking of the peoples of the United Nations to combine their efforts through the international organization . . . introduced formally the element of preponderance of power. And out went old man balance of power.[40]

There was a comedic element in Austin's artless attempt to banish "old man balance of power" by calling the new relationship between the United Nations and aggressor nations "preponderance of power." That NATO was fulfilling the purposes of the UN Charter by contributing to that preponderance was never a question in Austin's mind. In fact, he was saying nothing that Acheson had not stated more eloquently and probably more cynically.

The details that might appear to place the treaty at odds with the charter were the substance of the sharp criticism of Senator Donnell, who took full advantage of an invitation to participate in the hearing even though he was not a member of the Foreign Relations Committee. Acheson was putting it mildly when he said Donnell was not his "favorite senator. He combined the courtliness of Mr. Pickwick and the suavity of an experienced waiter with the manner of a prosecuting attorney in the movies—the gimlet eye, the piercing question. In administering the *coup de grace* he would do so with a napkin over his arm and his ears sticking out like an alert elephant."[41]

Acheson was more than a match for Donnell. The senator pressed him on whether the treaty's justification "would at least in part be in that portion of the United Nations Charter which refers to regional arrangements."

Secretary Acheson: No, it lies in article 51.

Senator Donnell: And not 52?

Secretary Acheson: That is correct.

Senator Donnell: So the application of "North Atlantic Treaty" did not in any sense indicate a desire on the part of those who framed the pact as being under the aegis, so to speak, of the regional arrangements contemplated by the United Nations Charter?

Secretary Acheson: That is correct. We were concerned with an area. This was not a universal commitment. . . . It had to do with a particular area, and an area of great importance to the United States.[42]

Donnell moved on to another topic, even though Acheson had not really responded to his query. Ambassador Austin was an easier target for Donnell's gimlet eye. Donnell forced Austin first to admit he did call the North Atlantic Treaty a regional arrangement and then to waltz around the definition by saying, "It is not necessary to define the organization of the North Atlantic community as exclusively a regional arrangement, or as exclusively a group for collective self-defense, since activities under both article 51 and chapter VIII are comprehended in the treaty." Donnell reminded him that Chapter 8, Article 54, required that the Security Council be fully informed of activities under regional arrangements. The following exchange between Donnell and Austin reveals the Missouri senator as prosecutor, about to pounce on his victim:

Senator Donnell: I understand your statement—and am I correct in this?—to say that activities under chapter VIII, that is to say article 52 and these other two articles, 53 and 54, are comprehended in the North Atlantic Treaty.

Senator Austin: Oh, yes.

Senator Donnell: So, that in the provisions of article 54, am I correct in understanding that the Security Council as an entirety, including every member, both Russia and the others, shall at all times be kept fully informed of activities undertaken?

Badgered by Donnell, Austin lapsed into incoherence, saying, "I do not regard this treaty as making a regional arrangement, fully panoplied regional arrangement . . . but it comprehends some activities that may get in there, and when you try those activities then you come under the restrictions in chapter VIII."[43]

Austin never did get out of the corner Donnell had backed him into, but it did not matter. The administration's team had the upper hand and the majority of votes. Acheson allowed critics from the Senate and from the public at large to express their opinions, firm in the knowledge that the treaty would survive the hearings and go on successfully to ratification. No matter how logical the counterarguments were, they had no more chance of succeeding in May than had the

Soviets' in the UN General Assembly in April. The Senate's and the public's conversion to an Atlantic alliance withstood attack from left and right with equal ease.

The opposition had no more luck on the Senate floor in July than it had at the hearings. Not that efforts to defeat the treaty were abandoned. Donnell had a formidable ally in Robert A. Taft of Ohio, arguably the most influential member of the Senate and a dedicated opponent of entangling alliances. To show his concern for the defense of Europe, Taft with Senator Ralph E. Flanders of Vermont, offered a resolution extending the protection of the Monroe Doctrine to Western Europe. This had little chance of passage, and the small band of isolationists knew it. Recognizing that the treaty had no offensive purposes in mind, Taft warned that the Franco-British alliance before World War I had also been defensive and yet, inevitably, led to war. Taft gave special emphasis to the military assistance that would follow the ratification of the treaty.[44]

Taft did raise the question of compatibility, without expecting the issue to have resonance. He merely stated that the treaty violated obligations under the UN Charter. Since it was obvious that Chapter 8 could not apply, he claimed, "because we do not propose to consult the Security Council as there contemplated, we do plan to take enforcement action without authorization of the Security Council, and we do not plan to keep them fully informed." So if the treaty can only be supported under Article 51, "it seems clear to me that the right is to be exercised only if an armed attack occurs." He concluded this line of reasoning by doubting if Article 51 encompassed the arming of other nations, a key factor in the treaty.[45]

While Taft's stature in the Senate allowed him more leeway than another senator might have had, he did not exercise his advantages in this cause as he had in so many domestic conflicts. Taft seemed resigned to defeat in a way that the feisty Donnell was not. To the very end of the debate on the Senate floor Donnell kept hammering away at the unacceptable assertions of the treaty's defenders that it created a regional association under Chapter 8 of the charter without having to cite the relevant Articles 52 to 54. His remained an exercise in futility. On July 21, the Senate ratified the North Atlantic Treaty by a vote of eighty-two to thirteen.[46]

The message in that vote was that the nation and its Congress had turned away from its isolationist past and accepted responsibility for the security of the West. The bipartisan element was evident in the persons of the prime mover in the Eightieth Congress, Arthur Vandenberg, and Tom Connally, his successor as chairman of the Senate Foreign Relations Committee in the Eighty-first Congress. Together they overcame the most significant charge against the treaty, namely, that NATO would signal revival of the alliance system that had led to European wars in the past. The conformity of the treaty to the charter in this context was the effort to demonstrate to the nation that the alliance fulfilled and did not destroy the new world order inaugurated by the United Nations.

Consequences

If there was a problem over compatibility it lay in the American tradition, not in the European. None of the agonizing over the two documents was evident in the allies' ratification process. The opponents, the communists in particular, would have opposed the treaty irrespective of its conflict with the charter, and its supporters had the more important objective of linking the acceptance of the treaty with the American pledge to defend Europe. When both Ernest Bevin and Winston Churchill spoke about the merits of the treaty, the House of Commons overwhelmingly voted for the treaty on May 12, 1949, by a vote of 333 to 6. Bevin easily dismissed critics who suggested that it was not consistent with the charter: "the answer to this criticism is plain and straightforward. The Treaty is not a regional arrangement under chapter VIII of the Charter. The action which it envisages was not enforcement action in the sense of Article 53 at all."[47] There was none of the soul-searching in the Commons that characterized the U.S. approach to the issue.

The treaty had a harder time in the French Assembly two months later. The debates were more vigorous, leading at one point to a fistfight on the assembly floor, but the opposition centered on the German question, military aid, and the extent of the U.S. commitment. The vote was 395 to 189 in the National Assembly on July 27, 1949.[48] But only the Communist Party, echoing Gromyko at the General Assembly, complained about the treaty's incompatibility with the charter, and this complaint was quickly squelched in light of Soviet behavior on the Security Council. The inherent contradictions between the treaty and the charter were not important enough to delay the ratification process in the allies' legislatures.

The European allies had more pressing concerns in mind when they signed the treaty on April 4, 1949, and when it came up for ratification before their national assemblies over the next few months. France's president Vincent Auriol could have spoken for all but the Canadians when he made it clear that the meaning of the treaty to his country was found in Article 3, involving military assistance, and in Article 5, the pledge of immediate response to attack. Conformity with the UN Charter went unmentioned in his diary on July 20, 1949, when the National Assembly considered ratification of the pact.[49] While the question created a storm in the United States, it hardly caused a ripple in Europe. When the Soviets failed to exploit the issue, it disappeared as a source of future conflict between NATO and the United Nations. Only the secretary-general and the president of the General Assembly appeared to worry about the implications of the differences between the treaty and charter outside the boundaries of the Cold War.

2

The Suez Crisis, 1956

No matter how intense the arguments over the conformity of the treaty with the charter, they had a limited shelf life. Soviet diplomats and U.S. senators may have clashed with the U.S. State Department spokesmen in the UN General Assembly and on the Senate floor, but the weight of public opinion in the United States and in the West's built-in majority in the UN had made the issue a dead letter by the summer of 1949. In fact, it seems the Truman administration's victory was accepted more quickly by the Soviet bloc than by the Taft-led Republicans in the Senate. For the NATO allies, compatibility with the charter had always been a minor consideration in the framing of the treaty.

This resolution did not mean that the Soviets accepted U.S. or NATO domination in the UN; the contest simply shifted to other issues, many of them on more favorable grounds for the communist side. And while the NATO allies quietly—and the British partner vigorously—supported the U.S. position on the matter of treaty versus charter, they were by no means quiet when their interests collided with the U.S. positions in the UN. The Soviet bloc was ever ready to deepen intra-NATO differences whenever the opportunity arose. Such was the case when the Suez crisis broke seven years later.

The termination of the Korean War in 1953, inconclusive as it was, allowed NATO to follow a course in its relations with the Soviet adversary that did not involve the United Nations. Nor was the UN the arena for intra-NATO problems, at least for a few years. When conflicts involving both organizations arose once again in 1956, the difficulties were not over East Asia. Rather, they concerned NATO's charges against Soviet behavior in Poland and Hungary, and (more painful) U.S. charges against its major allies over their intervention in the Suez Canal zone.

As in the Korean crisis in 1950, the UN secretary-general was a central if not controlling figure. Dag Hammarskjöld, a Swedish political economist and diplomat, succeeded Trygve Lie in 1954 and tried to present a different face of the UN from that of his predecessor. Historian Evan Luard noted that they displayed "two alternate styles in their service to the world organization."[1] Lie was the more aggressive as well as the more flamboyant, pressing his own agenda on such issues as his twenty-year peace program. He owed the extension of his position, from 1950 to 1953, to U.S. backing but completed his tenure without appreciation from the United States and with bitter animosity from the Soviet Union. He was a former foreign minister of a minor NATO ally, and neither Lie nor his office ever gained the respect that an internationalist of greater reputation might have received.[2] By contrast Hammarskjöld, a scholarly diplomat, was a skillful low-key negotiator always seeking ways to resolve difficulties among the UN members. His sudden death in an airplane crash in 1961 cut short a remarkable career. Although his efforts to mediate the Congo crisis was a likely factor in his posthumous Nobel Prize, there were limits to his ability to solve problems. He was instrumental in settling the Suez crisis in 1956 but could not bring the concurrent Hungarian crisis to a successful conclusion.

Under other circumstances Hastings, Lord Ismay, NATO's secretary general from 1962 to 1967, might have played an equally significant role in the Korean War and the Suez crisis. But the office of secretary general was not created until the Lisbon conference of the North Atlantic Council in February 1952, in the midst of the Korean War, as a civilian counterpart to the Supreme Allied command in Europe. The war broke out just as the alliance was seeking means to implement commitments made in 1949. The reconstituted organization was too preoccupied with European concerns, primarily with anchoring the Federal Republic of Germany into the West, to influence the course of the Korean conflict in any formal way. Conceivably, had the office been established early in the war, Lord Ismay, its first occupant, might have been a spokesman for NATO, as Trygve Lie was for the UN.

General Ismay came to NATO with an impressive record of military experience in India and Africa. In World War II he had been an influential adviser of Winston Churchill, his chief of personal staff at the Ministry of Defence. Ismay developed a close relationship with General Eisenhower at that time, which continued when Eisenhower was Supreme Allied Commander, Europe (SACEUR), and subsequently president of the United States.[3] Given his ties with NATO leaders, Ismay's diplomatic skills opened possibilities for influence on the world stage, yet his was a minor role in 1956, as NATO was marginalized in the Suez crisis.

The Setting

The Anglo-French invasion of Egypt exposed fault lines in the Atlantic alliance that extended far beyond the Suez Canal. The canal was not only Britain's connection to Asia—and to the oil of the Persian Gulf—it also symbolized Britain's role as a global leader. The canal itself was a product of Anglo-French entrepreneurship and engineering and one of the crowning achievements of Britain's imperial years during the Victorian era.

For the United States, British control of the canal was an irritating relic of colonialism, standing in the way of America's developing relations with the Arab Middle East. There was a perception in both Washington and London that the United States intended to replace Britain as the paramount power in the Mediterranean and the Middle East. The powerful American Sixth Fleet in the Mediterranean was an earnest of this intention. Historian Steven Freiberger attributed the final demise of British domination in the Middle East to President Eisenhower's pressuring Prime Minister Anthony Eden from office. By January 1957 it was the Eisenhower Doctrine that committed the United States to providing military and economic aid to any country in the area that felt threatened by communism.[4]

When Egyptian nationalists led by Colonel Gamal Abdel Nasser took control of the Suez Canal in July 1956, it not only set in motion a series of events that culminated in an abortive Anglo-French effort to retake the canal and overthrow Nasser. It was also the ultimate humiliation in Britain's post–World War II retreat from empire. By 1947 Britain had removed its presence from India, Palestine, and Greece but still maintained its position in Egypt, though this turned out to be short-lived. Instability in Egypt followed its defeat in the Arab war against Israel in 1948, and the repercussions were expressed in nationalist anger against the ruling elite and its British master.

Britain's refusal in 1950 to countenance Egyptian demands for evacuation of its Suez base led to Egypt's abrogation in 1952 of the Anglo-Egyptian treaty of 1936, the basis for Britain's presence in that country. Britain's hope—and that of the United States as well—was that troubles with Egypt could be subsumed under a new regional defense alliance directed against possible communist interference in the region. Such an arrangement could allow British troops to remain in the canal zone. This hope was not realized as riots shook Egypt in 1951, culminating with the overthrow of King Farouk in 1952.

Colonel Nasser, a veteran of the war with Israel and the driving force in the ousting of King Farouk, pushed the more senior General Mohammed Naguib aside and assumed the office of prime minister in 1954 and then of president in 1956. Young and charismatic, he confronted both Britain and the United States, winning popularity in the Arab world as the new Saladin. His immediate challenge turned on Britain's reluctant surrender of power over the canal zone.

The United States wished to satisfy at least some of Nasser's aspirations even if these clashed with Britain's position in the region. While the Eisenhower administration was always conscious of the importance of Anglo-American solidarity, the American partner became impatient with Britain's seemingly obsessive need to protect its shrinking interests at the expense of Egyptian sensibilities. Secretary of State John Foster Dulles felt it was imperative that the United States did not appear to "gang up with Britain against Egypt," as historian Burton Kaufman noted.[5] At the root of the problem between the two allies was the American perception that Britain's persistent colonial attitudes stood in the way of containing the Soviet threat. Britain in turn suspected that behind America's willingness to accede to Egyptian priorities was a wish to supplant British power in the Middle East.

This divergence of approaches to the canal issue also reflected mistrust between Eden and Dulles. The U.S. secretary of state came across as a moralistic, self-righteous, single-minded, coldhearted warrior in the eyes of the British foreign minister. Dulles's special animus against colonialism lay behind much of the troubles between the two allies. Even Sir Roger Makins, the British ambassador to the United States who saw Dulles as an honorable man who differed with Britain only on tactics, commented on "this deep-seated feeling about colonialism which is common to so many Americans, occasionally welling up inside Foster [Dulles] like lava in a dormant volcano."[6]

While Eden increasingly saw Nasser as the source of all the West's problems in the region, too willing to play off the West against the Communist bloc, Dulles was ready to explore opportunities to woo Egypt away from the Soviets. Granted that Dulles was alarmed at Nasser's arms deal with Czechoslovakia in 1955, he interpreted it as a challenge that the West should meet. As he informed Undersecretary of State Herbert Hoover, Jr., "We have a lot of cards to play with Nasser—although mostly negative." He meant that money would make the difference.[7] His cards included providing to Iraq funds that would have gone to Egypt. But they also included economic aid to Egypt so generous that Nasser would have to respond to U.S. largess. Such was the plan to fund with some 400 million dollars the building of the Aswan Dam on the Nile River, which would turn that river into a source of electric power and increase by a third the nation's cultivable area. Even more important, the successful completion of this massive project would give Nasser a personal triumph to crown his leadership of the Arab world.

A combination of factors doomed American sponsorship of the dam. Congress, unhappy with Nasser's behavior generally, objected to the cost of the project; anti-communists railed against a dictator who was so reluctant to join the West against the Soviets; and the Jewish lobby actively opposed aid of such magnitude to an enemy of Israel's very existence. Arguably, it was Nasser himself who was most responsible for the United States' withdrawal of its pledge when he threatened to turn to the Soviets if the United States backed away from its commitment. Convinced that Egypt was incapable of financing the dam by itself, Dulles was prepared to call Nasser's bluff about turning to the Soviets for funds. Furious about what he considered attempts at blackmail, the secretary of state personally rescinded the Aswan offer in his meeting with the Egyptian ambassador on July 19, 1956.[8] A week later Dulles had Nasser's reply: he nationalized the Suez Canal Company, largely British owned and operated since 1875. This action set in motion the Suez crisis.

The Negotiating Stage

In the summer of 1956 the United States and Britain seemed to be in agreement over both the importance of countering Nasser's abrupt seizure of the canal and the need to prevent a potential Israeli military strike against Egypt. The Eisenhower administration had given up its last hope of convincing Nasser to make peace with Israel and serve as a centerpiece of a Middle East complement to NATO. Instead, it was finally obvious that Nasser was playing the West off against the USSR as he sought to become the leader of Arab nationalism. In the course of Nasser's maneuvering, the United States wrote him off as a tool of Soviet communism.[9] For his part, expectations that arms from the Soviet bloc would replace Western funding for the Aswan Dam project clarified the direction Egyptian policies were taking.

Israel was a wild card in the deteriorating relations between the United States and Egypt. Tensions in 1955 arising primarily from continuing and increasing raids across the Gaza strip into Israel complicated Dulles's diplomacy. Nasser's belligerence appeared to Israelis to be in preparation for a renewed war. The destruction of the Jewish state would erase the stain of Egyptian defeat in 1948 and ensure Nasser's leadership in the region. Israel in turn appeared to threaten Egypt with French arms and the aggressive posture of Prime Minister David Ben-Gurion, as reflected in Israeli attacks on Gaza. So chances of a rapprochement between Egypt and Israel were steadily diminishing, and chances of a beleaguered Israel's starting a preventive war were rising, when Nasser made his move on the canal.

The Egyptian leader had calculated the odds against Western intervention when he took over the canal. Although he realized the British would interpret nationalization as a threat to their strategic interests, given that the Suez "was the jugular vein that fed Britain's colonies," Nasser counted on Eden's being too weak-willed to go to war. And the odds were on his side. The Soviets, Nasser felt, would see the advantages of serving as Egypt's patron, even though he was wary of having the Bear replace the Lion. Besides, he was sure that nationalizing the canal would give him the revenue needed to finance the dam. The Suez Canal Company had already given Egypt a percentage of the tolls. Why not take it all?[10]

Nasser's bombshell certainly surprised if it did not shock the Soviets almost as much as it did the Western allies. General Secretary Nikita Khrushchev was not privy to Nasser's intention and in fact was not happy with it. The Soviet leader fully understood that Nasser's ambition to become the paramount leader in the Middle East did not make him a communist. The Soviets preferred caution at this time, when unrest in Central Europe absorbed their attention. Khrushchev's denunciation of Stalin in his address in February 1955 before the Twentieth Party Congress had raised aspirations in the Warsaw bloc for more political freedom, particularly in Poland and Hungary. Khrushchev did not welcome a rash act on the part of Nasser that might invite Western intervention to complicate Soviet foreign policy. Yet, on balance, Khrushchev anticipated more difficulties for the West than for the Warsaw bloc in the wake of the nationalization of the canal. It could be another opportunity to spread Soviet influence in the area. And Nasser knew he had a useful ally even if he was not advertising his allegiance at this juncture.[11]

Britain's reactions were more predictable than the Soviets'. Nationalization of the canal was one more strike against British prestige in the Middle East, a concomitant of their pullout from bases in the canal zone. Eden was not going to repeat the appeasement policies of 1938 and wanted the concerted Western action that had been absent the generation before World War II. Basically, this meant deposing Nasser before he could become the Hitler of Eden's nightmares. By reversing nationalization, Eden envisioned that the resulting loss of face would lead to Nasser's loss of office. Such was the view that seemed to have been held by much of Eden's nation as well as by the prime minister and his Cabinet. That Eden recognized that a display of force was a necessary prerequisite to success was evident in his cable to Eisenhower on July 27, 1956, just a day after Nasser's action: "My colleagues and I are convinced that we must be ready in the last resort, to use force to bring Nasser to his senses. For our part we are prepared to do so. I have this morning instructed our Chiefs of Staff to prepare a military plan accordingly."[12]

Although France was a junior partner of Britain in the initial protests against Nasser, by October 1956, it had taken the lead in orchestrating arrangements for the overthrow of the Egyptian president, primarily through France's close links to Israel. French involvement in the Suez Canal Company was considerable: French investors owned about half the shares in the company, its main office was in Paris, and its general ambience was French.[13] But the key to France's behavior was its belief that Egypt was fueling the Algerian rebellion, now over two years old.

Nasser evoked the Hitler image for the French as well as for the British. Success in overturning Nasser's coup at the canal would help reverse France's string of military failures, from World War II to Indochina. French sympathy for and military support of Israel allowed none of the constraints that inhibited Britain from making common cause with Israel in confronting Egypt. Ultimately, it was the specter of Nasser in control of the canal that solidified Anglo-French determination to use forceful means to stop a "fascist dictator" in his tracks before he took the Middle East down Hitler's path. This sentiment was voiced in the French National Assembly in August. A month later Conservative MP Mott-Radclyffe echoed this fear: "'Let him have it' was the argument used about Hitler, to justify his occupation of the Rhine, the annexation of Austria and the Sudetenland—the slippery road to World War II."[14]

The United States was giving out mixed signals about the crisis, which derived primarily from differences in language and style between the president and the secretary of state. Despite the common assumption that Eisenhower was too frequently incoherent in his public statements, this was never true about his position on the nationalization of the Suez Canal. His voice was clear and consistent. It was Dulles the diplomat who appeared inconsistent, even duplicitous, in his relations with the two major European allies. And it was Eden who willfully or inadvertently misunderstood Eisenhower's position.[15]

Dulles was well aware of Eisenhower's views, and he shared most of them. As an international lawyer he knew that there was no legal way to rescind the nationalization of the canal. Nor was there a reasonable military option from the U.S. point of view. A presidential election was only a few months away, and a military strike would not only roil the waters of the campaign but remove any possibility of a peaceful solution. The dilemma for the United States was how to reconcile the Egyptian right to nationalize the canal with the need to respect the interests of its former owners.

In the short run it appeared that the summoning of an international conference on the future of the canal could be a way of resolving the problem. The British reluctantly accepted this approach, hoping that the result of failed deliberations would be a military solution. Dulles professed to agree with Eden that Nasser's seizure of the canal was intolerable and that it should be "disgorged." This was a term that Eden wanted to hear, and he would interpret it as U.S. support for whatever force was necessary. As Eden recalled, "Nasser must be made, as Mr. Dulles put it to me, to 'disgorge.'"[16]

This recollection reflected the prime minister's hopes. If it was not accurate, Dulles's delphic signals helped to reinforce the memory. The secretary of state was certainly as angry as Eden over Nasser's behavior, but his anger was qualified by the president's and his own commitment to the UN Charter, and further qualified by Egyptian assurances of compensation to the former owners as well as to worry about potential foreign interference in U.S. control of the Panama Canal. Still, all things considered, the United States should not have been surprised about Anglo-French intentions when they were so clearly expressed.

The American-driven effort to put off British and French military action had some initial success. The United States was the prime mover for calling a conference in London of the principal maritime powers using the canal (some twenty-four, including Egypt), in order to consider how to operate the canal in conformity with the Convention of 1888, which was intended to guarantee free passage to any nation in time of war as in time of peace. The U.S. objective was to create an international agency to safeguard the users but still to defer to Egyptian sovereignty. At this stage the three NATO allies wanted to keep the issue out of the UN Security Council where the Soviets could make mischief.[17]

It was an uphill struggle for Dulles to mobilize a conference in London that could cope with Egypt's objection to any international control and at the same time contain Britain's threat to use force if the conference failed to agree on international control of the canal. The secretary of state sought a delicate balance assuring free access to the canal without jeopardizing Egypt's operation of the canal. Egypt would receive an equitable profit while the former owners of the Universal Suez Company would be given appropriate compensation.[18] A Suez Canal Board would manage and develop the canal. Britain and France joined with the United States in this effort to resolve the crisis, but without any of the illusions nourished by Dulles.

Inevitably, Egypt claimed that the London proposal would infringe on its sovereignty. Equally inevitably, the Soviet Union sided with Egypt in opposing Dulles's plan. Undaunted by initial failure Dulles then proposed, on September 4, the establishment of a Suez Canal Users Association (SCUA) to serve as a vehicle to operate the canal, to maintain freedom of passage, and to negotiate with Egypt over disposition of tolls. In framing what he considered to be a balanced plan, Dulles believed he had the support of Britain and France; but if they seemed supportive, it was not because they believed SCUA would work. Rather, it would give them time to build up a force adequate to coerce Nasser into accepting genuine international control or (even better) set the stage for removing him from power. Dulles, by contrast, saw delay as a means of cooling tempers, and of paving the way for a diplomatic solution. He was heartened—and the British were disappointed—when Egyptian pilots showed they could operate the canal as efficiently as their British counterparts.[19]

The SCUA in Dulles's conception would ensure that the maritime powers would enjoy all the rights they were entitled to under the 1888 convention, and this assurance would temper Nasser's belligerence. The British and French were willing to go along with this plan on the assumption that U.S. blessing was vital for military action to proceed. Declining British dollar reserves meant there was all the more reason to appease the United States at this juncture. Initially, the European allies were encouraged by Dulles's idea of using transit fees to deflate Nasser's image. Instead, Dulles deflated British expectations by stating that none of the fifteen members of SCUA would have authority to withhold payments to Egypt, rather than to the new organization, if Nasser insisted. Despite these storm signals, SCUA was formally established on September 21, 1956.[20] England and France hoped that by accepting membership in SCUA they would guarantee the entanglement of the United States if the military option were employed, but these hopes were never realistic. The president could not have been more explicit than he was in a press conference on September 11, where he stated that "this country will not go to war while I am occupying my present post unless Congress is called into session and Congress declares such a war."[21]

At the UN

Given the level of confusion among the leading NATO allies, it was obvious that the British and French would only give lip service to Dulles's plan. SCUA did serve, however, to postpone the British intention to bring the UN into the controversy. But only for a while. Against U.S. wishes, Britain was now ready to take the case against Egypt to the UN. Again, the Soviet Union was a factor. Had the British not pressed the issue, the Soviets might have presented a resolution in the Security Council hostile to them. Dulles made a last-minute effort to hold off the British initiative by talking with Harold Macmillan, the chancellor of the exchequer, about "six ways" of getting rid of Nasser over a six months' period, long enough to have the presidential election behind him. He failed to convince Macmillan. The British called for a meeting of the Security Council on September 23 to condemn the Egyptians, only to encounter, not surprisingly, a Soviet veto (its seventy-eighth, as Foreign Minister Selwyn Lloyd noted) of the steps the British and French foreign ministers advanced toward settling the conflict with Egypt. The veto was in aid of Egypt's rejection of SCUA's terms.[22]

By this time the European allies had given up on any prospect of U.S. support for military intervention. The mistrust among the transatlantic allies was too deep to bridge. Consequently, Britain was ready to follow a French plan that would enlist Israel in an intricate plot to regain the canal and oust Nasser. The scenario would have Israel invading the Sinai, defeating the Egyptian army, and moving toward the canal. At this juncture the British and French would intervene to separate the Israelis and Egyptians on the pretext that the advancing Israelis would be a threat to the operations of the canal. The United States would be left in the dark, in light of the Anglo-French distrust of Dulles. The breakdown in transatlantic relations seemed complete.

While this conspiracy was entering its final stages, the secretary-general reported at a private meeting of the Security Council on October 12 that the foreign ministers of Britain, France, and Egypt had agreed to what was called "the Six Principles." These included the major points of the SCUA objectives, promising no discrimination on transit through the canal, insulating the operation of the canal from the politics of any country, and respecting the sovereignty of Egypt. Arguably, the key principle was that disputes between the company and Egypt would be settled by arbitration.[23] This apparent outburst of harmony was short-lived, however. It is doubtful if either side believed that the other took seriously the obligations under the six principles. The British and French were deep in their plans to use an Israeli invasion of the Sinai for retaking the canal. They would settle only for international management of the canal.

Unlike the situation of Britain and France, Israel faced an existential threat from Nasser that provided reasons for this vulnerable country's preemptive strike on October 29, despite some doubts about the motives of the European partners. The invasion of the Sinai itself was a surprise to most of the Foreign Office, which was no more privy to this turn of events than the American ally had been. British diplomats, like their American counterparts, were aware of rumors of French planes on Israeli airfields. They knew of hurried visits of French premier Guy Mollet to London and of Eden and Lloyd to Paris. When news broke of the Israeli attack, Lloyd's principal private secretary, Evelyn Shuckburgh, applauded: "Good, we thought, now let them chew up Nasser a bit and then the Security Council might order them back." But when Eisenhower condemned the Israeli assault, Shuckburgh thought his government would join the United States in honoring the tripartite agreement to punish any aggressor. He quickly learned that this was not the British position.[24] Two weeks before, Eden had accepted France's invitation to participate in the actions against Egypt.

An angry Eisenhower, cheered on by the Soviet adversary, had U.S. ambassador to the UN Henry Cabot Lodge present a resolution to the Security Council on October 30 demanding Israeli withdrawal to the 1949 armistice lines, calling upon all UN members to refrain from giving any economic or financial assistance to Israel, and asking the secretary-general to oversee compliance. It was a draconian condemnation but, in the U.S. judgment, in accord with the principles of the UN Charter and the Tripartite Declaration of 1950. In spite of the increasingly sharp divergence of policy toward Egypt on the part of the transatlantic allies, Lodge seemed surprised when the British ambassador at the UN, Sir Pierson Dixon, took the Israeli side and considered the tripartite declaration invalid in the present situation.[25]

The president may have been astonished by Dixon's assertion, but he had reason to be more astonished by the cascade of events that day. Britain and France vetoed the resolution. More than that, they announced the delivery of an ultimatum to both Egypt and Israel in light of a threat to the security of the canal. The rapid Israeli advance facilitated the implementation of the Anglo-French plan. The allies now had the excuse to strike at Egypt. The ultimatum on October 30 warned both Egypt and Israel to withdraw their forces to a distance of ten miles from the canal. The two allies then asked Egypt to agree to Anglo-French troops moving "temporarily" into Port Said, Ismailia, and Suez in the canal zone in order to assure separation of the combatants. Should either the Egyptian or the Israeli government fail to respond within twelve hours, British and French forces would intervene to assure compliance.[26]

By the end of the day British and French aerial bombardment had destroyed Egyptian planes on the ground, and the Egyptians in turn had blocked the canal by sinking ships to make it unusable. Selwyn Lloyd explained to Parliament why Britain had to act: "We say that in the present international system, where the Security Council is subject to the veto, there must be the right of individual countries to intervene in an emergency to take action in defense of their own nationals and their own interests."[27] Eden's excuse for the rapid response was that the immediate danger to the canal allowed no time for consultation. More candidly, he later admitted that he did not want to wait for compromises: "This was the last thing in the world we wanted, because we knew quite well that once palavers began, no effective action would be possible." Mollet put the case even more bluntly to the Americans: "If your government was not informed of the final developments, the reason . . . was our fear that if we had consulted it, would have prevented us from acting."[28] They were both right.

The British were taken aback by the promptness and vigor of the U.S. reaction to the Israeli move, and even more by its response to the Anglo-French collusion. Macmillan wondered why Dulles was so quick to denounce Israel when he had been so anxious to delay punishing Egypt for its refusal to accept the recommendations of SCUA. He wondered too why Dulles was so hysterical. Macmillan speculated that he may have felt betrayed by the allies' taking matters into their own hands. Or was it the specter of a nuclear-armed Soviet Union lurking in the background to endanger all the allies? More charitably, Macmillan sensed that the cancer that was to take Dulles's life a few years later had "affected his psychological and intellectual equilibrium." In any event, the prime minister felt that Dulles "clearly lost his temper; he may also have lost his nerve." It should have been galling to have the Soviets "acting together in an unnatural coalition."[29]

Unwilling collaboration with the USSR was galling to Dulles and to every other U.S. diplomatist. At the U.S. National Security Council meeting on November 1, they had to deal with the Anglo-French air attack on Egyptian air fields obviously in concert with the Israeli invasion of the Sinai. How to maintain NATO solidarity against the Soviet bloc without being identified with the colonialists posed a major dilemma. Dulles and Harold Stassen, U.S. representative on the UN Disarmament Committee and special assistant to the president, differed vigorously over the terms of the cease-fire resolution that the secretary of state wanted to introduce at the forthcoming meeting of the UN General Assembly. Long a rival of Dulles for the ear of the president on foreign affairs, and a former presidential aspirant himself, Stassen wanted to confine the resolution to just a cease-fire, without any reference to any side's responsibility. In fact, Dulles himself wanted to avoid such terms as "invasion" and "aggression" in deference to the sensibilities of close allies. Yet he repeatedly expressed irritation at Stassen's excessive deference to the British and the French. They deserved criticism, but how to deliver it remained a question that went unresolved. The president closed the meeting with the intention of doing "what was decent and right but still not condemn more furiously than we had to."[30]

The British were not appeased by U.S. efforts to soften its resolution. The British and French vetoed the resolution at the UN Security Council. France explained its veto by claiming that the council should not single out Israel for condemnation considering the Egyptians' open aim of annihilating that country. Egypt still considered itself at war and made its intentions clear by its continuing incursions from Gaza. The French delegate went on to excoriate Egyptian intervention in Algeria (possibly his primary reason for the veto) and associated Egyptian behavior in Algeria with the illegal seizure of an international waterway. Seven votes were in favor of the resolution, two against, and two abstained. The British and French managed to prevent any action by the Security Council. As might have been expected, the Soviets tried to exacerbate the frayed relations between the United States and its NATO partners by introducing its own resolution, aimed at Israel much like the original U.S. version. Predictably, the Soviets' resolution was also vetoed. They had never expected the British and French to accept it but had presented it simply to muddy the waters.[31]

In accordance with the Uniting for Peace Resolution of 1950, the Suez issue went to the UN General Assembly after the Security Council was unable to act. There at the first emergency special session on November 1, the full volume of communist abuse of Britain and France let loose, with the United States unhappily accepting the Soviets' approval. Macmillan felt it must have been extremely uncomfortable for the United States "to listen to the unctuous congratulations" the Soviet delegate showered upon his American colleagues. Dulles communicated some embarrassment by prefacing his resolution with a "doubt that any delegate ever spoke from this forum with as heavy a heart as I have brought here." Nevertheless, he asserted that the U.S. disagreement with "our oldest, most trusted, and reliable allies . . . cannot justify the resort to armed force which has occurred."[32]

The secretary-general was not neutral in this controversy. Hammarskjöld was as shocked as the Americans by the violations of the charter, particularly because he had played a central role in working toward a peaceful resolution of the canal question. At the beginning of the Security Council meeting on October 31, he expressed his dismay at the events of the past two days. More than that, he declared, "The principles of the Charter are, by far, greater than the organization in which they are embodied, and the aims which they are to safeguard are holier than the policies of any single nation or people. As a servant of the Organization, the Secretary-General has the duty to maintain his usefulness by avoiding public stands on conflicts between Member Nations." But he emphasized that "he must be a servant of the principles of the Charter, and its aims must ultimately determine what for him is right and wrong. For that he must stand." If the UN members had doubts about his stewardship, he implied, they should elect another leader.[33]

Two days later, after the General Assembly passed a cease-fire resolution by an overwhelming majority of sixty-four to five, the British and French without the power of a veto accepted the UN decision but with reservations.[34] Eden was upset by the world's condemnation and by the negative reaction in the House of Commons, but he and his French colleague were willing to stop their military operations only if the Israelis and Egyptians would agree to allow a UN force to keep the peace. They would also require both combatants to accept "limited detachments of Anglo-French troops to be stationed between the combatants" until the UN established a more formal peacekeeping arrangement.[35] These conditions were not satisfactory to the United States or to the secretary-general. Hammarskjöld explained the reasons in a press statement on November 2: "I do not believe that acts of violence, whatever the reason, lead to cooperation. I do not believe that victories, bought at the price of violations of treaty obligations, create confidence among neighbors. But I do believe that respect for decisions of the United Nations earns those concerned the support from the world community which every nation needs."[36] The secretary-general's words and attitude fitted Dulles's moralistic approach to the allies' actions. The Soviet Union—basking in the glow of righteous support of the UN, Egypt, and the mood of the Third World—enjoyed the troubles the Western allies were encountering, particularly since they diverted attention from the USSR's own behavior in Hungary.

Yet there was an opening from a Canadian initiative that could calm the waters and restore NATO harmony. While only Australia and New Zealand voted with Britain, France, and Israel against the resolution, four NATO allies abstained—Canada, Belgium, the Netherlands, and Portugal. Portugal's and the Low Countries' refusal to condemn the Anglo-French activities may have been related to concern about their colonial ties as well as their revulsion over Nasser's ambitions and their sympathy for Israel's situation. But Canada, a devoted partisan of the UN, was anxious to repair the damage done to intra-NATO relations. Foreign Minister Lester D. Pearson impressed upon Dulles the importance of linking a cease-fire with a political settlement that would be enforced by a peacekeeping force. Although Pearson failed to convince Dulles to broaden the scope of the resolution on November 1, he raised the possibility before the General Assembly of authorizing the secretary-general to raise such a force, pending the completion of a political settlement. He added that Canada would be a participant.[37]

The Hungarian Episode

What was particularly upsetting to Eisenhower and Dulles about their allies' deception over the Suez was the way it distracted the world's attention from Soviet handling of the Hungarian revolt. It was ironic that the British and French launched their attack on Egypt just as the UN was preparing to condemn the Soviet Union for its brutal suppression of the Hungarian uprising against the Warsaw Pact. For the Soviets, as historian Steven Freiberger observed, "Suez was a heaven-sent distraction from events in Budapest. It presented the Kremlin with the opportunity to recover its moral position by posing as the champion of the United Nations and an Arab country."[38]

It was not only Hungary that the Soviets wanted to remove from UN scrutiny. In Poland, a little more than a week before the Suez crisis broke, Wladyslaw Gomulka had been reelected Communist Party leader, against the wishes of Moscow. The Kremlin had good reason for their opposition. Gomulka seemed to favor the Yugoslav heresy when he declared to the party's Central Committee that "there are different ways and means to achieve socialism. There is the Russian, way, the Yugoslav way, and several others." The Eisenhower administration was poised to support the dissidents, at least verbally: "Our hearts go out to the Polish people, as they seek to win the right to choose their own regime."[39]

If Poland was a problem for the Soviet Union and the Warsaw bloc, Hungary was a far greater challenge to the communist world. Like Poland it was able to loosen Soviet control after the death of Stalin in 1953. Under Imre Nagy some reforms were enacted; then they were withdrawn when he was dismissed in 1955. The result was an explosion of popular resentment, touched off by student demonstrations, in October 1956. The repressive government of Erno Gero then brought in Soviet troops to suppress the dissidents, but in the face of an angry populace Gero turned authority over again to Nagy. In the last week of October, Nagy set up a coalition government with representation from noncommunist elements, thereby posing a threat to the future of communism in Hungary. Soviet troops and tanks returned to Budapest to overthrow the Nagy government and replace him with Janos Kadar, a more reliable advocate of the Warsaw bloc.[40]

These events were taking place as the Suez crisis was in motion and were brought to the attention of the Security Council. Two days before Israel entered the Sinai, the three NATO allies—the United States, Britain, and France—called for an urgent meeting of the Security Council to consider dealing with the Kremlin's intervention in Budapest. The allies accused the Soviets of violating the Paris treaty of February 10, 1947, that established peace between Hungary and the victors of World War II. U.S. ambassador Henry Cabot Lodge and his British counterpart, Sir Pierson Dixon, made identical charges against the Soviet invasion. Dixon asserted that it was "a situation which required immediate consideration in the world forum of the United Nations. This is why my government has joined with the United States and French Governments in requesting an urgent meeting of the Security Council."[41]

Over strenuous protests by the USSR, the council voted nine to one to put the Hungarian question on the agenda, a decision Premier Nagy's government "warmly welcomed," according to the Budapest radio. Only Yugoslavia abstained. In response to the vote the Soviets accused the United States of subverting the legitimate government of Hungary by "financing subversive activities in the People's Democratic countries." The Soviet representative on the Security Council charged that the Hungarian uprising was a domestic matter in which the UN had no jurisdiction. Lodge claimed that the United States had no purpose other than to allow people to have governments of their own free choosing. Even though the Warsaw Treaty was considered an excuse for Soviet intervention, its Article 8 could not be used to justify it. Nagy in his capacity as president of the Council of Ministers and acting foreign minister repudiated the Warsaw Pact and turned to the UN on November 1 for defense of Hungary's newly declared neutrality in the Cold War. The Soviets replied that the charges against it were a Western device to distract public attention from Anglo-French aggression in the Middle East.[42]

Three days later the situation in Hungary had changed. Soviet military reinforcements rushed in from the Ukraine to depose Nagy and install Janos Kadar, a former Nagy ally, to save Hungary from what they considered a counterrevolutionary Fascist government. Once again the United States called on the USSR to withdraw all its forces from Hungary, and once again the lone Soviet veto prevented the adoption of the resolution.[43]

The United States then submitted a draft resolution, supported by ten votes in the Security Council, to call a second emergency special session of the UN General Assembly in order to consider the plight of Hungary. At this time, November 4, Secretary-General Hammarskjöld placed on record the same views he had expressed on October 31 when he declared that while he must avoid public stands on conflicts between member nations, his primary obligation was to be "the servant of the principles of the Charter." Just as he had supported these principles against the Israel-British-French actions in the Suez, so he would apply them to the Hungarian crisis: "The observations I made on that occasion obviously apply also to the present situation."[44]

At the second emergency special session of the General Assembly, Kadar on November 4 asked the secretary-general to disregard Nagy's request for UN intervention. The new government, once again under the thumb of the USSR, objected to any discussion of the Hungarian question by either the Security Council or the General Assembly, "because the question is within the exclusive jurisdiction of the Hungarian People's Republic." Arkady Sobolev, the Soviet spokesman in the

General Assembly, seized on Kadar's cable to underscore his opposition to UN interference in a domestic matter.[45]

Ostensibly, the Warsaw bloc lost this particular contest with the West when the General Assembly backed a U.S. draft resolution not only calling upon the USSR to desist from all armed attacks against Hungary but also asking the secretary-general to investigate and observe the situation caused by foreign intervention. The USSR and the Kadar government would be asked to permit observers designated by Hammarskjöld to travel freely in Hungary and report their findings to him. At the same time, national and international organizations would be requested to provide food and other relief to the Hungarian people. This strong resolution passed by a vote of fifty to eight, with fifteen abstentions.[46]

Its strength was illusory, however; there were no means for the assembly to compel compliance. No resolution would change the behavior either of the Soviets or of the Hungarian government. Three and half months later, on February 20, 1957, the special committee established by the General Assembly issued an interim judgment, citing Hungary's—and the USSR's—familiar objection that visitations by its members violated the UN Charter. This was the outcome of promises to facilitate humanitarian aid. The report recognized its failure to budge the communist position despite assertions that the committee would persevere in its efforts to talk with Nagy and examine the precise facts concerning the Soviet intervention. The last sentences of the report reflected the committee's frustrations: "Parliament has played a central role in the history of the Hungarian people. It is significant that during the events of October 1956, the Government of Hungary was carried on from the parliament building. The parliament is now a subordinate agency of the Government and the Communist Party."[47]

The concurrent division within the West over the Suez crisis undercut any unity the NATO powers were able to muster over Hungary. With the unintended help of the United States, the Soviets were able to direct the UN's attention away from its blatant violation of another country's sovereignty by keeping the world's attention focused on the Middle East. On their side the communists had the advantage of numbers as well as of passion; the Asian and African countries were far less moved by violations in Central Europe than they were by comparable behavior in the Arab world, even if the charges against the offending powers were identical. Order was restored in Hungary at the cost of thousands dead or deported to the Soviet Union.

In Egypt it was a different story. Nasser may have been a failure as a military leader, but politically he emerged from the crisis a winner. He was able to preen as a victor before his audience. By contrast, Britain and France lost both face and status, and Israel only temporarily won some freedom from Arab attacks.

Resolving the Suez Crisis

Faced with the resentful opposition of the United States and the anger of the Arab and Asian worlds, the British and French quickly realized their position was doomed. It was not that Eisenhower and Dulles disagreed with their conviction that Nasser's seizure of the canal jeopardized the security and economy of the West. Nor were the Americans averse to the overthrow of the dictator. Privately, they had considered the possibility of a covert operation to oust Nasser once international attention had lessened. But the U.S. president was convinced that overt force would make a bad situation worse. As Dulles had noted on August 30, Eisenhower feared that if the United States were tainted by association with European imperialism, "the influence of the West in the Middle East and most of Africa [would be] lost for a generation, if not a century." Moreover, the Anglo-French action would only increase Soviet efforts to infiltrate the Middle East and, specifically, encourage it to send in its own military at Nasser's invitation. So, "regrettable as it might be, to see Nasser's prestige enhanced even temporarily, I did not believe the situation was one which should be resolved by force."[48] Not least among the issues widening the breach among the NATO allies was the U.S. presidential election, scheduled for November 6, two days after the General Assembly took responsibility for the Suez crisis.

The Anglo-French partners had to confront additional challenges. One of these derived from Soviet troublemaking and applied equally to Britain and to France. Initially, the USSR had kept relatively quiet as the Israel-Egypt conflict erupted and as Britain and France entered the war. But Nikita Khrushchev, the key figure in the Soviet hierarchy, realized that the USSR had to respond to Egyptian pleas for help or else lose the potential benefits of an intra-NATO split. Not even the Hungarian crisis could serve as an excuse to disappoint Nasser. Yet Khrushchev's means of contending with the Western allies in the Mediterranean were limited; the Soviet navy could not match the British and French counterparts. His answer was what he would employ again in the future—bluff.

Counting on Western fears of Soviet nuclear capabilities, he threatened to unleash Soviet medium-range ballistic missiles against targets in London and Paris. He sent telegrams on November 5 to the United States and India (to garner support from putative allies), as well as to Britain and France, with the message that the Soviets had "all types of modern weapons of destruction . . . to crush the aggressor and establish peace in the Middle East." Khrushchev was confident he could intimidate the United States as well as the Anglo-French allies.[49]

Britain also had to deal with opposition in Parliament, in the press, and from the public on grounds of morality and common sense, not to mention politics. The Labour Opposition was vocal in its damning of Britain's collusion with France and Israel. Eden had given his rivals an opportunity to flay the Conservatives for a

failed policy. Trade unions spoke of possible industrial action against the government's policies, and on November 4 there was a major demonstration in Trafalgar
Square representing all segments of public opinion.[50]

But it was not just partisan opponents who raised their voices against Eden.
The Cabinet itself was shaken by the government's response to the invasion, particularly in a conspiracy with the French and Israelis. Many of Eden's colleagues
wondered at the folly of deceiving the Americans. Few members of the Cabinet
were aware of the collaboration, including Foreign Secretary Selwyn Lloyd, who
had not known of Eden's plans until almost the last minute. Lloyd's private secretary, Anthony Nutting, was appalled at the invasion. Nutting felt this was a clear
violation of the Tripartite Declaration of 1950, made all the more reprehensible
because Britain was attacking the victim, not the aggressor. He noted that the
Anglo-Egyptian agreement of 1954 stipulated that troops would be sent to the
canal only at the invitation of Egypt. Nutting resigned his office in protest.[51]

Britain had an even more daunting challenge at this critical moment. A
financial crisis was looming. The loss of oil from Nasser's blocking of the canal
combined with Syria's sabotage of a key oil pipe line could cripple the planned
intervention in Egypt. The British needed U.S. help, and they were not to secure
it until they complied with Eisenhower's demands. But it was not only the oil
shortage that plagued the Eden government. The run on the pound sterling was
even more threatening. Britain's gold reserves had fallen by one-eighth in the
first week of November. Harold Macmillan, the chancellor of the exchequer, had
assumed that in an emergency he could count on a U.S. infusion of funds, but he
was mistaken. Instead of coming to Britain's aid, the United States used its influence in the International Monetary Fund to prevent Britain from stanching the
run on the sterling.[52]

The British took this turn in the Anglo-American relationship more seriously
than they did Soviet attempts at nuclear intimidation. Macmillan's recognition
of Britain's financial and economic plight signaled the end of the war and an
acceptance of the UN-brokered cease-fire. France was in a better economic position than Britain and was reluctant to cave in to U.S. pressure. Still, Mollet knew
that France could not continue military operations without British support.
Resentfully and reluctantly, the Mollet Cabinet assented to a cease-fire.[53]

The European allies needed a life preserver to get them back together with their
senior NATO partner, and Canada provided it—to the relief of the United States
as well as Britain and France. While Dulles would not accept Lester Pearson's suggestions on November 1 for a UN peace force, by the next day he had changed his
mind. Before the end of the General Assembly's session on November 2, Dulles
told its members that he wanted the Canadian delegate to formulate a concrete
proposal for a cease-fire that would be implemented by a peacekeeping force. The
secretary-general welcomed the idea.[54]

There was no question about U.S. anxiety to repair relations with its allies. When Canada, Norway, and Yugoslavia submitted the proposal to the General Assembly, U.S. Ambassador Lodge noted, "The United States earnestly hopes that the Government of Israel will agree without delay to the prompt withdrawal of its armed forces behind the armistice lines and will co-operate fully in carrying out the plan now being negotiated by the Secretary-General." Lodge had the same hopes for the British and French along with his "trust that the Government of Egypt, for its part, will be prepared to accept the temporary stationing within its territory of elements of the United Nations emergency force [UNEF] in order to preserve peace in that part of the world." As an earnest of the importance given the proposal by his government, Lodge promised that "the United States is prepared to help—and help in an important way—as regards airlifts, shipping, transport and supplies."[55]

Britain and France abstained from voting on the proposal. But fifty-seven nations voted for it, with nineteen abstentions. For different reasons Israel, Egypt, and the Warsaw bloc were among the members that abstained. It was not that the Anglo-French were opposed to a peace force. They wanted to have it on face-saving terms. They insisted that such a force was always their preference; their intervention was only to deal with an emergency the UN was unable to manage. British Ambassador Dixon "heartily welcomed the idea of sending a United Nations force to take over the responsibilities which we have felt bound to shoulder." But he also asserted that no immediate withdrawal was possible before the UN force arrived and took control of the canal zone. French ambassador Louis de Guiringaud also applauded the Canadian initiative and claimed to be especially gratified to observe that it is "an idea which was first suggested by France" during the Paris Peace Conference of 1919.[56]

The abstentions of the USSR and Egypt reflected their displeasure at the West's regaining the high ground by means of a peacekeeping force when they felt penalties should have been imposed on the three aggressors. Israel, too, abstained as it sought direct negotiations with Egypt. Otherwise, Israel feared that Egypt would continue to consider the armistices of 1949 "as a state of war, and it cannot be the function of the General Assembly to promote or to foster a system of war."[57]

The withdrawal of the Anglo-French forces, and particularly the Israeli forces ten miles from the canal, took time and tried the patience of the United Nations and the United States. Compliance did not come easily. Egyptian consent had to be won to allow the presence of a peacekeeping force. And it was vital that the UN force exclude any British or French contingent. Not until the end of 1956 did the British and French troops leave the canal zone, while the most vulnerable belligerent, Israel, delayed its departure from the Sinai and the Gaza strip until it had gained access to the Gulf of Aqaba. Promises for similar access to the Suez Canal were never fulfilled.

With Harold Macmillan as prime minister in place of the ailing Anthony Eden in January 1957, Britain resumed its close ties with the United States. While there would be serious differences in the future, never again would Britain strain the bonds of alliance to the degree it did over the Suez. France on the other hand followed a path toward Gaullism on the assumption that the United States was an untrustworthy ally. Although Nasser reluctantly accepted UNEF, the UN Emergency Force, he emerged as a hero of the Arab-Asian bloc—the man who stood up to the West, kept the canal closed to Israel, and bucked U.S. opposition in order to resume control of Gaza. The United States may have enjoyed a rare popular moment with the former European colonies in forcing Britain and France to end their intervention in Egypt, but their appreciation did not survive the decade. As for the Soviets, the Suez crisis was a providential action that permitted the world to turn a blind eye to their behavior in Hungary.

NATO and the UN

As the Suez imbroglio played out in the UN General Assembly, the voice of the Atlantic alliance was rarely heard in the efforts to extricate Britain and France from their quagmire. NATO's leading member did little to advance a position either in the North Atlantic Council or in the General Assembly, beyond proclaiming its virtue in defending the principles of the UN Charter. When the NATO allies wanted a communiqué in the December 1956 summit that would imply a consensus in NATO on a concerted policy in the Middle East, Dulles opposed their initiative. He managed to have his colleagues withhold any statement that might give the appearance of NATO "'teaming up' and taking positions in the UN as a bloc." The United States continued to worry about the taint of colonialism even as America sought to strengthen the alliance.[58]

Inevitably, concern about NATO's silence figured in discussions at the Paris meeting of the council on December 11–12, 1956. Halvord Lange of Norway shared the U.S. shock and dismay at the Anglo-French failure to advise their colleagues about their plans. He felt that the British and French actions would harm the NATO relations with Afro-Asian nations. But his object was less to rebuke the British and France than to use the occasion to emphasize the need for better consultation within the alliance, in keeping with the report of the "Three Wise Men," now sidelined by the Middle East crisis. Selwyn Lloyd for Britain and Christian Pineau for France tried to divert criticism by dwelling on Soviet violations of the UN Charter and by claiming that there would be no damage to NATO's image if UNEF was a success.[59]

Belgium's Paul-Henri Spaak followed Lange's line the next day to underscore the importance of the Wise Men's report, a plea to the larger powers to consult all the allies before taking action. The report was also intended to increase the powers of the secretary general as a means of emphasizing the purpose of the report. These recommendations may have been important to the smaller nations but did not register with the larger powers. The Wise Men's voices were drowned out by the concurrent conflict over Suez.

The summit meeting's communiqué, in December 1956, included a strong condemnation of Soviet behavior in Hungary while the Suez crisis appeared as a vague endorsement of a lasting peace in the Middle East. The only reference to the powers involved in the crisis was the emphasis on clearing the Suez Canal. Spaak's primary concern was to warn the council against allowing the issue of colonialism to govern NATO's decisions, since colonies such as the Belgian Congo were not prepared for independence. Portugal, conscious of its own African colonies, heartily concurred in this caveat.

The Danish and Dutch members of the council also expressed disappointment with the British and French, but Denmark's Hans Christian Hansen noted that his country "has refrained from indulging in public criticism," while the Netherlands' Joseph Luns observed that the Anglo-French motives were not dishonorable in any way; there was no intention of threatening Egyptian independence, "a fact which contrasts glaringly with brutal repression by Soviets in Hungary."[60] On balance, it appeared that the allies' rebuke to their European partners was milder than their feelings of neglect by the United States.

The voting pattern in the UN also displayed the mixed feelings of the NATO allies. Most of them supported the UN-sponsored resolution on November 2 demanding that the British, French, and Israelis withdraw their forces and accept an immediate cease-fire. But among the six countries abstaining were NATO allies Canada, Belgium, the Netherlands, and Portugal. Granting that their African colonies had some effect on the Belgian and Portuguese vote, the Low Countries abstained primarily in recognition of the damage that might be done to the unity of the alliance by the U.S. resolution.

Belgian Foreign Minister Spaak, a founding father of NATO, recalled his worry about "a possible break-up of NATO as a result of the differences between the British and French on the one hand and the Americans on the other." Knowing that Nasser had set the crisis in motion by illegally nationalizing the Suez Canal Company, Spaak lamented in a letter to the Belgian ambassador in Washington, "Let the Americans be in no doubt: if the British and French fail in Egypt, we shall blame this on lack of U.S. support. A severe blow will have been dealt to NATO and by the same token, the Russians will have won a victory and will gain indirectly what until now they have been unable to obtain by direct action." While praising Dulles as "a sympathetic mind and a generous soul," Spaak criticized him for his arbitrary division of the world into "absolute good and absolute evil in politics."[61] In brief, Spaak laid a good portion of blame for the Suez debacle on the U.S. secretary of state.

It was not surprising that Canada played the most important role in mitigating intra-alliance differences. As a North American nation, Canada had always positioned itself between a dominant U.S. neighbor and European allies whose interests often differed from Canada's. Its diplomatists were always concerned that their American ally might neglect Canada in favor of its new connections with the Old World. Suez was an opportunity both to save the alliance and to increase the prestige of Canada. The transatlantic parties were relieved to grab the life preserver Canada offered in the form of UNEF.

Some face-saving on both sides of the Atlantic was necessary before the Anglo-American entente could be reestablished, but by the spring of 1957 the entente was back in place. The USSR may have escaped consequences within the UN for its brutal suppression of the Hungarian revolt, but it failed to capitalize as much as it had anticipated on the West's troubles in the UN over the Suez crisis. In fact, Henry Cabot Lodge sounded complacent in June 1957 when he asserted that he was "not pessimistic regarding the influence of the Asian-African countries in the United Nations. The United States continues to occupy a unique position, which is not subordinate to any 'blocs.' This was demonstrated during the recent Suez difficulties. Moreover, the Asian-African nations are so diverse that it appears little likelihood that they will ever constitute a solid bloc."[62] There was an element of hubris in Lodge's statement that would shake his confidence over the next decade.

Two figures stand out in the turbulent events of October and November 1956. One is that of Secretary-General Dag Hammarskjöld, trying to calm the waters as best he could. Despite the usual cautious approach associated with diplomats, the secretary-general took a firm stand at a critical moment. When the British and French appeared unwilling to abide by any resolution from either the Security Council or the General Assembly, Hammarskjöld made it clear he would resign rather than accept the continuation of the Anglo-French intervention in Egypt. Despite his duty to avoid a public stand on conflicts between member nations, he proclaimed on October 31 that "the discretion and impartiality thus imposed on the Secretary-General by the character of his immediate task, may not degenerate into a policy of expediency."[63] This was a brave statement and was rewarded only in part. The "policy of expediency" that he deplored was not wholly abandoned. No matter how strongly he felt about Soviet aggression in Hungary, he had to accede to the realities of the time. No member, including the United States, was prepared to enforce UN resolutions directed against the Soviet Union.

The other figure was that of President Eisenhower, with a less conflicted role to play. His stand against his allies as well as the Soviet Union was unequivocal. Although he understood the provocations endured by the British and the French, for him the use of force was unacceptable. Eisenhower did not waver in spite of an election only a few days away.[64] Unlike the president's position,

Dulles's diplomacy produced too many ambiguities, leading the European allies to assume that no matter how angry the secretary of state was over their blind-siding him, he would still side with them when they made their move against Nasser. Had they listened more closely to the president they would not have remained under that illusion.

At another time NATO's secretary general might have been able to mediate among the allies and even present a united front at the UN. With all his diplomatic skills honed over four years in office, Lord Ismay had little to offer at this critical moment. The Anglo-French adventure in Egypt and their aborted challenge to the United States demoralized the alliance and deprived Ismay of an opportunity to exercise leadership of the contending members. It is noteworthy that his account of his stewardship from 1952 to 1957 makes no mention of the Suez crisis. Nor does his correspondence at the time pay much attention to it.[65] His absence from the scene contrasted vividly with the large presence of his counterpart at the UN.

Never again would the United States be so popular in the General Assembly. And never again during the Cold War were the NATO allies so divided. The alliance survived the mid-1950s only to come up against a new challenge at the UN, at the end of the decade, concerning the former Belgian Congo.

3

The Congo Crisis, 1960

Superficially, the turmoil in the former Belgian Congo resembled the Suez crisis of 1956. There were abundant similarities in the two cases, including the scene in Africa, the decolonization process, the threat of Soviet intervention, the division within NATO, and the United Nations' role as potential deus ex machina. There were other similarities as well. The American fear of alienating the African-Asian bloc in the United Nations by siding with its European allies was even more acute than it had been four years before. Seventeen new nations, mostly former colonies of Britain, France, and Belgium from Africa, joined the UN in 1960. And just as the Suez crisis produced the United Nations Emergency Force (UNEF), so the Congo anarchy in 1960 led to the establishment of Opérations des Nations Unies au Congo (ONUC).

The differences between the two cases are more important than the similarities, however. The sheer number of former colonies in the UN guaranteed hostile judgments of Belgian and Franco-British roles in the Congo. The opportunities afforded the Soviets to champion the new nations at the expense of the West were greater than in 1956, and they took advantage of them in ways they could not have done over Suez. Material aid to opponents of the central government was a factor absent in 1956 when the USSR had to cope with unrest in Eastern Europe.

The Warsaw Pact members never missed an opportunity in the UN General Assembly to link Belgian actions with a NATO conspiracy against Africa. The United States tried to dissociate itself from the imperial histories of its allies, but with less success than in the Suez crisis. The U.S. effort to channel all activity through the UN proved a problem when the UN secretary-general himself became the focus of Soviet and to some extent African-Asian opposition. The United States sided more consciously with the European allies, but without convincing them of its good faith. NATO, as in 1956, remained divided, unable to present a consensus at the UN General Assembly. When the North Atlantic Council (NAC) met in December 1960, the turmoil in the Congo went unmentioned.

Origins of the Crisis

No colonial power was less prepared than Belgium to disgorge its colonies in the 1950s. Unlike Britain and France, Belgium had taken over the territory from its proprietor, King Leopold II, in 1908 and ruled it from Brussels. Also, unlike the larger colonial powers, Belgium had made no provision for its colony's future self-government. Under a paternal government, the Congolese received social benefits, but economic development of the land's mineral resources was in the hands of such organizations as the Union Minière du Haut Katanga. There was no effort on the part of the Belgian government to promote settlement in the territory, although there was a white population of over a hundred thousand at the time of independence.

It was largely the pressure of decolonization elsewhere in Africa that forced Belgium to consider political reforms in 1958. These promises of change came too late to forestall serious riots in the capital, Leopoldville, however. Precipitously, a panicked Belgium decided in December 1959 to grant independence within five months. This sudden reversal of its previous management of the Congo was certainly inspired by fear of damage to the economy from newly energized Congolese nationalists. An uprising in the manner of Algeria's against France was also a frightening prospect. But there was hope that experienced Belgian administrators would be retained to guide the new republic, along the lines that President Charles de Gaulle was advocating for the new states of former French Africa.

National elections in the spring of 1960 produced a coalition government under President Joseph Kasavubu and Premier Patrice Lumumba. Each of the four provinces would have its own president, functioning under the authority of the central governments. Independence Day for Congo was June 30, 1960. It was to be a gala occasion. Belgian officials and diplomats from around the world—including Robert Murphy, head of the U.S. delegation—assembled in Leopoldville. King Baudouin of Belgium officially proclaimed the territory's independence. President Kasavubu delivered a gracious speech that fitted the occasion, expressing his country's goodwill toward Belgium. Premier Lumumba, on the other hand, offered a mixed message. Wearing the maroon sash of the Order of the Crown, Belgium's highest decoration, that he had received the night before, Lumumba lashed out at the former colonial master, reminding members of the new Parliament of the "ironies, the insults, the blows we had to submit to morning, noon, and night because we were negroes." The Soviet delegation seemed to enjoy the tirade as the premier called for the Congo to be the "rallying point of all Africa." Two hours later, at a state dinner, Lumumba toasted the king and praised Belgium for the magnificent work it had done in building the Congo.[1]

Given the mercurial temperament of the Congo Republic's premier, it may not have come as a surprise that within a week of its independence the country was in chaos. The Force Publique (the Belgian-officered Congo army) mutinied on July 5. The rebellion began innocently enough, with the soldiers demanding raises in pay and rank that they believed were being given to the civilian branches of government. To divert their anger, Premier Lumumba not only ordered automatic promotions for each soldier but also the removal of all Belgian officers in the Force Publique. In the ensuing disorders, panic spread among thousands of Belgian civilians as stories circulated of violence committed by leaderless soldiers in Leopoldville and other major centers. Conceivably, the Belgian officers might have suppressed the mutiny if they had not been constrained by their uncertain authority under the new Congolese government.[2] In any event these events, based on some facts and more rumors, led Belgium on July 9 to order its troops from the Kamina base in Katanga to intervene, first in friendly Elizabethville, Katanga's capital, at the invitation of its premier, Moise Tshombe, and then in other locations where Europeans were beleaguered. The announced purpose was to defend Belgian nationals against impending massacres. In so doing Belgium also claimed to be preserving the country from suicidal disorders.

At the instigation of Lumumba, Belgium was brought before the bar of world opinion and branded as an aggressor in the UN Security Council, even though that language was deleted in the subsequent resolution. The United Nations, now populated by an array of former colonized nations, seemed to accept without serious doubts Lumumba's accusation that the return of Belgian troops to Congo cities represented a plot to recolonize the Congo in the guise of protecting civilian lives. The almost simultaneous secession of Tshombe's mineral-rich Katanga was seen as evidence of the power of Belgian financial interests that reportedly guided Tshombe's behavior. In asking for UN troops on July 12, Kasavubu and Lumumba jointly accused "the Belgian government of having carefully prepared the secession of Katanga with a view to maintaining a hold on our country."[3] When Belgian paratroopers occupied the capital's airport, the Congolese leaders warned that, unless a UN force consisting of military personnel from neutral countries arrived without delay, they would appeal to Third World members and to the Soviet Union for help.[4]

All semblance of Congolese national sovereignty was now in jeopardy as Belgian paratroopers occupied key positions in the country. At the same time, Katanga declared its independence from the central government. That Belgium's military action was in violation of Congo's sovereignty was obvious. It was equally obvious that detaching Katanga from the country would impoverish the new republic. Katanga produced copper, along with 60 percent of the world's uranium and 80 percent of the world's industrial diamonds. Supporting Tshombe were powerful European mining companies that included French and British investors with a considerable stake in abetting his ambitions. Less than two weeks after winning independence, the Congolese witnessed the return of their former masters, seemingly ready to use force if not to negate their liberation at least to promote secession of a vital province.[5]

The scene was set for widening the crisis to embrace nations and organizations that in one form or another became entangled in the problems of central Africa. The most prominent inevitably was the United Nations and its secretary-general, Dag Hammarskjöld. With memories of his success in defusing the Suez crisis, he immediately thought of replicating the UNEF in Egypt with a counterpart in the Congo. As he demonstrated in 1956, he wished to take a strong stand on defending the charter, which he quickly found Belgium to be violating. His key aides in dealing with the Congo in 1960—Rajeshwar Dayal of India and Conor Cruise O'Brien of Ireland—shared his views, to the disadvantage of Belgium. His most devoted member of the Secretariat, Brian Urquhart, was confident that Hammarskjöld's "sureness of touch, and strength communicated to others the comforting feeling that in any situation he knew what to do, and how to do it, where he wanted to go and how to get there."[6]

Inevitably, the Soviet Union was happy to support Congo, particularly since the unsettled conditions seemed to provide an opportunity to embarrass the NATO powers and to assume the mantle of defender of the newly freed nations against the machinations of the capitalist colonial nations. This was not a new posture on the part of the Soviets; they had hoped to play the same role in the Middle East four years earlier. The Cold War became a part of the Congo crisis just as it had in the Suez crisis in 1956. The Soviets had allies in the new African nations Ghana and Guinea, radicalized by their colonial experiences and seemingly open to communist influence. While Kasavubu followed a more moderate response to Belgium's intervention, the volatile Lumumba was disposed to exploit the Soviet approach to Belgian aggression.

With Britain and France clearly on the side of Belgium, the United States once again occupied a sensitive position, hoping to balance its anticolonial history, most recently displayed in opposing the Anglo-French invasion of Egypt, against its obligations and loyalty to NATO allies. This was as difficult to manage as the path the country had chosen in dealing with Britain and France in 1956. Before the end of summer of 1960 Belgium was convinced that its trust had been betrayed by the leader of the Atlantic alliance in which Belgium had buried its independence. As waves of hostile world opinion dashed upon Belgium, the United States seemed to make no effort to stem the tide or to divert its force. Instead, America was seen to replay the experience in the UN of 1956 when it voted on July 14, 1960, alongside the Soviet Union to demand that Belgium "withdraw its troops from the Republic of the Congo," instead of defending its presence there. The two NATO allies on the UN Security Council abstained.[7]

Hammarskjöld's Intervention

That the secretary-general would take an early initiative in attempting to resolve the Congo crisis was prefigured in the history of the UN itself. Even before independence was granted to the Congo, the prospect of problems was evident, with the host of African countries entering the United Nations in 1960. The case of the Congo was just "the most crucial test" as a U.S. State Department paper on the forthcoming meeting of the fourteenth General Assembly recognized. The UN was charged with bringing order out of anticipated chaos, "in a country which has no experience in self-government," and with preventing "the area from becoming the arena of cold war conflict." This was a daunting challenge that might not be successful, but the UN "clearly offers the best hope of all the available alternatives." If successful UN help in the Congo could set an example of how the world organization might deal "with the myriad problems which may attend the attainment of independence in many formerly dependent areas of the world."[8]

It turned out that the situation in the Congo developed into the worst-case scenario all round—for the Congo, for Belgium, and for the UN. The qualified confidence of the State Department report was misplaced as the Congo descended into chaos. The Africanization of the Force Publique, renamed the Armée Nationale Congolaise (ANC), meant that inexperienced Congolese noncommissioned officers replaced the summarily dismissed Belgian officer corps. The new leaders could not command the obedience or respect of their troops, and the result was disunity and demoralization within the ANC that reflected the political and tribal disunity of the nation itself.

Into this confusion Secretary-General Hammarskjöld interposed himself, using Article 99 of the UN Charter as his justification. This article mandated that "the secretary-general may bring to the attention of the UN Security Council any matter which in his opinion may threaten the maintenance of international peace and security." It was a broad grant of authority, opening opportunities for extending UN authority to a degree not found in the Korean or Suez crises. In those cases it had been member nations that brought the matter to the UN, not the secretary-general.[9]

That Hammarskjöld's behavior was more than an unseemly grasp for power was obvious. It was Kasavubu, as commander-in-chief of the ANC, and Lumumba as minister of defense, not the secretary-general, who appealed on July 10 for UN technical military assistance to help restore discipline to the ANC. This was at the advice of U.S. ambassador Clare H. Timberlake. The Congo leaders also wanted U.S. troops to restore law and order, a request that was turned down on the grounds that the issue was in the hands of the United Nations.[10]

On July 12, Kasavubu and Lumumba changed the tone of their request and demanded the withdrawal of Belgian troops from the Congo within two days.

Now military aid was wanted in order to resist "external aggression" from "the colonialist regime." The telegram accused Belgium of violating the treaty that would allow its troops to intervene "only on the express request of the Congolese government." It linked Belgian aggression to the secession of Katanga, condemning the secession as a "conspiracy between Belgian imperialists and a small group of Katanga leaders."[11]

Such was the context of the Congo's appeal to Hammarskjöld. The secretary-general had clearly identified the functions of his office during the Suez crisis when he was ready to resign if his independence was in jeopardy. He made his point then. And after his appointment for a second five-year term as secretary-general in 1957, he amplified his belief that in the authority of his office, "the Secretary-General should be expected to act . . . without . . . guidance, should this appear to him to be necessary in order to help in filling any vacuum that may appear in the systems" for safeguarding peace and security.[12]

Given this background it is understandable that Hammarskjöld became the prime mover in having the UN Security Council provide the Congo with military assistance. He went beyond this response to establish a UN peacekeeping force that would not become party to any internal dispute or employ arms except in self-defense. Aside from this caveat there was the question of sending troops to the Congo. Only the United States had the capability of managing the logistical problems involved and did so with dispatch. Hammarskjöld reported on July 18 that thirty-five hundred troops in addition to substantial equipment from four African countries were en route to the Congo as a result of the resolution, which left implementation to the secretary-general. He understandably interpreted it in light of his experience with the UNEF. In the Sinai desert it was a much simpler matter to keep the activity of the UN troops separate from that of the Egyptians and to recognize a clear distinction between what was the UN's responsibility and what was the Egyptian government's. The Congo mandate, however, was less specific and was intertwined with the internal affairs of the country, making it difficult to draw a line between restoring law and order and interfering in the Congo's internal affairs.[13]

Hammarskjöld had the dual requirement of putting together a force to send to the Congo and of finding the means to get them there. The first task was the harder, the second the more contentious. While there was pressure from African countries to make the force an all-African affair, Hammarskjöld sought a compromise. African forces were too inexperienced to serve the purpose alone. The secretary-general wanted a broader representation of UN members based on the UN's status as an international organization. Besides Ethiopia, Ghana, Guinea, Morocco, and Tunisia, which had offered troops prior to the UN resolution, Hammarskjöld included such countries as Ireland and Sweden and appointed a Swedish general and an Indian chief of staff to lead the force. These countries had no history of colonialism and were acceptable to African members.[14]

Once the composition of the force was settled, the problem was how to transport it. Ethiopia, Ghana, Morocco, and Tunisia were already in Leopoldville. Some six hundred Swedish troops were expected to arrive by July 20.[15] This was an impressive achievement, of which the United States boasted in its report in support of the July 14 resolution. This action was also one that was bound to fuel Soviet efforts to arouse African suspicions of the secretary-general's motives. While the United States noted that "it had been necessary to send a small number of United States technical and service personnel to Leopoldville" to support the airlift, the Soviet permanent representative to the UN, Arkady Sobolev, made a formal "protest against the sending of United States troop units to the Republic of the Congo on any pretext and insists on their immediate withdrawal." If the Soviet charges were accurate, the Americans were violating Hammarskjöld's intention of excluding troops from "any of the permanent members of the Security Council."[16]

At the same time, Belgium, in league with France and Britain on this issue, was equally suspicious of Hammarskjöld's motives, because of his seeming tilt toward the Lumumba position on July 13. His language was skeptical of Belgium's contention that it returned to the Congo only to protect lives and restore order: "It is not for the Secretary-General to pronounce himself on this action and its legal and political aspects, but I must conclude from the communications received from the Government of the Congo that the presence of these troops is a source of internal, and potentially also of international tension. In these circumstances, the presence of Belgian troops cannot be accepted as a satisfactory stopgap arrangement."[17] While this statement helped to justify a UN force, Belgium found it prejudiced against their humanitarian actions to protect lives of threatened Europeans. The removal of language in the resolution that had identified Belgium as the aggressor did not appease the European allies even as the United States tried its best to quiet their concerns.

Given the toxic environment created by the anti-Belgian passions in the Congo and by that government's reactions, it was understandable that controversy dogged the passage of the Security Council resolution. The USSR had the backing of the African-Asian states in branding Belgium an aggressor and in presenting a deadline for its troops to be withdrawn. The Soviet presumption to speak for the government of the Congo in the Security Council led U.S. ambassador Henry Cabot Lodge to ask why the USSR had intervened to seek a meeting of the council on the Congo's behalf: "I am curious as to how it happens that Mr. Sobolev [the Soviet representative on the Security Council] has become a spokesman for the Government of the Republic of the Congo when they are perfectly able to speak for themselves and yet have not asked for this meeting." The British and French members of the council added their own jabs at the Soviet Union for its gratuitous partisanship.[18] The Cold War was alive and well in the Congo crisis in July 1960.

To set the peacekeeping process in motion, Hammarskjöld had to walk a fine line. On the one side was Lumumba, the angriest of the Congo leaders, supported by African neighbors and by the Soviet Union, all wanting quick action directed at the Belgian occupation. On the other was Belgium, quietly backed by France and Britain, that wanted appreciation as well as support for its rescue efforts of European civilians. The secretary-general spelled out the way he would handle the potentially explosive differences in his first report on July 18, less than a week after Congo had asked for aid. He emphasized that the UN force was a "temporary security force," serving "as an arm for the maintenance of order and the protection of life—tasks which naturally belong to the national authorities and which will pass to such authorities as soon as, in the view of the government, they are sufficiently firmly established." But until that time, Hammarskjöld underscored the point, the security force (ONUC) would be "under the exclusive command of the United Nations, vested in the secretary-general by the Security Council."[19]

Tunisia sponsored a compromise resolution that called upon Belgium "to remove its troops" from the Congo and that authorized the secretary-general "to take the necessary steps, in consultation with the Government of the Congo, to provide the Government with such military assistance as may be necessary."[20] The inflammatory language wanted by the Soviets—and repeated a week later—was taken out of the resolution. The moderate approach of Mongi Slim, the Tunisian representative at the UN, did not deter the Soviets from introducing another resolution demanding the "immediate cessation of armed intervention against the Republic of the Congo and the withdrawal from its territory of all troops of the aggressor within a period of twelve days." This resolution was inspired by news that the United States was transporting some twenty-five hundred foreign troops—mostly Tunisian—on U.S. planes, which the Soviets interpreted as U.S. army troop units sent in support of Belgium.[21]

The NATO allies on the UN Security Council—France, Britain, the United States, and Italy—had reservations about the clause in the Tunisian resolution requiring Belgian withdrawal of troops, in light of the statement of the Belgian representative that its forces would leave when UN forces were in a position to assure order and security. The United States could swallow Mongi Slim's skepticism about Belgium's sincerity while the European allies remained uncomfortable with the initial language. The USSR and Poland, on the other hand, wanted both condemnation of Belgian aggression and the immediate withdrawal of troops. The USSR offered two amendments making its points, which were rejected by a vote of seven to two, and a third amendment providing military assistance from African member states, which was rejected by five to four.[22]

Ultimately, the Tunisian draft was adopted unanimously by eight to zero, with France and Britain both abstaining despite more moderate language in the final text.[23] It is noteworthy that, as in the Suez crisis, the United States and the Soviet

Union voted on the same side. Unlike in 1956, the American vote here was reluctant, concerned with appeasing the African members of the UN and hoping that the careful language of the resolution would not antagonize the Belgians. France and Britain did not exercise their veto power, but their abstention was a token of their concern for Belgian sensibilities and interests. The Soviet affirmative vote was not a sign of confidence in the plans of the secretary-general. It was essentially a recognition that there were limits to how far and how fast the USSR could proceed in radicalizing the African states and neutralizing American influence. The USSR understood that aggressive opposition to Hammarskjöld could alienate Third World countries that valued UN membership and their influence in the UN. The strong support of the African-Asian bloc for the July 14 resolution forced the Soviets to vote for it despite their misgivings about UN military aid.

The USSR continued to press the thesis that Belgian aggression was part of a larger NATO plot to control Africa on behalf of its members' economic interests as well as to remove Soviet influence from the region. As Khrushchev responded to a Congo plea for help on July 15: "The bayonet was Belgian, but the bosses were the United States, Belgium, British and West German big monopolies." Convinced that Hammarskjöld and the UN were in the service of the West, Moscow moved for open military support to Lumumba. When on September 17, the secretary-general backed a resolution from Ceylon and Tunisia eliminating all intervention in the Congo outside UN channels, the Soviets vetoed it. Deadlock in the UN's Security Council brought the Congo problem into the General Assembly's special session, which replicated the Security Council resolution on September 20, prohibiting all military aid except through the UN, by a vote of seventy to zero. The Soviet bloc and France abstained.[24]

Soviet alienation from the UN deepened as its client, Lumumba, was first removed from his post, then arrested in December, and murdered in February 1961. Kasavubu and his strongman, Joseph Mobutu, were the victors in this struggle, as was the secretary-general in this period. Once again, the Third World recognized that the UN, not the Soviet Union, was the path to influence in world affairs—at least in this particular contest. Soviet frustration over being outmaneuvered by the West was expressed in the USSR's denunciation of Hammarskjöld and a demand that his position be replaced by a troika of the major powers.[25]

Just as the Soviets viewed the Congo crisis as a zero-sum contest with the United States, so U.S. behavior was governed by Cold War concerns. Its rejection of the Congo's requests for U.S. military aid rested on fears that the Soviets would use this action as a pretext for substantial aid to Lumumba's faction. This caution did not signify lack of interest in the affairs of the Congo. More time and energy in Washington was devoted to that country than to all the rest of Africa combined. Among other reasons for the Congo's importance was its position as the arena for conflict in the Kennedy administration between the State Department's dominant European bureau and the newer emerging African bureau, led by such activists as the former Michigan governor G. Mennen Williams, assistant secretary of state for African affairs under President John F. Kennedy. The way out of the old dilemma of being simultaneously anti-imperialist and a faithful ally of imperialist powers was to have the UN serve U.S. aims. Recognizing that the communists would always work to tie the United States to colonialism, successive administrations found the UN to be a way of unloading responsibility while reaping the benefits of the stability that the UN could provide. The United States was to be the most devoted adherent of UN peacekeeping in the Congo.[26]

The Katanga Problem

From the outset of UN intervention, the United States had no choice but to back the UN even at the expense of ties to its NATO allies. The attempted secession of Katanga was a case in point. The Soviets may have failed in their campaign to elevate Lumumba to power, but they still were able to exploit the connections between Moise Tshombe and the Union Minière in order to win African applause for their stance against colonialism and capitalism. NATO was the link between Tshombe and the Union Minière. The ambivalent positions of Britain and France in their abstention from the Security Council resolution of July 14 seemed to prove the Soviet charges. While Belgium never formally recognized the independence of Katanga, the powerful European mining interests left no doubt about their intentions to back Katanga and the mercenary troops they had recruited for Tshombe.

Belgium might have been as unhappy with Britain and France for their failure to veto the establishment of ONUC as it was with the United States. The NATO allies recognized the need for immediate action, which the UN could supply, despite their unease over international intervention. And the Belgians recognized that their allies' concern over ONUC stemmed in part from the precedent its establishment would create for similar action in Rhodesia. This British federation shared an eleven-hundred-mile boundary with Katanga and also possessed rich mineral deposits in Rhodesia. British investments in the Union Minière were a critical factor in dampening Macmillan's hopes of keeping ties with the new nation of Africa and supporting Hammarskjöld's mandate.[27]

The Katanga lobby—composed of right-wing Conservatives and corporate leaders of Rhodesian and Katangan mineral industries—was a powerful voice in determining British policy. Their sympathies as well as interests were with Tshombe. Still, apart from the pressure of the Katanga lobby, the British Foreign Office was constantly worrying over the possibility that the UN force might enlarge its mission. Deposing Tshombe would open Katanga to the same chaos that afflicted the rest of the country and would jeopardize economic interests in that region. These arguments were widely circulated within the Conservative Party throughout 1960 and 1961. Until Hammarskjöld's death, Britain was wary of employing UN force against Tshombe and joined France in criticizing UN representatives Conor Cruise O'Brien and Rajeshwar Dayal for their hostility toward Katanga. Yet Britain's weight ultimately fell on the UN side. Unlike France, it never withheld financial support for ONUC. Like the United States, Britain wanted to avoid a Cold War clash in the Congo while keeping it out of communist control.[28]

It was Harold Macmillan, Eden's successor as prime minister, who had to wend his way carefully through the minefields laid by political opponents in Parliament. He tried to explain to Parliament why Britain was in favor of the July 14 resolution and yet still abstained in its final form: "Her Majesty's Government did not feel that it would be right in the present state of knowledge of the situation in the Congo to call for Belgian troops to withdraw without any qualification." The Labour leader Hugh Gaitskell did not hesitate to blame Belgium for not taking steps "earlier to bring the people of the Congo toward self-government." Nor was there an easy way to respond to Liberal Jo Grimond's observation that the UN was not to interfere in the internal functions of a sovereign country: "Is that not inevitably what they are doing in the Congo?"[29] Macmillan himself summed up his difficulties with the observation that the Congo

> became a convenient arena for rivalries and fears of the great powers. The communists undoubtedly intended, by turning the Congo into a satellite country, to form this territory into a base from which to spread Marxist gospel throughout the continent, the Americans and British were equally determined to circumvent these plans. In a sense, the task of the British Government was the more complicated because, although in full agreement with Washington's purpose, London was more affected by various conflicting interests.[30]

France's position was less ambivalent. Like Britain it had a constituency with investments in Katanga's minerals, and also like Britain it had a long-term interest both in political stability and in the prevention of communist intervention. The major difference was in the role of President de Gaulle in minimizing UN interference in the Congo. The Gaullist position was to have the whole issue resolved through a troika of the three major NATO powers. The concept was unacceptable to the United States, with respect to the management of NATO itself in 1958; it was equally so in the 1960s with respect to the Congo. The result was that the French, like the Soviets, refused to contribute funds for the ONUC force and, aside from the July 22 resolution, abstained in all others at the Security Council. De Gaulle made it clear through his own pronouncements and through France's representatives in the council that it was in full sympathy with Belgium's military actions in the summer of 1960. As Armand Bérard asked at the Security Council, "Which of our governments would have acted differently if it had been placed in the same position?" More specifically, he labeled the notion of Belgian aggression a myth and said that Belgian actions were in conformity with the Belgian-Congolese Treaty of Friendship of June 29, 1960, a claim that Belgium itself was hesitant to make.[31]

U.S. perplexity over France's stance in the Congo emerged in a letter from Eisenhower to de Gaulle at the end of August 1960. Referring to the French president's complaint that the United States was not consulting sufficiently with France, Eisenhower claimed that "the differences we have had as for instance in past Security Council votes, have not been the result of any lack of consultation with one another. I have, in fact, been struck by the frequency and fullness of the consultations that have taken place among our representatives on virtually a daily basis in Paris, here in Washington, and in Brussels." Eisenhower doubted "that any more formal or elaborate tripartite arrangement at whatever level could have altered this. I cannot believe that our differences were in large measure responsible for the disorder and anarchy in that country." He granted that the U.S. attitude toward the role the United Nations should play had been different and that France might hesitate to rely upon the UN, but "I believe it is a fact that in our consultations on the Congo, France did not present alternatives to a resort to the UN."[32] Secretary of State Christian Herter, Dulles's successor, made the same point to France's ambassador to the United States, Hervé Alphand, the next month when—"with his kind smile," as Alphand put it patronizingly—he rebutted the French reproach about not being consulted on the Congo with the charge that France proposed no alternative beyond talking about a troika. Alphand responded diplomatically that there was no real discord between the two countries, just a difference over methods, notably over the appropriate role of the United Nations.[33]

De Gaulle, characteristically, was more blunt than either the president or the secretary of defense in noting Franco-American differences over the Congo in the summer of 1960: "once the independence of the ex-Belgian Congo had been recognized and Patrice Lumumba's government formed, we openly disapproved of the action instigated by Washington under the umbrella of the General Assembly of the United Nations which led that organization, contrary to its own charter, to intervene militarily and financially in the internal affairs of the new State."[34] De Gaulle was mistaken about which UN organ authorized ONUC—it was the Security Council, not the General Assembly—but his message was unmistakable. The Congo for him was one of many issues that separated France from its NATO ally.

The French and Belgians continued to ask for a joint strategy to deal with the Congo, in order to thwart Soviet penetration. But they did so on terms the

United States could not accept. Although they sided with the Americans in the Kasavubu-Lumumba split in November 1960 and were relieved to see the marginalization of Lumumba's faction, they objected to the U.S. plan in January 1961 to have the ONUC neutralize all Congolese troops, if necessary by force. Such action would give improper emphasis to the UN, precisely the hope nourished by the United States in the difficult period following the assassination of Lumumba. Yet, as the British recognized, "it would be embarrassing to oppose it outright, but we certainly would not want to see it take effect immediately," at least not until Kasavubu could defeat the pro-Soviet Gizenga forces.[35] Yet pressures from the African members of the UN for more energy in the expulsion of Belgium made the UN all the more important as a way out of the U.S. dilemma.

Belgium's Grievances: The NAC and Article 4

Arguably, Belgium's troubles with America over the Congo derived from attitudes as much as from actions. Its leaders looked with suspicion upon the initial U.S. statement on the mutiny, which said, "What is required is an instantaneous response to the urgent requests of the Congolese government rather than the ill-advised or malicious attempts to make political capital out of the serious difficulties of the Congolese people." The Belgian government complained that it was the Congolese people, not the Belgian people in the Congo, to whom Americans showed concern; it was the "malicious" Soviet and "ill-advised" African or Asian efforts to exploit Belgium's difficulties—not the injustice of the accusations against Belgium—that agitated the United States.[36] Behind the guise of fairness to both sides, Belgians could see prejudice against them.

Anticipating a difficult relationship with the American ally, Belgium's ambassador to the NAC, André de Staercke, requested an emergency meeting of the council on July 14 under the rubric of Article 4 of the treaty in order to solicit the support of its allies behind its intention to withdraw its forces "as soon as the United Nations forces were able to ensure the security of the white population." Belgium hoped that the allies would use their influence to deflect the demand that Belgian troops be withdrawn before the UN forces were in place. The allies initially expressed complete sympathy with Belgium's position, recognizing the danger of the advantage the Soviets could take from divisions within the alliance. Yet, before the special sessions ended, the Belgians were concerned over Norway's asking that NATO not make any public statement unless the Soviets threatened war with Belgium. Given the U.S. emphasis on UN action and its wish to avoid antagonizing the African-Asian bloc, de Staercke worried that the United States might adopt the same policy in the Congo that it had on Suez. The British representative found the Belgians to be "very lonely and quick to suspect United States purposes, especially when stated by Cabot Lodge." The U.S. delegate, in response, vigorously asserted his nation's support of Belgium in the debate over the UN resolution, and that its affirmative vote for UN involvement was the best available solution.[37]

The U.S. concern was over possible Soviet advantage in the crisis. In their eagerness to anticipate and combat Soviet taunts, Americans frequently slighted the feelings of their allies. For example, Ambassador Lodge's responses to Soviet charges against Belgium in the UN Security Council suggest that the need to make debaters' points against the Soviet adversary ranked as high as the defense of Belgium's position. Should Belgians feel properly grateful for gracious congratulations for their cooperation with UN resolutions when, in the same speech, the U.S. delegate assailed the Soviets for linking the United States with Belgium as NATO allies exploiting the Congo? The explanation that the two countries were allies only in the defense of Europe could have given Belgians scant comfort, even though the U.S. commentary was literally accurate.[38]

But no matter how misguided or muddled U.S. policy toward the UN and the Congo might be, Belgium recognized just how limited its response could be. The American-educated premier, Gaston Eyskens, exhibited as much sorrow as anger over U.S. behavior. Certainly he could not turn to the Soviet Union, which relished his country's plight, or to a Swedish form of neutralism when Belgium's defense was inextricably tied to NATO. Former premier Paul-Henri Spaak, then NATO's secretary general, agreed that "the treatment we received in the United Nations was disgraceful. Our best intentions were distorted and our mistakes— unfortunately we did commit some—were exploited beyond measure." The most serious mistake was the Belgian government's failure to assure the support of its allies in determining its actions in the Congo.[39]

Yet some means had to be found to redress a situation in which, as minister of foreign affairs Pierre Wigny put it, "Even our friends have kept silence, and we alone are regarded throughout the world not as victims but as traitors." One answer was to strike back through NATO. A week before the crisis, a leading Socialist deputy complained to the Belgian Parliament about the U-2 flights and about the allies' inability to affect U.S. decisions in NATO's relations with the Soviet Union.[40] The Congo problem was merely a more humiliating example of Belgium's inferiority in the alliance.

The Parliament left it to the Belgian premier, Gaston Eyskens, to find a way to attract America's attention to Belgium's concerns. After NATO allies had approved—or at least did not disapprove—Hammarskjöld's demand that Belgium withdraw its troops, Eyskens noted with some bitterness that Belgium had established the bases in the Congo at NATO's insistence. Perhaps, in implementing the UN Security Council's decision, Belgium not only should evacuate those bases and save 70 million dollars annually but should also save even more money by canceling its plans to buy 100 million dollars' worth of Starfighter aircraft? He added, "I do not want to say that Belgium should disassociate itself from the Atlantic Alliance, but I declare that gestures of generosity do not pay. If we are a small country, we are also a sovereign country, which will take in the military sphere the necessary decisions."[41]

The trouble with this reaction was its lack of credibility. The only action that would have compelled America's attention would have been the denunciation of the North Atlantic Treaty and departure from NATO. For Belgium to take or even to promise drastic change would mean punishing the European allies more than the United States. Many of the contracts affected by a reduction of military expenditures would be those of the Dutch, German, and British suppliers rather than the U.S. economy. The government quietly abandoned its threats against NATO. When Spaak went directly from his post as NATO's secretary general to head the foreign ministry in a Social Christian–Socialist coalition in the spring of 1961, he calmed some of the tensions between Belgium and its allies.

A realistic appraisal of Belgium's strategic position did not preclude other means of manifesting Belgian displeasure with U.S. leadership. An attractive solution could be to follow like-minded European allies, uneasy over their dependence on a potentially unreliable ally. Britain's qualified acceptance of the UN initiative and France's vigorous defense of Belgium's position in the Congo evoked special appreciation. Perhaps the best hope for Belgium would be to join de Gaulle and West Germany's Konrad Adenauer in remaking a Europe that could stand up to the United States as well as to the Soviet Union. But these views were no more than ritual gestures of defiance, no more credible than retaliation against NATO. It was not forgotten that at a critical moment neither Britain nor France had the strength or the will to veto the resolution of July 14. And if they had, would the Europe of de Gaulle be more understanding of Belgian interests than that of the U.S.-led alliance? Some members of the Belgian Parliament in a spirit of resignation and others with cynicism observed that there had always been solidarity of the great powers against the weak, and as a victim of international intrigue Belgium could do little more than "continue to bear the cross."[42]

Both the Belgian government and the press also continued to look for explanations behind U.S. actions against their interests. Simplistic anticolonialism was one explanation for American gullibility about the efficacy of the UN intervention in the Congo and the character of its new leaders. The treatment of Premier Lumumba in Washington at the end of July 1960 was an example of the problem. By this time most Belgians had identified the new premier of the Congo republic as the source of their troubles and traced the problems of Congo's independence to his erratic but charismatic genius. At the very moment of Belgium's humiliation in the United Nations, the United States, eager to win favor in the Third World, followed its anti-Belgian actions in the UN Security Council with a reception for

Lumumba that was fit for "a prince regent." Feeding his ego in the hope of winning him over to the West, the Eisenhower administration lodged him at the Blair House in preparation for a meeting with the president. Belgians believed that Americans honored a dangerous adventurer, from whom the United States had as much to fear as Belgium, as if he had been king of the Belgians himself. For those who conceded good intentions to Americans, the best that could be said was that the politics of "boy scouts" was inapplicable to the real world.[43]

For other Belgians, U.S. anticolonial policies had more sinister meanings. For them the United States was serving as a dupe of the communist world conspiracy. From the beginnings of the Congo mutiny, the Soviet Union had engineered a plot that would bring the Congo into the communist orbit. Soviet attacks on Belgium were never more than thinly disguised attacks on NATO and on the United States itself, with Lumumba as its agent. Yet Americans were too naïve to recognize this reality in the summer of 1960. When the Eisenhower administration finally became disillusioned with Lumumba, Belgian commentators took some satisfaction in reporting the premier's verbal assaults against the United States: "The trouble for certain of these people is that the arm they employed to throw us out is turning against them."[44]

Despite this belated awakening to the dangers from communist plotting and Lumumba's demagoguery, the United States was slow to learn from experience, according to the views of conservative Belgians. The Americans, they asserted, had served the interests of the Soviet Union in its campaign against Tshombe in Katanga, which led to the Katanga premier's removal in the winter of 1963. They drove into exile—at least temporarily—the one Congolese who respected Western civilization and stood as a bulwark against communism. If only a Dulles could emerge again in the United States to give vigor to American anticommunism, mused one Belgian newspaper.[45] This wistful note was uttered while President Eisenhower was still in office; under his successor, John F. Kennedy, there was greater anticommunist vigor, but to the horror of many Belgians it was applied to misdirected ends—at least in Africa.

In much of the criticism there was an element of condescension over the Americans' inexperience and ineptitude in handling Congolese relations. But this element was notably lacking in the area of U.S. financial interest in the Congo. Here condescension yielded to suspicion, as the United States was credited with shrewdness and guile usually denied it in other matters. In brief, many Belgians were convinced that U.S. behavior in the Congo reflected the demands of its financial leaders to replace Belgian capital investments with their own. The Union Minière in Katanga was the target. Economic advantage seemed to provide a credible reason for America's precipitate plunge into African affairs. This would explain its subsequent support of the UN force against Katanga, and its continuing vendetta against Tshombe.

This argument gained currency immediately after Congo won its independence when Premier Lumumba contracted with Edgar Detwiler, an American industrial promoter, to exploit the mineral resources of the Congo. Lumumba professed to have the moral support of the State Department in his ventures.[46] For Lumumba the major benefit would be a non-Belgian company to perform a vital task on terms presumably more favorable than the Union Minière would offer. For the American investors there would be the lure of enormous profits blessed by the State Department, which would welcome the Detwiler operation as a means of removing Soviet competition in this region. Such, at least, was the expectation attributed to the Detwiler operation. The grand design involved 2 billion dollars, with five hundred workers and technicians prepared to proceed immediately to the Congo. The first projects were already earmarked—large hydroelectric and aluminum plants near Inga at the mouth of the Congo River.[47]

But Detwiler's scheme quickly dissolved. The revelation that Detwiler was essentially a speculator with a record of failed ventures in Guinea and Liberia may have had some bearing on the Congo's abandonment of the contract. Undersecretary of State C. Douglas Dillon pointed out to Lumumba that "this man had no connections with the United States Government and no access to the United States Government funds." More likely, pressures from other African countries forced Lumumba to back off from his commitment with the excuse that no contract was valid without the Congo parliament's endorsement.[48]

What is significant about this aborted project was its impact on Belgian public opinion, from Premier Eyskens to the man in the street. Even though the influential right-wing Catholic *La Libre Belgique* acknowledged that the U.S. government was not in collusion with Detwiler and that he was not a serious figure on Wall Street, the paper raised the image of hostile, opportunistic American financiers ready to profit from Belgium's misfortunes. Two weeks after the collapse of Detwiler's plans, *La Libre Belgique* warned about "a vast political-financial intrigue from the other side of the Atlantic." And at the end of August the liberal paper *La Nouvelle Gazette* clearly referred to Americans when it editorialized that "sooner or later other people would take over what Belgium abandoned." Fairly or not, in Belgium the Detwiler deal became the symbol of American capitalist intervention in the Congo, and an explanation of the U.S. use of the UN to serve its own interests. ONUC's function then was to unify the Congo on America's behalf.[49]

The U.S. Role

The overheated rhetoric in Belgium's press and Parliament reflected the tensions of the time. The serious plight of Belgian civilians in the Congo was genuine, and the nation's emotions were understandably aroused. The United States, striving to avoid the taint of colonialism, welcomed Hammarskjöld's intervention, but without condemning the terms—withdrawal of Belgian forces—in the spirited language used by the French and British governments. The European allies appeared to be on Belgium's side, but not the senior NATO partner.

Of the charges that accompanied Belgium's disappointment with U.S. behavior, most disappear under scrutiny. In the Detwiler case it was not just that Eyskens and the Brussels press knew how insubstantial Detwiler's project was. The *New York Times* had publicized Detwiler's business dealings and reported the spotty record of his activities in other African countries. In no sense was he regarded in the United States as the vanguard of the American financial community's invasion of Africa. In fact, at a meeting of the National Security Council on July 25, 1960, Allen Welsh Dulles, director of the Central Intelligence Agency (CIA) expressed his worries about Detwiler's activities in the Congo. Detwiler had the reputation of not finishing anything he started. Secretary of Defense Thomas S. Gates, Jr., added that Detwiler "was a fabulous promoter who has not really promoted anything."[50] Washington did not appear to be behind this putative assault on Belgian mineral resources in Katanga.

The Lumumba visit to Washington had even less substance. Lumumba came to the United States on his own initiative in order to secure funds and make friends, but without the endorsement of the Eisenhower administration. Secretary of State Christian Herter claimed to find it "difficult to understand why Lumumba was in the U.S." But as long as he was in the country, and a potentially dangerous symbol of African nationalism, Secretary of the Treasury Robert B. Anderson suggested it could be to U.S. advantage to keep him away from the Congo for a while. The president then said that a three-week tour of the United States could be provided "on a modest basis."[51]

Given that Lumumba's visit coincided with the Republican National Convention in Chicago, it was hardly surprising that official Washington's attention was focused on the convention city rather than on the visit of an obscure leader of a new government. Instead of greeting Lumumba at the airport or anywhere else in Washington, President Eisenhower went directly from Chicago to his summer retreat in Denver. In fact, the president was never in Washington during the premier's short stay. No record of a royal reception being accorded to Lumumba exists.

In retrospect, the most Lumumba was able to extract from the U.S. government in the course of his two-day stay in Washington was the continuation of U.S. economic assistance to the Congo. But even before he left the city, the State Department was disturbed over Lumumba's claim that his correct reception was a sign of U.S. approval of the Congo's accusations against Belgium. The department was even more disturbed when the U.S. ambassador to the Congo, Clare

H. Timberlake, arrived during the premier's visit to confirm the ugly reports of pillage and rape by mutinous Congolese soldiers that Lumumba had derided. The upshot did not reflect a triumphal capture of Washington. It was instead a communiqué expressing restrained good wishes to Lumumba's Congo, along with a pointed statement of appreciation of Belgium's fulfillment of its promises to withdraw its troops.[52] Good wishes were to be for only a very short period. Within a month the United States used its influence to support President Kasavubu in his efforts to depose Lumumba.

That the romance with the Congo, whether under Republican or Democratic auspices, was tentative and fragile became evident almost from the beginnings of the U.S. involvement in the Congo. Granted that at the moment of independence, U.S. congressmen had welcomed the new member into the international community with the observation, as one congressman noted on June 30, that "For long our friendly relations with the mother countries in Europe have largely sufficed for the conduct of our relations with Africa, but they will not suffice for long in the future."[53] But most legislators would share Senator Leverett Saltonstall's (R-MA) qualified approval, warning that "the African states must free themselves from political bondage without breaking ties of friendship and assistance from their former masters which are critically necessary to their own strength and success."[54]

What Belgians did not appreciate was just how shallow this support was. When news circulated, with the help of Belgian propaganda, of Congolese atrocities against Belgian civilians, U.S. senators were outraged on their behalf. Senators Allen Ellender of Louisiana and Ernest Gruening of Alaska were quickly convinced that "largely primitive African people" were not fit for self-government. Gruening suggested that "some of them are scarcely 'out of the trees,'" to which Ellender added that "in fact, many of them are still cannibals."[55] The plight of the civilians seemed to uncover a vein of racism that accompanied sympathy for Belgium.

Senator Thomas Dodd (CT-D), later Katanga's and Tshombe's strongest U.S. champion, raised the question of Lumumba's pro-communist sympathies. Katanga in this context could be a major object of Lumumba's ambitions, and Tshombe by contrast, with his pro-Belgian connections, was a defender of the West. Dodd could understand why Belgium talked of reducing its modest contributions to NATO because of the Congo situation. The chaos in the Congo showed some congressmen a clear path to communist power, under the auspices of Patrice Lumumba.[56] The United States was a naïve pawn of a political process that could deliver the Congo to the Soviet Union.

The Eisenhower administration tried to follow a course that respected African nationalism without antagonizing Belgium and its U.S. defenders. To do this meant staying as close as possible to Hammarskjöld's intentions of using ONUC to maintain the unity of the Congo. This meant not only opposing Katanga secession but halting Soviet military aid to dissidents such as Lumumba. Proponents of Hammarskjöld's policies such as Senator Clifford Case (R-NJ) wanted to have the Senate issue a resolution expressing the sense of the Senate that a UN force be established as a permanent arm of the United Nations, ready to act even more rapidly and effectively than ONUC had done in the Congo crisis. Senator Francis Case (R-SD) was able to draw on journalist Roscoe Drummond's admiring judgment of Hammarskjöld as a leader who "at critical moments—and the Congo is only the latest . . . finds a way to tell his superiors what to tell him."[57]

U.S. uncertainty was reflected in its reaction to Khrushchev's proposal to the UN General Assembly on September 23, 1960, asking for immediate independence for remaining colonial territories. The Soviets—unlike the Americans—had no qualms about the appropriate role of the UN; in their view there was none. They were opposed to the secretary-general's assertion of authority in the Congo and were hopeful of winning the African-Asian bloc in order to achieve the goal of marginalizing that office and isolating the United States and its NATO allies. Perhaps it came as a surprise to the Soviets that the U.S. delegation strongly supported Khrushchev's declaration in favor of immediate statehood for African territories. With delegate Mary Lord cheering the passage of the Declaration on Decolonization along with eighty-eight other UN members, it was humiliating then for the U.S. delegation to find the State Department reversing its approval in the face of the negative reaction of NATO allies. Senator Wayne Morse (D-OR), also a delegate, accused the State Department of rejecting "our own history" by "allowing the Communist bloc to champion the cause of the millions of people who are trying to gain their independence."[58]

U.S. abstention on the Soviet resolution appeased neither NATO allies nor African nationalists. But Belgians were mistaken in believing that the United States had abandoned them. Admittedly, the U.S. view of Congo's independence frequently sounded like a reflex action of traditional anticolonialism. Some State Department officials were attracted by the prospect of Lumumba's becoming an African Ataturk, but neither the familiar attitudes of the past nor the romantic hopes for the future dominated policy-making for the Congo in 1960. The key to U.S. behavior was the need for an immediate solution to the crisis produced by the mutiny of the Force Publique. ONUC was to be the answer. Should this fail, the Eisenhower administration feared the resulting chaos would open all Africa to Soviet intervention.

The Soviet Union appeared to be the winner in this particular Cold War contest. This was the session of the General Assembly at which Khrushchev pounded the table with his shoe to demonstrate the depth of his support of the new nations. Yet appearances were illusory. Khrushchev failed to capitalize on the success of the resolution; his theatrics were excessive. The Soviet attack on the UN as an institution and on the secretary-general as its leader repelled the former colonial nations. Their status and potential influence on the world stage rested on their presence in a viable United Nations General Assembly. Soviet fury against Hammarskjöld became an obstacle to Third World ambitions. The U.S. policy of doggedly supporting ONUC and the secretary-general despite occasional tensions succeeded in minimizing the Soviet role in Africa, even if it did not bring the Congo into the community of democratic nations.

From the beginnings of the crisis U.S. actions were designed to restrain the Soviet impulse to profit from Belgium's difficulties in the Congo. If the USSR initially joined the United States in accepting UN's help in the Congo, this was for purposes if its own, and the joint effort lasted only as long as those purposes were being served. Failing to control events in Africa, the Soviets turned violently against the United Nations, which after August 1960 they bracketed with Belgium as a lackey of American imperialism. Against the threats of the communist bloc, both immediate and potential, the United States' continued affirmation of the UN's actions in the Congo was more than a quixotic gesture of anticolonialism or a bid to keep the African-Asian countries on the U.S. side. It was in the national interest as well as in the interest of NATO to secure a genuinely neutral Africa. Without the role played by the UN, the Soviet Union might have succeeded in a unilateral intervention, which in turn might have converted equatorial Africa into another battlefield of the Cold War.

NATO, the UN, and the African-Asian Bloc

The Congo crisis, like the Suez crisis four years before, divided the NATO allies, but this time a different member was arraigned before the bar of world opinion. Belgium as a smaller member of the alliance was more vulnerable to pressure from the senior partner than Britain or France. Three other elements were in play in 1960. First, the Soviet Union was not distracted by its problems with Warsaw Pact members and was readier to intervene on behalf of potential allies. Second, the African-Asian countries were a much more visible presence in the UN General Assembly. Third, the United Nations under Dag Hammarskjöld's leadership had the confidence gained through its peacekeeping experience in the Middle East to play a primary if not decisive role in dealing with the chaos in the Congo. The European allies, those with their own colonial history, looked apprehensively at the aggressive UN role and the Third World's rallying behind the Congo against Belgium. Their sympathies were with the Belgians, but the most the larger powers could do in the UN Security Council was to abstain from condemnation.

The European allies could expect no help from NATO's secretary general. Paul-Henri Spaak, Ismay's successor in the office, as a Belgian was vulnerable to being charged as a spokesman of national interest, despite his prestige as a statesman devoted to the advancement of NATO. He was right to ask, "Can we remain united in one part of the world and work at cross-purposes, or even as adversaries in another? Can we[,] thanks to NATO, maintain a common policy on European questions and at the UN oppose each other on all others?" As NATO's secretary general in 1960, Spaak could supply no answer. Even as he conceded mistakes made by the Belgian government in the Congo, he cast more blame on Hammarskjöld than on the United States, for Hammarskjöld's eagerness to "indulge in risky policies and take too much upon himself. . . . His idea was to chance his hand in an experiment which, if it succeeded, would perpetuate the glory of the UN. In actual fact, the operation was beyond the Organization's means." As Spaak prepared to leave the office, Spaak recognized that NATO could not stand in unity against the authority that the UN secretary-general, with U.S. blessing, gave to the UN's involvement in the Congo.[59]

The key player once again was the United States. Despite Belgian cries of betrayal, the senior partner's alliance with the UN served both the UN's and NATO's interests. U.S. policy over the next four years remained constant. The recognition was, first, that the Belgian presence could not be sustained in any form; second, that the United Nations would fill the vacuum as peacekeepers—and peacemakers as well—and as conduits for economic and technical aid; and third, that the unity of the Congo must be preserved at all costs. It is worth noting that these decisions were made by an administration whose prestige had recently been damaged in its handling of the U-2 affair with the Soviet Union and whose attention was directed primarily toward a critical presidential election. The Kennedy administration subsequently confirmed the judgments of its predecessor. If anything, its pressures were more vigorous than those of the Eisenhower administration.

4

The Vietnam War, 1961–1965

Problems between the United Nations and NATO members continued to be a staple of the Cold War, with the Soviet bloc eager to complicate the relationship at every opportunity. The Anglo-French intervention in Egypt in 1956 drove a schism in the alliance, with the United States and most of the smaller allies separating from their major partners. The Congo crisis of 1960 drove a wedge once again into the alliance, this time between the United States on one side and Belgium, encouraged by the British and French, on the other. Unlike Suez, the chasm between the allies caused by the Congo crisis was not as wide; and the UN's creation of peacekeeping forces in both instances helped to bridge the gaps.

The longer conflict in Southeast Asia that could be traced to the end of World War II came into focus in the mid-1960s. On this issue the United States was the party on the dock. Its allies, though alienated by the violence and worried about its impact on the alliance, expressed their dissent without having to cast votes in the UN Security Council or General Assembly. There was no UNEF or ONUC to provide a UN blanket to cover up the differences. The UN was a peripheral player in this long-drawn-out war. The penultimate act took place on March 8, 1973, when an international peace conference on Vietnam met in Paris. The UN secretary-general was invited to attend those meetings so that they could be held in his presence and recorded in the final act.[1] But neither NATO nor the UN was to be seen, two years later, as the last Americans left Saigon under the gun of the victorious North Vietnamese. Yet the United Nations and its secretary-general, the Burmese diplomat U Thant, were always present, though behind the scenes. While the United States emerged as the offending party in this war, the Johnson administration was usually anxious to present its case before the world organization.

U Thant as Secretary-General

Arguably, had Hammarskjöld been in office in the mid-1960s the role of the United Nations in the Vietnam conflict might have been different. His prestige might have brought the belligerents to the peace table before 1973. But a counterfactual historian could also envision more divisions within the alliance if the secretary-general had pressed the United States for greater effort to end the war and urged NATO Europe to distance itself from the senior ally.

Hammarskjöld had the personality and the energy to impress his stamp upon international disputes in a manner that his successor, the Burmese diplomat U Thant, was unable to do. Although U Thant may have judged the belligerent parties much the same way, there was a basic passivity, a reluctance to impose himself, that reflected a Buddhist temperament. He was a devout believer in the Teravada form of Buddhism, whose tenets emphasized both detachment and equanimity.[2] These qualities were necessary in abundance when Thant assumed office. Soviet hostility to Hammarskjöld over his policies in the Congo led the USSR after his untimely death in 1961 to support a troika, in which each bloc—NATO, the Warsaw Pact members, and the Asia-Africa alignment—would have a veto. U Thant and the new majority of emerging nations along with the United States and the West all opposed this scheme. For the new nations the General Assembly of the United Nations was their seat of power, and any effort to dilute its role was unacceptable to them.

Given the newly empowered voices of the African-Asian bloc in the General Assembly, it was hardly surprising that Hammarskjöld's successor would be chosen from that group. No matter how unhappy the Soviets were with the assertiveness of his predecessor, they lacked the votes and the incentive to prevent an Asian from becoming secretary-general. Both NATO and the Warsaw powers had reasons to appease the new majority. Had France and the Soviet Union not been opposed to Tunisia's Mongi Slim, his moderating influence in the Congo crisis would have made him a perfect candidate. U Thant, then Burmese ambassador to the UN, favored his appointment. U Thant himself was an acceptable second choice. With experience as a teacher and lawyer in Burma, he was also an intimate of that country's first prime minister, U Nu. As a diplomat he had burnished his credentials by chairing the UN Development Fund, presiding over the Congo Conciliation Commission, and by participating as a member of the working committee on Algerian freedom.[3]

Like U Thant but unlike the two professional politicians who were his immediate predecessors as NATO secretary general, Manlio Brosio was steeped in the traditions of diplomacy. A native of Turin, he had served in the Italian army in World War I and was an articulate opponent of fascism during the Mussolini years. He served briefly in postwar cabinets, but his skills as a negotiator offered him a diplomatic career as ambassador to Moscow, London, Paris, and Washington. Most of his energies in the Vietnam years were spent on the problems emerging from the Gaullist challenge to the United States and NATO.[4]

Secretary-General U Thant understood the aspirations of former colonized nations and identified Vietnam as one of them. His temperament, not to mention his sense of limited authority, predisposed him toward modesty in looking for solutions to the war in Indochina. But there was no doubt of his unhappiness with U.S. activities in Southeast Asia and with French behavior in Algeria. He made a distinction between neutrality, which he espoused, and impartiality, which he felt himself forced to abandon in the case of the Vietnam War. There were always limits to his philosophy of tolerance.[5] But the efforts he made prior to 1964 to open up channels of negotiation were mostly secret, conducted as private conversations working behind the scenes as an individual rather than as secretary-general.

U.S. Expansion of the Conflict, 1964–1965

Vietnam was not at the head of the UN agenda when U Thant took office in 1961. Nor was it an important issue for America's NATO allies. South Vietnam under the autocratic rule of the Diem family seemingly had achieved relative stability after the conclusion of the Geneva Accords in 1954 dividing the country at the seventeenth parallel. When elections to unify the two halves did not materialize, communist North Vietnam worked to undermine the Diem government by supporting the disaffected Vietcong in the South. U.S. assistance in the form of military advisers helped to stave off dissolution of the Diem regime, but the excesses as well as the incompetence of the South Vietnamese government made it vulnerable to Vietcong subversion, as well as to a hostile communist regime in North Vietnam.

Efforts to insulate the South from communist influence through land reform failed to stem the increasing pressure of the communists, abetted as they were by a stream of men and materiel from the north infiltrating through Laos. President Ngo Dinh Diem who had assumed power in 1955 was a Catholic and an authentic nationalist. But by 1953 he was an increasingly autocratic ruler who had lost support from most of the country, particularly by his repression of the Buddhist majority. When a coup in November 1963 cost him his life, the United States bore some responsibility for his violent death; its representatives were giving signals to the generals who toppled the regime.[6]

Instead of restoring order and encouraging anticommunist resistance, the bumbling military leaders who succeeded Diem only encouraged communist activity against the successive governments. The United States in turn was forced to increase its aid and in fact, by the summer of 1964, was prepared to assume the burden of fighting a war against the Vietcong and North Vietnamese that the Republic of Vietnam was unable to undertake for itself. With only one-fifth of the country under control of the government, there seemed to be little choice: either the United States intervened or Vietnam and probably all of Southeast Asia would be lost to communism. On uncertain reports of North Vietnamese attacks on U.S. vessels in the Gulf of Tonkin in August 1964, President Lyndon B. Johnson ordered secret air strikes against North Vietnamese naval bases and supply depots and then pushed through a congressional resolution, the Gulf of Tonkin Resolution, authorizing the president to "take all necessary measures to repel any armed attack against the forces of the United States and to prevent further aggression" in Southeast Asia.[7] The scene was prepared for the full Americanization of the Vietnam War without the necessity of a formal congressional declaration of war.

The United States might have detached itself from the failing South Vietnam state. Under John F. Kennedy the assumption was that U.S. aid could do only so much; the burden of self-defense should fall on the South Vietnamese. If they were unwilling or unable to follow the advice of the American patrons, the United States spoke of leaving the country to its own devices. But the stakes were too high; the domino scenario haunted the Kennedy and Johnson administrations. Even neutralization, though conceptually viable, might have led to complete communist control of South Vietnam. Fear of losing Vietnam, as China had been lost, inhibited the United States. Increase of military advisers and, particularly, bombing of the offending North Vietnam were the fateful choices that had been made by the end of 1964.

U Thant's Role

By this time the Vietnam conflict had the full attention of the UN secretary-general. Earlier the conflict had been a peripheral matter. The subject came up at his first press conference on December 1, 1961, when he was asked, as acting secretary-general, whether the United Nations could alleviate "the tense situation in Southeast Asia." He responded in a way that was habitual to him—cautiously—with a statement that he did not think "he should make any observations" since the matter had not yet come up in the General Assembly. He was somewhat more forthcoming two years later when the Diem regime disregarded his denunciation of its mistreatment of Buddhists.[8]

There was never any doubt where the secretary-general stood privately on the war in Vietnam. As an Asian whose country had thrown off British colonialism, he was never convinced that Ho Chi Minh was primarily a communist. U Thant saw him as a nationalist contending with the Americans who had succeeded the French as colonialists. Nor did he believe that the problem was essentially military; it was political, and only diplomacy could resolve the conflict.[9]

As the United States poured men and resources into Vietnam after 1965, U Thant did not accept the premise that the National Liberation Front (the Vietcong) was a surrogate, let alone a stooge, for North Vietnam. The opponents of the Saigon regime were genuine patriots, seeking reforms that the Diem family and its successors were unable or unwilling to instigate. The secretary-general questioned whether the survival of South Vietnam was vital to the security of the West. He saw the struggle as an Asian affair quite apart from the demands of the Cold War. The country posed no threat to international peace and security. Rather, its leaders of all factions "are obsessed with the principle of non-alignment."[10]

But the United Nations in his judgment was not the place or the instrument to resolve the troubles in Indochina. He came to a very different conclusion concerning the authority of the UN from that of his predecessor, Dag Hammarskjöld. It was not that U Thant ignored Article 99 of the UN Charter, which stated clearly that "the Secretary-General may bring to the attention of the Security Council any matter which in his opinion may threaten the maintenance of international peace and security." Rather, it was that the Security Council was not the arena where the issues should be thrashed out. From a practical point of view the Cold War divide, with the Soviets lining up on one side and the United States on the other, ensured deadlock. And if the conflict moved into the General Assembly, U Thant foresaw controversy over the absence of the principal parties—North and South Vietnam—from membership in the United Nations. Whether this was a legitimate obstacle is open to question. Article 99 was a vehicle he might have cited if he believed that the United Nations could manage the problem. Failure would tarnish an organization already in difficulty over France's and the USSR's unwillingness to bear the costs of peacekeeping.

U Thant's approach then was to reconvene the Geneva Conference, the body that had determined, without UN involvement, the division of Indochina in the wake of France's defeat at the hands of the Viet Minh. He would lobby for its venue in private conversations with the world's leaders without making a public declaration of his preferences. He made a point of saying that he made no proposals. "I just thought aloud," he claimed, "because in my position as Secretary-General of the United Nations, I do not think it would be proper for me to come up with any proposals regarding the solution of the crisis in Southeast Asia."[11]

U Thant's circumspection was certainly understandable. Neither North Vietnam, the National Liberation Front (NLF), nor China would deal with the United Nations directly, and all had some suspicion that he served as a tool of the United States. Yet his modesty was suspect in this context. He was being disingenuous when he disavowed any intention of proposing solutions to the problem. Simply the suggestion of reconvening the Geneva Conference was itself a clear indication of his position. There would be no direct UN intervention as peacemaker in Vietnam, but the direction in which he would move negotiations would fulfill the stymied process of 1954 when Vietnam was divided at the Geneva Conference. This path presumed that communism was not the prime mover of the people of that region.

Escalation, 1965

The dam restraining full Americanization of the war was finally breached when U.S. troops, not military advisers to South Vietnamese forces, took over the full conduct of the war. Escalation was rapid in 1965. Secretary of Defense Robert S. McNamara orchestrated the conversion of Americans from advisers to active combatants. Two battalions of marines at Danang in March 1965 rose to 70,000 army and marines by mid-June, and fifteen battalions were not sufficient. President Johnson announced in July that 100,000 troops would follow. By the end of 1966, there were 267,500 American military personnel in Vietnam, compared with 150,000 in Central Europe in that year.[12]

Operation Rolling Thunder, involving massive air attacks against North Vietnam, opened a Pandora's box that the Johnson administration was unable to close. The bombing exceeded the numbers of World War II, with far fewer results. In 1965, U.S. pilots flew 25,000 sorties over North Vietnam and dropped 33,000 tons of bombs. In the following year, as the war intensified, 128,000 tons fell on the North in the course of 79,000 sorties. Targets in South Vietnam in this period were expanded. From 3,600 sorties in April 1965, the number of targets had risen to 4,800 by June. The price for the United States was high. For every dollar of damage to the enemy the country spent $9.60. The number of U.S. planes shot down in 1965 and 1966 numbered 489.[13]

There were other costs to be paid also. The suffering of the Vietnamese people increased exponentially with the war of attrition. The use of herbicides such as Agent Orange, designed to deprive the enemy of sanctuary by defoliating forests, had devastating effects in South Vietnam. One-quarter of South Vietnam's population was rendered homeless by chemical warfare, and one-half of South Vietnam's timberland was destroyed.[14] While body counts of enemy soldiers gave McNamara's Pentagon a sense of progress, supplies and men from the North continued to pour into the country, further alienating the people of South Vietnam. Only the Vietcong benefited from this campaign. It is difficult to refute U Thant's conviction that U.S. escalation of the conflict served to minimize the differences between the Soviets and the Communist Chinese, as both powers competed in their drive to help the North Vietnamese. The war impacted prospects of improving relations between the United States and the USSR, as the Soviets had to demonstrate that "Chinese accusations of 'betrayal' of the interests of socialism" in Vietnam were unfounded. Bombing Haiphong harbor in 1967 while Soviet premier Alexei Kosygin was in North Vietnam was hardly the way to advance peace negotiations.[15]

There was never an open break between the secretary-general and the United States. Rather, lack of trust in America's intentions in Indochina on the one side and U Thant's secretive efforts to nurture a North Vietnam connection on the other fostered an atmosphere of mutual suspicion that never fully dissipated. Yet both the Johnson administration and the UN secretariat continued to seek ways out of a conflict that could spread beyond the region. On April 7, 1965, President Johnson seemed to open a path of rapprochement in a speech at Johns Hopkins University when he proposed "unconditional discussions" and an offer of a billion dollars in aid of a cooperative effort for economic development of Southeast Asia. If only the communists would not interfere with an independent South Vietnam, tied to no alliance and serving as "a military base for no country," then "we will never be second in the search for such a peaceful settlement in Viet Nam. . . . We have stated this position over and over again, fifty times and more, to friend and foe alike. And we remain ready, with this purpose, for unconditional discussions."[16]

Although this was the passage endorsed by U Thant, the part of the speech that the communist adversaries read was the president's avowal to continue air attacks against North Vietnam "as a necessary part of the surest road to peace." Secretary of State Rusk made it clear in a press statement on May 17, 1965, that the United States would not suspend raids on North Vietnam. Rusk rejected suggestions that suspension could lead to an end of aggression from the North. "Now our best judgment tells us it would only encourage the aggressor and dishearten our friends who bear the brunt of the battle."[17]

President Johnson's blessing of U Thant's activities on behalf of Asian development, along with the secretary-general's appreciation of the president's partial opening of the door to negotiation, did not respond to the request made a week before by the seventeen heads of non-aligned governments for the United States to start negotiations without preconditions. The communists were even less impressed. The Chinese were convinced that U Thant was now in America's pocket. It was this negative reaction from Beijing that deterred U Thant from either making an open appeal for a cease-fire or undertaking a mission to China or North Vietnam. Speaking with UN correspondents in mid-April 1965, U Thant did not see "any point in discussing the possibility of my visit to Peking." Still, he insisted that "I shall continue my efforts to find a peaceful solution to the Vietnamese problem, as I have been doing all along. I feel that my usefulness has not ended."[18]

He was true to his word, as he continued to seek some opportunity to bring the hostilities to a close. While the Johnson administration remained as wary of his initiatives as he was of its putative attempts to solve the Vietnam problem, U.S. officials and the president himself from time to time saw the UN Security Council as an arena in which to put the communist adversaries on the defensive, or at least to prevent them from placing the United States in the dock. In February 1965 General Maxwell D. Taylor, then U.S. ambassador to Vietnam, linked a proposal of "a joint GVN/US program of measured and limited air action against selected military targets in the southern part of the Democratic Republic of Vietnam (DRV)" with "presentation to the United Nations Security Council of the case against the DRV as the aggressor, accompanied by an indication of readiness to discuss ways of bringing the DRV aggression to an end." Taylor's approach to the UN was to take "the initiative from those countries who might wish to call us before the UN bar as the guilty party." The increased use of air strikes made a preemptive diplomatic strike necessary.[19]

It was the increasing attention to U.S. bombing of sites in North Vietnam that undercut both the private steps of the secretary-general in both the Johnson and Nixon years in office and the fitful, often painful attempts by the U.S. administrations to bring the United Nations and the NATO allies into the peacemaking process. In celebrating the twentieth anniversary of the first session of the General Assembly, President Johnson recognized that the United Nations "must be concerned." He informed the member nations that "we will support effective action by any agent or agency of the United Nations." But he emphasized that "the processes of peaceful settlement are blocked by willful aggressors contemptuous of the opinion and will of mankind." Nowhere in this address did Johnson allude to the U.S. war against North Vietnam as a reason for the failure to achieve a peaceful solution.[20]

Questions in Congress

In essence, the Johnson administration was frustrated by the absence of any clear path toward resolving the war in Vietnam in 1965. Expanded military operations only exacerbated the problems, as allies were horrified over the casualties inflicted on civilians in the North and the South without seeming to have any effect on the war-making capacity of the Vietcong or North Vietnamese. If the enemy refused to take seriously U.S. proposals for peace it may have been, the administration reasoned, because of the communists' expectation that they could wait out the American adversary and achieve a solution on their own terms, abetted as they were by Soviet and Chinese allies. The Vietcong could also take heart in the inability of the United States to win over its own opinion-makers. Johnson told his key Cabinet advisers that "they have no idea how much I've talked to the Fulbrights and Lippmanns. They're not coming aboard."[21]

The president may have been too hard on J. William Fulbright. The Arkansas senator, chairman of the Senate Foreign Relations Committee, was reluctant to differ with the administration in public. In response to Johnson's request in the middle of June to make a public statement in support of the administration's policies in Vietnam, Fulbright did so on the floor of the Senate, noting that the president was showing "steadfastness and statesmanship" in managing the war in Vietnam. The administration did not appreciate, however, the caveats that accompanied his support, notably his assertion that a military victory would not be worth the cost. The thrust of his message was to urge a compromise settlement with major concessions on both sides. While continuing to sustain the South Vietnamese army, "we must continue to offer the Communists a reasonable and attractive alternative to military victory."[22]

Walter Lippmann, the most influential of U.S. pundits, was the most serious loss to the administration. In a critical column in June 1965, just a week after Fulbright expressed his conditional assent, Lippmann reported the impact of the escalation of the war was having on European allies, which he encountered in Europe. "Does it really matter what other peoples and governments think of what we are doing in Southeast Asia?" He believed it did, noting in the last seven months "a spectacular decline in respect for United States foreign policy." He feared a decline of solidarity with the NATO partners that might result in their disillusionment with U.S. leadership of the alliance. Consequently, he felt that West Europeans, and Germans in particular, were bound to look "more and more to a settlement that they themselves negotiate with the Soviet Union."[23]

This reaction was similar to the kind of criticism that Fulbright and Wayne Morse (D-OR) had begun to express on the Senate floor. Morse was upset at the Republican demand for more escalation, bombing the capital, Hanoi, and nuclear installations in China. This would lead to war with the Soviet Union, he was convinced: "I say to the President, 'We cannot bomb Hanoi without killing Russians, and the Russians have as much right in Hanoi as we have in South Vietnam.'" As for Republican demands for a wider war, "watch them when public opinion starts to turn. They will trample each other in trying to get off your ship of state." His recommendation was to "lay the issue before the United Nations in keeping with the procedures of the charter and ask the other signatories of the charter—which countries have exactly the same moral and legal obligations as does the United States—to assume their fair share of responsibility for bringing a peaceful settlement to this war-torn part of the world, that day by day, threatens the peace of the world."[24]

NATO and Vietnam: In Support, 1961–1964

The defection of NATO allies from the U.S. policies in Southeast Asia was an unexpected blow, even though the potential had always been in the background. From the U.S. perspective, the European allies should have cheered the constancy of the American role in Southeast Asia. By aiding South Vietnam in its fight against the internal threat from the communist Vietcong and the external intervention of North Vietnam and its communist allies the Soviet Union and the People's Republic of China, the United States thought it was serving the common cause against communist aggression everywhere. Should South Vietnam fall to communism, the independent nations of Southeast Asia—Laos, Cambodia, and Indonesia—would collapse like so many dominoes. U.S. firmness in Asia should have been translated into its equally firm stance in Europe, and appreciated as such. And it was—or seemed to be—for a considerable time. While there were occasional signs of some concern about America's involving itself in an area so far from Europe, there was always recognition that communism was a global menace, and that NATO recognized the many dimensions of communism.[25]

NATO's long-term threat assessment always included Asia. China's invasion of India in 1962, combined with its first nuclear detonation, not only kept the communist peril alive but placed a special emphasis on that part of the world. As an expert working group reported to the North Atlantic Council in May 1963, "The primary problem in the Far East remains communism. While the communist cause as a whole has suffered somewhat by virtue of the Sino-Soviet rift, neither Soviet nor Chinese power 'per se' have shown evidence of any reduction of their capability to influence or undermine, if not overpower individual countries in the area."[26]

South Vietnam in this context was just one of many danger spots in the area. If U.S. involvement was mentioned at all in NATO circles in the early 1960s, it was in a positive light. The expert working group in May 1963 credited the "considerable extension of United States aid" for improvement in the military situation.[27] The violent deaths of the Diem brothers in November of that year and the succession of coups in 1964 tested this optimism and induced the United States to seek help from its NATO allies. On May 12, 1964, Secretary Rusk made a point of blaming North Vietnam and China, along with "at least political support by the Soviet Union" for the vigor of the Vietcong insurgency in South Vietnam. He expressed the hope that none of the allies doubted "Hanoi is specially and in detail directing these operations in the south." Later that day the French foreign minister, Maurice Couve de Murville, weighed in with qualified sympathy for the difficulties of the United States in Vietnam and of Britain in Malaysia. But he also reminded his allies that France had endured these problems in Indochina and Algeria for a longer period in the past and implied that his country did not receive the understanding being sought by the United States.[28]

France's intervention at NATO sessions always reflected some satisfaction over the morass into which the Americans had deservedly fallen. Before 1964 de Gaulle's was the only European country to condemn the United States for its policies in Vietnam. From de Gaulle's point of view, Vietnam was a symbol of America's domination of the West. He wanted its power to be checked in NATO as well as in Southeast Asia. De Gaulle's carefully plotted withdrawal from NATO's military structure had its counterpart in his campaign for a neutralist solution in early 1964 when he supported the ambitions of prominent South Vietnamese military figures, former members of the French military establishment in Indochina, who pressed for this approach. He repeated his proposal for unification of a neutralized Indochina on January 31, 1964, two days after a coup in Saigon, but this idea was anathema to the Johnson administration, which equated neutralization with ultimate surrender to communism. De Gaulle's initiative touched a raw nerve—already exposed after France had recognized the People's Republic a few days earlier and then wanted to include China in future guarantees of Indochina's security. Whatever de Gaulle's intentions may have been, they fit into U Thant's recommendations on Vietnam. The mutual admiration between the secretary-general and the French president only confirmed the Johnson administration's judgments on both leaders.[29]

France's particular bias against the United States was not shared by most allies on the problems either in Asia or in Europe. The Canadian delegate on the NAC, Paul Martin, represented a country with some reservations about U.S. policy in Vietnam, but he nonetheless responded with sympathy to Rusk's plea in December 1964 for those allies who recognized Beijing to "make it clear that they were in full support of the effort of the South Vietnamese to ensure the security of their country." Martin then reminded NAC that "it is our United States Allies who are bearing the bulk of the military burden there in Indo-China and who are faced with the most difficult political and military decisions in the face of the deteriorating situation in South Vietnam."[30]

It was hardly surprising that Britain should be in America's corner, appreciating its increasingly active defense of South Vietnam. Britain's experiences with communist-backed aggression in Malaysia ensured empathetic treatment of U.S. difficulties. The "special relationship" seemed all the more relevant when Defense Minister Denis Healey expressly linked his country to the United States in their common struggle in Southeast Asia. Their allies may not have realized, he pointed out at the NAC December 1965 meeting, "the disproportionate share in the defence of the free world outside Europe which was carried by the United States and the United Kingdom alone. Few ministers realized that the United Kingdom had as many men in Malaysia as in Germany, and that the United States would soon have as many men in Vietnam as in Western Europe."[31]

Healey in effect was repeating the official line of the Harold Wilson government.

When Operation Rolling Thunder intensified the war, the British prime minister made "absolutely plain our support of the American stand against the Communist infiltration of South Vietnam." Healey could portray the many peace initiatives Wilson had made in 1965 and following years as extensions of the U.S. offers to negotiate without conditions for peace in Vietnam. Granted that there was skepticism over Wilson's motives on the part of President Johnson, who felt that the prime minister's pro-American stance was a mere formality disguising his unwillingness or inability to take meaningful action in Vietnam. Granted, too, that Wilson's initiatives were designed to pacify the increasingly vocal criticisms of Labour backbenchers in Parliament. Still, Britain's voice until the mid-1960s was consistently pro-American.[32]

Two other NATO allies—Greece, with its memories of the civil war that inspired the Truman Doctrine, and Portugal, facing explosions in its African possessions of Angola and Mozambique—identified their experiences with communist subversion with the experience of South Vietnam. Remembering the key role played by the United States in coping with its adversaries, Greece applauded the defense of a similarly afflicted country. In response to the Gulf of Tonkin challenge, the Portuguese representative agreed with U.S. ambassador Henry Cabot Lodge at the NAC meeting in August 1964 that NATO should not limit itself to any specific geographical area if its interests were affected. The Greek delegate was equally enthusiastic in support of the U.S. response to the Gulf of Tonkin crisis. He felt that Greek experiences were similar to those of South Vietnam in standing fast against communist aggression.[33]

Most of the other NATO allies at least gave lip service to the U.S. cause. As late as October 1965, after a dramatic buildup of U.S. troops in the summer and fall of 1965, NATO secretary general Manlio Brosio, addressing the NATO Parliamentary Conference in Brussels, warned that a setback of the United States in Asia, for example, in Vietnam, would also be a grave setback for the whole of the West. An American retreat or a humiliating compromise in Vietnam, far from ending U.S. commitments in Asia, would extend them on an even greater scale to all sorts of other areas, from Thailand to the Philippines.[34] As for the effect on Europe, Helmut Schmidt, a German delegate at the conference, spoke four days later about the prospect of the United States' withdrawing troops from Europe in order to fight in Asia. He was convinced that "Europeans can count on America to hold its course in Europe. There may be, and probably will be, alterations as far as the Asian theaters are concerned, but as long as political developments do not serious[ly] affect the European situation, there will be no major changes in the U.S. strategy concerning Europe, and Europeans ought to understand that, I think."[35]

Schmidt's last clause, almost an aside, reflects doubts about the United States already held by Europeans. Would the United States, a late convert to alliance with Europe, one day turn its back on Europeans? Early in the decade, new U.S. vulnerability to Soviet missiles (symbolized by Sputnik) was one reason for concern. The Vietnam War in turn revived an old European fear, namely, that America's historic orientation toward the Pacific arena would drain the Atlantic alliance of its vitality as well as of U.S. troops. Would lack of support for the war in Vietnam even lead to America's abandoning NATO? These questions helped to inform Europe's public reactions to the war.

Troubling symptoms of estrangement were evident in Anglo-American relations prior to the escalation of 1965. Johnson's testy response to Wilson's offer of advice in February 1965 was related to Europe's, particularly Britain's, actual rather than professed behavior. When the State Department asked U.S. allies for some material and manpower contribution for the common cause, the response, as historian Fredrik Logevall put it, was "underwhelming, to say the least."[36] The campaign to bring NATO into the Vietnam War, begun by the State Department in April 1964 under the name of "More Flags," was a failure.

German chancellor Ludwig Erhard was always steadfast in his appreciation of American policy but did little to bring substantive aid to South Vietnam. Conceivably, the Germans were inhibited by their continuing efforts to collaborate with de Gaulle, even as both Adenauer and his successor, Erhard, sought to distance themselves from his anti-American posture. In May 1965 Foreign Minister Gerhard Schroeder offered a particularly German rationale for supporting the war in Vietnam. He feared that Soviet pressure on Berlin was designed to force the United States to reduce its commitment to Vietnam. "Withdrawal or defeat of the United States in Vietnam," he asserted, "would have an effect on the situation in Europe, and especially Berlin, comparable to that of the test of strength over Cuba in 1962 on the situation in Berlin." Recognition of Soviet motives made it imperative for Germany to support a policy on Vietnam that would prevent a negative impact on Europe—by protecting NATO allies "against attempts to extort concessions from them in South-East Asia through the application of pressure in Europe."[37]

Notwithstanding this perception, the sense that neutralization was the only genuine path toward peace governed actions of the Federal Republic. Certainly, Adenauer's warning to Henry Kissinger in June 1965 that "Vietnam was a disaster," that "Europe was the decisive area and instead we were getting sucked deeper into the morass in South East Asia," reflected the sentiments of the governing elite, if not that of the public at large. In light of German behavior in World War II, the prospect of sending troops to Saigon was impossible to conceive, but even the Southeast Asian development program that President Johnson had included in his Johns Hopkins address in April 1965 garnered only 30 million dollars, not the 75 million the administration had anticipated.[38]

It was British unwillingness to provide even a token troop commitment that most disturbed Johnson. It was important to the president to have the U.S. press feature the deaths of a few British soldiers in Vietnam so the American public could see that their primary U.S. ally in Europe was contributing its share of sacrifices in the common effort. Wilson never delivered, and circumstances were such that the United States had to accept his reasons. He could always use the British struggle in Malaysia to deflect criticism. An even more compelling argument was the need to stem the tide of criticism in Parliament from the left wing of his own party.[39] It is noteworthy that the United States did not exert the kind of financial pressure to ensure compliance that the Eisenhower administration had employed so effectively in the Suez crisis. In fact, on the eve of the NAC meeting on December 14, 1965, Rusk told news reporters that he was not going to raise the point of trade with North Vietnam. He brushed off the issue by noting that "a number of allies have done something about ships going to Hanoi."[40] By the end of 1965 the United States had given up any expectation of NATO "flags" joining its forces in Vietnam.

NATO and Vietnam: In Opposition, 1965

Any sympathy the European allies felt for the U.S. role in Vietnam did not survive the escalation of arms and men in 1965. The uneasiness on the part of the European allies, expressed elliptically in the failure of the "More Flags" appeal and in a barely concealed wish to remove Vietnam from a NATO agenda by means of neutralization, became explicit in the summer and fall of that year. The steep buildup of U.S. forces in Vietnam evoked vocal opposition from Scandinavian and Dutch members of the North Atlantic Council. Usually it was cloaked in diplomatic language. The Dutch foreign minister, Joseph Luns, gingerly touched on the implications of the U.S. troop buildup when he urged greater consultation among the allies before events outside the NATO area produced a wider conflict involving all the members. While sensitive to "the enormous sacrifices the United States was making to stave off the Communist take-over of South Vietnam," he asked the Americans to repeat at regular intervals their "readiness to enter into negotiations unconditionally, as they have done many times in the past."[41]

The Danish foreign minister, Per Haekerrup, was less circuitous in his approach to American activities in Vietnam. At the December NAC meeting, he noted the rising opposition in his country to the escalation of the war in Vietnam. Much of the opposition was driven by press reports by U.S. correspondents of how badly American soldiers treated "the poor people of Vietnam." Although he recognized the absence of press accounts of the crimes committed by the Vietcong, he had to take into account Danish public opinion directed against the United States. The Scandinavian leaders did not want to push the United States too far or too openly, but they were doubtful about the sincerity of U.S. intentions to negotiate without prior conditions. What triggered these doubts at this time, according to Haekerrup, "was an announcement by a very well-known US paper . . . later accepted by the US Government, that some feelers had been put out from the Vietnam side, a long time ago. I think it was in the middle of the election campaign, but . . . this was not published so that nobody knew it."[42]

These events were taking place at the same time that the United States proclaimed it was willing to enter negotiations unconditionally. The Danish foreign minister said he was "very happy to hear again, which I never doubted that, as Mr. Rusk has said, it is the firm policy of the US Government to go into negotiations without prior conditions." This reference to Rusk's firmness may have been ironical. The Norwegian defense minister, Otto Grieg Tideman, apparently thought so when he expressed the hope that "the present lack of willingness to negotiate will be overcome by continued and increasing efforts so that the final solution can be found which will bring peace to the people of Vietnam."[43] The implication in this statement was clearly that American professions of willingness to negotiate were not credible.

Unhappy as many of the delegates were with the conditions in Vietnam, none was ready to condemn the United States in the language of the French spokesmen. The French rapporteur at the NATO Parliamentarians meeting in May 1965, even before the major buildup of U.S. forces in Vietnam, assailed the United States for its systematic large-scale military actions against North Vietnam, observing that its unilateral steps "taken without inter-allied consultation" damaged the alliance in the eyes of unaligned nations and weakened the "moral standing of the free world." Even such a friend of the United States as British delegate Sir Geoffrey de Freitas feared the consequences of any precipitate U.S. action, "which was out of proportion to what had provoked it." He worried about reactions in Asia and Africa where "NATO stood for a club of rich, white, countries."[44]

U.S. delegates to NATO sessions, whether in the NAC or in the Parliamentary Assembly, recognized the complexity and confusion in their allies' reactions and for the most part limited their demands to understanding the common goals their nation was serving. But there was resentment over Europe's insensitivity to America's concerns. One U.S. member of the NATO Parliamentarians Conference, former congressman Charles Chamberlain of Michigan, pleaded in 1965 and in subsequent years for more understanding of the U.S. role in Vietnam on the part of the NATO allies, particularly in light of France's "high-level criticism of the sort usually reserved for one's enemies."[45]

Secretary General Manlio Brosio, as noted, did recognize America's unhappiness over the way its allies treated its Vietnam policy and warned the NATO Parliamentarians in October 1965 that "a setback for the United States . . . in Vietnam would be a grave setback for the whole of the West."[46] A master diplomat by experience and temperament, Brosio was able to win the respect of all parties not only where Vietnam was concerned, but also over the potentially damaging implications of France's withdrawal from the military arm of the alliance. His diplomatic skills notwithstanding, Brosio was unable to make a common NATO case to the UN since he was unable to speak for the senior partner. Consequently, Brosio was not in a position to exercise NATO's influence as an organization. Even though there was no venue in the UN for the secretary general to make his presence felt, he might have engaged in private conversations with U Thant, much as the UN secretary-general did with the United States. Conceivably, the crisis in Europe over de Gaulle's increasing challenge to the alliance in the mid-1960s diverted Brosio's attention from the lesser issue of the Vietnam War—at least lesser from the perspective of a Europe-oriented leader.

Despite eruptions of anguish and outrage in Europe over the events on the ground, the U.S. State Department was relatively complacent about the outcome of the NATO ministerial meeting of December 1965. In his assessment of the sessions, Secretary Rusk granted that while the meeting may not have itself produced the results the administration wanted, "at least NATO governments may display even greater sensitivity to the depth of US feeling on Viet Nam in public statements they make on [the] subject." Although he saw "few signs of increased readiness [of] NATO countries [to] participate meaningfully in Viet Nam," he could take comfort in their support of the U.S. policy of seeking a peaceful solution through unconditional negotiations.[47] Rusk was taking comfort in an illusion. Unconditional negotiations had never been on the table, and the European allies were well aware of this fact. But for the sake of the survival of the alliance during the Cold War, they were all (save the French) prepared to go along with Rusk's illusion.

NATO and the UN

If the NATO allies toned down their criticism of U.S. Vietnam policies at NAC meetings in 1965 (their discontent with military escalation, the lack of progress in negotiations), they were even more restrained in the UN's Security Council and General Assembly meetings. There were reasons enough for quiescence over Vietnam. The escalation of the conflict in the summer of 1965 may have been the most important development on the international scene, as Secretary-General U Thant observed in the introduction to his annual report to the General Assembly's twentieth session on September 20, 1965. But the war in Vietnam did not offer opportunities for the UN to take constructive action. The Geneva settlement of 1954 provided no formal role for the United Nations. Neither North nor South Vietnam were members of the organization. Nor had countries with direct interest in the Vietnam conflict found the United Nations to be the setting for a solution.[48]

Yet the exclusion of Vietnam from any formal discussion did not preclude its intrusion into debates at the Security Council and General Assembly. The United States and the Soviet Union exchanged accusations throughout the year, with the USSR charging the United States with aggression against North Vietnam, in particular accusing the United States of using poison gas against the people of South Vietnam. U.S. replies over the year asserted that the materials used were not toxic and were in use by police forces elsewhere in the world. These replies were not convincing. Its more spirited response in January 1966 maintained that the United States never had territorial ambitions but only wanted to honor its pledge to keep South Vietnam free in a way that would tell other peoples they could count on America if they were attacked. At the same time U.S. representatives repeatedly reaffirmed the nation's willingness to enter into negotiations without conditions. The United States threatened no rights and wanted no territory; it sought no wider conflict, only the termination of Hanoi's aggression against the Republic of Vietnam.[49]

Where did NATO stand in this indirect contest over Vietnam? There was no common NATO response as a bloc; there was no need for such action since Vietnam was never on the agenda in 1965 or later. Secretary General Brosio's defense of the United States at NAC meetings in 1965 reflected his reasons for keeping Vietnam off the table. Had NATO's voice been required, unstinting support of the United States would have been unlikely. There was too much turmoil within the different public opinions of the allies over the damage to the civilian population of the country, too much fear that the war would exacerbate international tensions, too many doubts of U.S. sincerity about negotiations, and too much visceral suspicion that the increasing U.S. absorption in Vietnam would take both U.S. troops and U.S. commitment from Europe.

None of the emotions that erupted in NAC meetings in 1965 surfaced in the UN General Assembly meetings in that year. Rather, the tone was to seek ways to bring the contending parties to the peace table, without attaching blame to either side. In plenary meetings of the twentieth session of the General Assembly in September and December 1965, the delegates from NATO countries, speaking for their individual nations, pleaded for the revival of the Geneva Conference of 1954 as a step toward resolution of the conflict. These views were in tune with the views of the UN secretary-general. Invariably, they deplored the suffering of the peoples of the region and asked for cessation of bombing North Vietnamese targets and negotiations, without conditions. But unhappy as the allies were, there was no inclination in the wake of the escalating war in 1965 to unload the responsibility wholly on the United States, as Soviet Foreign Minister Andrei Gromyko vehemently did before the UN General Assembly in September when he declared that "whatever version of events the United States Government may have, it is clear to everyone that . . . United States armed forces have invaded Vietnamese territory in order to impose a political order which suits the United States in a land where the Vietnamese people alone is entitled to be master."[50]

At the same meeting the Canadian delegate, Paul Martin, declared that, on peacekeeping, his government has "a right to give some advice on this matter because we have participated in every one of the peacekeeping operations of the United Nations." And Canada's advice was to recognize that "if the cease-fire provisions agreed to in 1954 had been fully observed, the tragedy and danger we now face in that part of the world would not have occurred."[51] Less than a week later, the Italian delegate to the General Assembly, Giacinto Bosco, weighed in with the observation that "Italy is prepared, as it has repeatedly stated, to support any steps—particularly by the United Nations—which may really lead to negotiations for a speedy and peaceful, and at the same time, equitable and lasting solution of the questions which provoked the hostilities." French foreign minister Maurice Couve de Murville, President de Gaulle's spokesman at the General Assembly, could not resist mentioning "first, most feelingly, the human suffering and human destruction which this war is bringing to the Viet-Namese people, whom the French nation knows well, with whom it worked for so long and with whom it has maintained a variety of ties since Viet-Nam attained independence—a people, in a word, whom it knows to be still its friend." But having separated France from the other NATO allies, especially the United States, in asserting a special relationship with all of Vietnam, the French representative spoke much as the others had done about the wish to achieve a settlement that assured independence and neutrality. Unlike the Soviet message and unlike French comments in other venues, the foreign minister did not use the occasion to blame the United States for the war in Indochina.[52]

Prime Minister Harold Wilson, speaking for Britain in December 1965, recognized the value of reconvening the Geneva Conference. He understood that the problem could not be managed in the UN Security Council, let alone in the General Assembly, and he paid tribute to the failed efforts of the secretary-general to open new channels. "It is a terrible commentary on man's impotence that, while we can reach out to the moon or to more distant planets, while astronauts can rendezvous in outer space, the whole power of the United Nations is incapable of establishing a dialogue between the leaders of two parts of the same country and between others concerned with this dispute." As for responsibility for the plight of Vietnam, Wilson assigned it, not to U.S. intervention, but to "Hanoi, where alone this matter can be decided."[53]

Granted that 1965 was the watershed year in the Vietnam War. It was the year that found the United States fully in control of the war, as evidenced in the spectacular rise in numbers of U.S. forces in that country. The rapid escalation of the conflict damaged U.S. relations inside the United Nations, not least among its own NATO allies, as European public opinion turned violently against the Johnson administration's policies. Yet the allies—and the global community—were unable to arrive at any means to end the war during the 1960s.

Denouement

The burden of the war became heavier in the last years of the Johnson administration, however, as the United States sought unsuccessfully to extricate itself from the quagmire in Southeast Asia. Only after the North Vietnamese Tet offensive in 1968 and the subsequent withdrawal of Johnson from the presidential race did negotiations begin. It still required five more years under a new U.S. administration and a new UN secretary-general before a treaty was made, with some United Nations involvement. The process included failed efforts through nuclear intimidation to manipulate the Soviet Union into brokering a peace with North Vietnam. Indeed, the violence and the protests in all the NATO countries intensified in the wake of the U.S. incursion into Cambodia in 1970 and a more indiscriminate bombing campaign against North Vietnam in Richard M. Nixon's first administration.

U Thant was never able to use his personal powers of persuasion to affect any of the parties. He remained convinced that the United States was the primary offender as an Asian people tried to assert control of their own destiny. His position won little appreciation from the communist powers. The European publics, like their American counterpart, were as alienated from the U.S. position under Nixon and Kissinger as they had been under Johnson and McNamara. But the voices of their representatives in the United Nations were muted as they realized that the demands of the Cold War excluded a break with U.S. policy. Their hope was placed, not in a potential UN presence, but in the negotiations among the belligerent parties conducted in Paris in the years of the Nixon presidency.

Only at the end of the process, on January 27, 1973, was the United Nations acknowledged in the agreement ending the war and restoring peace in Vietnam. Even this acknowledgment was grudging and patronizing. U Thant's successor in 1971, the Austrian Kurt Waldheim, was even more cautious in his exercise of leadership than his predecessor, arguably the result of his personal history as an SS officer in World War II, which made him vulnerable to pressure from those powers that knew his secrets. He quickly backed off from his condemnation of U.S. bombing of North Vietnamese dikes in 1972 when President Nixon rebuked him. His hasty retreat was in keeping with his disposition to please the major powers in the UN. The secretary-general was included among the conferees in the twelve-nation conference who were to guarantee the peace, but the United

Nations itself played no significant part in the process. Waldheim was not even asked to chair the concluding session at which the protocols were signed in his presence.[54]

According to the terms of the agreement the secretary-general, "having received messages from the United States and the Democratic Republic of Viet-Nam requesting him to attend the Conference," informed the president of the Security Council that he would accept the invitation. And in his presence, the participating governments signed the agreement on February 13, 1973. Potentially even more significant was Article 6(b) stipulating "that the signatories forward information regarding implementation of the agreement to the Secretary-General, with the understanding that any violation of the cease-fire in Vietnam be reported to the United Nations."[55] But this was only lip service to the authority of the United Nations.

The Vietnam War ultimately was notable for the failure of the United Nations to serve the peacekeeping function it had begun with the Suez and Congo crises. It also revealed the inability of the NATO allies to play a visible role in ending the conflict. Joseph Luns, Brosio's successor as NATO secretary general in 1971 and a seasoned former foreign minister of the Netherlands, was notoriously pro-American in his conservative positions. As an admirer of Secretary of State Henry Kissinger, Luns provided no NATO obstacle to the U.S. policies in Vietnam.[56] Like the UN, NATO was a negligible factor in the Paris negotiations. As a post-script, the unraveling of the 1973 accords took only two years, ending in the collapse of the Republic of Vietnam and the humiliating departure of U.S. officials from a North Vietnam–controlled Saigon.

5

The Afghanistan War, 1980

The Yom Kippur War, 1973

Two crises in the final twenty years of the Cold War marked the continuation of conflicts within NATO that were manifested in the UN arena. Both of them involved the United States and the Soviet Union as central figures. Arguably the more bitter, if not the more significant, was the Yom Kippur War of 1973 in which the Soviet Union was a key partisan of the Arab cause, anxious to replace the United States in the Middle East and to stir up as much trouble as possible within the Atlantic alliance.

It is noteworthy that NATO's voice in the UN was silenced by the divisions between the United States and its European allies over the Middle East. Essentially, dependence on oil, along with national interests in the Arab world and sympathy for the Arab cause, trumped considerations of aggression in October 1973. In all the proceedings the UN secretary-general played only a minor role. Hobbled by a compromised past, Waldheim was in no position to attempt to exercise the kind of leadership Hammarskjöld and even Lie had displayed in the UN's first decade.

A deeper political issue was at work within the alliance. Repressed resentments against U.S. hegemony had been loosened by the Vietnam War, and the Israel-Arab conflict was an opportunity for the allies to vent their feelings. Although the NAC could not express these sentiments clearly, the European Community (EC), where the European NATO powers functioned outside U.S. scrutiny, could and did. Europeans felt that Americans did not appreciate their dependence on secure access to Middle Eastern oil. They were convinced that American leaders sacrificed their partners' vital interests to the imperatives of domestic politics. America's bias toward Israel then was responsible for the turmoil in the Middle East.

There was little understanding of European sensibilities in the American reaction, which in essence saw the United States as being on the brink of confrontation with the Soviets just as the European allies were abandoning their senior partner. The Cold War had not ended, and the Europeans recognized the continued need for the alliance. But visceral fears of the Soviet bloc along with the respect for U.S. leadership had diminished to the point where the Europeans could act more freely in challenging the senior ally.

Background of the Soviet Invasion

Six years later, another crisis in the Middle East confronted the United Nations when the Soviet Union in December 1979 dispatched troops to Afghanistan. This time it was one of the two superpowers, the Soviet Union, and not a surrogate nation that initiated the crisis. On one level conflict grew out of a bilateral arrangement between two communist powers. In fact, the regime that the Soviets supported as well as its predecessor were both in the communist orbit. But much of the noncommunist world including the Arab bloc and the United States saw the Soviet invasion as a repression of the Afghan people and a threat to international peace. The United States feared that the Soviets were using turmoil in Kabul as an excuse to move into the Persian Gulf, and into control of the oil resources of that region. NATO allies joined the majority of UN members in denouncing the Soviet intervention but, even more than in the Arab-Israel war, they distanced themselves from the meaning the United States gave to the Soviet invasion. There was no NATO voice in the UN deliberations. In fact, the European Community offered a clearer reaction than NATO to the crisis.

Afghanistan itself had long been a prize contested in the "Great Game" of the nineteenth century between an expanding czarist Russia and an imperial Britain worried about the defense of India. In the Cold War this land-locked mountainous country of fiercely independent tribesmen had tried to balance the new players of the "game," the Soviet Union and the United States, by accepting military aid from both sides after the departure of Britain from India in 1947. Obviously, the Soviets had a stronger interest in the neighboring state than the United States, whose interests centered on Iran and Pakistan. And accordingly, Afghan governments both before and after the overthrow of the monarchy in 1973 tried to accommodate the Soviets.[1]

The balancing act ended in 1978 when Marxist officers seized power in a violent coup with a pro-Moscow faction under Nur Mohammed Taraki assuming the offices of president, prime minister, and secretary-general of the party. Despite a treaty with the USSR that provided arms and military advice to the communist regime, armed resistance by tribal groups led Moscow to increase military aid and advisers to shore up the Afghan army, and Taraki's inept governance induced the Soviets to support another member of his coup, the foreign minister Hafizullah Amin. Chaos in the countryside continued. After Taraki's death in September of that year, Amin inherited the presidency.[2]

Amin displayed more independence of Soviet control than his predecessor but proved no more capable of coping with insurgency. The Soviets then orchestrated his violent removal and intervened with 30,000 troops in late December 1979. The Afghan insurgency continued under the presidency of the more submissive Babrak Karmal, inducing the Soviets to enlarge their forces to 80,000 (and ultimately 120,000) before the guerrilla war ended. As the Soviets overran the country, the insurgents increased their pressure with the help of external aid, including weapons from the United States.[3]

Why the Soviets felt it necessary to intervene with a massive deployment of troops in December 1979 is still an open question. The continuing insurgency may have been the major factor. Additionally, they felt that Amin's strident nationalism may have compromised his communist identity. The leaders of Afghanistan had all professed loyalty to communist ideology and friendship with the Soviet Union. Certainly, concern about rising Islamic fundamentalism that fueled the insurgency and might infect Soviet Moslems across the border may have played a part. Concern also about the dwindling supply of petroleum, which would be solved by the assurance of cheap natural gas from Afghanistan, may have played a role in the Kremlin's decision. Or, was it a target of opportunity opened to the Soviets at a time when the United States was embarrassed by its broken relations with Islamist Iran? That neighboring country had shown its contempt for its former ally by taking the U.S. embassy staff hostage in Teheran in November 1979. American weakness may have been a factor in emboldening the Soviets to take control of its southern neighbor in a fashion it had not attempted before. The so-called Brezhnev Doctrine, however, did not apply to Afghanistan, which was not a member of the Warsaw Pact. Soviet subjugation of the country was a new step in what appeared to be a pattern of aggression. Fifteen years later, evidence from Soviet archives revealed that there was no Soviet master plan to reach the Persian Gulf. Rather, the Kremlin was reacting to developments in Afghanistan at the time.[4]

The U.S. national security adviser to President Carter, Zbigniew Brzezinski, reminded Soviet ambassador Anatoly Dobrynin a month before the invasion of the alliances that imperial Germany's "assertive policies" brought on World War I: "Today, Soviet policies were generating growing anxiety, and this could have the effect of creating an alliance, spanning the United States, Western Europe, some friendly countries in the Middle East, and even Japan and China."[5] Brzezinski was not far off the mark. The USSR's lame excuse was that they were in Afghanistan at the invitation of President Amin, but everyone knew it was Moscow that eliminated Amin and took over military control of the country. If the Soviets really believed that rebel forces backed by China, Pakistan, Saudi Arabia, and the United States threatened the survival of Amin's government, the charge backfired.[6] Most of the nations represented in the UN branded the USSR as the aggressor. It was not an "alliance" that now confronted the USSR, but it was a close approximation over this issue at this time.

The approach that had worked in Hungary in 1956 and in Czechoslovakia in 1968 now failed in 1980. There was no Suez issue to divert attention from the Soviet's crude intervention in Afghanistan. Nor was there the U.S. quagmire in Vietnam to check the West's unhappiness with the suppression of the liberal Czech government twelve years later. The Soviet Union stood unmasked in the face of hostile world opinion. Its effort to accuse Amin of being an agent of the United States lacked credibility. Amin's successor arrived in Kabul on a Soviet transport plane, and from the outset Babrak Karmal was identified as a Soviet puppet.[7]

USSR before the Bar of the UN

It was Afghanistan's neighbor Pakistan that, as early as December 31, 1979, took the initiative to assemble other Islamic countries to condemn Soviet intervention in Afghanistan. As Pakistan's representative at the UN made clear, "we are concerned as a non-aligned, as an Islamic country, and as a next-door neighbor. But above all, our concern is based on respect for the fundamental principle of nonintervention and nonuse of force."[8]

Cheering from the sidelines at this point were the United States and the NATO allies who happily let the Third World nations take the lead in bringing the issue to the attention of the UN Security Council. China, however, made the specific charge on December 31 that the Soviet action was an interference in Afghanistan's internal affairs, and it demanded the withdrawal of Soviet armed forces. Among other unintended consequences, the Soviets' invasion sharpened their differences with China. On that same day, another former ally (indeed a client of the Soviet Union), Egypt, ended its efforts to improve relations with the Soviets by having its assembly register its condemnation over "the Soviet attempt to impose a Marxist regime on the people of Afghanistan."[9]

From January 27 to 29, a special session of the Islamic Conference of Foreign Ministers, responding to a request from Bangladesh, met in Islamabad to raise its voice against the Soviet invasion. Thirty-six members including NATO's Turkey, the Palestine Liberation Organization, and rival Middle East powers Iran and Iraq joined in the chorus of disapproval. The conference demanded "the immediate, unconditional and total withdrawal of Soviet troops from Afghanistan." South Yemen, a Marxist country and Soviet ally, was notably absent from the conference, and its lonely position underscored the extent of the Islamic world's hostility to the Soviets and its solidarity with the Afghan insurgents. By contrast, the conference's expression of support for the Palestine cause as well as condemnation of

Egypt's normalizing relations with Israel lacked the passion inspired by the plight of Afghanistan.[10]

Islamic opposition to the Soviet intervention was reflected also in the large numbers of Muslim countries ranging from Egypt to Indonesia that joined fifty-two UN member states on January 3, 1980, in asking the president of the UN Security Council to convene an urgent meeting of the council in order to consider the implications of the Soviet invasion of Afghanistan for international peace and security. Only France's name was missing from the list of NATO members that signed the request, and this was only because the French member, as president of the council, needed to maintain a nonpartisan posture.[11]

No attention was paid to the protest of the Afghan foreign minister the next day against the UN's interference in the internal affairs of a member nation.[12] The Soviet voice in the six meetings the UN Security Council held between January 5 and 9 had to be heard. The Soviet representative not only repeated the complaint of the Afghan foreign minister but added that the USSR's decision to send limited military forces into that country was a response to urgent requests from the Afghan government in compliance with treaty obligations to repel external armed intervention. The Soviets charged that the insurgency in that country drew its strength from foreign sources, particularly the United States and China, which were fomenting counterrevolution in that country.[13]

Although the Soviet objection was shared by its Warsaw Pact ally East Germany, the USSR had to contend with arguments that thirty-two members of the General Assembly presented to the UN Security Council. They discounted the communist claim that the temporary armed presence of Soviet forces did not present a threat to international peace and security. Pakistan and Singapore among others joined Britain in pointing out that the estimated fifty thousand Soviet troops hardly amounted to a limited response to Afghanistan's request. The United States was relatively modest in criticism when it accused the USSR of planning the invasion of Afghanistan because of dissatisfaction with the behavior of its communist client. It is noteworthy that it was China along with Chile and Somalia, and not the United States at this moment, that attributed Soviet actions to an attempt to reach the Indian Ocean and control oil-producing areas.[14]

A group of non-aligned nations on the UN Security Council—Bangladesh and the Philippines from Asia, Jamaica from the Caribbean, and Niger, Tunisia, and Zambia from Africa—drafted a resolution on January 7 deploring the armed intervention as a violation of the sovereignty, territorial independence, and non-aligned status of Afghanistan. They asked the council to call for the immediate and unconditional withdrawal of foreign troops from the country and the secretary-general to report in two weeks on the progress in implementing the resolution. The veto power of the Soviet Union defeated the council efforts to condemn its intervention, however. The draft resolution received twelve votes in favor, with two against and one abstention in a vote on January 9, 1980. Only East Germany joined the USSR in opposition.[15]

The UN Secretary-General

Given the lack of unanimity among the permanent members, the UN Security Council called for an emergency special session to examine the situation in Afghanistan and the implications for international peace. Once again the veto power of a permanent member had forced the transfer of proceedings to the General Assembly where seventy-four delegations made statements from January 10 to 14, 1980. During this period the secretary-general, Kurt Waldheim, remained in the background much as U Thant had done in the long Vietnam conflict of the 1960s. Waldheim made little effort, however, to make his voice heard in the informal meetings with the principals, in the manner U Thant had adopted during the Vietnam War.[16]

The contrast between Waldheim's behavior and that of Dag Hammarskjöld in the Suez crisis is stark. Waldheim entered office in 1971 seeking to enhance the United Nations' reputation by emphasizing public relations. One means of raising the image of the UN, it seemed, was to project his own image as leader. He relished the trappings of his position and felt that an imperial style lent distinction to the office. Among his first acts as secretary-general was to seek an apartment on Fifth Avenue with at least five bedrooms and sufficient room for two maids. His quarters should reflect the significance of his role in the United Nations, he thought. When he complained of rumors about his extravagance, he insisted it was important to let the world know of what the UN was doing.[17]

But his concern for his image and that of the UN was made a mockery by the fallout from the revelation in January 1980 that he had lied about his activities in World War II, and particularly about his service in the Balkans as a Nazi intelligence operative.[18] This exposure initially took place at the very height of the Afghan crisis. Details followed over the next half dozen years. There was suspicion that Waldheim's record was known to the Soviets as well as to the Western allies, and that his unaccustomed reticence over Afghanistan was a response to Soviet blackmail. Those who knew Waldheim well believed there was no need for blackmail to explain his desire to please. There is no evidence that the Soviets, the British, or the Yugoslavs blackmailed him on the strength of their knowledge of his wartime record. Rather, critics found that his efforts to please all parties made him susceptible to pressure from all sides. He "bent with the prevailing winds of the moment," as Seymour M. Finger and Arnold A. Saltzman observed, which earned him the title of "headwaiter." He gave away perquisites to countries of all ideologies and used his UN position as a means of ingratiating himself with as many governments as could serve his needs.[19] He would not raise a voice against the Soviets whose favor was needed for reelection.

Full disclosure of his wartime record did not appear until 1986, after he had left the United Nations, but the record had always been available. It simply was never given close inspection as Waldheim rose through the ranks as an Austrian observer at the UN in 1955, as ambassador to Canada in 1958, and as Austria's permanent representative to the UN in 1962. The reason his compromised past—about which he lied repeatedly, according to Urquhart—was not revealed may be seen from a U.S. perspective. His experience as a Wehrmacht intelligence officer made him an asset to the CIA. The Soviet incentive for inaction was based on Waldheim's susceptibility to exposure that guaranteed his turning a blind eye to Soviet aggression.[20] A vigorous stance over the Afghanistan issue could antagonize powers he was anxious to placate.

Waldheim's disgrace only reinforced the low esteem the U.S. government and the general public held for the UN in this period. The organization was perceived to have been hijacked by the Arab bloc in collaboration with the Soviet Union and the non-aligned nations. It is ironical that the USSR's Afghan venture revived the U.S. reputation in the world and gave the United States an opportunity to reclaim some of the luster it had enjoyed in the 1950s. The United States found itself sharing the sentiments of the vast majority of the UN members in the General Assembly. The Afghan crisis, then, should have been an occasion for the United States to bond not only with the Third World members but with its own unruly allies in NATO, but America failed to exploit this unanticipated opportunity.

Ambivalence of the Non-aligned Bloc

As recorded in the proceedings of the UN Security Council, the Soviets could count only on their allies in the Warsaw Pact and their client states, such as South Yemen and Vietnam, and on Afghanistan itself. The situation was much the same in the General Assembly. The Afghan minister for foreign affairs insisted that there was a misconception about developments there. These involved only domestic and bilateral issues that constituted no threat to any other country. In response to armed attacks supported by foreign interests, Afghanistan insisted it was only exercising its inherent right of self-defense in conformity with the UN Charter and that it had invited Soviet military help in conformity with the 1978 Afghan-Soviet treaty. Soviet allies echoed these arguments, adding the need to defeat counterrevolutionary forces that had infiltrated the Afghan government. The USSR representative contended that the very survival of the April 1978 revolution hung in the balance, and such military assistance as was given to the government was in full accord with the right of individual and collective self-defense as defined by the charter. Had the Soviets failed to respond to the request of its neighbor, the southern border of the USSR would have been exposed to serious danger and Afghanistan itself abandoned to imperialist designs.[21] The Soviets might have observed that the right of individual and collective self-defense, under Article 51 of the UN Charter, was the very principle on which both NATO and the Warsaw Pact were framed.

It was Grenada, a client of Castro's Cuba in the Caribbean, that made the specific point that Soviet troops in Afghanistan were there legitimately under Article 51. Grenada's delegate accused the Western powers of orchestrating "in a hysterical manner a return to the worst features of the cold war." Many supporters of the Soviet action, such as the German Democratic Republic, resorted to the extravagant language often used in Soviet propaganda to justify Soviet behavior. The East German delegate asserted that the draft resolution of January 14 "is designed to help to continue the slanderous campaign launched against the Democratic Republic of Afghanistan and the USSR . . . to render the Afghan people defenceless against imperialist machinations."[22]

The communist voices were drowned out by the sheer numbers of nations who were unhappy with or fearful of the Soviet actions in Afghanistan. The USSR and its allies were oblivious to the heart of the UN's objections, namely, that the government of Afghanistan did not represent the people of the country who were ready to rise up in the name of their faith against the communist overlords. The range of countries lined up against the Soviet Union was impressive. Communist Albania, China, and Yugoslavia voted in concert with the large Islamic bloc and the Western allies. There was a total of 104 nations who adopted the Resolution ES-6/2 A/ES-6/L.1, introduced by Pakistan on behalf of 24 sponsors on January 14, 1980. There were 18 in opposition, and 18 abstentions.[23]

The first speaker to address the General Assembly was not from either the Arab or the Western bloc but from the Dominican Republic. That the offender was "from one of those countries that were represented at San Francisco and signed the Charter there, a country that is also a permanent member of the Security Council, is a scandal of incalculable dimensions." The delegate went on to assert that "it is deplorable, and indeed paradoxical, that just a few weeks ago it was that very Power that has now committed aggression against the sister country of Afghanistan that produced a draft resolution to prohibit hegemonism in international relations. Today we see that that initiative was nothing but sheer hypocrisy, with absolutely nothing of substance behind it."[24]

The Dominican Republic's delegate spoke for many in the Third World who felt betrayed by the actions of the Soviet Union. That presumed champion of the colonized world was now reduced to the stature of the American superpower. In the Cold War contest, the USSR at this moment replaced the United States as the oppressive imperialist for many of the non-aligned countries. Nigeria also expressed its disillusionment with a country that had been such a friend of the Third World. And Papua New Guinea felt that the Soviet Union's claim to be a champion of world peace was in tatters. How meaningful were the votes condemning the Soviets in January 1980? A number of delegations explained their supporting votes in ways that raised questions about their willingness to implement the resolution. Guyana and Malta explained that their votes in favor of the resolution rested on fear that the alternative might be an escalation of the crisis. Guatemala and Santa Lucia felt that the resolution had little more than moral value. Others based their vote on their disbelief in USSR's explanations.[25]

But the eighteen delegations that abstained from voting connoted problems of enforcement that might arise in the future. Zambia as a member of the UN Security Council was conspicuous in its lone abstention from the council's resolution on January 9. The vote on the draft resolution sponsored by Mexico and the Philippines was twelve to two, with East Germany joining the USSR in opposition.[26] Zambia's abstention may have reflected the uneasiness of some Third World nations in condemning a country that had been seen as their bulwark against the Western colonial powers, even as they protested Soviet behavior. Even Cuba, a long-standing client of the Soviet Union, felt compelled initially to join the non-aligned nations in condemning the Soviet action.[27]

This alignment with the West and particularly with the United States did not last. After fifty-six non-aligned nations voted in the General Assembly in January for a strong resolution against the Soviet Union, calling for "immediate and unconditional withdrawal of all foreign troops from Afghanistan," they were ready in March to remove "unconditional" from their compromise proposal. No mention was made of the Soviet Union or Afghanistan in the statement of the non-aligned nations. Much as they may have wanted Soviet evacuation from Afghanistan, they were more interested in the quick resolution of the conflict. The communist bloc essentially won the day by accepting a compromise that "hopes that the legitimate aspirations of the people of Afghanistan would be realized" and that withdrawal of all foreign troops would follow from these aspirations. No country's activities were deplored or condemned nor was any action asked of the ninety-two nations in the non-aligned group.[28]

The ambivalent stance of India prefigured the weakening of the Third World's resolve. On January 23, 1980, India's president did deplore the "intervention of outside forces" and the "introduction of armaments" into the region. But as for the Soviet Union, the president intended to "deepen and extend" the friendship and cooperation between the two countries.[29] Prime Minister Indira Gandhi clarified India's position when U.S. President Jimmy Carter called to congratulate her on her reelection as prime minister. She showed no interest in discussing anything of substance with respect to Afghanistan, and for good reason. In a speech to the Indian parliament she blamed both superpowers for the tensions in the world but seemed more worried about the warming of U.S. relations with Pakistan than with the Soviet military presence in Afghanistan. "What happened in Afghanistan," she said, "is an internal matter of that country." India's representative at the UN General Assembly was as "strongly supportive of the Soviet invasion" as were the Czech and Vietnamese delegates.[30]

When Afghanistan surfaced again at the General Assembly in the fall of 1980, the vote of condemnation appeared to reflect the continuing disapproval of Soviet behavior. The Saudi delegate in October wanted to "reaffirm that the Soviet Union's armed intervention in Afghanistan was unworthy of a country which professed to be the champion of the right to independence." He appealed to all countries, particularly the Muslim members, to adopt decisions in support of the Afghan people.[31] The voice of the non-aligned nations in fact appeared even more heavily weighted against the Soviets in November than in January. Of the forty nations in the bloc, thirty-one voted in favor of the resolution as opposed to twenty-eight in January; two voted against, compared with one in January; seven abstained or were absent, compared with eleven in the earlier vote.[32]

Yet the language of the resolution was weaker than in January, reflecting the pressures of pro-communist members despite the overwhelming vote in the General Assembly. The resolution called for "the immediate withdrawal of foreign troops," but not "the immediate, *unconditional* and *total* withdrawal" asked for in the indignant resolution of January 14, as proposed by forty-two powers.[33] Pakistan, the prime mover whose delegate was the chairman of the Islamic group, admitted that if the language had not been softened, an estimated fifteen to twenty-five votes might have been lost. The hope expressed by the Muslim delegates was that the larger number voting to condemn would be a psychological boost to Afghan mujahideen in their war against the Soviets.[34]

The Carter Doctrine

The U.S. reaction to the Soviet invasion was in some respects the opposite of the reaction among the Muslim and non-aligned members of the United Nations. The first letter to the secretary-general denouncing the Soviets and asking for an emergency meeting of the UN Security Council came from China, Bangladesh, and Chile. Indeed, it was Chile that initially raised the specter of a Soviet drive to the Persian Gulf area, not the United States. It was not that the U.S. voice was silent. Its delegate made the point that the invasion was no Cold War squabble. It was open aggression that violated the only principle that all nations could invoke to protect themselves from the more powerful members. The United Nations was obligated to respond. But the United States seemed to be only one of the many in opposition. There was no sense of leadership in their responses in the Security Council, or subsequently in the General Assembly, either in January or in November. If so, this unusual deference to smaller nations was a sensible attitude; a loud denunciation might have been counterproductive as well as unnecessary.

In reality, the U.S. reaction was anything but muted. It may not have been audible in UN circles, but within the Carter administration there was deep concern that led to a series of initiatives demonstrating just how far-reaching the U.S. response would be. A connection initially was made to the Iranian detention of U.S. hostages in the U.S. embassy in Teheran since November 4, 1979, less than two months before the Soviet action in Afghanistan. The world was sympathetic to the U.S. situation but not willing to take up arms to free the hostages. In the midst of deliberations over Afghanistan at the General Assembly, a Soviet veto in the Security Council on January 11, 1980, prevented acceptance of a U.S. draft resolution calling on the Iranian government to release the hostages and imposing sanctions in the event Iran did not comply.[35]

It was the Iranian behavior in Teheran and Soviet obstructionism that exacerbated relations between the United States and the Soviet Union. Iran's association with the majority in the General Assembly over the Afghanistan issue was no balm to the United States. Too many members agreed with the Soviets that Iran's actions did not threaten international peace and security. The dispute with the United States was bilateral and did not fall within the purview of Chapter 7 of the UN Charter. This seemed to have been the judgment of the Islamic Conference of Foreign Ministers in January 1980, when its members, while wishing that Iran and the United States would resolve their differences peacefully, declared solidarity with the people of Iran in choosing whatever system they preferred.[36] The United States continued to pay a price for its identification with the hated Shah.

In one of the few instances where the secretary-general played a central role in this period, Waldheim called a meeting of the Security Council on November 25, 1979, under the auspices of the charter's Article 99. Despite the lack of response from Iran, the Security Council, and particularly the United States, wanted Waldheim to use his office to resolve the problem. His visit to Teheran produced no results and further isolated the secretary-general from the major crises of the day.[37]

The Iran confrontation provided much of the background for the vigorous U.S. responses to the Afghanistan invasion outside the halls of the United Nations. While taking no specific action against Iran, aircraft carriers were dispatched to the Persian Gulf at the end of 1979 to send a message to the Iranians and to the Soviets of the importance of the area to the United States. Unlike most of the nations outraged by the Soviet intervention, the United States from the outset of the invasion envisioned the Soviet action as a pretext for moving into the Persian

Gulf area with its vast oil and natural gas resources. As noted, this was not the perception expressed in many of the speeches in the General Assembly at the time. But it was a scenario that Carter's national security adviser, Zbigniew Brzezinski, had long anticipated. A report from Harvard professor Samuel Huntington warning that the Gulf region would be the most likely area for a confrontation between the United States and the Soviet Union had reached Brzezinski three years before.[38] If it had not been acted upon in 1977, this was largely because Carter's early foreign policy centered on rapprochement with the Soviets and on the miseries of the Third World as opposed to the Cold War rivalry with the Warsaw Pact. That perception of the Soviets, held more by Secretary of State Cyrus Vance than by Brzezinski, had fully dissolved by 1979 as the harder line of the national security adviser prevailed in the expanding defense budget of the last year of Carter's term in office. As early as March 1979 Brzezinski had warned the president that the Soviets' "creeping intervention" in Afghanistan could put them "in a position, if they came to dominate Afghanistan, to promote a separate Baluchistan [from Pakistan], which would give them access to the Indian Ocean while dismembering Pakistan and Iran." This scenario with its implicit demand for action separated the national security adviser from the secretary of state as much as their celebrated differences over Iran. Contingency options in the event of Soviet military operations were already in place by the fall.[39]

The U.S. response to the events in Afghanistan followed the Brzezinski line. More painful to Carter than any of the subsequent measures was the indefinite postponement of the SALT II (Strategic Arms Limitation Talks) agreement with its intention to deescalate the nuclear contest between the superpowers. In light of the new tensions of the day, no SALT agreement could pass muster in the Senate. As Carter pointed out in his memoirs, "The worst disappointment to me personally was the immediate and automatic loss of any chance for early ratification of the SALT II treaty." Brzezinski, knowing how deeply Carter felt about SALT, tried to console him by saying that he "understood his desire to go down in history as a President Wilson" but added that "before you are a President Wilson you have to be for a few years a President Truman."[40]

In his Address to the Nation on January 4, 1980, the president asserted that "the successful negotiation of the SALT treaty has been a major goal and a major achievement of this administration. . . . However, because of the Soviet aggression, I have asked the United States Senate to defer further consideration of the SALT II treaty." Suspension of progress toward completion of SALT agreements, although regrettable from the perspective of Carter and Vance, was no problem for the Congress or the public. Carter hoped that the treaty could be submitted at a more propitious time. Despite the deteriorating relations with the Soviet Union, he promised in his State of the Union address on January 21 that the effort to control nuclear weapons would not be abandoned.[41]

Far more difficult politically was the decision to impose a grain embargo on the USSR. The president claimed that the grain was not intended for human consumption but for building up Soviet livestock herds. This measure was accompanied by requests to Canada and Australia (subsequently granted) not to replace the grain the United States would withhold. His troubles with this action were not with the grain-producing rivals (even Argentina initially acceded) but with U.S. farmers. Vice President Walter Mondale from Minnesota worried about the injurious effect domestically but was mollified by the president's assurance that farmers, elevator operators, and grain dealers would all be protected when the government substituted for the Soviet Union in the purchase of grain. As Carter noted in his January 4 address, "The undelivered grain will be removed from the market through storage and price support programs and through purchases at market prices."[42]

Even more controversial was the administration's decision to pull out of the summer Olympics in Moscow, as an expression of America's outrage over Soviet behavior in Afghanistan. This was in accord with the president's intention not to conduct business as usual with the USSR. He announced the decision about the Moscow Olympics on a *Meet the Press* interview on January 20.[43] This action more than such economic penalties as refusing to allow Soviet ships into U.S. coastal waters and cutting Soviet access to high-technology equipment aroused controversy in the United States and in Europe. The national security adviser, against the advice of the secretary of state, saw this as an opportunity to deny the Soviets an occasion "to stage a major propaganda festival." The Moscow Olympics evoked memories of the 1936 Olympics when Hitler used the games to trumpet the success of his Nazi regime, as Vance recognized.[44]

Understandably, many of the U.S. athletes were unhappy with this decision, as was the International Olympic Committee. A majority of the representatives on the advisory council to the U.S. Olympic Committee opposed the U.S. boycott of the Moscow Olympics and speculated about their participating without official backing. However, the president of the international committee, Lord Killanin, dismissed as impractical the idea of U.S. athletes' entering the Olympics as individuals.[45]

Arguments over the boycott were aired in U.S. political and academic circles. Some students of Soviet affairs felt that the presence of thousands of Western tourists would expose the weaknesses of the USSR to the wider world. Governor Ronald Reagan of California, a potential Republican candidate for president in 1980, felt that the United States was "in a poker game with the Soviet Union," and the boycott was "not responsive to the Soviet call of our hand."[46] At hearings on the subject before the Senate Foreign Relations Committee Charles Percy (R-IL) felt that "if we allow the games to go ahead in Moscow . . . we would be handing the Soviets one of the greatest propaganda weapons they could have," while Ted Stevens (R-AL) was convinced that "the decision as to whether or not we should boycott the games in Moscow should be made by the athletes who participate in those games."[47] Objections notwithstanding, the boycott went ahead, to identify the Soviet Union as a pariah among the nations.

The Carter administration's response also extended to changing judgments of nations whose behavior in the past had elicited condemnations. The People's Republic of China was a particular beneficiary of changing perceptions. Its firm denunciation of the Soviet behavior, both in January immediately after the invasion and in the fall when the matter was again before the General Assembly, deserved appreciation and received it. The day after the president delivered his State of the Union Address, the Department of Defense announced that the United States was willing to sell military support equipment (though not weapons) to China. This was a departure from American policy toward China and a direct response to Soviet intervention in Afghanistan. At the same time the Congress approved a most favored nation status, putting into effect a trade agreement drawn up in 1979.[48]

These steps complemented Carter's words in 1979 in conversations with Soviet leader Leonid Brezhnev: "After thirty years normalization of relations between the United States and the People's Republic was long overdue. This new relationship can contribute to peace and stability, not only for our two countries, but also for the entire region and perhaps the world." But the president did add that "these improvements will never be at the expense of Soviet-American relations."[49] Brzezinski was particularly pleased with the new approach to China and observed that in the course of 1980 China was "transferred by the Commerce department from the Warsaw Pact country group 'Y' category to a new country group 'P' category, making China eligible for wider exports, particularly in such sensitive areas as transport aircraft, long-distance communications equipment, and military-type helicopters." Such was the meaning given to "military support equipment." The national security adviser observed that "what had started as an exercise in even handedness by 1980 became demonstrably a tilt, driven by stark strategic realities."[50]

The heart of the State of the Union Address was the president's promulgation of what was to become the Carter Doctrine. This rested on an assumption that the Soviet aggression in Afghanistan threatened the Persian Gulf region: "The destruction of the independence of Afghanistan government and the occupation by the Soviet Union has altered the strategic situation in that part of the world in a very ominous fashion. It has brought the Soviet Union within striking distance of the Indian Ocean and the Persian Gulf." The president laid down a gauntlet, expressed clearly in his address before a joint session of the Congress two days later. "Let our position be absolutely clear: An attempt by any outside force to gain control of the Persian Gulf region will be regarded as an assault on the vital interests of the United States of America, and such an assault will be repelled by any means necessary, including military force."[51]

The tone of the Carter speech was in sharp contrast to the optimism of his first major foreign policy address in May 1977, when he told the graduating class at the University of Notre Dame that "we are now free of that inordinate fear of Communism which once led us to embrace any dictator who joined us in that fear. . . . We hope to persuade the Soviet Union that one country cannot impose its own social system upon another, either through direct military intervention or through the use of a client state's military force."[52] Three years later he spoke of reviving the draft, of providing military aid to Pakistan, and increasing the U.S. naval presence in the Indian Ocean. The link to the hostage crisis in Iran and the concomitant failure of Iran to serve as a stable ally in the Persian Gulf helped to account for this role reversal. These sentiments fit Brzezinski's perception of the problems in the region but conflicted with Vance's fear that any increase in U.S. naval forces would lead to a corresponding Soviet buildup.[53]

The State Department's caution did not prevail in 1980. Vance lost stature in the Cabinet, though his resignation was precipitated not by Afghan policy but by the abortive rescue attempt of the hostages in April 1980. Senator Edmund Muskie (D-ME) succeeded him as secretary of state. The president determined that the building of a rapid deployment force would serve to inhibit Soviet designs on Iran and Afghanistan. The removal of the Iran bastion as a U.S. ally under the Shah was a vital factor in promoting the Carter plan. He asserted in the State of the Union message to the Congress on January 21 that "the Soviet invasion of Afghanistan has eliminated a buffer between the Soviet Union and Pakistan and presented a new threat to Iran. These two countries are now far more vulnerable to Soviet political intimidation. If that intimidation were to prove effective the Soviet Union might well control an area of vital strategic and economic significance to the survival of Western Europe, the Far East, and ultimately the United States."[54]

Soviet aggression in Afghanistan appeared to have set in motion actions that had been germinating in the councils of the national security advisers long before 1980. These included an increase in the U.S. defense budget, new weaponry for European allies, naval deployments in "remote areas of the world," aid to threatened areas such as Pakistan, and "above all enhancing US ability to respond rapidly to non-NATO contingencies wherever required by our commitments or when our vital interests are threatened." The means of achieving these objectives was through new flexible rapid deployment forces, ranging from "a few ships or air squadrons to formations as large as 100,000 men, together with their support. Our forces will be prepared for rapid deployment to any region of strategic significance."[55]

The NATO Response

Given the impressive chorus of voices denouncing the Soviets, the Carter administration seemed justified in anticipating appreciation and support from the global community, and particularly from U.S. allies in NATO. And the support seemed forthcoming. An emergency meeting of the North Atlantic Council on January 1, 1980, even found the German ambassador to NATO raising the question of boycotting the Moscow Olympics as a possible NATO riposte to the Soviet intervention. Remembering the Nazi summer games in Berlin in 1936, he wondered if concerted action then might have changed the course of events leading to World War II. The NATO secretary general, Joseph M. A. H. Luns, declared at this session that the situation required "solidarity and unity of purposes and decision among the allies."[56] Although no NATO policy flowed from the German suggestion, its surfacing signaled NATO's need not to do business as usual with the aggressor.

The votes on the UN Security Council and later in the General Assembly should have confirmed the alliance's common revulsion against Soviet aggression, in line with the U.S. reaction. But even as they lined up to condemn the Soviets, France insisted it could not join fifty-two other nations in urging a council meeting on the crisis in Afghanistan. As president of the UN Security Council, the French delegate reasoned that his country must adhere to strict neutrality.[57] When the issue went to the General Assembly, the French representative did vote in favor of the resolution demanding immediate, unconditional, and total withdrawal of Soviet troops. But he also expressed reservations about the resolution's preamble, employing the language of the 1950 "Uniting for Peace" resolution, which, France felt, usurped the functions of the Security Council. As the French spokesman pointed out, "we regard [the preamble] as illegal because it changes the rules regarding a competence which are set out in our Charter."[58] This relatively minor dissent presaged more serious divergences between Europe and America.

The question of implementing measures against Afghanistan reopened fissures within NATO that had been made during the Vietnam War in the 1960s and the Israel-Arab conflict in the 1970s. The array of sanctions proposed by President Carter went beyond actions the allies were prepared to take. At a time when Western Europe was anxious to complete arrangements for a natural gas pipeline from the USSR, the U.S. intention to restrict trade seemed excessive and economically unsound. Europe's refusal to impose sanctions immediately against Iran's continued detention of U.S. embassy personnel, despite the Security Council's passage of Resolution 461 by an eleven-to-zero vote on December 31, 1979, was a harbinger of their positions on Afghanistan. Secretary Vance recognized that although the allies "did not want to leave us in the lurch . . . none of them wanted to risk a long-term disruption of their Persian Gulf trade and oil links."[59]

The Olympic Games became the most dramatic indication of divisions among the allies. While the idea was broached by Germany immediately after the invasion, it was the United States that trumpeted its boycott decision as one of the more important measures against the USSR. Pressures from U.S. Olympic athletes, angry over their government's disregard for years of training gone to waste, did weigh upon political leaders. Despite the decision of the Italian government not to send any official delegation to Moscow, it did not prevent the Italian Olympic Committee from allowing its athletes to compete in the Olympic Games. At the government's insistence, they would not carry the Italian flag and the national anthem would not be played in Moscow. Ultimately, only West Germany, Norway, and Canada supported the American-sponsored boycott.[60]

Germany's official compliance with the United States over the Olympic boycott could not disguise the frequently expressed hostility toward U.S. leadership during the Carter years, and particularly toward the U.S. national security adviser, Zbigniew Brzezinski. From the outset of the Carter administration Chancellor Helmut Schmidt, a defense expert in the Social Democratic Party, both disparaged the president's leadership in the alliance and urged for a more European-based NATO policy. Brzezinski felt insulted by Schmidt's manner when they met in London in 1977, where the chancellor berated him for U.S.-supported Radio Europe operating on German soil. By 1980 Schmidt tried to get Brzezinski fired.[61] At the highly visible forum of London's Institute for Strategic Studies, the German chancellor spoke out against what he perceived to be a drift in U.S. policy in 1977. While the Carter administration pressed the NATO partners for a 3 percent increase in each ally's defense budget beyond its current plans, Schmidt assailed the United States for failing to deal with the Soviet intermediate-range nuclear threat to Western Europe. Instead of standing up to the Soviets, Schmidt claimed, Carter supported a strategic arms limitation agreement that "will inevitably impair the security of Western European members of the alliance vis-à-vis Soviet military superiority in Europe."[62] Schmidt was suspicious of a possible Soviet-American deal over nuclear deescalation at the expense of Europe's security.

This was only the beginning of the souring German-American relationship during the Carter years. The failure of the U.S. administration to produce the neutron bomb was a further cause of friction, although Schmidt was unwilling to offer German territory as a site for its deployment. The consequence was a reputation for ineptitude that Schmidt helped to impose on the president, even when the administration through the dual-track initiative in 1979 agreed to couple détente with new intermediate-range nuclear weapons.

The administration's position on Afghanistan did little to repair the transatlantic relationship. The series of measures advocated by the United States to counter the Soviet invasion ruffled the sensibilities of the allies, most notably the German chancellor's. At a private meeting of his parliamentary caucus he complained about the unpredictability of U.S. responses to Soviet initiatives, as well as America's failure to consult with the allies before promulgating measures.[63] Revival of the Cold War by embargoing agricultural products from the United States or by boycotting the Olympic Games appeared to be a cosmetic reaction to Soviet behavior, with little likelihood of accomplishing anything beyond stiffening Soviet opposition.

What rarely surfaced openly in NATO meetings was the importance that Europeans attached to economic connections with the Soviet Union. The Afghanistan invasion should not be a reason to jeopardize the delicate negotiations for multibillion dollar plans for building a natural gas pipeline from Siberia to Western Europe. This understandable wish to downplay excessive punishment for Soviet actions rested on the assumption, never shared in the United States, that the Cold War was a thing of the past, and that the Soviet Union essentially was a normal adversary motivated less by communist ideology than by national interest. Afghanistan after all had long been a Soviet preserve. The invasion itself followed an invitation from a communist government whose coup replaced another communist government that Moscow felt was out of control. Was the United States overreacting, with Carter focusing on Afghanistan to ward off both right- and left-wing critics as the presidential election dominated U.S. policy? The unresolved hostage situation in Iran aroused more emotion among the American electorate than the suppression of a Muslim population in a faraway land.

Arguably it was the Carter Doctrine and its implications that became the most divisive issue within NATO at that time. Testifying before the Senate Foreign Relations Committee in February 1980, Clark M. Clifford, secretary of defense in Johnson's administration and currently a special envoy in Europe for the Carter administration, criticized the allies for their reticence in supporting the sanctions the United States was initiating against Moscow. Clifford suspected that the Soviets would derive comfort from the divisions within the alliance over the Afghan issue.[64] He was referring to the restriction of exports and the boycott of the Olympic Games but did not acknowledge that a major reason for the Europeans' reluctance to embrace U.S. actions was their disagreement with the Americans over the assessment of Soviet designs. Europeans in general felt that the Americans were mistaken in envisioning the end of the Soviet invasion being only when the Soviets reached the Indian Ocean in a position to threaten the Persian Gulf states, including Iran.

While all the allies publicly professed solidarity with the United States in the winter and spring of 1980 over the Soviet challenge, their behavior suggested reservations if not dissent from U.S. leadership. This is what Clifford perceived in his visits to Europe. Secretary of State Vance, more sensitive to European concerns than many of his colleagues were, recognized that the allies did not share the U.S. conviction that, as "the first example since World War II of Soviet military occupation of a non-Communist-bloc country, the security interests of the West dictated that we act cohesively and promptly to demonstrate to the Soviets that such behavior was not [an] acceptable part of the East-West competition." But the allies realized they were more vulnerable than the United States, since "the invasion moved Soviet ground and air forces several hundred miles closer to the gulf and the West's jugular vein of oil."[65]

This divergence between Europe and America explains why the European allies were so reluctant to make the kind of contributions to containing Soviet expansion that the Americans were asking of them. They did agree in principle that Soviet aggression should be deterred, and they supported limited sanctions and diplomatic actions such as formal condemnation of the Soviets in the United Nations. And the allies did actually participate to some degree in strengthening security in the Persian Gulf even if they were skeptical about Soviet ambitions in the area. Great Britain expanded its naval and air facilities on the island of Diego Garcia in the Indian Ocean; and Western European powers collaborated with the United States in a financial consortium to assist Pakistan's defenses. But when it came down to expanding their military budgets and enlarging their military forces in order to compensate for America's diversion of its forces from Europe to the Persian Gulf and the Indian Ocean, or initiating trade sanctions that might jeopardize their economies, they demurred.[66]

These differences represented problems more complicated than the mutual dislike of Schmidt and Brzezinski, or the patronizing attitude of the professional military expert Schmidt toward the amateur Carter. They reflected the worldviews of the transatlantic partners. Communism was still an American obsession, while the Europeans seemingly had transcended that fixation. The United States had nightmares of the Soviets conquering the West through their control of the resources of the Middle East, while the Europeans judged the Soviet invasion as a deplorable but understandable reflex action of a superpower worrying about the potential loss of a neighboring client. There was no way that a common NATO position on Afghanistan beyond a ritual denunciation of Soviet aggression would play out in the United Nations.

Discord over the meaning of the Afghan crisis did not mean that the communiqués of NATO summit meetings would put the differences on display. In fact, every pronouncement emerging from NATO meetings in 1980 emphasized the importance of solidarity. At a key meeting of the Defense Planning Committee on May 13 and 14, the ministers agreed that the Soviet invasion "made it more than ever necessary to maintain solidarity, cohesion, and undiminished strength throughout the Alliance." They "further agreed that the stability of regions outside NATO boundaries, particularly in the South West Asia area, and the secure supply of essential commodities from this area are of crucial importance. Therefore, the current situation has serious implications for the security of the member countries." In this context, "special relationships of Allies with the regional countries are in the interest of the West as well as of the countries of the region."[67]

Six months later, as the war in Afghanistan between Soviet forces and the Islamic insurgents continued unabated, the defense ministers repeated their condemnation and again "acknowledged that this use of force in pursuit of political aims can bear directly on the security of all member states."[68] Yet it is worth noting that, despite frequent allusions to the relationship between Afghanistan and the Gulf states, NATO had no intention of including any out-of-area countries within the protection of the organization. Secretary General Luns made this position clear at a symposium sponsored by NATO and the U.S. Naval Academy in June 1980 when he asserted that a widening of the alliance's area would both impose an excessive burden on the allies' defense spending and increase the risk of a general war. Luns's voice, while strongly favorable to U.S. positions, was not a major factor in NATO policies, as Ryan Hendrickson has observed. Arguably, had his voice been raised more often in opposition to U.S. policies, he might have had more influence in NATO councils. References to the secretary general rarely appeared in the memoirs of U.S. policy-makers.[69]

But the annoyance of U.S. leaders over the actions as opposed to the words of the allies also continued unabated. The words were clear enough. At the June 1980 summit meeting in Ankara, "The ministers agreed that the international crisis . . . calls for a resolute, constant and concerted response on the part of the allies . . . and there could be no question of accepting a fait accompli resulting from the use of force."[70] The military expert of the *New York Times*, Drew Middleton, noted in February how little help the European allies were actually willing to give. Of the naval powers, only Britain had shown any interest in providing naval support in the Indian Ocean. France with the strongest military presence in the region was unlikely to use its assets to support the United States in a confrontation with the Soviet Union. Rather than seeing the Soviet intervention in Afghanistan as the first phase of a Soviet move into the Persian Gulf, France was assuming that the future easing of the situation would open the way for a renewed approach to détente.[71]

Despite the language of solidarity, the communiqués implicitly accepted this judgment. The Ankara summit's communiqué in June 1980 combined its earlier condemnation of Soviet behavior with a reaffirmation of NATO's attachment to détente, even as the ministers noted the serious damage the Soviet Union had done to that relationship.[72] Although the Carter administration agreed with the need to revive détente, it could not have been comfortable with the emphasis placed by the allies on "the United States contingency plans" for sending its rapid deployment force to the Persian Gulf area. Even though the allies also agreed it would be essential for them to prepare for diversion of NATO-allocated forces to safeguard the alliance's interests outside the North Atlantic Treaty area, there was no immediate plan to implement this intention, beyond recognizing "that the developing situation would entail a suitable division of labour within NATO."[73]

These statements were made not in the aftermath of the invasion but at the end of the year in which only the United States was providing military aid to the Afghans and deploying its naval forces in the region. In May 1980 the NATO communiqué noted that the burden of defense measures had fallen "largely upon the United States" but implied that the European members' increases in their individual defense capabilities in NATO Europe would be an appropriate division of labor.[74]

Given the depth of the transatlantic gulf, it is not surprising that no NATO voice was raised in any of the UN deliberations. Would France subscribe to any particular course of action? Would the allies accept the package of measures the United States was prescribing? NATO members were all represented in the resolutions denouncing the Soviet Union, but in the NATO councils assembled in 1980 there was no consensus that would encourage its members to present an institutional message at the UN. Britain was a vocal presence at the UN Security Council meetings in January 1980, but its delegation at the Moscow Olympic Games and its resistance to U.S. appeals for specific actions against the Soviets were more genuine measures of British sentiments. The United States was not without strong support in opposing the Soviets in Afghanistan, but support was expressed more passionately from China and the Muslim world than from the European allies.

By contrast the more cohesive European Community did speak out on more than one occasion in this period. The Italian delegate at the General Assembly delivered the formal rebuke to the Soviet Union on January 17, 1980, as presiding officer of the EC: "The nine members of the European Community have focused their attention on the Afghan crisis" and "reaffirmed their grave concern with regard to the crisis created by the military intervention of the USSR in Afghanistan." However, besides urging the Soviet Union to respect the UN resolution of January 14, calling for immediate and unconditional withdrawal of its troops, the Europeans had no action to recommend. In fact, the message was watered down by affirming their devotion to the cause of détente, which required Soviet conformity with the standards and principles of the United Nations Charter.[75] In essence, the EC was not willing to allow Soviet aggression in Afghanistan stand in the way of continuing negotiations for détente in Europe.

In April 1980 the heads of state and foreign ministers of the EC, meeting as the European Council in Luxembourg, declared its "grave concern" that Soviet troops had not yet been withdrawn from Afghanistan. It asked that Afghanistan be allowed to remain outside the boundaries of the Cold War and "return to its traditional position as a neutral and non-aligned state." While they were ready to support any initiative, and particularly from the Islamic countries, there was no political or military action implied in their statement. They reiterated their "deep concern" in June as the Soviets expanded their operations in Afghanistan. The June letter concluded with the hope that the great powers would refrain from interfering in the country's internal affairs but went no farther than to associate the EC with whatever the Islamic states would propose.[76]

There were no comparable statements to the United Nations from the NATO partners, although the sentiments as well as the unwillingness to act were certainly expressed in NATO meetings. The primary reason for the absence of any formal NATO statements in the UN may have been the European allies' resistance to U.S. pressure for the steps the superpower was taking, a form of passive aggression against policies that endangered the economic well-being of NATO Europe but complied with U.S. views on Soviet intentions in Afghanistan. The authority once wielded by the United States in Europe had eroded over the years, particularly since the Vietnam War.[77] Despite their unhappiness over the Soviet behavior in Afghanistan, the European allies were unwilling to have that misadventure stand in the way of détente, a policy the alliance had clarified in 1979.

There was still another dimension in NATO Europe's reactions. The European allies had a well-established fear that the United States might abandon Europe in favor of its long-standing interests in Latin America and East Asia. The Carter Doctrine had added the Persian Gulf area to America's center of attention, even though the resources of that region were of as much concern to Europeans as they were to Americans. Europe's eye, though, was primarily on Soviet ambitions in Europe where U.S. nuclear power was still needed to cope with the Soviet counterpart. In this context Europe's view of the United States was schizophrenic: on the one hand, the European allies deprecated the danger in Southwest Asia by turning their backs on the senior partner's position, and on the other hand, they demanded continued reassurance of America's ability to cope with Soviet nuclear bullying. According to the dual track decision of 1979, defense efforts coexisted with the pursuit of détente. It was an uneasy coexistence that prevented a NATO voice, comparable to the EC's, from being heard in the United Nations in 1980.

This relatively relaxed reaction to what Europeans agreed was Soviet aggression reflected, even more than during the Yom Kippur War, a sense that no matter how offensive Soviet behavior was, it still lacked the menace the Soviet empire of the 1950s and 1960s had signified to the West. It was this changing perception, combined with a considerable loss of respect for American leadership of the alliance, that encouraged the allies to place their own economic interests, again as in 1973, above the common interest as defined by the United States. American opposition to a natural gas pipeline that would bind the West more closely to the East went unheeded, and the American call for a boycott of the summer Olympics in Moscow elicited mixed results: Canada, Germany, and Norway joined the United

States in withdrawing from the Olympic Games, but the majority of the NATO allies—Britain, France, Italy, the Netherlands, Belgium, and Denmark—did not.

Consequences

The last decade of the generation-long East-West conflict witnessed no crisis on the order of Suez or Afghanistan, although the targeting of Western cities by Soviet intermediate-range weapons and the response of the United States with its own nuclear weapons in Europe assured the continuation of tensions. The Afghanistan War ground on through the 1980s, with few prospects for Soviet success. A new secretary-general, Javier Perez de Cuellar, performed his bureaucratic duties in convening the UN Security Council, but his was a passive role, like Waldheim's before him. The Cold War remained in the background, always able to nullify any actions the majority in the Security Council might wish to take.

The arrival of Mikhail Gorbachev to power in the mid-1980s brought first a genuine détente between the superpowers and ultimately a dissolution of the Soviet empire in 1991. Afghanistan was not the quagmire for the Soviets that Vietnam had been for the United States. This image was more suitable for jungle flatlands. Rather, Afghanistan's losers fell into a mountain abyss. The Islamic mujahideen, drawn from all parts of the Islamic world and aided by lethal U.S.-supplied anti-tank weapons, deepened the chasm into which the Soviets fell. The situation required the authority of Gorbachev to begin the Soviet disengagement from Afghanistan. His agreeing to the presence of a team of UN observers gave that organization a role to play, finally, in assuring Soviet removal of one hundred thousand troops by 1989.[78] This was arguably the first step in the dissolution of the Soviet empire unwittingly initiated by Gorbachev. The new bonds between Reagan and Gorbachev permitted the deescalation of the Cold War, with limited involvement of the United Nations. Only after post-Soviet Russia on the UN Security Council removed the constant threat of veto from its resolutions was there to be opportunity for NATO to engage in a serious relationship with the UN.

6

The Persian Gulf War, 1990–1991

Prelude: End of the Cold War

The sudden termination of the Cold War in 1991 offered an opportunity for the United Nations to redefine its role as the leading actor in maintaining peaceful relations in the world. The steps taken by Mikhail Gorbachev to relax controls over the Soviet Union's Warsaw Pact partners as it reduced the size of its nuclear arsenal prefigured the dissolution of the Soviet empire in that year. The resulting warmer relations between the Soviet Union and the United States revived the possibility of the UN Security Council's winning the consensus needed to deal with such crises as the invasion of neighboring Kuwait by Iraq's Saddam Hussein in August 1990. Although the end of the Cold War left NATO without the mission it had held for almost two generations (the containment of Soviet-led communism), it did encourage positive connections between NATO and the UN. Since the Atlantic alliance was questioning its very reasons for survival at that juncture in time, the United Nations appeared poised to provide a leadership in peacekeeping that it had been unable to assert during the long contest between the U.S.-led alliance and its Soviet counterpart.

If NATO was primarily a defense against potential communist aggression, the removal of that threat could have made the alliance irrelevant in coping with future crises in Europe. The UN even had a military instrument built into its charter expressly to serve as the keeper of peace in the world. This was the long-neglected Military Staff Committee (MSC) that had been established under the rubric of the charter's Article 47: "to advise and assist the Security Council on all questions relating to the Security Council's military requirements for the maintenance of international peace and security." The MSC was the product of a British initiative to create a standing general staff along the lines of World War II's Anglo-American Combined Chiefs of Staff.[1]

But even before the developing Cold War sidelined the MSC, there had been no discussion on how the military might be employed, who would command the forces, and how much national sovereignty would be sacrificed in the process. These questions created problems for U.S. military leaders outside the parameters of the Cold War. For Americans there was always a gap between the grant of new powers to the UN and, as historian Jonathan Soffer observed, "the promise to the American public that the UN would not infringe on US sovereignty."[2] A generation earlier the fight in Congress over Article 10 of the League of Nations Covenant—requiring each member to preserve the territorial integrity of all its members—had doomed U.S. acceptance of the league. Its memory effectively removed the question from consideration when the Truman administration sought to maintain congressional support for the UN Charter.

The Joint Chiefs of Staff had no intention of making the MSC their surrogate. If the new committee had any function at all, it would be for minor operations against minor disorders. Given the onset of the Cold War, no consensus between NATO and the Soviet Union was likely, even with respect to a minor offender. There was even less likelihood that the Soviet Union would have accepted a viable military staff committee in 1945. On the assumption that the United States and its allies would control the UN machinery, the USSR would see the committee as an instrument of U.S. domination. Small wonder that the MSC never came to life, remaining "a high-level husk for forty-five more years."[3]

In 1990 a new world order was in prospect, affecting NATO and Gorbachev's Soviet Union. The language of the NATO communiqué at the London meeting of the North Atlantic Council on July 4–5 was almost ecstatic in anticipation of such a new world order: "Europe has entered a new, promising era. Central and Eastern Europe is liberating itself. The Soviet Union has embarked on the long journey toward a free society."[4] President George H. W. Bush shared this optimism in his news conference following the London summit meeting: "The London Declaration will bring fundamental change to every aspect of the alliance's work. This is indeed a day of renewal for the Atlantic community. For more than 40 years, we've looked for this day—a day when we have already moved beyond containment, with unity on the continent overcoming division. And now that day is here, and all peoples from the Baltic to the Adriatic, can share its promise."[5]

For the Soviet Union in the midst of its perestroika, the future offered dramatic possibilities, particularly in relations with the United States and Western Europe. The Soviet Union had opened the way by permitting independent governments to rise out of the Warsaw Pact—and even permitted, with reservations, the incorporation of the German Democratic Republic into the Federal Republic. By the summer of 1990 the Cold War had terminated, and the UN should have been in a position to exercise a leadership denied it in the past. Such certainly was the view of Soviet foreign minister Eduard Shevardnadze. Writing in the year of the Persian Gulf crisis, he emphasized, "There is nothing more rational and effective in the world community than the United Nations. Even in terms of the future, the U.N. is still the only possible true guarantee of international stability. It must be allowed to fulfill this function. No country will allow a single state to impose order by force. The new world order can be built only collectively."[6]

The crisis over Kuwait took place at a time when the old negative Soviet view of the UN, symbolized by the 114 vetoes it cast between 1945 and 1975, had been replaced by a new vision. As early as 1987 Gorbachev, writing in *Pravda*, expressed interest in the UN role in promoting peace and security.[7] His use of the UN to supervise Soviet withdrawal from Afghanistan in that year seemed to have been an earnest of his intentions.

Although there was no mention of the UN in the NATO communiqué from the summit meeting in London on July 5–6, 1990, it was reasonable to assume, in light of the blossoming relationship between the United States and the Soviet Union, that there would be potential for consensus among the veto-holding powers in the UN Security Council that could enhance the UN's authority in a future crisis. Iraq's invasion of Kuwait in August 1990 was just such an opportunity, even though it was not specifically an occasion for NATO-UN collaboration. The war over Kuwait was outside the geographic boundaries of Article 6 of the North Atlantic Treaty. There would have to be future crises "out of area" before Article 4 (dealing with threats to the territorial integrity and security of any ally) could be used to justify NATO action. Yet Saddam Hussein's aggression did open the way for the United States to mobilize a coalition that included most of the NATO partners to punish Iraq for its violation of a vital tenet of the UN Charter.

Notwithstanding a devastating seven-year-long war with Iran, Saddam Hussein seemingly had few qualms about taking on neighboring Kuwait with its vast oil resources. The initiative appeared to be relatively risk free. The United States after all had not been an enemy of Iraq in the 1980s; in fact, it had provided considerable aid on the assumption that Iraq's assault against Iran struck a blow at an enemy that had humiliated America in its seizure of hostages in 1979 and that was considered the major obstacle to stability in the Persian Gulf region. As for the Soviet Union, it had long been an active supporter of Iraq.

As late as July 1990 expert opinion in the United States assumed that Saddam was only bluffing in his extravagant claims against Kuwait, in order to intimidate the emirate of Kuwait into making economic concessions. If there should be any danger of precipitate action, a U.S. carrier task force dispatched to the Arabian Sea should make the Iraqi dictator aware of how seriously the United States took the crisis he was inciting. U.S. ambassador April Glaspie subsequently was the scapegoat—unfairly, according to both the president and the secretary of state—for failing to impress Saddam sufficiently with the depth of U.S. concern. Following an interview with Saddam on July 15, a week before the invasion, Glaspie concluded, "We have fully caught his attention, and that is good. I believe we would now be well-advised to ease off on public criticism of Iraq until we see how the negotiations develop."[8]

Congressional Reactions

Glaspie was not alone in misjudging Saddam. Secretary of State James A. Baker III recognized that, had President Bush bluntly informed the Iraqi president that if he invaded Kuwait the United States was willing to go to war, "members of Congress would have been muttering impeachment."[9] Baker was not far off the mark. In the months between Iraq's conquest of Kuwait in August 1990 and military action in February 1991, the administration's efforts to win over a skeptical Congress were arguably as difficult as they were to put together a coalition of willing nations.

Fundamentally, Congress was as upset with Iraq's aggression as the administration was. In support of the actions taken by the president, including the deployment of U.S. forces troops to the Persian Gulf, the Senate passed a resolution with an overwhelming majority of ninety-six to three. Yet an underlying uneasiness about the extent of presidential power was expressed when Senator Herbert Kohl (D-WI) felt that the president "should have sought congressional approval for the actions he has taken." Memories of the Vietnam War were reflected in Senator John Kerry's (D-MA) pointing out that "this resolution is not a Gulf of Tonkin resolution on the Persian Gulf. On the contrary, this resolution reflects the near unanimity of the global community in condemning this aggressive act by a brutal dictator."[10]

Kerry was correct in his observation about the almost universal condemnation of Iraq, and he was right too to distance U.S. congressional response from the Gulf of Tonkin resolution. Yet as senators rallied behind the administration there were cautionary notes, such as Senator Nancy Kassebaum's (R-KS) that the resolution adopted by the Senate was not a "blank check to the President" for any unilateral military action. Senator Terry Sanford (D-SC) felt that too much emphasis was placed on getting Iraq out of Kuwait. He wanted the United Nations, with the prompting of the United States, perhaps, to go a step further toward the new world order and to require, as part of the price for lifting the embargo, "the destruction of his weapons and onsite verification for any ensuing years the United Nations deems appropriate."[11] Senator Daniel Moynihan (D-NY) agreed but expressed some skepticism about the administration's newfound appreciation of international law and of the United Nations itself: "there has not been such an invocation since Harry S. Truman. The term ['international law'] almost disappeared from the vocabulary of the American Presidents and from the vocabulary of American Secretaries of State." Secretary Baker made it clear that despite the new relationship with the United Nations "we would have difficulties with a United Nations command, representing as we do at this stage at least, such a disproportionately large element of the multinational force."[12]

The Bush administration still had to deal with the public. Vietnam was certainly on the minds of former Senator George McGovern, antiwar Democratic presidential candidate in 1972, and of former secretary of defense Robert S. McNamara, remorseful but not yet ready for a public confession of blame over his role in that war. McNamara predicted a casualty toll of thirty thousand, and McGovern fifty thousand, of the six hundred thousand U.S. forces massed in Saudi Arabia by January 1991. Conservative columnist Robert Novak saw Kuwait as a lost cause, abandoned by its Arab neighbors. Liberal journalist Mark Shields felt the administration was deluding itself in thinking it would be a short war: "This is an administration in trouble, it really is. It's bereft of ideas . . . reminiscent of nothing so much as Jimmy Carter's in 1978."[13] The liberal *Christian Century* criticized the Bush administration for going far beyond asking the UN and Arab states to support a boycott of Iraq. Abandoning a cautious approach, the United States sent a "vast armada" into this region, "acting, Bush told an appreciative Pentagon audience, to defend 'our way of life.'" This kind of jingoism, the editors feared, would take in "a wooden horse filled with 'Muslim rage'" and undo efforts to undo Iraq's aggression against Kuwait.[14]

The stakes were too high in 1990 for critics to have their way. Iraq's aggression jeopardized the security of the entire Middle East with special implications for the oil resources of the region. This factor was uppermost in the mind of Secretary Baker, although he admitted he made a mistake in trying to define "a principled stand against unprovoked aggression . . . as a simple economic calculation—jobs."[15] Given the ease with which the Iraqi army defeated and annexed Kuwait, it was hardly surprising if all the powers concerned, particularly those in Western Europe, assumed it would be difficult to dislodge the invader. But despite the customary hostility with which the majority in the General Assembly greeted a superpower's policies, the very visible leadership now assumed by the United States might have been a critical factor in putting together a coalition to oust the aggressor.

What was surprising at this time was how little of the familiar opposition to U.S. policies was heard in the UN halls. The tide that had been turning in America's favor in the Afghanistan War continued to rise as the Cold War ebbed. There was near unanimity in the Security Council over condemnation of the Iraqi conquest, even though the resolutions—twelve in number between August 2 and November 29, 1990—originated in Washington, then were faxed to New York, and were distributed to the other ambassadors by Ambassador Thomas Pickering. An admiring French diplomat observed that Pickering "knew how to negotiate with the members so they would feel part of the process. He might change a word here, a word there, nothing substantive, but it would enable a delegate to save face."[16] It was not simply the case of a shrewd diplomat successfully twisting arms that produced the results. Rather, the world community seemed to have been ready to accept a U.S. leadership that would have been impossible to visualize ten years before.

The resolutions passed in the UN Security Council were draconic. Only five days after the invasion, the council decreed a total embargo on all trade with Iraq, except food and medicine, unless it withdrew its forces from Kuwait. The resolution passed by a vote of thirteen to none, without dissent from the Soviet Union or China. Only Cuba and Yemen, communist clients of the Soviets, abstained. Of the twelve resolutions, five passed unanimously, Cuba voted against three of them, Yemen against two. This was a remarkable expression of the world's sentiment, which might have cowed a tyrant less self-confident than Saddam Hussein.[17]

The Soviet Factor

Equally striking was the joint letter on August 3 from the two Cold War antagonists to the Security Council condemning the Iraqi dictator's strike across his border.[18] This letter might not have been sent at that critical moment had it not been for the fortuitous presence of Secretary Baker in Moscow. His friendship with his Soviet counterpart made it possible. It was not an easy decision for Eduard Shevardnadze when he met with Baker at the Vnukovo II Airport. Indeed, he confessed, "It was one of the most difficult decisions I ever had to make." He knew there would be resistance from the Arabists in the foreign ministry. He also knew that the traditional Soviet role of patron could be fatally compromised: "We had to carry the ball down the whole field. But it was no longer a game of American football, which was being questioned, and not even a Soviet-American game. The question of the world's future was in the balance." The Iraqi invasion, he felt, "threatened to undermine the practice of the new thinking, the tendency toward disarmament, the entire course of building new international relations."[19]

National Security Adviser Brent Scowcroft understood how important the joint statement was: "It dramatically put the two superpowers on the same side of a major crisis for the first time since the Cold War began." The fact that Scowcroft identified the Soviet Union as a "superpower" was an important factor in Shevardnadze's signing the letter with Baker, and in Gorbachev's accepting its consequences.[20]

But despite all the good feelings between the two foreign ministers, they still had to confront the misgivings of their colleagues. Only two days after dispatching the joint statement, Shevardnadze informed Baker that the USSR would not support any further UN resolutions until the Iraqis were given sufficient time to withdraw from Kuwait. President Bush did his part to worry the foreign minister when he announced he was dispatching U.S. troops to Saudi Arabia at the request of that monarchy. Baker's explanation that the deployment would be temporary and implied no permanent U.S. presence did not appease the Soviet foreign minister. As the secretary noted, an angry Shevardnadze asked, "Are you *consulting* us or *informing* us?"[21] His language and tone were reminiscent of NATO allies' reactions to unilateral U.S. decisions during the Cold War years.

Baker calmed his friend with the suggestion that the United States would welcome Soviet participation in the multinational force being planned. Shevardnadze countered with the idea of using the Military Staff Committee as the umbrella, under the rubric of the Security Council, in which the Soviets would play a prominent part. Not surprisingly, Baker found strong resistance to both proposals in the State and Defense departments. These proposals violated the tenets of U.S. diplomatic efforts over a generation to minimize Soviet influence in the Middle East. The president and national security adviser shared these misgivings, but the secretary of state's argument convinced the president. Baker emphasized the risks that Shevardnadze was taking in agreeing to a joint statement, but in addition to feeling a sense of obligation toward the Soviet foreign minister, he pointed to "the significant plus to have the Soviets in the military coalition. It would certainly ruin Saddam's day to learn that his primary arms supplier might now be prepared to join in military operations with the Americans."[22]

U.S. willingness to accept the Soviets as a partner in what would be called Operation Desert Shield was a successful ploy even though Gorbachev rejected the invitation to participate in the coalition. Remembering the Soviet experience in Afghanistan against Muslim fanatics—a version of the U.S. Vietnam complex—and perhaps distrustful of a junior partnership, he would not join. He did agree that "the Persian Gulf crisis proved to be essentially the first serious experience with the new relations then being established between the Soviet Union and the United States. And we withstood the test of this experience, although the situation was not an ideal one."[23] Ultimately, the Soviets did send a few ships to monitor the blockade as a token of their solidarity with the opponents of Saddam.

In turning down an active role, Gorbachev disarmed Baker's critics in Washington by relieving them of having to deal with the Kremlin's military contributions to the growing coalition. The rejection also disarmed Shevardnadze's enemies in Moscow. Furthermore, the interaction raised Gorbachev's morale. The point was not that he accepted or rejected the U.S. invitation. Rather, it was that the Americans offered it and the world could see the United States continued to respect the Soviet Union as a superpower. As President Bush recorded in his diary on August 6–7, "They want some standing, some face, and it's so important in the world. . . . He's against what Iraq did. They disapproved of [the invasion] in the United Nations, but now if they see us go rushing in carrying the ball, and they have no role, then they just look like bit players or unimportant."[24]

For Shevardnadze the outcome was personally less satisfactory. The Arabists in the Kremlin led by Yvgeny Primakov continued to assure Saddam Hussein that his old patron had not abandoned him. Without consulting the foreign minister, Primakov visited Baghdad as a personal envoy of President Gorbachev, ostensibly to remove some five thousand Soviet technicians remaining in Iraq. Primakov, a Middle East expert, sympathized with Saddam's sense of isolation and felt he would not be moved by threats.[25] Primakov's visit to Baghdad, one of many in the fall of 1990, was designed to broker a settlement between the USSR and Iraq. If successful it would be a major coup for Soviet diplomacy, a goal Gorbachev would value even more highly than Shevardnadze's services. There was little chance that Primakov's efforts could succeed. What he and his Kremlin colleagues did manage was to drive the foreign minister out of office in December 1990. However, there were limits in 1990 and 1991 beyond which the Soviets felt they could not challenge the United States. Their votes on the UN Security Council never varied from those of the transatlantic superpower, when Desert Shield became Desert Storm in February 1991.

The Coalition

The Soviet Union was only one piece, although arguably the most important one, in the mosaic coalition that the United States was assembling in the summer and fall of 1990. Almost as important as the Soviet Union was China, which also enjoyed veto power and was opposed to the use of force against Saddam. At the same time China was reluctant to antagonize the United States, particularly in the wake of the world's reaction to the Tiananmen Square massacre, by overt dissent from the U.S. position. In August China was part of the majority condemning Saddam Hussein for his invasion of Kuwait. Its foreign minister spoke clearly at the General Assembly in September, saying that Iraq's action, "in China's view, constitutes a violation of the United Nations Charter and a gross trampling on the accepted norms governing international relations." But he also emphasized "a political settlement of the Gulf crisis," with the dispute to be resolved "through peaceful negotiations."[26] But when the time came, on November 29, for an ultimatum that would involve force, the Chinese wavered. Security Council Resolution 678 set a deadline of January 15, 1991, after which "all necessary means" may be used to implement Resolution 660 of August 2, 1990, demanding withdrawal of Iraqi forces from Kuwait. Abstention was the best the United States could get on this critical vote. Cuba and Yemen opposed, as they had in earlier, less drastic resolutions. China abstained.[27] By refraining from vetoing the resolution, the Chinese implicitly accepted it—and U.S. leadership of the coalition.

Britain and France, the other major powers, took different routes to the same end. Prime Minister Margaret Thatcher had few qualms about action. If she had had her way, the coalition's stance would have been unequivocal and more militant. She was the first leader among the United States' NATO allies to raise the question of forcibly removing Iraq from Kuwait. Her immediate response was to ask all UN members to "stand up and be counted." And it was Britain that was most consistent in backing Washington's increasing pressure on Iraq into war itself. The British contribution to the coalition forces when the time came was greater than that of any other member.[28]

Thatcher's close friendship with Reagan and to a lesser extent with his successor, George Bush, helps explain this demonstration of the "special relationship." Britain's investments in Kuwait's resources as well as its ties with Saudi Arabia reinforced Thatcher's resolve to play a prominent part in liberating Kuwait. Should Iraq attack a NATO ally, Turkey, in the course of a war, Article 5 would be a clear and appropriate response. But this was not a key factor in Britain's behavior. Rather, the point was made by Foreign Secretary Douglas Hurd, the American connections allowed Britain to "punch above its weight" in a world where Britain's role in the new Europe could be diminished by the enlarged post–Cold War Germany.[29] Britain supplied thirty-five thousand troops and three hundred tanks to the common effort. More important, it placed its forces under U.S. command in the conduct of the war.[30]

France, as always, made difficulties for the coalition even as it supported all the resolutions. Although not to the degree of the Soviet Union, it had been a strong supporter of Saddam Hussein's military machine and its use in the Iran-Iraq war. France had prided itself in the distance it kept from U.S. foreign policies while it tried to consolidate its position as Europe's leader in the European Community and as the primary challenger to American suzerainty over NATO. Added to this was concern for the ties France had made with the Arab world since its break with Israel in 1967. In joining the Anglo-Americans in war President François Mitterand had to face sharp criticism from opponents such as the Rassemblement Pour la République (RPR) spokesman, Philippe Seguin, who asserted that "this war is a stupidity. It is absurd. France has everything to lose in it. We are giving the U.S. tremendous power and leeway, without knowing where this will lead us."[31]

Yet France was a partner in the war, no matter how reluctant it may have been to occupy a secondary role. President François Mitterand's relatively Atlanticist postures help to explain French reasoning. Just a few years earlier he had supported the U.S. deployment of Cruise and Pershing II missiles in Germany, but not in France, in order to counter the Soviets' targeting West European cities with medium-range nuclear weapons. Despite all efforts to identify a Europe separate from America, France was as concerned as any NATO ally about the United States' abandoning its allies if they did not participate in the war against Iraq.

A cartoon in *Le Monde* on the day of the invasion depicted a ravenous Saddam ready to gobble up tiny Kuwait.[32]

Having proved its commitment to freeing Kuwait, supporting the embargo, and even dispatching troops, France still hoped that its ties with Iraq and reputation of relative independence from U.S. control might serve to extricate Saddam from war. Such was an expectation of the Iraq ambassador to Paris. Mitterand's speech at the UN General Assembly meeting on September 24 was an opportunity to raise the prospect of a peace conference to follow Iraq's withdrawal from Kuwait. His demand that the Emir of Kuwait could be restored only after democratic reforms were in place could have divided the coalition. His speech was a ploy to show the world that France had its own agenda.[33]

This initiative revived U.S. suspicions about France's place in the coalition. The genuine military contributions France made to the buildup in the fall of 1990 (13,500 troops, 110 tanks, 2,500 vehicles, and 120 helicopters) were frequently deprecated. But even as the combat operations became inevitable, Mitterand could accept placing French forces under a unified American command only with ground troops; French air forces would not participate in the coalition's air campaign. France did participate as an ally, but always with the understanding that it was an ally with a difference.[34]

The two other NATO allies of major significance to the coalition were Germany because of its relative invisibility and Turkey because of its vulnerability. With all its dominance in Europe, magnified by the unification of East and West, Germany was in no position to become a participant even on the ambivalent order of France. The date for unification was set for October 1990, and with elections in December, domestic issues fully absorbed the attentions of the German public and government. Beyond this consideration was the legacy of Germany's ugly history and the constitution of the Federal Republic, which limited its military forces to self-defense within the confines of the Atlantic alliance. The answer from the perspective of Chancellor Helmut Kohl's government was to revise the constitution in order to permit a German presence in the coalition. The justification would be conformity with the UN's condemnation of Saddam's action and solidarity with its allies.[35]

Some accommodation was made under U.S. pressure to resist opposition from the Social Democrats and Greens. Reports circulated in August that Germany would consider sending minesweepers to the Gulf as part of a Western European Union (WEU) force. But despite Kohl's party's bond with NATO allies, the government was unwilling to challenge the idea of German forces operating outside NATO territory. The Kohl government did make some concessions. In August Germany agreed to send five ships to the Mediterranean to replace U.S. ships of the Sixth Fleet that had left for the Gulf. In the next month Kohl provided a package of aid in the form of civilian aircraft and commercial ships to transport U.S.

troops from Germany to the Gulf and allowed the use of U.S. bases in Germany to transport troops and supplies to the region. The U.S. Congress, which was well aware of the 8 billion dollars Bonn was prepared to provide in order to repatriate Soviet troops from Germany, felt that Germany could afford to do more. And it did. Germany ultimately gave over three-fourths of a billion dollars to the common effort.[36]

Germany's ambivalence toward the coalition manifested itself in its attitude toward the defense of Turkey in the event that Iraq struck at its northern neighbor. When the Turks sought assurance from its NATO partners that the alliance would come to its defense, Germany first tried to evade the question by saying that NATO's reach was restricted to East-West issues. It justified its stance on Article 5 by saying that U.S. use of Turkish bases to strike Iraq could be construed as a provocation that would relieve Germany of its obligation to aid Turkey if Iraq retaliated. The German government retreated from this position after encountering an angry Turkish reaction. Turkey charged that if Iraqis attacked with chemical weapons, it would hold responsible the German companies that produced the weapons. To defuse further criticism, Germany provided jets, pilots, support staff, and some air defense batteries, but only after foot-dragging and continued resistance from the Social Democratic and Green parties.[37]

Turkey's position was different from those of the other allies. It was both a Muslim nation (though determinedly secular) and an uneasy neighbor of Iraq. In brief, Turkey was on the front line. While there was no difficulty in mobilizing its membership in the coalition, it was concerned about the economic cost that the sanctions imposed on Iraq would have on its economy. Iraq's oil pipelines supplied the West, and Turkey's action would come at the price of a 7 billion dollar loss. The government of President Turgut Ozal was divided, even though his party controlled parliament. Public opinion as well as the voice of the powerful military opposed going to war against Iraq; the chief of the foreign and defense ministers along with the chief of the general staff resigned, while polls indicated that two-thirds of the population agreed with them and preferred a policy of neutrality. Ozal faced hostile elements from the left and the right.

The U.S. stake in Turkey's collaboration with the coalition rested in part on the important Incirlik air base, five hundred miles from the Iraq border, from which U.S. planes would be launched. The Turkish Cabinet wavered over the use of the bases before allowing them for humanitarian and logistical support. Once the war began, U.S. planes struck Iraqi targets from the base with parliamentary approval. Much of Turkish hostility was not founded on sympathy for Saddam. Even as polls showed 70–80 percent of the public opposed to U.S. use of the air base, two-thirds saw Saddam as a threat. Baghdad protested but took no further action, grateful perhaps that the coalition did not launch a second front from Turkey.[38]

A vital component of the coalition were the Arab countries, threatened by the precedent of Iraq's seizing a neighboring country with impunity but leery of an entanglement with U.S. foreign policy. Egypt, Syria, and Saudi Arabia were the principal parties. The key was Saudi Arabia, which served as the host for the massive buildup of U.S. troops, which the Saudi royal family felt was vital in order to deter aggression from its Iraqi neighbor. The Saudis were the most enthusiastic adherents of the coalition, and with good reason. They feared the Iraqi seizure of Kuwait was only a prelude to an attack against Saudi Arabia. The United States was the Saudi bulwark against potential Iraqi aggression, and the Saudis responded, as did Egypt, with money and troops for the coalition.[39]

Inevitably, there were caveats on the Arab side. The prospect of waging war against fellow Arabs reputedly disturbed Syria's Hafez al Assad, even as he relished the defeat of his Baathist Iraqi rival. As Baker observed, "The Syrians wanted the political benefits of participating, but only discreetly at a safe distance."[40] With U.S. agreement they settled for entering Kuwait as a strategic reserve, ready to help the Egyptians if necessary. There would be no offensive operation against Iraq. When the Arab League sent troops to participate in the war, it did so (in the manner of France) as a separate command but not under the joint Anglo-American command.

Jordan was more of a problem than other leading Arab states. Despite the Western leanings of King Hussein, the proximity to Iraq, dependence on its oil supplies, and fear of Iraqi revenge kept Jordan out of the coalition and in continued collaboration with Saddam Hussein. The king was desperate for a compromise that would not alienate him from the West. He failed to secure an international peace conference through which Saddam might have withdrawn his forces from Kuwait. The sentiments of the Jordanian public, which shared the Palestinian appreciation of Saddam as the new champion of the Arab cause, were another barrier against participating in the coalition.[41]

A major issue in the Arab role in the coalition was the status of Israel. Should Israel be provoked by Saddam to strike back, the Arabs could desert the cause or their regimes would risk being overthrown by the Arab "street." Saddam was counting on the breakdown of Saudi, Syrian, and Egyptian solidarity with the United States if Israel retaliated. Heroic U.S. efforts kept Israel from entering the war on its own behalf, after Iraqi Scud missiles rained down on Israel when air operations began in January. Ultimately, the Arab states accepted Israel as a beneficiary in the war against Saddam, as long as it remained a silent partner.[42]

The UN's condemnation of Saddam's action was translated into meaningful military form not only by the Anglo-American forces, the Saudi-led Arabs, and an always ambivalent France but also by ground troops from Niger and Pakistan and by naval forces from Australia, Argentina, and Poland. NATO allies Belgium, France, Italy, Denmark, Germany, Greece, the Netherlands, Norway, Portugal,

Spain, Britain, and the United States, comprising most of the original signatories of the North Atlantic Treaty, could claim credit for the success of the war, even though it was not a NATO operation.[43] Discordant notes—from France over relations with U.S. forces and, initially, from Germany over defense of Turkey—were only minor irritations. The coalition represented multilateral diplomacy at its best. From the earliest Security Council resolution in August to the ultimatum of November to the air campaign of January and finally to the four-day war in February, the United States managed to keep together an uneasy combination of disparate nations with disparate interests. It did so with the mixed blessing of the United Nations.

The UN and the Iraq War

Ostensibly, the defeat of Saddam and the restoration of Kuwait was a triumph for UN leadership. The coalition operated under the umbrella of UN approval, in conformity with the terms of its charter. Secretary-General Javier Perez de Cuellar had no problem with the need for action against a regime that "flagrantly contravened international law and the Charter of the United Nations, to which Iraq as a member state was committed." Perez declared that "there never was a question in my mind that this aggression must be repelled."[44]

Yet the secretary-general had problems with the way the coalition functioned under U.S. leadership. His style as secretary-general, low key and usually deferential, did not always make his discomfort clear. He claimed that "Saddam Hussein's aggression might well have been prevented." Although he did not have any information beyond press accounts, the major powers did know "in advance that a very large Iraqi force was moving toward the Kuwait border." If only the United States or the Soviet Union had warned the Security Council of the threat, or "if they had given [him] the benefit of their satellite intelligence" he could have gone to the Security Council, which would have issued a warning statement and sent a fact-finding mission to Baghdad. Perez felt this would have had a restraining influence on Saddam's behavior.[45]

Beneath Perez's agreement with the coalition was a sense of grievance manifested from time to time in passive aggression. The secretary-general felt that the United States exploited the United Nations as an instrument to justify actions it might have taken without the approval of the Security Council. The Bush administration (as the Thatcher government did also) believed that Article 51 of the charter, with its blanket approval of individual and collective self-defense, could have been used.[46] The secretary-general resented that his role was marginal, but he was never in a position to challenge the coalition leaders directly. The best he could do was to deny it the use of the UN flag.[47]

Despite the many Security Council resolutions, the military operation was not a peacekeeping operation as in Cyprus, Lebanon, or Namibia. Nor was it really a collective security action under Article 42 of the charter, which allowed the Security Council, if other measures failed, to "take such action by air, sea, or land forces as may be necessary to maintain or restore international peace and security." Rather the U.S.-led multinational coalition was "a type of subcontract acting on behalf of the organization." Since the member states never provided the Security Council with the military force needed to give meaning to the authority provided in the charter, there was no alternative to the action the Security Council took against Iraq. This was "an improvisation to permit enforcement of the council's will."[48] The United States was not responsible to a UN authority, nor were UN personnel participants in the decision-making. During the bombing raids and ground action that took place in January and February 1991 the United Nations was not even in the picture.

It was not that the secretary-general was invisible in all these months. He kept in the background during Security Council meetings, avoiding comment on the resolutions, in the hope of serving as a mediator. By appearing to be above the fray, he sought to be the decisive voice in persuading Saddam to evacuate Kuwait. He was conspicuously absent from the Security Council when it voted to enforce the embargo. To avoid the final step of war, he traveled to Paris, then to Amman and Baghdad, to seek a peacekeeping force that would monitor Iraq's withdrawal from Kuwait and then establish a mechanism for negotiations between the two countries.

What he found was an adamant Saddam and his equally inflexible foreign minister claiming to want an "Arab solution." In frustration Perez cried out that the UN resolutions were not his to negotiate: "I cannot make concessions on what does not belong to me. I'm not a merchant. I can discuss without negotiating. I rely on the political will of all concerned." But even after his last meetings with Saddam on January 12 and 13, 1991, before the coalition's deadline, he continued to believe that the Iraqi dictator would not have moved had there been a strong Security Council warning before the invasion. His last-minute effort failed.[49]

What Perez undoubtedly had in mind was the role Dag Hammarskjöld had projected with the United Nations serving as an unbiased peacekeeper to moderate tensions among all parties, including the superpowers. Whatever forces the United States and the Soviet Union could provide would only be acceptable to the majority of the UN members if they had "an indisputable U.N. identity." Unlike the organization of the coalition in the Gulf War, Perez would have preferred to have the secretary-general appoint a UN commander, with troop contingents from member states serving under national officers taking orders from the UN commander, who in turn would report to the secretary-general.[50] He told a BBC correspondent a week after the war started that the war was not justified. Even though Security Council resolutions underpinned the action, this did not mean it was a UN war conducted in accord with the charter. Only if the UN had command and control of the forces could the coalition's war over Kuwait be called a UN war. As Perez noted, the involvement of the Security Council was limited to giving the American coalition "a very large mandate."[51]

Whether Perez himself had the personality to exercise this kind of leadership is open to question. Granted that his personal qualities were more attractive than those of his predecessor, Kurt Waldheim, whose willingness to accommodate the powers that would keep him in office undercut any prospect of a genuinely independent secretariat. Perez was cut from different cloth. Like U Thant he was closely allied with the government of his country, Peru. As such he had an "unofficial place at the heart of the Third World elite."[52] As president of the non-aligned group of 77, he served as Peru's ambassador to the United Nations before joining the UN staff under Waldheim where his diplomatic skills advanced talks between Greeks and Turks in Cyprus. When Waldheim campaigned for a third term as secretary-general, he found Perez was his chief rival. The Peruvian's selection as secretary-general was a product of Waldheim's overreach and Peru's diplomatic effort rather than Perez's own politicking.[53]

The secretary-general was not quite as marginalized in 1990 as he indicated during the Persian Gulf crisis. In his annual reports for the war years, he could bask in the recognition that 1990 and 1991 had witnessed a series of events "marking a great turning-point in history." The end of the Cold War, the implosion of the Soviet Union, and the dissolution of the Warsaw Pact were what he most appreciated. They ended, as he noted, "the long season of stagnation for the United Nations."[54] After years of estrangement, the Soviet Union under Gorbachev had realized the value of UN mediation; it even paid its past dues. The United States had been only slightly less hostile to the United Nations under Third World sway during the Cold War and now embraced the organization and its charter. When President Bush was interviewed in *U.S. News and World Report* in December 1990, he made a point of identifying the significance of the showdown with Saddam Hussein: "What's at stake here is whether we can have disputes peacefully resolved by a reinvigorated United Nations. Or will the United Nations, its peacekeeping function having been elevated to its most promising height since 1948, be sent back into the Dark Ages because we failed to fulfill its mandate?"[55] Perez's grievances against the United States notwithstanding, he could reflect at the end of his term in office that "with its return from the doldrums, and with its role no longer peripheral, the United Nations has come nearer to the vision of its Charter. Everyone who contributed to the process is entitled to a measure of exultation and I, for my part, to a feeling of fulfillment."[56]

NATO and the UN

A case may be made that in the anticipated new world order ushered in by the end of the Cold War, NATO would play a more prominent as well as a more harmonious role within the United Nations. NATO members, led by the United States, dominated the coalition. In fact, almost every member—with the exception of Iceland, which had no military arm, and Luxembourg, whose military force was integrated with Belgium's—made some contribution to the coalition. While only the United States, Britain, and France supplied ground troops, the other allies were all represented by naval forces. Turkey's particular vulnerabilities precluded an active role, although there was no doubt about its government's opposition to Saddam Hussein. NATO achieved a consensus over the Iraq invasion and annexation of Kuwait that had been lacking in all the crises after the Korean War. The skepticism concerning U.S. measures against the Soviet Union over Afghanistan in 1980 had dissolved a decade later, aside from the traditional French knee-jerk reaction to any U.S. initiative. Yet NATO as an institution played no part in the debates and resolutions over Iraq in the months leading up to war.

By contrast, the European allies within NATO did raise their voices institutionally within the United Nations. The European Community (EC) under the presidency of Italy dispatched a letter of outrage in the name of its twelve member states on August 2, 1990, the day Iraqi troops crossed the border. A second letter followed on August 6, endorsing an embargo on oil imports from and on sales of arms to Iraq. On August 12, the EC at the extraordinary ministerial meeting in Brussels declared to the UN Security Council their readiness "to take further initiatives, in the framework of the United Nations Charter" to contain the conflict. The last letter from the EC transmitting more declarations on the continuing crisis was on December 17, 1990. While Italy was not a member of the Security Council, it was able to participate in council deliberations in order to speak for EC members.[57]

The EC's voice was heard in the UN Security Council. The EC even joined with the USSR in September to express satisfaction at the high degree of consensus in the Security Council and in the international community as a whole over the importance of ending the invasion as well as increasing efforts to resolve other conflicts in the region. As the deadline for Iraqi response drew near, the EC still had hopes of using its influence in the Security Council's attempts to sustain a dialogue that could avert war. The EC wanted the Arab countries to use their contacts with Iraq's foreign minister to implement the Security Council resolutions.[58] Despite a tone of moderation and its wish for mediation, the EC took a harsh line in August when it rejected the Iraqi demand that its members close their missions in Baghdad. The EC warned Saddam that harm to any EC citizen would be taken as an aggressive action against the entire community and provoke a united response to such an offense.[59]

That the Iraqis were intimidated by EC's protests and warnings is doubtful. The EC as an institution lacked the military capabilities to pursue any military option. The European powers, however, did have a vehicle to implement their concerns with at least a limited military capability. This was the Western European Union (WEU), the unappreciated offspring of the Brussels Pact's 1948 creation, the Western Union. When NATO appropriated many of its committees and most of its raison d'être in 1949, the WU became moribund until it was revived as the WEU in 1954, to usher Germany into NATO. It came to life once again as a means of fleshing out the EC's intentions in 1990. In August France, acting on behalf of WEU members, transmitted to the Security Council the final communiqué of the WEU's ministerial session in Paris concerning the situation in Iraq. The WEU vowed to offer its resources to the growing coalition.[60]

The WEU made good on its offer, although compared with the Anglo-American contribution it was modest. Apart from France and Britain, the support of the other members under the aegis of the WEU was limited to naval forces. Even if their presence was more symbolic than effective, it did represent a concerted European show of solidarity. Germany, distracted by the pangs of reintegration at the end of the Cold War and by its constitutional constraints, provided significant financial assistance to the coalition. While the British would have preferred to make the Persian Gulf a focus of NATO activity, they could use the WEU as a coordinating instrument. Unlike NATO, the WEU did allow for operations outside Europe. France as chair of the WEU at this time identified the French role in that organization as an earnest of its participation in a multilateral enterprise, while Belgium and Italy would not have made their contributions outside a European framework. Positive as these developments were, they could not circumvent the WEU's lack of any command system, rules of engagement, or mechanism for burden sharing. The WEU could not serve any more than the EC as a serious partner in the war against Iraq.[61]

Only NATO had the military capacity to take on the Persian Gulf crisis, and it did so informally through its senior partner. NATO's formal presence at UN debates and in the activities of the coalition was conspicuous by its absence. It was not that the NATO allies ignored the war or its consequences. In December 1990 both the Defense Planning Committee (DPC) and the North Atlantic Council saw Iraq's aggression as a warning to the world. But the closest NATO involved itself in the conflict was in a statement that the demands of the Gulf crisis demonstrated the importance of Article 4 of the treaty, which called for consultation whenever a member's security might be threatened. The DPC congratulated the coalition's support of the UN resolutions in which "Alliance members have participated." The communiqué also recognized that risks to NATO's "security can arise from instability in Eastern and Central Europe, and *from elsewhere.*" The implication was clear enough. There were dangers to the alliance in the Middle East, and they would have to be addressed even though they were obviously "out of area."[62]

When the war ended, the DPC agreed in May 1991 that the Gulf War was an example of a risk that "can also arise from elsewhere," as its members "warmly welcome the success of the international coalition forces." The communiqué also commended "the effectiveness and prompt action taken by the Alliance." But these actions did not refer to U.S. forces in Iraq or to those of its allies in NATO. Rather, they involved the deployment of "naval and air forces to its Southern region to deter any possible attack on its members." There was no connection between NATO and the UN in this communiqué. There was no mention of the UN at all. Not even the UN Security Council resolutions applauded in the December meetings seemed worthy of mention.[63] A senior NATO official thought that there was no consideration of a NATO role in the Persian Gulf conflict "because the idea that NATO would go 'out-of-area' was 'unthinkable' at the time, particularly in a combat role."[64]

If the prospect of a hangman's noose concentrates the mind wonderfully, Iraq's occupation of Kuwait in August 1990 should have had a similar effect upon the activities of the North Atlantic Council. The breakup of the Soviet empire in that year and the concurrent termination of the Cold War had required a new look at the justification for NATO's survival—as the allies recognized at their London summit in July 1990. Since the containment of Soviet expansionism was no longer relevant, NATO's future was in doubt. The shock of the Iraqi invasion, however, illustrated the dangers that still lay ahead in the post–Cold War 1990s, which NATO could help to contain. The crisis in the Persian Gulf raised to the forefront the question of an "out-of-area" role for the allies, a question that had not been resolved, or fully confronted, in the forty years of NATO's history.

But a revitalization of NATO through a common policy toward the Middle East in the UN context was not a consequence of this crisis. What took place was an American initiative, backed by the UN Security Council and with some reluctance by a weakened Soviet Union, to mobilize its own forces and those of the more conservative Arab states in a militant confrontation with Iraq. The stated purpose of the coalition's intervention was the stability of the area and the defense of Saudi Arabia and other oil-producing countries from the control of Saddam Hussein. By this action the United States was serving the interests of its European allies who were more dependent upon Middle Eastern oil than the United States. If ever there was an example of commonality of NATO's concerns, it was over Kuwait in 1990.

Yet NAC and other NATO bodies were almost invisible in this crisis. The voices raised in support of action against Iraq were those of individual members such as Britain or of Europe speaking through the EC, but not of NATO itself. France in its independent fashion did dispatch its own forces (army, navy, and air) to Iraq—never fully coordinated with the Anglo-American allies. Belgian and Italian warships in the eastern Mediterranean delayed their departure to the Persian Gulf until the WEU had given its blessing.

The reason for hesitations and divisions over—even opposition to—a common NATO front stemmed initially from the dictates of the North Atlantic Treaty itself, which made explicit just what territory was to be defended. Article 5 had its elliptical elements, but there was no doubt that an attack against any member would be considered an attack against them all. Article 6 defined the area in which an attack would demand a united response, and conflict outside this area would not come under the rubric of Article 5. If Iraq had attacked Turkey, the obligations of the members would have been clear, although Germany's constitution might have inhibited that country's response.

Such was the provenance for NATO's abstention from action in the Persian Gulf, outside the area of Article 6. There was a justification, however, for a loose construction of the treaty that might have been used—but was not—by NATO over Iraq, particularly in the case of Turkey. This was the provision in Article 4 for consultation in the event that the "security of any of the parties is threatened." Granted the passivity implied in the word "consult," Article 4 opened the door to a new NATO relationship with the United Nations that developed in the Balkans later in the 1990s, and in the Middle East and Asia in the twenty-first century.

7

The Balkan Wars

Bosnia, 1992–1995

NATO and the UN: A New Relationship?

The sudden end of the Cold War did not bring an equally sudden end to the distant relationship between NATO and the UN, but it did remove the impasse between the United States and the Soviet Union on the UN Security Council. After the implosion of the Soviet empire in 1991, a weakened Russia was unable to resist the power of the West in the UN. The Gulf War demonstrated that the UN, with Russia and China reluctantly agreeing, could condemn Iraqi aggression without having to worry about the reactions of Saddam Hussein's former patrons. This change did not immediately close the gaps between the two organizations, but it narrowed the differences considerably. The UN was able to work with NATO countries and especially the United States, if not with NATO as an institution, in repelling the Iraqi invasion of Kuwait. The new atmosphere opened the way for collaboration in the future between NATO and the UN.

But the euphoria in the wake of the victory of the "coalition of the willing" had its critics. Not long after the Serbs succumbed to U.S.-driven NATO pressures at a conference in Dayton, Ohio, Sir Brian Urquhart, now retired from his influential post at the United Nations, leveled a broadside in December 1995 against the major Western powers, particularly the United States, for misreading the lessons of the Gulf War. To Americans, he felt, Desert Storm showed that appropriate military action under the umbrella of the United Nations could solve all post–Cold War problems. After neglecting (when not denigrating) the UN during most of the Cold War years, the United States through its NATO identity was ready to use the world organization as a vehicle for maintaining global peace: "Desert Storm . . . was a huge success in the use of preeminent force. Particularly on the television. It looked terrific. And people began to think, 'Ah, now that the UN is united once more, it can do anything by force. They forgot that it's one thing to agree on a solution to a problem, but it's quite another to put it into effect."[1]

The United States and its allies, Urquhart asserted, then exaggerated the powers of the UN and misunderstood the nature of the conflicts in the Balkans. "What they were getting into weren't conflicts between nation states. . . . These were civil, ethnic, and sometimes religious wars." But the UN Security Council put traditional peacekeeping operations into the former Yugoslavia "because none of the Europeans, and certainly not the United States, wanted to go in and fight the Serbs. So they set up this sort of fig-leaf operation of the UN which was bound to fail . . . which everybody could then blame for not fighting the Serbs though that wasn't what they'd been sent down to do in the first place, because peacekeeping forces are supposed to be impartial."[2] Urquhart was bitter in his denunciations of the United States for setting the UN up for a fall in the Balkan crises, then pushing the UN aside as NATO effectively replaced the Security Council and the secretary-general in the military campaign against the Bosnian Serbs in 1995.

UN Secretary-General Javier Perez de Cuellar shared Urquhart's unhappiness over the position assigned to the United Nations during the Balkan Wars of the 1990s. His emphasis was on the EC's pressure rather than NATO's, but the implication was clear, namely, that in the Gulf crisis the UN was manipulated by the major powers to the detriment of the organization's mission. Perez's "strongly held position" shared by all his senior advisers was that there should be no peacekeeping operation in Yugoslavia until a cease-fire was in place and all fighting had stopped. Even if a UN or a UN-authorized force had been given a mandate to "*enforce* an EC-brokered cease-fire," Perez doubted "that the Security Council could have been persuaded to authorize such action at this time, nor would I have recommended it, having been then, as I remain now, doubtful of the wisdom of using peacekeeping troops whether UN or UN-authorized, for enforcement purposes in internal conflicts."[3]

NATO's New Strategic Concept

While the leaders of the United Nations had grounds for their cynicism, they had to recognize that NATO was enlisted in 1992 to perform a function the UN was incapable of filling, namely, contributing military power to give credibility to UN Security Council resolutions. The UN's weakness made for an unequal and often contentious, if intimate, relationship with NATO. Crisis management, a concept that blossomed almost simultaneously with the Gulf crisis, was first broached at the London summit of the North Atlantic Council in July 1990, at a moment when the Soviet Union was on the brink of disintegration. A new rationale was needed if the alliance were to survive. At the London summit the allies debated the possible future missions of the organization, and then in Rome in November 1991 the ministers reaffirmed the importance of arrangements existing "within the alliance for consultations among the allies under Article 4 of the Washington treaty, and, where appropriate, coordination of our efforts including our responses to such risks."[4] Without formally abandoning Article 5 of the treaty, which mandated collective defense against an aggressor, the allies opened the way for a broader mission for NATO by invoking threats to a member's "security" as a reason for action. Unrest to the point of civil war outside the boundaries of the alliance's formal commitments could present just such a threat.

The NATO allies also recognized that "the challenges we will face in this new Europe cannot be comprehensively addressed by one institution alone, but only in a framework of interlocking institutions tying together the countries of Europe and North America. Consequently we are working toward a new European security architecture in which NATO, the CSCE [Committee for Security and Cooperation in Europe], the WEU and the Council of Europe complement each other."[5] Little room in this communiqué was made for the United Nations in the new security architecture in Europe. The UN was barely mentioned. Should crises arise in Europe, "the European pillar within the alliance will reinforce the integrity and effectiveness of the Atlantic Alliance."[6] The North American pillar appeared to be less relevant at this juncture. If the UN were to be involved, it would simply be to give its blessing to the EC's activities, much as it was doing to the informal gathering of the "willing" in the Gulf crisis of 1991.

The dissolution of Yugoslavia with the consequent splitting into its component parts was inevitably a logical area of NATO concern under the rubric of its new strategic doctrine that centered on a loose construction of Article 4. The Gulf crisis might have fit the criteria if the Rome summit's proposals had been on the table in August when Saddam Hussein's Iraq army invaded neighboring Kuwait. Saddam certainly threatened resources vital to the West's economy. Unlike the Iraqi challenge, the Balkan conflict appeared to be a regional issue. Still, Article 4 was relevant. Yugoslavia was a neighbor to a number of present and future NATO members, and internal disorder there could lap over onto NATO territories.

The language of the Rome communiqués pointed to Europeans' responding to European problems growing out of the breakup of the Yugoslav federation: "We urge all parties to cooperate fully with the European Community in its efforts under the mandate given to it by the CSCE, both in the implementation of ceasefire and monitoring agreements and in the negotiating process within the Conference on Yugoslavia."[7] Managing this conflict seemed made to order for Europeans to solve, with minimal participation of the United States. There was no oil in the Balkans to attract U.S. attention. Secretary of State James Baker expressed the American attitude toward events there when he used a homely Texas saying—"we don't have a dog in this fight."[8] U.S. national interests were not at stake. Making the Yugoslav conflict a NATO matter was not an issue the United States wished to press on its colleagues. Rather, it was more a matter for European organizations such as the WEU or the EC (renamed the European Union in December 1991) to take the major responsibility for action, as the Rome communiqués recommended.

The NATO ministers elaborated on this theme. In a special communiqué, "The Situation in Yugoslavia," they recognized the "grave danger" to the region that was posed by the crisis in Yugoslavia. It is noteworthy that the statement specified "European Community"—not NATO or the UN—as the central actor. The communiqué went on to condemn such acts as the attacks by the Serb-dominated Yugoslav army on Dubrovnik and other Croatian cities that were out of all proportion to the requirements for protecting Serb minorities in Croatia. The UN was mentioned in NATO's "support and appreciation for the efforts of the European community, the CSCE, and the Security Council of the United Nations to resolve this crisis." But the primary reference to the UN was in the last paragraph of the communiqué, where the allies consigned a role for the UN high commissioners to provide humanitarian assistance to victims of the war.[9] NATO as an organization and the United States as its most prominent member were conspicuous by their absence.

NATO Europe and the Balkan Wars, 1991

Responsibility for the calamitous breakup of the federal republic of Yugoslavia rests largely with the leaders of the constituent states. The country itself had been cobbled together after World War I into a kingdom of Serbs, Croats, and Slovenes. This uneasy combination of South Slavs broke down in World War II, as Croatia embraced the Nazi invaders and the Serbs, for the most part, comprised the resistance. The Serb-Croat division arose from their separate identities. The Croats and Slovenes had been part of the Austro-Hungarian empire and Roman Catholic in religion, while the Serbs reflected their heritage as part of the Eastern Orthodox Church under the Ottoman empire. A substantial Muslim population was largely ignored or designated as "Turks" by the Serbs and Croats. Their common language and, after World War II, their membership in the victorious Communist Party under the leadership of a Croat general, Josip Broz (better known as Tito), kept the postwar federation together.

Tito's death in 1980 precipitated the slow disintegration of both the Communist Party and the republic itself. All the toxic passions of the past, which had separated the Eastern Orthodox Serbs from the Roman Catholic Croats, revived. Nationalist leaders of the two ethnic groups inflamed their followers as each exploited traditional enmities in order to secure their power. Memories of the fascist Croat state that was responsible for the slaughter of thousands of Serbs remained alive among the more populous Serbs who dominated the Yugoslav army. The existence of a large Serb minority in the Krajina sector of Croatia made that area a flashpoint of conflict between the two nations. Given the Serb sense of persecution going back to the Turkish conquest of Serbia in 1389, they would not forget this or any other injustice. The last U.S. ambassador to Yugoslavia observed that "their tragic defect is an obsession with their own history." They had, he felt, a "lugubrious, paranoid and Serbo-centric view of their own past."[10]

The Serbian president was Slobodan Milosevic, a former communist apparatchik turned virulent nationalist who took full advantage of this obsession. Equally intent on following a nationalist part was the Croat president, Franjo Tudjman, who was a former Yugoslav general and like Milosevic a communist leader. If he was the lesser offender, according to Ambassador Warren Zimmermann, it was because he was driven by narrow nationalism and not by a lust for personal power. The only leader supportive of a genuinely federal Yugoslavia was the Bosnian Muslim Alija Izetbegovic, president of Bosnia-Herzegovina. Devout but not an extremist, and no more a democrat than his counterparts in the former Yugoslavia, he recognized the dangers to multiethnic Bosnia facing an expansionist Serbia on the east and an expansionist Croatia on the west. The Muslims comprised the largest portion of the population of Bosnia, some 40 percent, with 32 percent Serbs, and 18 percent Croats.[11]

The Balkan Wars of the 1990s began on June 25, 1991, when Slovenia and Croatia unilaterally declared independence in the wake of referendums in both states. The Yugoslav People's Army (JNA), controlled by Milosevic's Serbia, dispatched troops to suppress the disengagement of the two republics from the federation. Given Slovenia's homogeneous population and Western orientation, the JNA withdrew from that country after a short-lived war, less than a month after Slovenia's break with Yugoslavia, but Milosevic had no intention of doing the same in Croatia with its substantial Serbian population in the Krajina region.

Within the West there was division over the course of action. The United States and, to a lesser extent, Britain, agreed that responsibility for some kind of intervention lay with the EC, not with NATO. "This is Europe's hour," as Luxembourg's Jacques Poos proclaimed when the EC launched its mediation effort in August 1991. Understandably, the United States did nothing more than applaud the EC's initiative. It considered the destabilizing events in the Soviet Union and the Persian Gulf more urgent challenges to post–Cold war stability.[12]

Nevertheless, the United States was discomfited by Germany's persistent lobbying on behalf of Slovenian and Croatian independence—based on, as Misha Glenny noted, "ties of culture, economics and religion for many centuries." The EC and Germany considered irrelevant the Croat failure to guarantee the security of the minority Serbs, a factor that seemingly justified the JNA's invasion. Peter Carrington, former British foreign secretary and former NATO secretary general, was the EC's representative in the Balkans in the effort to end the conflict.

Dispirited over his inability to reconcile the contending parties, he later told U.S. negotiator Richard Holbrooke that he had never met such liars in his life as the peoples of the Balkans.[13]

Successful or not, the EC role was particularly fitting given Chapter 8 of the UN Charter, which gave priority to mediation by regional organizations before any problem was turned over to the UN Security Council. Only after the EU admitted defeat did the Balkan Wars become a UN issue. The United States joined the EC in supporting the unanimous Security Council Resolution 713 in September 1991 that imposed an arms embargo on all factions.[14] The weight of UN disapproval seemed to have had a positive effect. In November Serbs and Croats agreed to accept the deployment of UN peacekeepers as prescribed in UN Security Council Resolution 721. The council appointed former U.S. secretary of state Cyrus Vance as personal envoy of the secretary-general, joining Lord Carrington in the peace effort.[15]

Despite professions of compliance with UN resolutions, the dominant Serbs, buoyed by their control of the Yugoslav army, paid little attention to UN requirements. Serbia's war with Croatia raged throughout the fall of 1991. The leaders of both sides were either unwilling or unable to implement agreements they had signed, while the world witnessed the humanitarian crises the war had brought on, most notably the destruction of Dubrovnik, the historic center of Croatia. Television coverage brought the suffering of the city's population into the public's homes.

The UN secretary-general's report of December 11, 1991, reflected his disappointment over the inability of the warring parties to end their hostilities. Depressed over the failure to win the adversaries' respect for cease-fire agreements, Secretary-General Boutros Boutros-Ghali felt that conditions for a peacekeeping operation did not yet exist. In the annex to his report he made a point of warning the EC against any "early selective recognition" of the former republics of Yugoslavia. As a result of his pressure, the UN Security Council adopted Resolution 724 on December 15, which strongly urged "all States and parties to refrain from any action which might contribute to . . . impeding or delaying a peaceful and negotiated outcome to the conflict in Yugoslavia."[16]

Although the EC knew that recognizing the independence of Croatia and Slovenia would mean extending the war, Germany ignored the risk and did precisely that. Despite efforts of Carrington and the U.S. State Department to stop the rest of the EC from following Germany's lead (and thus making "a bad situation worse," as Secretary Baker put it), they failed. But the United States, preoccupied with events in the crumbling Soviet empire and with preparations for war in the Gulf, confined its efforts to "tepid public statements and low-level diplomatic messages." When the EC recognized the two republics on April 6, 1992, the United States did the same the following day. Presciently, Carrington predicted that EC recognition of Slovenia and Croatia "might well be the spark that sets Bosnia-Hercegovina alight."[17]

The UN, NATO, and Bosnia, 1992–1994

Carrington's prediction was all too accurate. Between 1992 and 1995 there was almost constant warfare between Bosnian Serbs and Muslims, and from time to time between Bosnian Croats and Muslims. The failure of European efforts to stop the carnage in Croatia dumped the problem of Bosnia into the UN's lap, even if the responsibility for much of the trouble lay squarely with the EC. That NATO would not assume the burden in Bosnia was made clear by the attitude of its senior partner. So if the Balkan Wars could not be managed by the newly established European Union (EU) and would not be taken up by NATO, then by elimination there was no other choice but the UN. Chapter 8, Paragraph 2, of the UN Charter legitimized the transfer by its understanding that, if regional organizations could not handle a breach of peace, then it would become the UN's responsibility.[18]

In fact, the UN had been involved with the Balkans in 1991 in the person of Cyrus Vance, the secretary-general's special envoy to Yugoslavia. To the extent that he was able to work out a cease-fire in January between Croatia and Serbia, the UN efforts were successful, at least temporarily.[19] Bosnia presented a greater challenge. This region of Yugoslavia had never had an independent existence in the past, and the Muslim majority was vulnerable to pressures from both Serbs and Croats, each of them aspiring to annex its territory. The intermixture of populations induced Milosevic's Serbia to use the Yugoslav army to encourage Bosnian Serb operations against the Muslims.

When the JNA formally withdrew from Bosnia, it left behind troops and equipment to create a formidable Bosnian Serb force. Milosevic's objective after the secession of Croatia was to link Croatian Serb areas with the motherland itself to create a Greater Serbia. In his way was the Muslim population of Bosnia, which was to become the victim of ethnic cleansing. From 1992 until checked in 1995, the Bosnian Serbs in collusion with Serbia embarked on a program of uprooting Muslim communities, a program marked by atrocities. The Muslim president, Alija Izetbegovic, had reluctantly led Bosnia to declare independence in 1992, realizing the dangers that lay ahead. He rested his hopes on the UN's ability to preserve the status of the new state. When the decision for secession was made, the Bosnian Serbs, led by a fiery psychiatrist, Radovan Karadzic, boycotted the elections, refusing to accept separation from the Yugoslav Federation (now composed only of Serbia and Montenegro). By the end of the year, the heavily armed Serbs controlled 70 percent of Bosnia, with the Bosnian government holding on to only 10 percent. The remainder was falling to Bosnian Croats, who were at odds with both Muslims and Serbs.[20]

No matter how ineffective the results of its activities, the UN was fully engaged in Bosnia throughout 1992. Its chief instrument was the UN Protective Force (UNPROFOR), which the Security Council established on February 21, 1992, in accordance with the recommendations of the secretary-general. Its headquarters was in Sarajevo, the Bosnian capital, with a mission to provide protection of the civilians, primarily Muslims.[21] At the same time the UN continued its mediation efforts, along with those of the EU and CSCE. They had little to show for their work. Bosnian Serb forces continued their shelling of Sarajevo as they persisted in attempts to remove Muslims from what they intended to be exclusively Serbian territory.

The original function of UNPROFOR was to ensure the implementation of the mandatory arms embargo in Bosnia. The UN Security Council expanded its charge in March 1993 to include security of "safe areas" that had been bombarded by Serb artillery.[22] It never succeeded in the latter objective and had doubts about the wisdom of lumping Muslims with Serbs in the arms embargo. The UN General Assembly's Resolution 47/121 of December 18, 1992, displayed its dissatisfaction with the behavior of both Serbia and the Bosnian Serbs when it strongly condemned "Serbia and their surrogates in the Republic of Bosnia and Herzegovina for their continued non-compliance with all relevant United Nations resolutions." Because the arms embargo hurt the Muslims and had minimal effect upon the well-armed Serbs, the resolution recommended exempting Bosnia from the arms embargo and urged the establishment of an ad hoc international war crimes tribunal.[23] A war crimes tribunal did emerge from UN deliberations, but lifting the arms embargo against the Muslims did not materialize until 1995.

Arguably, the most demonstrative diplomatic activity in 1992 was the instituting of the International Conference on the Former Yugoslavia in Geneva, which involved the UN, EU, OSCE, and the Organization of Islamic Conferences. The conference appointed a steering committee co-chaired by Vance and David Owen to coordinate peacekeeping and humanitarian aid. Like Carrington, Owen was a former British foreign secretary and Carrington's successor as representative of the EU presidency. The most important achievement of this conference was to back the ambitious Vance-Owen peace plan in January 1993, which divided Bosnia into ten provinces, three each to Serbs, Croats, and Muslims, and a fourth jointly administered in Sarajevo. In this arrangement the Serbs would have 43 percent, the Muslims 36 percent, and the Croats 21 percent. Although a division of the country based on ethnic considerations was later to be the pattern followed, the plan had little chance of success in early 1993. The Serbs, who had overrun most of Bosnia, spurned it. The Muslims, anticipating a better deal under a new U.S. administration, turned it down initially. Only the Croats responded favorably.[24]

The Clinton administration, focused as it was on domestic issues, initially continued the Bush policy of abstention from problems in the Balkans. The new president and his secretary of state, Warren Christopher, had no intention of assuming leadership at the UN or in NATO in order to enforce UN resolutions in Bosnia. Christopher described the Bosnia conflict as "the problem from hell."[25] Richard Holbrooke, by contrast, celebrated the UN choice of Vance as mediator for he had worked with Vance in the Carter administration. The more influential Clinton advisers, however, opposed using U.S. military force in the Balkans irrespective of Vance's kinship with many of them. The rugged mountains of the Balkans, they believed, were not comparable to the deserts of the Middle East as an arena for U.S. tanks. These voices were echoing the Powell Doctrine, which drew from the experience in Desert Storm and from memories of the Vietnam War to the effect that, as General Colin Powell, chairman of the U.S. Joint Chiefs of Staff during the Gulf War, expressed it: "We must not . . . send military forces into a crisis with an unclear mission they cannot accomplish." Military force must be matched against political objectives and then applied with preponderant power. Powell carried more weight in this matter than such figures as U.S. ambassador to the United Nations Madeleine Albright, who wanted a more active U.S. posture toward Serb atrocities.[26]

Historian Randall Woods has suggested that Clinton was influenced by his mentor, Senator J. William Fulbright (D-AR) who had been an articulate critic of Lyndon Johnson's Vietnam policies as chairman of the Senate Foreign Relations Committee in the 1960s. Fulbright had argued repeatedly that the United States had no duty or ability to impose a settlement on a nation where there was no consensus on war and peace. If the European NATO allies, closer to the scene in the Balkans, were reluctant to intervene, the United States should be even more hesitant.[27]

Clinton unwittingly reinforced this caution by launching an ill-fated U.S.-led and UN-sanctioned military intervention in Somalia as a result of public opinion appalled over the televised violence and chaos in that African state. But six months later, the equally televised dragging of the bodies of U.S. troops on the streets of the capital resulted in a hasty evacuation and termination of the mission. It was a cautionary experience that certainly did not invite repetition in Bosnia.[28] It underscored the importance of the Powell Doctrine.

Notwithstanding the prevailing sentiment in Washington in both the Bush and Clinton administrations, the United States endorsed NATO decisions in 1992 that trumped U.S. efforts to avoid involvement in Bosnia. The United Nations needed help to give meaning to the many resolutions aimed at stopping Serb aggression and rolling back their gains in the area. In June 1992 the NATO allies made a point of congratulating the UN for its "valuable contribution" to peacekeeping and welcomed the presence of NATO members in UNPROFOR. The

Balkan Wars were not singled out as such, but the implication was clear: NATO was getting ready to join the UN in actively seeking peace in Bosnia.[29]

By December 1992, the NATO allies had done precisely that: in July 2002 they agreed "in principle" to use naval forces to monitor compliance with Security Council Resolutions 713 and 787. On December 17, 1992, they put the principle into practice when NATO foreign ministers announced that they were prepared to support the "initiatives that the UN secretary-general might take to seek Alliance assistance in the implementation of UN Security Council Resolutions." NATO's secretary general then would make the appropriate contacts with his counterpart in the UN regarding the role NATO could play. The NATO delegate noted that, "for the first time in its history, the alliance is taking part in UN peace-keeping and sanctions enforcement operations."[30]

These activities included enforcing the UN's economic sanctions against Serbia and Yugoslavia as well as an arms embargo against all the republics of the former Yugoslavia, and specifically employing NATO's early warning aircraft (AWACs) to monitor the "no fly zone" over Bosnia and Herzegovina, as mandated in the Security Council's Resolutions 781 and 786, adopted unanimously on October 9 and 10, 1992, respectively.[31] It appeared that a centripetal movement toward collaboration between NATO and the UN, which had begun during the Gulf crisis and been propelled by the end of the Cold War, had now matured during the Balkan Wars. It remained to be seen how firm the connections would be as the war in Bosnia continued unabated.

NATO Secretary General Manfred Woerner was eminently suited to assume leadership in fostering military links with the UN. He had been in office since 1988 after six years of service as West Germany's defense minister in Chancellor Helmut Kohl's Christian Democratic Union. He was pro-American in his outlook and a supporter of President Reagan's defense policies, and his credentials were more impressive to Americans than to Europeans. He was the first German to hold the office at a time when his positive views of the United States made him a controversial candidate for the office.[32]

Woerner provided vigorous leadership as the Cold War came to an end. He recognized that the new strategic doctrine formulated in Rome in 1991 had, in Bosnia, a situation where NATO should depart from the constraints of the treaty's Article 5. He also recognized that the post-Soviet Russian presence on the UN Security Council meant more cooperation with the West but still entailed problems that would limit the council's freedom to intervene in the Balkans. Emphasizing these limitations, he was not hesitant about pushing the NAC and the United States into a more active role in Bosnia in light of the atrocities being committed by Bosnian Serb forces. As he pointed out in a speech at the NATO Defense College in Rome in May 1993, "We all wish that diplomatic means alone would succeed. But diplomacy needs to be backed up with a determination to use force if it is to be credible." An "overstretched and underfunded" UN could not perform this function.[33]

If the United States had been willing to press the allies to lift the embargo that was hurting the Bosnians but not the well-stocked Serbs, Woerner would have seconded the motion. Although there was considerable feeling in Congress in favor of lifting the embargo in order to allow arms to the Bosnians and to use allied air strikes to reinforce sanctions, the Clinton administration responded to public opposition against direct military intervention. Woerner also encountered even more opposition from the European allies, who resented the absence of a U.S. presence in the European-dominated peacekeeping force.[34]

Given his propensity for action, the NATO secretary general welcomed NAC's instructions to work with his counterpart at the United Nations. It was not an easy assignment. The personalities and backgrounds of the two men were strikingly different. Boutros Boutros-Ghali was an upper-class Egyptian, a Coptic Christian with a tradition of public service at the highest levels. His grandfather, a prime minister assassinated by radical Muslim nationalists, represented the Westernized elite who lived privileged if insecure lives within an Islamic society. Boutros-Ghali lived a comfortable life as a wealthy academic after Nasser's Arab nationalism sidelined his political career. Only after President Anwar Sadat's more liberal regime took power did he return to public life, as acting foreign minister in the successful negotiations with Israel in 1979. Although his role in the Israel-Egyptian peace treaty subjected him to the charge of treason for his dealing with Israel, Sadat's successor, Hosni Mubarak, kept Boutros-Ghali on as state minister for foreign relations and deputy foreign minister, which served his candidacy for UN secretary-general in 1991.[35]

Boutros-Ghali's long experience as a leader without the power that might have been his in another society led him to distrust his colleagues when he did achieve power. He wanted to be involved in every major decision. In Madeleine Albright's sardonic view, the secretary-general was "hyper status-conscious and seemed to believe that administrative tasks were beneath him." In this respect his attitude toward his office and its benefits was reminiscent of Waldheim's. But unlike Waldheim, he was a hard worker and a keen analyst of international crises, even if his manner was often professorial. Peacekeeping was at the top of his agenda. During his first six months in office he prepared an "Agenda for Peace," setting down proposals to improve the UN's capacity for peacemaking and peacekeeping.[36]

There was an inevitable wariness in his relations with the NATO secretary general. Boutros-Ghali was as interested as his counterpart in military affairs and equally aggressive in asserting the autonomy of his position. It was galling for him to accept the reality that only the United States, through its authority in NATO, had the potential to make a difference in Bosnia. He was fully aware of the difficult position the UN occupied as an impartial peacekeeper in the Balkans and at the same time an opponent of Serb—and from time to time, Croat—aggression. It was all the more distressing to him when the United States demanded more action from UNPROFOR while remaining unwilling to dispatch its own troops. In his "Agenda for Peace" in 1992 Boutros-Ghali emphasized the importance of each member nation's setting aside special forces for rapid deployment missions, calling to mind the MSC that had never been utilized since its incorporation into the UN Charter as Article 47. In brief, his plan would enlist troops as peace enforcers, maintaining cease-fires, rather than as just peacekeepers. Boutros-Ghali repeated these sentiments in a revised version of this "Agenda for Peace" in 1995, in which he castigated the UN membership for failing to provide military support when needed.[37]

The secretary-general's revised agenda angered U.S. officials, particularly Ambassador Albright, who took exception in a news conference to his assumption that "every success is due to the United Nations, and every time there is a failure, it is due to the member states."[38] Woerner had died of cancer by this time, but he might have concurred with Albright's sense that Boutros-Ghali was trying to arrogate more power to himself than his office merited. But Woerner also might have shared the UN secretary-general's annoyance with the United States' persistent unwillingness to employ its military power to stop Serb atrocities. Unlike Boutros-Ghali, Woerner was less concerned with the UN Security Council's approval of a NATO intervention.

U.S. officials were too willing to blame Europeans for doing too little to help the Muslims. They criticized the Vance-Owen plan for giving away too much to the Serbs and did not recognize the impact of Secretary of State Warren Christopher's indecisiveness in his visit to NATO headquarters in May 1993. Christopher's attitude may have convinced the Serbs that the United States—and NATO—would not stand in the way of their ethnic cleansing in Bosnia. Woerner was disappointed in the U.S. reaction when he told Christopher he was ready to ask the NAC to endorse a "lift and strike" policy against the Serbs. Woerner referred to lifting the embargo against the weaker Muslims, then using U.S. aircraft to strike the aggressors. David Owen reported that the secretary of state was startled by the boldness of Woerner's proposal and preferred to hold bilateral meetings first with the allies, "almost as if he was afraid for the US to take the lead on this issue."[39]

Instead of accepting some responsibility for the U.S. failure to influence its allies over the embargo, the Senate Committee on Foreign Relations, in the words of Senator Joseph Biden (D-DE), saw only a "mosaic of indifference, timidity, self-delusion and hypocrisy." Biden went on to accuse the Europeans of codifying a Serb victory in Bosnia. The arms embargo against the Bosnian Muslims, according to Biden, was "an act of moral rape."[40] Yet, it should have been obvious that the timid actions as opposed to the extravagant rhetoric of the U.S. partner was a part of the problem. It was not that the NATO allies under U.S. leadership were not taking measures against the aggressors. It was that these measures were insufficiently robust to be credible to Bosnian Serbs, to Milosevic in Belgrade, and to the Croats whose struggle with the Serbs did not preclude ambitions for a Greater Croatia. Nor were the measures a balm to the Muslim victims who felt abandoned by the West.

Since NATO was unprepared to undertake peacekeeping operations on its own initiative because of a lack of consensus among its members, it was essential that the allies work closely with the UN, so it might do what it could. NATO's deputy assistant secretary general John Kriendler cited such peacekeeping activities as "monitoring ceasefires and withdrawal of forces; supervising disarmament and control of weapons; supervising disarmament and control of weapons." This confession by a senior NATO official underscored the symbiotic relations now being fashioned between the two organizations. If, as Boutros-Ghali reluctantly conceded, the UN needed NATO, so NATO needed the UN to complement its contribution to the peacekeeping effort.[41]

Yet the actions of both organizations in 1993 and 1994 were never enough to impress the belligerents in Bosnia. Only when newspaper and television accounts of particularly egregious Serb behavior aroused the public did NATO finally strike. Serb planes bombed Srebrenica in March 1993, and Serb artillery firing from heights overlooking Sarajevo killed sixty-eight civilians in a Sarajevo marketplace in February 1994. These outrages shocked the UN and NATO into action that temporarily relieved these cities. But these strikes were in response to particular provocations and were not part of any coherent strategy to compel the violators into compliance with UN resolutions.

The UN mission that NATO was enlisted to protect served only to contribute to the problems. The peacekeepers were tasked with the protection of the "safe areas" where refugees could gather free from danger of attack. Srebrenica, flooded with Muslim refugees from areas of Bosnia overrun by Serbs, became a visible symbol of the limits of UN and NATO protection. The Serb forces besieged supplies and prevented them from entering the city, creating a humanitarian nightmare that shamed the Security Council into declaring the city a "safe area" in June 1993, along with Sarajevo and other Bosnian cities, and dispatching peacekeepers to ensure its status.[42] A small contingent of Canadians in Srebrenica convinced the Serbs to call off their attack—at least for the time being.

The inability of NATO to act without prior approval from the UN (the so-called "dual key" arrangement) was a constant frustration to the NATO military. Winning approval from the UN key holder, the cautious Japanese diplomat Yasushi Akashi, was always difficult. He had won laurels as a peacemaker in Cambodia and always sought more negotiations before using force. Security Council resolutions, such as Resolution 836 on June 4, 1993, were often confusing and contradictory.

This resolution seemed to allow UN member states to use airpower to support the security of the safe areas. Up until this time UNPROFOR could use force only to guarantee delivery of humanitarian aid to Bosnia. But the resolution was never clear as to how far the UN's reach could extend. Was it just for self-defense, or could NATO airpower and UNPROFOR force the withdrawal of Serb forces from areas outside the safe zone? The European NATO allies with their vulnerable troops in Bosnia preferred a limited range, which suited the temperament of Akashi. He was not alone in his concern.[43] The peacekeepers on the ground were understandably fearful that an air strike would provoke the Serbs to retaliate.

Boutros-Ghali further muddied the waters in February 1994 after the Sarajevo marketplace massacre by authorizing close air support—but not air strikes, which would require a further decision by the Security Council. The secretary-general specifically delegated authority to his special representative (Akashi) to approve a request from the commander of UNPROFOR for close air support for the defense of UN personnel in Bosnia. The trouble for both the UNPROFOR commander who held one key and his counterpart in NATO who held the other was the difficulty in finding agreement between the holders of the two keys.[44]

According to Kofi Annan, undersecretary-general for peacekeeping operations, there was room for optimism in the UN-NATO relationship. Celebrating the forty-fifth anniversary of the UN's peacekeeping operations, Annan listed a record of accomplishments in an article in the October 1993 issue of the *NATO Review.* He traced their evolution from monitoring buffer zones in the Cold War years to "peacekeeping with teeth. When lightly-armed peacekeepers were made to look helpless in Somalia and Bosnia, member states and public opinion supported more muscular action." It was in this context, Annan noted, that the UN partnership with NATO became important, with "member states operating in the NATO framework . . . providing protective air cover for UNPROFOR troops operating on the ground to deter attacks against the safe areas established by the Security Council." He envisioned a continuing cooperative arrangement whereby "the Council could, in the Bosnian case, ask the Secretary-General to exercise his responsibility by providing overall political and strategic guidance through his Special Representative, leaving the tactical and operational decisions to a UNPROFOR Theatre Commander who would use NATO command structures and assets in leading a force which, in the main, would be composed of NATO troops." He qualified this rosy scenario by inserting a subtext that could—and did—lead to future conflict between the two organizations: "Understandably, for NATO, it is critical to determine at what level of its own political and military hierarchy command and control should be submitted to the authority of the Security Council through the Secretary-General of the United Nations."[45]

Aside from caveats that undercut the credibility of his optimism, Annan erred in identifying NATO as a "regional organization." NATO was not a regional organization under the provenance of the UN Charter's Chapter 7, despite Annan's sweeping assumption, and hence was independent of the UN hierarchy. NAC's communiqué from Istanbul in June 1994 recognized the difference: "The alliance has demonstrated its readiness and its capacity to support on a case by case basis, peacekeeping and other operations under the authority of the United Nations Council. We will work for further improvement in the mutual understanding and the close cooperation between NATO and the UN."[46] The operative phrase is "on a case by case basis." The careful wording of the North Atlantic Treaty used only Article 51 to proclaim its association with the United Nations. Had the framers included Article 53 of the UN Charter in the text, making it specifically a regional organization, they would have had to submit the alliance's deliberations to the UN Security Council where the Soviet Union had a voice and a veto.

That there was work to be done in codifying UN-NATO relations in 1993 was obvious. NATO leaders chafed over the authority of the UN in the management of the Bosnian conflict, even as they agreed "with the position of the UN Secretary-General that the first use of air power in the theatre shall be authorized by him."[47] The obstacles to UN-NATO collaboration were visible from the outset of the Balkan Wars. Arguably, they may be traced to the Bush administration and the early months of the Clinton administration when the United States left the Balkans for the Europeans to handle. When the Europeans failed, Americans blamed their partners for condemning the Serbs without providing credible penalties for their actions even though they had been implicated in the disintegration of Yugoslavia. But fairly or not, the European allies agreed with Lord Owen that, had the United States given more than lukewarm approval to the Vance-Owen peace plan, Bosnia might have been spared the miseries of 1994 and 1995.[48]

Given the divisions within NATO, the United States had too little leverage to exert the leadership it felt necessary in Bosnia. The "dual key" arrangement required UN approval before NATO airplanes could begin bombing Serb positions, and impatient U.S. generals had to face both the UN bureaucracy and their allies in the UN before they could bring their airpower into play. The misgivings of UNPROFOR commanders about air strikes provoking Serb retaliation carried weight because of the weakness of their troops on the scene. The UN could deliver food and supplies only when the Serbs permitted. It was never in a position to change the conditions that made humanitarian aid necessary. The civilian holder of the UN key, Yasushi Akashi, could hold up decisions for effective air strikes, insisting on more patience and more attempts to negotiate, and could even then veto the NATO proposal to force Serb compliance with UN Security Council resolutions.[49] It was rarely a matter of the UN's frustrating NATO. More often it was the NATO European allies, sensitive to the vulnerability of their troops in the safe areas of Bosnia, that sanctioned delays.

The deadlock between the UN and NATO was guaranteed to render impotent any efforts to enforce the "no fly" zones over Bosnia and to prevent Serb forces from flouting UN resolutions. Even after the worldwide horror over the massacre at the Sarajevo marketplace on February 5, 1994, brought U.S. aircraft into action against Serb artillery, the effect was minimal. Serb mortars were stilled only for a moment. The NAC meeting four days after the incident issued specific orders calling for "the withdrawal, or regrouping and placing under UNPROFOR control, within ten days, of heavy weapons . . . of the Bosnian forces located in an area within 20 kilometres of the centre of Sarajevo."[50] This clear-cut decision sounded as if NATO and the UN had judged the continuing Serb siege of Sarajevo to be intolerable and intended to make their condemnation effective.

This conclusion would have been mistaken, however. The lull in violence was only temporary. Boutros-Ghali and Akashi were always reluctant to give up their "key." They would allow military force to be used only as pinpricks, thereby neutering NATO threats to subject Bosnian Serb arms and depots to sustained air strikes if they continued to attack UN-designated safe areas. The NATO threats were hollow.[51] The secretary-general disclosed his intentions to friend and foe alike when he stated in September 1994, "I stand firm in my conviction that a durable solution to the problems plaguing the former Yugoslavia can only be reached by peaceful means. Any settlement imposed on one side or the other by military means might, at best, result in a temporary halt of hostilities and would eventually draw the international community into even more troubled waters."[52]

Akashi dispelled any doubts the Bosnian Serbs might have had about NATO's functions in support of UN missions in Bosnia when he reassured the Bosnian Serb leader, Radovan Karadzic, in December about the limits of NATO airpower: "Except for self-defense, NATO aircraft will not conduct air-to-ground operations without advance authorization from the Special Representative of the Secretary-General. NATO will not use force except in pursuit of these missions, or in self-defence when aircraft are directly threatened by anti-aircraft fire, surface-to-air missiles, locking-on of anti-aircraft weapon tracking radars, or attack by aircraft. No automatic firing of missiles will occur."[53]

The Akashi letter only added to the confusion experienced by NATO pilots. They might be allowed to act if threatened but not "necessarily fired on," but were not clear about the meaning of "no automatic missiles will occur." What was the message the UN was sending to the Serbs? Whatever warning was intended, it was ameliorated by an assurance that there was nothing to fear from NATO. Even if the Serbs fired first, NATO commanders at AFSOUTH in Naples would need "dual key" approval, coordinating their strikes against surface-to-air weapons sites with UNPROFOR over a "proportional response."[54]

Less than two weeks before this exchange, Senator John McCain, former naval pilot and veteran of the Vietnam War, raised a question to Lieutenant General

Howell Estes, chief Pentagon planner for Bosnian operations, testifying before the Senate Armed Services Committee: "If there is a request for an air strike, that air strike then is endorsed or not by NATO, is that correct? And then does it need final approval by the Secretary General of the United Nations?" When McCain then asked Estes if "that is a good way of doing business," the general replied that "you clearly cannot operate for two masters and that is what you are doing in this case." Obviously exasperated by what he considered the absurdity of the situation, McCain asked rhetorically if NATO could "ever operate, frankly, with a UN master who has neither the equipment, training, background, staff, or support to make that kind of battlefield decision."[55]

These handicaps did not deter the secretary-general six months later from making a bad situation worse. In May 1995 he accepted Akashi's conclusion that air strikes were ineffective, but not for the reasons U.S. and NATO commanders judged. Boutros-Ghali then summarily removed the authority from the UNPROFOR commander in Sarajevo to ask for air strikes. In the future he would make the decisions himself from his headquarters in New York.[56] This was not a position that either McCain and his Senate colleagues or the NATO commanders found acceptable.

NATO over the UN, August 1995

The consequence of cross purposes within NATO and the UN was that the Bosnian Serbs and their master in Serbia, Milosevic, had little respect for UN authority or for NATO military capabilities. It seemed that the Serbs believed they could freely ignore UN mandates. Bosnian Serb forces under General Ratko Mladic underscored their contempt by taking UN peacekeepers hostage when the UN backed off from its toothless threats. And until August 1995 this happened all too frequently. So contemptuous were the Serbs of the peacekeepers that they could humiliate them without fear of retribution. It was this kind of pusillanimous behavior that incited the Serbs to capture three hundred peacekeepers in order to halt NATO bombing of Sarajevo in June 1995. They succeeded in this instance. Ultimately, they went too far; the massacre of eight thousand Muslim men and boys in July 1995 after they occupied the "safe area" of Srebrenica took place while the Dutch peacekeepers were held hostage.[57]

Not until August 1995 was there to be a resolution of the differences between the UN and NATO over the conduct of the Bosnian conflict. When the resolution was made, a new NATO secretary general had been in office since September 1994. After a long struggle to keep the alliance focused on Bosnia, Woerner succumbed to the ravages of cancer in that month. On one level he had failed in his efforts to push the senior ally into more forceful action against the Bosnian

Serbs. But at the time of his death, NATO's patience with the UN's caution was badly frayed. Woerner's successor, former Belgian foreign minister Willy Claes, had to contend with the many loose ends in the Balkans, particularly the preference of the European allies to keep the UN as the leading player in the Bosnian imbroglio.

Claes's service as president of the EU in the second half of 1993 burnished his credentials as a candidate for secretary general. Arguably, the backing of France on the basis of his advocacy of a strong EU foreign policy was a major factor in his prevailing over Norway's Thorvald Stoltenberg, Vance's successor as personal representative for Boutros-Ghali in Bosnia. Although Claes faced pressures from the Clinton administration to confront the UN, the continuing refusal of the United States to accept troop engagement in the Balkans meant that Claes had to display more caution in his stewardship than the more charismatic Woerner had done. In his early months in office, Claes's manner was reserved. The Norwegian ambassador to NATO observed that Claes came across as nervous and uncertain at his first meeting with NAC. In his inaugural address at NATO headquarters, he professed confidence in the smooth cooperation between NATO and the UN, despite sufficient evidence that this confidence was not warranted.[58]

Claes's confidence grew as he became accustomed to being in office in 1995, and as Bosnian Serb behavior became more outrageous, his voice blended with the U.S. administration's and most of NATO's military leaders' in articulating his opposition to the Bosnian Serbs and their manipulator in Belgrade. Indeed, according to the U.S. ambassador to NATO, Robert Hunter, and the supreme allied commander in Europe, General George Joulwan, Claes was ahead of the Americans in recognizing the absence of alternatives to military force in the summer of 1995. If the UN stood in the way, Claes made the point repeatedly, "NATO is more than a sub-contractor of the UN."[59]

Claes became an important agent in moving NATO out of the UN orbit and into an independent military confrontation with the Serbs that essentially dispensed with UN approval. National Security Adviser Anthony Lake felt that Claes was supportive of U.S. efforts to push NATO into more aggressive military action. Holbrooke credited the secretary general with bypassing the NAC and authorizing the NATO commander to strike the Serbs, on August 29, 1995, at a critical moment in an assault against Serb positions above Sarajevo. This was "one of those bureaucratic decisions whose importance is lost to most outside observers."[60]

A bribery scandal in Belgium, in which Claes was involved, prematurely ended his tenure as secretary general in November 1995, but not before he had become "an instrumental player at NATO," in the words of Ryan Hendrickson, "as it adapted to new missions and roles in transatlantic security."[61] The most significant player in the drama unfolding in Bosnia, however, was the energetic U.S. diplomat Richard Holbrooke, who had been entrusted to field a team that would "end the war" (the title of his memoir on Bosnia). Holbrooke had been in the diplomatic service since the Vietnam years and had served as U.S. ambassador to Germany during the Clinton administration. He had a "brash, pushy image," the charisma of a "sort of diplomatic Lone Ranger," with a liking of the limelight and an aggressive style that made him as many enemies as admirers. In fact, it was his very style that made him the right person for the job, and as a reviewer of his memoir observed, he put together a loyal and able team of diplomats.[62] The scene was set for the resolution of the Bosnian civil war.

A series of events in the summer of 1995 precipitated the decision to inaugurate "Operation Deliberate Force," the NATO assault against the Bosnian Serbs that led to Milosevic's intervention on behalf of the defeated aggressors. The most traumatic event was the slaughter of some eight thousand Muslim men and boys after the fall of Srebrenica, which had been one of the "safe areas" protected by UNPROFOR. The capture of the city and the brutal treatment of its population took place while four hundred Dutch peacekeepers were held hostage. This was a brazen challenge to the authority of the UN, and one that the UN was unable to handle.[63]

In a sense this was a self-inflicted blow. The UN in fact invited the disaster by accepting the vulnerability of its UNPROFOR units in areas where they were at a serious military disadvantage against the more numerous and better-armed Serbs. The secretary-general had encouraged Serb disrespect for the UN when Boutros-Ghali and Akashi decided in May 1995 that air strikes were ineffective. This message was implicit in Boutros-Ghali's report to the UN Security Council, which recommended that UNPROFOR confine itself to peacekeeping duties and not enforcement. Such irresolution on the part of the UN leadership gave currency to suspicions that the European allies, particularly the French, were making deals with the Serbs to stop air strikes in return for the release of UNPROFOR hostages. General Mladic's tactic had been to seize troops in response to the bombing of ammunition dumps. The exposure of UN troops to such blackmail made such arrangements likely.[64]

The NATO European allies whose troops were the victims of this behavior were painfully aware of their weaknesses. The British Cabinet in June 1995 spoke of withdrawal of its troops by winter, but it was the French president, Jacques Chirac, who pressed for a NATO response when he visited Washington in mid-June. On the table was seemingly a choice between either removing the source of vulnerability by removing all UNPROFOR troops or reinforcing them with a rapid reaction force. The strengthened force had been discussed in NAC on June 3 and was welcomed by the United States in a press communiqué of the Defense Planning Committee and Nuclear Planning Group five days later. Chirac recommended that the allies either punish the Serbs with a rapid reaction force or leave the scene. This was a less than subtle hint that the Americans must join in this support of the troops at the risk of losing a French contribution to UNPROFOR.[65]

Once again, the United States hesitated, or so it seemed. The Pentagon had drawn up a plan to dispatch twenty thousand troops to Bosnia, not so much to fight the Serbs as to assure a safe withdrawal of UN forces. According to Holbrooke's recollection, this plan had the approval of the North Atlantic Council, but not the president's imprimatur. Actually, NAC's action was ambiguous. In Brussels, a week before Chirac's visit, NAC "took stock of contingency planning to conduct a NATO-led withdrawal of UN forces if requested by the UN," but the council still asserted strong support for maintaining the UN presence in Bosnia, "strengthened to carry out a clear mission and with their safety assured."[66]

In the United States there were mixed feelings about involvement as the president vowed to provide 100 million dollars to finance a rapid reaction force of 12,500 British, French, and Dutch soldiers irrespective of whether the Congress provided an appropriation. That the United States should lift the embargo was another matter. Propelled by public opinion and a new Republican majority in the Senate, Congress passed a bipartisan bill by a veto-proof majority to lift the embargo and provide 100 million dollars in military assistance to Bosnia. Even as he agreed with the provision of military assistance and with the general thrust of the message, the president vetoed the bill because of the complications it raised with the allies. The issue then became moot when massive NATO air strikes began against the Serbs. But the obvious reluctance of the United States to put its troops onto the ground was not lost on the Bosnian Serbs. No less a personage than Senator Edward Kennedy (D-MA) agreed with his colleagues who deplored the "massive human tragedy" in Bosnia but opposed unilateral lifting of the arms embargo because it might leave the Muslims in a worse situation.[67]

These steps toward more active NATO engagement in the Balkans were sufficiently tentative for the Serbs to resume attacks against Sarajevo. Although Serb behavior inspired British prime minister John Major to call an emergency meeting of NATO allies in London in July 1995, this gathering was expected to do no more than postpone the withdrawal of peacekeepers. But the meeting did far more than hold the rationalized alliance positions: it set the final stage for military intervention in Bosnia. NATO "drew a line in the sand" around the Goradze "safe area," invoking, as Holbrooke noted, the language President Bush had used in the Gulf crisis. More specifically, NATO challenged the UN by repudiating the "dual key" arrangements. Decisions on the use of airpower over Bosnia would be NATO's, not the UN's.[68]

To give substance to NATO's intentions, the United States would back the peace plan proposed by the Contact Group, consisting of France, Germany, the Russian Federation, Britain, and the United States, a group established in February 1994. Without much encouragement from any of the key member states, the Contact

Group had been seeking a territorial division of Bosnia. Now the plan was revived in 1994, with Bosnia to be 49 percent Serb and 51 percent controlled by a Croat-Muslim federation that would end the war. With the United States offering a military contribution, there would be far more muscle behind the new plan than in the rejected Vance-Owen plan, which had given the Bosnian Serbs a larger share of territory. The primary U.S. planner, the national security adviser Anthony Lake, sketched out a program on August 1, 1995. In the words of General Wesley Clark, the Pentagon's member of the U.S. negotiating team, "There would be an offer of U.S. forces—up to 35,000 troops—as part of a NATO force to help enforce a territorial division between Serbs and the federation. If the Bosnians and Croats didn't agree we should stop providing them support; if the Serbs didn't agree we would do 'lift and strike' against them, as we had threatened for years. There would be positive and negative inducements for each side."[69]

Up to this time the Serbs had been on the offensive and all too successful in their campaign to uproot Muslims and Croats while intimidating the UN mediators. Now for the first time the Serbs found themselves on the defensive. The Croats in cooperation with Muslim troops launched an offensive in early August 1995 that quickly regained the lost Krajina region of Croatia and moved ahead into Bosnia with the quiet acquiescence of the United States. Their offensive was accompanied by qualms among U.S. officials about its implications. But as U.S. negotiator Robert Frasure observed, "This is the first time the Serb wave has been reversed."[70]

The surprising aftermath of this new military surge was Milosevic's passivity in the face of what was becoming a changing balance of power. The NATO allies—European and American alike—did not anticipate this behavior; they were still fearful of a dangerous riposte from Belgrade and formally opposed the Croat offensive. Yet Milosevic did not intervene, giving rise to hope within the Holbrooke team that a show of force could induce the Serbs to lift their siege of Sarajevo.

The tragic deaths on August 19, 1995, of three senior members of the negotiating team (including Frasure), which occurred when their vehicle slid off a dangerous mountain road, raised the level of NATO's anger. This was not the first accident on a road to Sarajevo that was taken only because the Serbs, in maintaining their siege of the city, had blocked more suitable access. The emotions generated by this event stiffened U.S. pressures on the wavering Europeans—as well as some members of the Clinton administration—who were still worried about Croat advances jeopardizing the security of peacekeepers. There was less need for concern after the commander of UNPROFOR accelerated the redeployment of his troops to more defensible sites. Removing the fear of Serbs' seizing hostages as they had done so often in the past, UNPROFOR also removed a main obstacle to NATO air strikes.[71]

Even after the changing mood of the NATO allies was becoming evident, the Serbs continued their bombardment of Sarajevo and, in doing so, precipitated the attacks that brought the former Yugoslav republic in all its parts to the peace table, marginalizing the UN in the process. On August 28, 1995, a mortar shell struck down thirty-eight people in a Sarajevo marketplace. This act appeared to be a reprise of the shelling and carnage of February 1994 and showed how little effect all the declarations of the UN and NATO had had on the Serbs in the intervening eighteen months.[72]

This was the last straw. The difference in the West's reactions between 1994 and 1995 was the unwillingness of the United States and NATO to accept the halfhearted Bosnian Serb efforts at appeasement and to accept UN authority over NATO's actions. The Serbs could no longer use the UN as cover. In New York Kofi Annan, in charge of UN peacekeeping operations, issued instructions that UN civilian and military officials in Bosnia give up any authority to veto air strikes, nominally for a limited period of time. This permission was in fact a bow to reality; NATO had already renounced the "dual key" arrangement. The initiatives would now be in the hands of SACEUR General Joulwan and Admiral Leighton Smith, commander of NATO's southern flank. They had the blessing of Secretary General Claes, who authorized the NATO commanders to take appropriate steps without calling a NAC meeting to ratify the decision. The UN's role in this last act before the unleashing of Operation Deliberate Force was now minimal.[73]

NATO versus the UN, 1991–1995

The abrupt termination of the Cold War should have been the occasion for a reevaluation in both organizations of how they could together serve the maintenance of world peace and stability. But the implosion of the Soviet empire happened too suddenly to allow immediate change in what had been a distant and uneasy relationship. It took time before the United States realized that the Russian presence on the Security Council did not mean deadlock, and that a weakened superpower would not automatically obstruct U.S. or NATO initiatives in the UN. The first post–Cold War challenge might have witnessed NATO acting in lockstep with the Russians. But this did not happen, and only partly because Russia and China were unreliable partners with the West. More important was the Gulf crisis as a testing ground for NATO-UN collaboration. In August 1990, NATO had not yet come to grips with a post–Cold War posture and was unsure it could justify a mission so far "out of area." While the "coalition of the willing" that conducted the operation against Saddam Hussein consisted of mostly NATO members, the operation was never a NATO action. Nor was the UN—which gave a cautious blessing to the military campaign against the Iraqi aggression against Kuwait—sure of what its proper stance should be.

The breakup of Yugoslavia a year later and the subsequent wars among the former constituent states of that country should have been an easier decision for both NATO and the UN to make. The scene of conflict was in Europe, not Asia; and the threat to NATO members in the neighborhood should have been sufficient to warrant early summoning of Article 4. While the fighting in the former Yugoslavia did yield a flurry of UN resolutions condemning violence, the Security Council established a peacekeeping force on the assumption that this was a civil war calling for neutrality on the part of the peacekeepers. This approach limited the response that the UN gave to Bosnian Serb aggression. Its presumption was always that UN military action should be subordinate to diplomacy, no matter how outrageously any of the parties to the conflict behaved. Reluctantly and hesitantly, the UN leaders recognized that military means had to be deployed, and only NATO was equipped to do this.

NATO for its part was no more interested in intervention than the UN was, partly because its senior partner believed the troubles in Yugoslavia in 1991 were Europe's affair to resolve. And while NATO Europe had some responsibility for the dissolution of Yugoslavia, it too saw the conflict as a civil war, not simply a war of Serb aggression. Only when televised scenes of the horrors of war penetrated public consciousness in the United States did the Clinton administration—initially immersed in domestic problems and as averse as the Bush administration had been to active engagement in the Balkans—exert pressure for action in the UN and with its NATO partners. U.S. initiative succeeded to the extent of responding to the UN invitation with NATO air and naval support against the Bosnian Serbs. In 1992 the UN and NATO had established a symbiotic connection for the first time, with NATO filling needs only it could supply, and the UN providing the umbrella of legitimacy for NATO operations. NATO communiqués not only emphasized its importance to the UN's mission but also identified other organizations, such as OSCE and WEU, as collaborators. All would give formal obeisance to the UN as the final authority in managing the conflict.

The next two years, however, were marked by tensions among NATO members and between NATO and the UN that delayed if not subverted their common objectives. NATO was deeply divided between the United States, which wanted more active efforts to suppress the aggressors but would not contribute troops on the ground, and Europe, which resented U.S. pressure for actions that potentially jeopardized the security of European troops on the ground in Bosnia while its own pilots were safe in the skies. This dispute among the allies was as important as any other factor in preventing the Security Council where European NATO members had seats from endorsing a more vigorous posture against the Bosnian Serbs and their patron in Belgrade.

This division among the allies facilitated the UN's ability to keep NATO in its place, as a subordinate to UN authority. While the UN secretary-general recognized the organization's dependence on NATO's military power, he sought with considerable success to maintain control of NATO operations. Not until the summer of 1995 did NATO, now essentially united under U.S. leadership, free itself from a UN veto on where and how NATO aircraft could strike the Bosnian Serbs. The new outrage in Srebrenica in July 1995, combined with the U.S. decision to contribute its own troops to the area, led to NATO's sidelining the UN as NATO undertook a sustained assault at the end of August that year. For the time being, NATO removed the UN from its authority in the Balkans. By now, the uneasy partnership between the two organizations seemed to have dissolved into mutual hostility.

8

The Balkan Wars
To Kosovo, 1995–1999

Dayton and NATO

When Secretary-General Boutros Boutros-Ghali reluctantly turned over responsibility to NATO for military action against the Bosnian Serbs in August 1995, he appeared to be doing more than simply turning over the key to NATO supreme commander George Joulwan for NATO's airpower to bring the aggressors to the peace table. The UN action symbolized both the inability of the UN to manage military crises and the indispensability of NATO as the only agent to perform this role. The collaboration between the two organizations over Bosnia had collapsed in the assault over Sarajevo as the UN lost its authority in the area. That the conference concluding the hostilities took place across the Atlantic at the Wright-Patterson Air Force Base in the midwestern city of Dayton, Ohio, was a testament to NATO's superiority. More to the point, it was a testament to the weight of the United States in NATO.

Granted that the revived fortunes of the combined Muslim-Croat campaign against the Bosnian Serbs degraded the Serb military machine and rendered it vulnerable to a robust NATO air offensive, it was the U.S. resolve to unleash a sustained air assault against Serb positions in Bosnia that finally terminated the conflict in such a short time. Without the U.S. presence it is unlikely that Milosevic would have turned on his surrogates as rudely as he did to take over Bosnian Serb control of the delegation that met in Dayton for three weeks in November. The Bosnian subordinates had no choice but to follow the Yugoslav president's initiative. Anxious to relieve Serbia of the damaging economic sanctions, Milosevic had no qualms about distancing himself from the Bosnian Serbs. He proclaimed his readiness to attend a conference with Croatia's president, Franjo Tudjman, and the Muslims' president, Alija Izetbegovic, to "settle everything" as he told Richard Holbrooke, the U.S. chief negotiator, two days after the heavy bombing of Serb positions around Sarajevo.[1] Operation Deliberate Force had begun with sixty planes operating out of air bases in Italy and an aircraft carrier in the Adriatic. The planes were joined by artillery from the French and British Rapid Reaction Force that had been mobilized over the summer of 1995. It seemed that only two days after the massive assault against the Serbs' positions, NATO had won its objectives. And it was very much a U.S. victory, with Holbrooke controlling the NATO partners as firmly as Milosevic controlled the Serbs. The United Nations appeared an irrelevant entity in this settlement.

David Owen who had been the European Union's representative for the Bosnian crisis admitted as much when he blamed U.S. inaction from 1993 to 1995 for the plight of the Muslims and the depredations of the Serbs.[2] Only when the United States was prepared to dispatch its own troops to Bosnia were the Serbs—and the Europeans—prepared to find a path to peace. Had the Clinton administration made the commitment to engage its forces in Bosnia in 1993, Owen asserted, it would have spared Bosnia the two years of carnage that followed. Fairly or not, Owen blamed U.S. inaction on Clinton's assumption that U.S. involvement would have jeopardized the success of his new administration. The irony in the ultimate results at Dayton was NATO's acceptance of the basic Vance-Owen formula for peace under the auspices of the five-member Contact Group that had initially been rejected in 1993, namely, a nominally unitary state composed of a Croat-Muslim federation coexisting with a Bosnia-Serbian state.

The important difference between the Vance-Owen plan and the Dayton agreement was that both the Serbs and the Muslims had rejected the territorial apportionments in 1993, whereas in 1995 all three contending parties accepted the final arrangements. Equally important was the multinational Implementation Force (IFOR) to which the United States contributed a third of the total force (some twenty thousand troops) in order to enforce the agreements. This did take some time and considerable arm-twisting on the part of Holbrooke. Just a week after the initiation of the intense bombing campaign, the five-member Contact Group met in Geneva for the first of numerous meetings that would carry negotiations from Moscow to Rome before they culminated in Dayton on November 1, 1999. Unlike in 1993, when the Bosnian Serbs were occupying 70 percent of Bosnia and 22 percent of Croatia, the Croat-Muslim offensive had won back most of the territory lost in the previous two years.[3]

While it required only three weeks at Dayton to complete the arrangements, the very composition of the participants at Dayton—the three NATO European powers, Russia, and "Yugoslavia," with Milosevic speaking for the Bosnian Serbs—inevitably opened fissures among the allies that could have benefited the Yugoslav leader. Holbrooke's objective was to prevent the Balkan representatives from playing European powers against each other at U.S. expense. At no time were the Western Europeans or the Russians or the Serbs able to breach the chain of command that ran directly from the troops on the ground in Bosnia to the Supreme Headquarters Allied Powers, Europe (SHAPE) and the NATO headquarters in

Brussels. The experience of UNPROFOR when a UN diplomat could block military action would not be replicated.[4]

The enthusiasm of the U.S. public for forceful action in Bosnia was matched in Congress by those who had faulted NATO allies for their seemingly fruitless reliance on diplomacy. Senator Robert Dole (R-KS) spoke for a bipartisan majority when he said that the NATO assault was "long overdue: . . . The world has finally done what it should have done a long, long time ago."[5] But when the realization dawned on legislators that U.S. lives would be at stake if the United States intervened, there were more sober reactions. Congress wanted to know just what was the U.S. mission in Bosnia, and how long its troops would have to stay. The administration had to convince Congress and the public that the commitment was for a limited time only—and to do so without creating new doubts among the Europeans of how resolute the U.S. decision was for involvement in the Balkans.

A critical factor in the U.S. decision was Senator Dole's backing of the administration at a time when he was positioning himself to seek the Republican presidential nomination in 1996. He argued that deployment of U.S. forces was in the national interest and that a premature exit date would be a repudiation of the troops. By suggesting a flexible timetable, "approximately a year," he managed to win Senate approval (by a vote of sixty-nine to thirty), as well as a rejection (by fifty-two to forty-seventy) of a resolution opposing the dispatch of any troops.[6] The close vote on December 13, 1995, suggested that not even Dole's influence would carry the day without some kind of exit strategy put in place.

The Dayton Accords themselves made it clear that Operation Deliberate Force lived up to its name. Its intention was indeed deliberate. The objective was not to overthrow the Milosevic regime but to demonstrate sufficient power and resolve to allow the establishment of a viable Bosnian nation and to force the Serbs to respect the many UN resolutions it had flouted in the past.

If there were qualms in Washington about the imposition of the U.S. presence in the Balkans, it was hardly surprising that the European parties to the Dayton agreements had their own reservations. Always in the background was the plaintive grievance of David Owen that the United States was both late in coming to the aid of Bosnia and hypocritical in its criticism of Europeans for their failures on the ground in UNPROFOR while the United States employed only airpower invulnerable to casualties. And when America did become fully involved, it escalated the attacks without consulting its allies. Such was the subject of a special meeting of the NAC on September 11, 1995.[7] But the primary annoyance was over the highhanded way in which the Americans managed the diplomatic process. After a temporary halt of the bombing, the Contact Group agreed to a meeting in Geneva. Although the EU's Carl Bildt, successor to Owen, was co-chair, the Europeans were annoyed by the United States' choosing the site (the American Mission in Geneva) rather than a UN building, which the Western allies preferred. The Americans acted, then consulted.[8]

None of the foregoing slights could compare with the ultimate insult of removing negotiations from Europe and transporting the principals to the United States, to the remote air force base in southwestern Ohio where U.S. influence could be fully exercised. True, the allies were certainly represented through the EU, but there was never any doubt about which NATO member would be threatening and cajoling Milosevic and the three ethnic leaders in Bosnia into a settlement. Holbrooke as master of ceremonies intended to keep the reluctant Europeans sealed off from the outside world at the air base until the work was completed.

Discontented with being stuck in the middle of America, France in particular expressed its unhappiness at being slighted by the superpower. Foreign Minister Hervé de Charette refused to call it "an American peace, even if President Clinton and the Americans have tried to pull the blanket over to their side." The Americans had in fact blocked the progression of peace by distancing themselves so long from the troubles of former Yugoslavia. But even as de Charette had to concede that Europe really was not present in the conclusion of the conflict, he could take satisfaction in having the final peace settlement signed in Paris on December 14, 1999, the appropriate place for any peace celebration. At least the Dayton Accords would be known as the Treaty of the Elysée, and, as the French foreign ministry insisted, the speakers at the formal signing ceremony made no mention of Dayton.[9] Given the role of Paris in U.S. diplomatic history, at peace conferences in 1783, 1800, 1898, and 1919, it would have been churlish for the Americans to dispute this title.

Of the major European powers, the most troubled was Russia, the traditional protector of Serbia, whose support of the Contact Group's campaign against Milosevic was always problematic. While the escalating pressure on the Bosnian Serbs through use of cruise missiles and the targeting of military centers in other parts of Bosnia in September occasioned some criticism among the NATO partners, it sparked an angry response from the Russian defense minister who threatened to withdraw military cooperation and even come to the support of the Serbs if the bombing did not stop. Russia went so far as to propose a UN Security Council resolution to suspend the bombing, but this failed to win support.[10]

Nevertheless, Russia was too important to ignore. Its participation in the future IFOR was vital to the success of a peace agreement. What the Russians wanted in essence was respect from the West commensurate with Russia's sense of its own importance on the international scene. Holbrooke credited Strobe Talbott, Clinton's senior adviser on Russian relations and later deputy secretary of state, with attributing Russian behavior to "the Rodney Dangerfield syndrome," a consequence of being denied due respect.[11] But there were limits in this period beyond which Russia would not go in challenging the United States. Russian military leaders did not abandon the view of East-West relations that they had entertained during the Cold War. Post-Soviet Russia competed with the U.S.-led NATO for power in Europe, and at least for the time being, a weaker Russia had to defer to a stronger America. The Russian general responsible for planning all military operations once told General Clark, then the Pentagon's representative on Holbrooke's team, "we know what you Americans are up to. You are coming into Bosnia because it's in our part of Europe and you want to be there. And you say you will be gone in a year, but you won't be; you will stay." When Clark protested, he was interrupted: "Please, please. Do not be offended. We Russians understand you. And if we were in your position, we would be doing the same thing."[12]

This exchange did not necessarily signify submission to U.S. will, just a recognition of the realities of the time. Russia was willing to participate in the U.S.-led IFOR in 1996 but only if its brigade remained—at least nominally—under Russian control. Unlike other non-NATO forces participating in IFOR, the Russian troops would remain under the national command of a Russian general through the intermediary of the Russian deputy to SACEUR General Joulwan. Although this special relationship created considerable technical problems, the NATO allies and particularly the United States felt the concession was needed to keep Russia connected with the Dayton Peace Accords.[13]

Dayton and the UN Secretary-General

In light of the conflicts between the UN and NATO in 1995, personified by the toxic relations between UN Secretary-General Boutros Boutros-Ghali and U.S. secretary of state Madeleine Albright, it is difficult to remember that NATO's actions from August through December 1995 conformed with the mandates of the UN Security Council. The assault against the Bosnian Serbs was authorized by the United Nations, and no matter how reluctantly the secretary-general had handed the Bosnian civil war to NATO, Kofi Annan's instructions to UNPROFOR to turn the UN key over to NATO seem to remove the UN from the scene. The subsequent bombardment was outside the UN's control. More important, the management of peace negotiations was the responsibility of NATO, which was made abundantly clear by the way the senior partner handled the negotiations that led to the Treaty of Elysée.

Holbrooke's opinion of Boutros-Ghali was reflected in his offhanded observation that the former secretary-general was present at the ceremonies in Paris, "oddly, a man whose actions had contributed so little to the ending of the war."[14] He attributed Boutros-Ghali's behavior over Bosnia in large measure to the patrician's contempt for the backward Balkans and his impatience over the diversion caused by the Bosnian conflict of UN resources from other parts of the world. At the same time the secretary-general was unwilling to surrender authority to NATO except under duress. When Boutros-Ghali did condemn Serb shelling and ordered his military commanders to take appropriate action, Holbrooke was convinced that such an order, "typically, meant almost exactly the opposite of what it seemed to say." Boutros-Ghali would avoid action whenever possible, leaving his senior representative in the former Yugoslavia, Yasushi Akashi, to be a scapegoat for his actions, or inactions.[15]

At the UN, Ambassador Madeleine Albright was equally critical of Boutros-Ghali's style and his views. Moreover, she was in a better position to do something about her objections to his stubborn defense of the "dual key" system and to his patronizing description of the Bosnian conflict as a "rich man's war." Boutros-Ghali's failure to win a second term as secretary-general was primarily the fallout from his standing within the United States. He consistently alienated the Senate by his "imperial manner."[16]

Although the secretary-general had originally pledged to serve only one term, he changed his mind before the term was up and actively campaigned for re-appointment in 1996. Given his Third World background, the natural endorsement of Egypt's president, and the important support of France on the Security Council, Boutros-Ghali had reason for optimism. He was raised in the francophile environment of upper-class Egypt, and it was hardly surprising that he would fit French standards. The brewing conflict with the United States made his candidacy all the more attractive to France, as well as to others who were put off by the United States' dismissive treatment of the United Nations. The Organization of African Unity rallied to Boutros-Ghali, for example. But when the resolution giving the secretary-general a second term came before the Security Council on November 19, 1996, the United States vetoed it, the lone voice against fourteen in favor of Boutros-Ghali. Bosnia was not the only element in the U.S. rejection of Boutros-Ghali, but it played an important part in the decision.[17]

The hostility between the United States and the UN secretary-general was not one-sided. In his memoir Boutros-Ghali claimed that the United States and NATO exploited the United Nations by making it a scapegoat for their own initial refusal to take responsibility for resolving the Bosnian conflict. By calling it a "humanitarian" crisis, the United States, he asserted, removed it from NATO's charge. And after administering a death blow to the Vance-Owen plan that would have given the Serbs 43 percent of a unified territory, the administration "took pride" in the Dayton agreement almost three years later, which not only gave the Serbs 49 percent of an essentially partitioned Bosnia but did so after tolerating years of unnecessary horrors.[18]

As the bombing campaign produced promising results, he claimed credit for turning the task of managing the Bosnian crisis over to NATO but was miffed by the lack of appreciation from its most influential ally. When Holbrooke chaired a meeting to negotiate an end to the Bosnian crisis in early September 1998, Boutros-Ghali charged that the United States' exclusion of his chief diplomatic envoy for the former Yugoslavia, Norway's Thorvald Stoltenberg, was "an unworthy and gratuitous insult to the United Nations." At the same time he professed a warm welcome to the U.S. diplomatic initiative, noting that he had always felt "member states and regional organizations, such as NATO, were far better suited to the task of dealing with the Bosnian crisis than was the United Nations."[19]

There was a passive aggressive element in this message, as there was throughout his memoir, and just as there was in his official report to the UN Security Council in September 1995. By identifying NATO as another "regional organization," he was disparaging of its importance even as he claimed to be the key figure in establishing its presence. In his report to the UN General Assembly on the work of the organization, as of October 17, 1995, he observed that "the Council's determination to . . . strengthen cooperation between the United Nations and relevant *regional* organizations, in particular the European Union and the North Atlantic Treaty Organization still offers the best hope of bringing to an end the human tragedy in the former Yugoslavia."[20]

The secretary-general was quick to urge the allies to declare a permanent suspension of bombing after the Serbs withdrew their artillery from Sarajevo, a position that led to confrontation with NATO secretary general Willy Claes as well as with NATO military and civilian leaders.[21] His NATO counterpart was as aggressive, perhaps even more so, than NATO's military leaders in moving the organization toward military action in Bosnia—and by extension into confrontation with Boutros-Ghali. When UNPROFOR general Bernard Janvier of France wanted to extend the initial cease-fire after two days of bombing, Claes was as impatient as Holbrooke and SACEUR's General Joulwan to restart the bombing. As political scientist Ryan Hendrickson noted, Claes was contemptuous in his references to the UN.[22]

In brief, the United Nations had been not only sidelined but essentially removed from involvement in the settlement of the Balkan conflict. Boutros-Ghali had turned military control over to NATO; his primary aide, Akashi, was removed from authority; and his expectation of a co-chair in the negotiations was thwarted. His personal representative, Thorvald Stoltenberg, was grudgingly allowed a place at Dayton on condition that his participation be confined to matters involving eastern Slavonia.[23] Small wonder that the secretary-general chose to minimize NATO's role in resolving the crisis in Bosnia and to maximize what he considered to be the UN's primary contributions.

The Dayton Accords

No matter how annoying his attitude was toward the United States and NATO, the UN secretary-general was justified in asserting the UN presence into the events leading up to the assault against the Bosnian Serbs and the events following the completion of the Dayton Accords. NATO's functions in the summer and fall of 1995 were all authorized by the UN Security Council and the results were indeed submitted and ratified by that body. The North Atlantic Council in its ministerial meeting on December 5, 1995, acknowledged as much: "Decisive action by the alliance in support of the United Nations in the Former Yugoslavia, together with a determined diplomatic effort, broke the siege of Sarajevo and made a negotiated solution possible."[24] In fact, the communiqué lacked the air of triumphalism that filled the pages of Clark's, Holbrooke's, and Albright's memoirs. It paid full tribute to increasing ties with the WEU and especially to the OSCE (Organization of Security and Cooperation in Europe), which was expected to be "a valuable partner in the Alliance in the implementation of a peace settlement in Bosnia." The OSCE would have a central role in "the election process, in monitoring human rights, and in establishing confidence and security-building measures and arms control in the Former Yugoslavia."[25]

Even a casual glance at the Dayton Accords would explain why the NATO allies paid their respects to a variety of organizations, which were all necessary for the successful implementation of NATO objectives. There were eleven annexes to the peace settlement, and only one of them dealt with military aspects. Granted the importance of the NATO-led IFOR, it is worth noting that its composition included sixteen countries outside the alliance from Europe, North Africa, the Middle East, and Asia.[26] As for the other annexes, number 10 referred to the important role of the European Union whose Special Representative for Bosnia was also the High Representative, an ad hoc international institution in charge of overseeing the civil life of Bosnia, promoting a democratic reconstruction "to ensure that Bosnia and Herzegovina evolve into a viable democracy on course for integration into Euro-Atlantic institutions." The designated High Representative's responsibilities would include humanitarian aid and economic reconstruction.[27]

The ongoing responsibilities of the Security Council were continued—even expanded—as a result of the General Framework Agreement for Peace in Bosnia and Herzegovina. The United Nations was prominently mentioned in the framework agreement itself, where "the parties agree to cooperate fully with all entities, including those authorized by the United Nations Security Council, in implementing the peace settlement." More specifically, the UN was requested in Annex 11 to establish a UN International Police Task Force (IPTF) to carry out training and advising of local law-enforcing personnel as well as monitoring law enforcement activities. The IPTF would be headed by a commissioner appointed by the UN secretary-general. And the UN would continue to be the lead agency for coordinating humanitarian relief, particularly in planning for the return of displaced persons.[28]

The agreement contained a host of loose ends that required the international organization's involvement, even beyond the military issues remaining unresolved in the Dayton Accords. Foreseeable disputes over disarming Bosnian Serb forces and over conflicts within the Croat-Bosnian entity and between that portion of the Bosnian Federation and the Serb Republik Sprska called for more than a NATO presence. The UN Security Council officially authorized the transfer of authority from UNPROFOR to IFOR in Resolution 1031 of December 15, 1995. UNPROFOR itself was dissolved when its mandate expired on January 31, 1996, but seventeen thousand of the "blue helmets" were incorporated into IFOR.[29] The former UNPROFOR commander would become deputy commander of IFOR. He would retain UN authority over those UNPROFOR units not transferring to IFOR, until they were withdrawn from Bosnia.[30] Given these circumstances, it seems the UN secretary-general had a right to be present at the signing ceremony in Paris.

The UN and NATO after Dayton

That the Dayton Accords were full of contradictions was obvious from the awkward linkage of two entities in one country. Within one of those entities was a tradition of hostility between Croats and Muslims that inevitably bred new tensions. NATO remained stuck in the middle of these problems. Its functions were military, and yet it faced police problems when it came to apprehending Bosnian criminals identified for trial in the International War Crimes Tribunal for Yugoslavia at The Hague. IFOR refused to accept this assignment, and major figures such as Karadzic and Mladic remained free, if nominally in hiding, It took a dozen years before Karadzic was sent to The Hague for trial; Mladic remains at large in 2009.

The IFOR assignment itself was too optimistic if it assumed that its mission would last only a year. Actually, there was little choice at the time. The U.S. Congress would not have tolerated an indefinite existence, but there was no question that the deadline would have to be extended, though under a new name. The Stabilization Force (SFOR), with fewer troops (some thirty-six thousand) replaced IFOR (with its sixty thousand) in November 1996, and President Clinton promised that the new force would complete its mission by June 1998. The smaller numbers suggested some measure of success as well as a way to mollify U.S. concerns about the American contribution. Nevertheless, Secretary of State

Albright had to persuade the president to continue military deployment without a deadline for withdrawal.[31]

A case has been made that in spite of SFOR's limited capabilities it enjoyed more successes than failures in the years before the Kosovo crisis. Colonel John L. Cirafici suggested that historians may identify 1997 as a watershed year for NATO operations in the Balkans. Not that the need for SFOR was gone in that year. The UN had extended its presence twice, with deadlines for U.S. withdrawal from Bosnia come and gone, but it had managed to use its units from thirty-seven different countries to implement the General Framework Agreement. The force was evenhanded in presenting its position as that of an honest broker to the three major factions—Serb, Croat, and Bosnian Muslim (or "Bosniac")—without becoming a fourth faction. SFOR succeeded, too, in creating conditions for successful elections in 1997. Granted that it took more than a year before OSCE was able to ascertain those conditions, which included allowing displaced persons to vote for local government in the communities from which they had fled or been expelled. More than seven hundred thousand refugees who had relocated in neighboring countries returned home.[32] IFOR and SFOR between them managed to separate the armies of the belligerents, place their weaponry in cantonment sites, and reduce their size to peacetime levels.

Still the fragility of the two entities was undeniable, not only in 1997 but into 1999 when Kosovo diverted attention from Bosnia Croatia, and Serbia continued to exercise a baneful influence upon the republics. SFOR could not be disbanded. As Berlin think-tank analysts Gerald Knaus and Marcus Cox noted, five years after Dayton, "Bosnia is not yet a self-sustaining structure and the consequences of premature withdrawal could be catastrophic, not just for Bosnia, but across the region." Government institutions remained so weak that the international mission with the Office of the High Representative as well as the OSCE became "central pillars of the constitutional order."[33] Middle East scholar Fouad Ajami was even more doubtful about the future of Bosnia, as he emphasized the fate of Muslims caught between Croats and Serbs and the resentment this engendered in the Muslim world. He emphasized too U.S. reluctance to become and stay entangled in Bosnia, with the United States providing only one-third of the SFOR force and Europeans bearing a burden five times greater than the Americans had assumed. Dayton codified, he claimed, "partition in all but name"[34]

NATO remained a factor in Bosnia throughout the decade, but in a diminished role. The contributions of European as opposed to U.S. troops increased, as the size of the U.S. force declined. SFOR was truly an international enterprise, far less under U.S. control than IFOR had been. The UN by contrast increased its visibility. When implementation of the Dayton Accords began in Boutros-Ghali's last year in office, the United Nations was a central figure.

The new NATO secretary general, Javier Solana, acknowledged the UN's centrality in the reports that IFOR delivered to Boutros-Ghali for distribution to the Security Council. In Boutros-Ghali's report to the Security Council on June 21, 1996, the subject was progress of the activities of the UN Mission in Bosnia and Herzegovina (UNMIBH) in which NATO and IFOR played no part. The UN secretary-general emphasized the importance of "my Special Representative," who arrived on the scene in 1996 to coordinate the work of the police task force and civil affairs offices and to work with the special envoy of the UN High Commissioner for Refugees (UNHCR).[35] IFOR and OSCE were recognized as entities in association with the UN, but not superior to the roles of UN representatives. The United Nations in a very short time had come a long way from the pariah it had been in Dayton.

The departure of Boutros-Ghali in 1996 may have accounted for relaxing tensions between the NATO and the UN, certainly from the standpoint of the United States. His successor was Kofi Annan, an old hand at the UN who was appreciated by NATO for his quiet but effective support of NATO initiatives against Bosnia in 1995. Educated in the United States with his graduate studies in Geneva, he had been a member of the UN bureaucracy for most of his career. For four years prior to his appointment as secretary-general he had been undersecretary-general for peacekeeping and had distinguished himself in Bosnia for his graceful management of the transition of peacekeeping operations from UN to NATO forces.[36]

Annan's relationship with NATO was further smoothed by the appointment of Javier Solana as NATO secretary general after the sudden resignation of Willy Claes. Like Claes, Solana came out of a socialist background but without the pro-NATO sympathies that had characterized Belgian socialists since the days of Paul-Henri Spaak, even though he had an American background with a doctorate in physics from the University of Virginia. Spanish socialists had opposed joining NATO in 1992 because of their memory of Franco's close links to the United States. Solana had been foreign minister from 1992 to 1995 in the Socialist Workers' government. While Senators Bob Dole and Jesse Helms objected to his socialist ties and his former opposition to the alliance, their reservations did not occasion controversy over his selection. The French had their own objections to other nominees. The Dutch candidate appeared to be insufficiently informed about Bosnian issues, and the Danish candidate was not comfortable with the French language. Solana became the compromise choice in December 1995, and he turned out to be as supportive as Claes on the Balkan problems and as influential as Woerner in dealing with the allies. Arguably, he was more effective than either in his relations with the UN secretary-general.[37]

But it was less the accommodating personalities of the secretaries-general than other priorities that now demanded NATO's attention. The years from 1995 to 1999 were filled with efforts to keep Russia in the Western fold. Boris Yeltsin, the first genuinely democratic leader, was restive over failed promises made in 1990 under the North Atlantic Cooperation Council (NACC) to contain NATO's presence in a unified Germany. Yeltsin was even more uncomfortable with NATO enlargement, which had been solemnized in the Madrid summit of 1997. New arrangements to pacify Russia in the Founding Act of that year had to accompany the admission of such former members of the Warsaw Pact as Poland, the Czech Republic, and Hungary, all scheduled for formal adherence in 1999. These major issues of the alliance inevitably downsized the importance of Bosnia in the hierarchy of NATO concerns. They helped to account for the more prominent role the UN occupied in the Balkans, even as IFOR morphed into SFOR.

The NATO ministers gave as best they could a positive gloss to the UN-NATO record in Bosnia at the end of 1999: "The alliance remains committed to supporting a peaceful future for Bosnia and Herzegovina." SFOR succeeded at least to the point of placing "next year, a smaller, more flexible force . . . fully capable of carrying out its mandate. SFOR will continue to contribute to the maintenance of a secure environment and to give targeted and focused support to civilian implementation."[38] In essence, it did not matter which organization was effectively in control in Bosnia. Without SFOR and NATO and the United States, the uneasy balance in that divided country would have collapsed. The military power of SFOR made it possible for the other agencies, including those under direct UN authority, to function. Yet NATO acknowledged that it was the UN Security Council that legitimized the role of NATO in the Balkans.

Kosovo, 1998

Unlike the case of Bosnia where the UN and NATO shared responsibilities under the oversight of the UN Security Council, NATO's war against Serbia over Milosevic's behavior in Kosovo was waged outside the orbit of the UN Security Council. The threat of a Russian veto on the council, joined presumably with China's, effectively forced the Western allies to plunge ahead without UN cover. This is the image that was projected in 1999 when NATO under the leadership of SACEUR's General Wesley K. Clark opened NATO's Operation Allied Force on March 24, 1999, to begin a war that ended in a NATO victory seventy-eight days later.

But how wide was the distance between NATO and the UN over Kosovo? Unlike in Operation Deliberate Force, in this case NATO acted without UN authorization. UN Secretary-General Kofi Annan seemed to recognize the reasons for NATO's actions, even as he regretted their necessity. In the midst of the war Annan deplored the UN's marginalization in Kosovo when he spoke at The Hague commemorating the centenary of the first international peace conference.

He criticized the United States for attacking Serbia without the blessing of the Security Council but included Russia and China in his criticism for ignoring the ethnic purging that had provoked NATO's bombing.[39] But looking back a few months later, Annan concluded that the war had raised a genuine dilemma, which was resolved without a happy ending:

> Kosovo has cast in stark relief the dilemma of what has been humanitarian intervention on the one side, the question of the legitimacy of an action taken by a regional organization without a UN mandate; on the other, the universally recognized imperative of effectively halting violation of human rights with grave humanitarian consequences. The inability in the case of Kosovo to unify these two equally compelling interests of the international community—universal legitimacy and effectiveness in defense of human rights—can only be viewed as a tragedy.[40]

The defeat of Serbia and the reversal of ethnic cleansing signified an unhappy ending to the Kosovo War. Its success continues to be a matter of debate in light of the ongoing tensions between Serbia and the international community over the future of Kosovo. Equally debatable is the assumption that the NATO allies, and particularly its senior partner, had sufficient international legal justification to take military action against Milosevic's continuing violation of human rights in Kosovo. The Clinton administration in 1998 suppressed its doubts. Secretaries of state and defense Madeleine Albright and William Cohen asserted that the United States could employ air strikes against Serbia even if neither the UN nor NATO authorized them. Albright and Clinton made this claim in June 1998 when NATO authorized flights over Serb territory in order to deter Milosevic from his ongoing effort to expel the Albanian population in Kosovo.[41]

Whether this claim conformed with international law is another matter. Without NATO's intervention, there would have been no resolution (or at least no military resolution) of the crisis in Kosovo. Rather than elevate the contribution of either the Security Council, the UN secretary-general, or NAC, a more accurate assessment of the situation in 1998 and 1999 might give pride of place to the NATO secretary general, Javier Solana. NATO scholar Ryan Hendrickson was convinced that, beginning in March 1998, "the crisis catapulted Solana into a new and different leadership role for the alliance. The systemic political conditions that evolved in 1998 provided Solana with unique opportunities to shape policy on many of the alliance's political and military decisions for the war."[42]

If the NATO secretary general enjoyed unusual influence as NATO moved toward intervention in Kosovo, it was not simply because his views accorded with U.S. military and civilian officials. He was unencumbered by the uncomfortable legacy of the Bosnia conflict, which had left the perpetrator of the Kosovo tragedy in undisputed control of Serbia and the former Yugoslav army. Although the

NATO allies knew that Slobodan Milosevic had been the manipulator behind the scenes of the Bosnian Serbs' aggression against the Muslims, they accepted his pretense of neutrality in the Bosnian civil war and allowed him to negotiate at Dayton as an equal partner in the arrangements for Bosnia's future. His shrewd combination of bluster and bonhomie disarmed U.S. negotiators even as they recognized the deceit behind his façade. Milosevic was a Serbian nationalist who would take advantage of whatever weaknesses he could detect within the NATO alliance in order to advance his objectives.

Holbrooke, who had more opportunities than most Western diplomats to meet with Milosevic, recognized his charm but also understood his duplicity and opportunism. Nevertheless, he felt he could work with him on Kosovo just as he had at Dayton. In discussing war criminals, Holbrooke named names, particularly those of Mladic and Karadzic, and was impatient with the inability or unwillingness of Milosevic to bring them to trial. But Holbrooke did not equate the Yugoslav president himself with the Bosnian leaders and in 1998 did not hesitate to seek to deal with him in order to solve the problems of Kosovo. In brief, the allies knew of Milosevic's unreliability, but he was all they had to work with. The Dayton negotiations showed that as a blustering bully he would back down if confronted with force and that he was willing and able to push the Bosnian Serbs into a settlement that was satisfactory to the West.[43]

But Kosovo was a different matter, and the allies were slow to realize the difference. Kosovo was the historic epicenter of Serbian nationalism. It was near the present-day capital, Pristina, where the Ottoman Turks had defeated the Serbs in 1389, a date never forgotten by the Slavic Serbs. A subsequent battle in Kosovo in 1448 along with the fall of Constantinople in 1453 sealed the fate of Kosovo, which remained part of the Ottoman empire until the twentieth century. Serbia itself did not free itself from the Turks until the early nineteenth century. Even though the Serbs were a minority in a population dominated by ethnic Albanians by the time Yugoslavia was created after World War I, Kosovo remained integral to the Serbs' national identity.

In the Tito years, Kosovo had enjoyed special status in the Yugoslav federation, with a measure of autonomy that included Albanian language schools. But the Yugoslav Federation dissolved in 1991, and Milosevic, president of Serbia since 1987, two years later stripped Kosovo of the autonomy it had enjoyed under Tito. Milosevic's brutal efforts to force the emigration of Albanians into neighboring countries led to resistance, first in the form of the moderate Democratic League of Kosovo (LDK) and ultimately the radical Kosovo Liberation Army (KLA). Under the leadership of Ibrahim Rugova, the Kosovo Albanians countered Serb repression with a parallel state structure—in the hope of winning the kind of external support for independence that had been achieved by other former Yugoslav territories.[44]

There was little prospect during the Bosnian civil war that the concerns of the Kosovars would resonate with the world community or with the NATO allies specifically. First, Kosovo was not a republic of the former Yugoslavia. It was a province of Serbia, and external interference could be considered intrusion into the internal affairs of a sovereign nation. Second, turmoil in Albania, though created by Belgrade, stimulated guerrilla attacks against Serbs and the Yugoslav army, with the blame falling on Kosovars. Third, and most important, Milosevic's repression in Kosovo coincided with the wars of conflict in the other Yugoslav republics and diverted attention from Serb behavior in Kosovo.

Not until the spring of 1998 did NATO and the UN begin to pay serious attention to the ethnic cleansing that had been taking place in Kosovo while these organizations were preoccupied with Bosnia. For Milosevic and most Serbs it did not matter that 90 percent of the province was populated by Albanians. For them Kosovo would always be a symbol of their victimization by the outside world, as Milosevic proclaimed in a dramatic speech at the Field of Blackbirds, the putative site of the Serb defeat six hundred years earlier. It was no coincidence that this speech was given at a time that the Serbian legislature was preparing amendments to the Yugoslav Constitution of 1974 that would undermine Kosovo's autonomy. The consequence of this outburst of Serbian nationalism were decrees from Belgrade removing vestiges of Albanian autonomy.[45]

The Western allies were aware of what was taking place in the Kosovo province, primarily because of their concern that unrest among Albanians could spread to Macedonia, another former Yugoslav republic with a large Albanian minority, and to Albania itself, destabilizing the whole area. President Bush in December 1992 had dispatched a "Christmas letter" to Milosevic, seconded by President Clinton in 1993, warning that a violent crackdown against the Albanians could lead to military action against Serbia. Milosevic was able to ignore these threats, at least until 1995.

Unfortunately for the Albanians, the Croatian and Bosnian conflicts with Serbia held center stage for the West in the next few years. That Kosovo was regarded as an integral part of Serbia further lowered the priorities for involvement of the UN or NATO in the relations between Serbia and its Kosovo province. Although Holbrooke at the end of the Dayton negotiations did bring up the Christmas warning to Milosevic, his seemed to have been a pro forma statement hoping for some relaxation of pressure rather than a prelude to implementing the Bush and Clinton threats.[46]

Arguably, the United States, and Holbrooke in particular, should have used the Dayton Accords, with the U.S. promise of troops to enforce them, as a means of pressing Milosevic to respect the rights of Albanians. The NATO allies were no longer dependent on Milosevic to resolve the crisis in Bosnia and, presumably, were free to threaten sanctions if not war if he did not change his policies.

Sanctions in the form of blockade or embargo had considerable effect in distancing Milosevic from his associates in Bosnia, but it was questionable whether these tactics would be as successful in Kosovo. The importance of that province to Bosnian nationalism trumped any threat the allies might make. Milosevic remained confident to the end of his ability to charm or bully the West, assuming divisions within NATO and support from Russia. He could also count on the fact that worries raised by aggressive Albanian militants among the NATO allies would moderate the allies' opposition to his ongoing campaign to rid Kosovo of its Albanian population. And for a time Milosevic managed to have his way. He took full advantage of the violent KLA attacks, which were designed to win world attention by goading Serbs into massive retaliation.[47]

The six-member Contact Group that had an ongoing if peripheral role in Bosnia became involved in Kosovo in March 1998 when the Serbs were held responsible for the deaths of fifty-three Albanians, half of them women, children, and old men, part of an extended family whose head was accused of controlling the KLA. Secretary of State Albright, long an adversary of Milosevic and an advocate for strong measures against him, was convinced he had gone too far this time. She was quoted as saying, "We are not going to stand by and watch Serbian authorities in Kosovo do in Kosovo what they can no longer get away with in Bosnia." Her British counterpart, Robin Cook, agreed on sanctions, but neither Albright nor Cook could win over the French, Italian, or Russian delegates. The French foreign minister wanted to delay sanctions and include a condemnation of KLA provocations, as well as a statement opposing Kosovo independence. The Italian member felt that sanctions would lessen rather than hasten Milosevic's cooperation, while the Russian had no interest in the meeting under any circumstance.[48]

A watered-down rebuke to Milosevic did come out of the meeting. On paper the Contact Group sounded forceful in its statement of March 9, 1998. It demanded that Milosevic act within ten days to halt attacks against the civilian population and to withdraw all police units from Kosovo. The ministers brought the United Nations into play by requiring Serbia to allow the UNHCR to visit Kosovo in order to monitor the implementation of Serb commitments. Russia would not join the other five members of the Contact Group in considering such additional measures as a complete arms embargo and freezing Serb-held funds abroad. But the operative term in the Contact Group's statement was only to "consider" implementation, and Serbia's patron Russia would not even consider this step. Although Western pressure produced withdrawal of some Serb military from Kosovo, in the face of these tepid responses Milosevic proceeded with his destruction of Kosovo villages as part of his larger mission of making room for a future Serbian majority in Kosovo.[49]

The Pentagon was slow to take up this challenge despite General Clark's protestations in his capacity as commander of U.S. troops in Europe. Clark felt that the Joint Chiefs of Staff not only had other priorities but faulted him for going to the secretary of defense without first consulting the chairman.[50] He found a more sympathetic ear in Solana. The NATO secretary general agreed that Milosevic had to be stopped, but he had to admit that the NAC was not prepared to do more than express solidarity with the Kosovars, without alienating Milosevic, "who remains crucial to the success of the Dayton Accords and stability in Bosnia."[51]

Some NATO partners had no objection to the United Nations' participating in the effort to force Milosevic to back off. Britain initiated a draft Security Council Resolution 1160, imposing an arms embargo against Yugoslavia. Secretary Albright, however, called it "well intentioned but not well conceived." It did win unanimous approval at the council's 3868th meeting on March 31, 1998, and the resolution sounded even more serious than the Contact Group's statement. It called upon Yugoslavia to take the necessary steps to achieve a political solution through dialogue and, at the same time, called upon Kosovar Albanian leaders to condemn terrorism and to pursue their goals through peaceful means.[52] The trouble with this resolution was its lack of ability to enforce an embargo, as well as its equation of Serbian behavior with Albanian reaction without reference to enforcement beyond the Security Council's appointing a committee to report on its implementation. Small wonder that the resolution won unanimous endorsement.

A close look at Resolution 1160, and at 1199, which repeated the demands of 1160, disclosed that there was no immediate prospect of compulsion following Milosevic's failure to respect the Security Council's resolutions. This may explain why both resolutions won Russian approval. Six months later Annan reported to the council that neither resolution was observed. He noted that the international community had witnessed appalling atrocities in Kosovo, reminiscent of the recent past elsewhere in the Balkans, without being able to take any steps to stop the violence from either the Serb military or the Albanian guerrillas. All that he could hope for was a resumption of negotiations between the parties in Serbia and Kosovo to find a comprehensive political solution.[53]

There was little prospect of NATO's stepping in either on its own initiative or through an arrangement with the UN Security Council in the spring and summer of 1998. The NATO ministers at the meeting of the NAC in Luxembourg in May 1998 were "concerned" about the situation in Kosovo and "deplored" violence both in the Serbs' suppression of Kosovo's dissent and in Kosovo's pursuit of change. They did charge Milosevic with "a special responsibility to ensure that steps are taken to achieve a political solution in Kosovo." They also promised military advice in support of UN and OSCE monitoring and noted "NATO preventive deployments" in the neighboring countries of Albania and Macedonia to contain expansion of the instability in Kosovo.[54] None of these statements appeared meaningful enough to deter Milosevic from his continuing destruction of the Albanian communities of Kosovo.

NATO's cautious approach to the violence in Kosovo became bolder in the face of Milosevic's increasing Serbia's uprooting of Albanian villages in the summer of 1998. Solana exercising influence behind the scenes feared that Milosevic was damaging NATO's credibility by his persistent depredations in that province. Serbia's behavior forced Solana to take a more militant stance in his relations with Milosevic.[55]

The secretary general's willingness to consider military force inspired the allies to take seriously the threat of military action that could be read into Security Council Resolution 1199—to "implement immediately" withdrawal of security units used for civilian repression. Still, over the summer, the "preventive options" mentioned in the June 1998 NATO communiqué were not translated into action, even as plans for military strikes were maturing. As Serb repression accelerated despite Milosevic's promises not to attack civilians, the NAC on September 24, 1998, issued "an activation warning" for limited air strikes (ACTWARN). In the words of a senior Pentagon official, this decision "is not a decision to use force," but "it will allow the Alliance to move within a matter of days from a situation of being ready to execute."[56]

In all these deliberations NATO was aware of the importance of its relations with the UN. Its members recognized that Russia and China would veto any mandate from the Security Council to use force against a sovereign country. This recognition raised the question as to whether UN's explicit authorization had to be a prerequisite to intervention. Whether the humanitarian crisis combined with the inability of the Security Council to act justified an exception to a UN mandate was not resolved until Solana claimed on October 10, 1998, that there was sufficient legal basis. He did so without defining its terms. In essence, Solana was endorsing the understanding that UN resolutions, particularly SC Resolution 1199 in September 1998, gave NATO the authority to employ force if necessary. Although SC 1199 failed to contain Milosevic, Solana's use of the resolution marked a turning point, as Ryan Hendrickson observed, in elevating the role of the secretary general in NATO affairs.[57] The NAC still was not ready to act on Solana's judgment.

To break the impasse within the alliance, the Clinton administration sent Holbrooke back again to negotiate with Milosevic. As at Dayton his mission seemed a success, as Milosevic agreed to the presence of a civilian group to verify the Serbs' compliance with UN demands and to assure Kosovo autonomy while its final status was worked out over a period of three to five years. Holbrooke, familiar as he was with Milosevic's tricks, managed to prevent further stalling, saying that only acceptance of his propositions would hold off NATO's air strikes. An important element in the agreement was the presence of a Kosovo Verification

Mission to verify compliance with Resolution 1199, underscored by the deployment of two thousand Polish unarmed verifiers.[58]

In these intense negotiations, the significance of UN approval was always implicit—and at times explicit. Solana accompanied by the chairman of the Military Committee, General Klaus Naumann, and SACEUR General Clark went to Belgrade in October 1998 to deliver "a simple but strong message to President Milosevic; he must comply fully and immediately with the requirements of the UN Security Council Resolution 1199."[59] Germany and Italy now joined with the other allies in seeing the UN Resolutions 1160 and 1199 as the authority for NATO preparations for war, if not for war itself. The Security Council on October 24 endorsed the agreements between Holbrooke and Milosevic that created the Verification Mission under OSCE auspices.[60]

The next day Generals Clark and Naumann won an agreement from Milosevic to comply "unconditionally" with SR 1199. These arrangements encouraged the NATO ministers at their meeting in December to hope for an end of violence and a lasting political settlement. They also noted violent incidents in November from both sides, blaming "both the Belgrade authorities and the armed Kosovar elements" for failing "to comply fully with the implementation of Security Council Resolutions 1160, 1199, and 1203."[61] As the year ended, there may have been division within NATO over the need for UN approval before launching military action, but there was no division over the importance of a close connection between the two organizations.

Kosovo, 1999

Milosevic's capitulation was always suspect in the minds of those who had dealt with him over the years. He had no intention of giving up his plans for Kosovo and counted on a pretense of compliance to drive a wedge into the alliance's solidarity, such as it was, in 1999. It was not just that the allies were hesitant to engage in combat; they had shown their determination to use force over Bosnia in 1995. Rather, a number of issues gave Milosevic confidence that he could keep his adversaries at bay. The UN Security Council was always a weak reed, as Russia with Chechnya and China with Taiwan in mind were unwilling to interfere in the internal affairs of a sovereign country. NATO's posture was potentially more dangerous, but Milosevic recognized that many of its members had no wish to embrace Albanian aspirations for independence. Like Russia and China, Turkey had a Kurdish minority and Spain a Basque minority that could be emboldened by Kosovo's independence. Moreover, the European NATO partners shared fears that Kosovo could become a hotbed of Islamic fundamentalism, if not ungovernable criminal gangs, as the KLA was often labeled. Accompanying all these obstacles to a NATO strike against Serbia were the elaborate alliance plans to welcome three new members in April 1999 at the fiftieth anniversary of the signing of the North Atlantic Treaty.

Still, the violence in Kosovo could not be ignored. The discovery of a massacre of forty-five ethnic Albanians in January led to fears of another humanitarian disaster. Neither NATO nor the UN could avert their eyes from the latest atrocity in Kosovo. Solana, speaking for the NAC on January 17, 1999, issued a ritual denunciation of the crime but at the same time appealed to "both sides to cease hostilities immediately and to begin negotiations toward a lasting political solution which provides greater autonomy for Kosovo and which preserves the territorial integrity of the FRY [Federal Republic of Yugoslavia]."[62]

This concession to the legitimacy of Serbia's control over its Kosovo province may have given confidence to Milosevic to proceed in his campaign of terror, but it was not the end of the matter. Public opinion in the West was fired up much as it had been over Sarajevo in 1995, and Secretary General Solana, reflecting the rising passions of the NAC's constituencies, warned that the allies were ready to take military action to stop further violence. Yet Solana may have sent the wrong message by blaming both sides. Unlike the rhetoric of the previous year, however, the British and French spoke of their willingness to send ground forces to extract a political settlement. Given a commitment of this sort, the United States was under pressure to be part of a peacekeeping mission that might be produced by a settlement. What was evident in these threats was the conviction that force would be necessary to impose a peace.[63]

As NATO seemed on the verge at last of acting on its pledges, it now found the UN secretary-general speaking to the North Atlantic Council on the same day that the NATO ministers issued their new warning. Kofi Annan applauded NATO as an active partner in creating "a new architecture of preventive proactive policies for peace." Allowing for the necessary politesse that accompanies such an occasion, he emphasized that it "was critically important for us to draw on each others' strengths in pursuit of peace and security" and suggested that "the success of the NATO-led mission operations under a United Nations mandate is surely the model for future endeavors." In brief, he admitted the necessity of military action to impress Milosevic: "The bloody wars of the last decade have left us with no illusions about the difficulty of halting internal conflicts—by reason or by force—particularly against the wishes of the government of a sovereign state." Annan went on to say that the conflicts had also left the world community with no "illusions about the need to use force when all other means have failed. We may be reaching that limit, once again, in Yugoslavia." This statement was not specifically a demand for war but it was close, as the secretary-general had come to accepting war as the solution, as it had been in 1995.[64]

Unlike most of his predecessors, Annan had a good working relationship with regional organizations, among which he always included NATO. He recognized that they could intervene in conflicts the UN could not manage by itself.[65] While trying to balance the humanitarian justification for intervention against the danger of undermining the UN's authority, he did what he could to keep the UN as much in the forefront as possible. At no point did he unreservedly cede UN fundamental responsibility for peacekeeping in Kosovo or elsewhere in a fractious world. It was a delicate balancing act. In Kosovo the humanitarian cause seemed to trump the legitimacy of national sovereignty. But, as he noted in his ambiguous comments during the seventy-eight-day war, he continued to worry about a diminished status for the UN.

Their warnings to Milosevic notwithstanding, the allies still looked for a way out of a commitment to force. The Clinton administration had to cope with a public unhappy with the extended troop deployment in Bosnia, and Clinton himself, distracted by impeachment proceedings launched by the Republican party, preferred not to test Milosevic's mettle. The administration also had to cope with the allies' hesitation, even after the revelations of the massacre in Racak on January 15, 1999, to act on the resolutions they had supported. The Europeans were suspicious that the KLA appeared to seek out opportunities to bait the Serbs into harsh retaliation in the hope that it would damage Milosevic in the world's eyes. On both sides of the Atlantic there was no appetite to identify ground forces as a credible means of influencing Milosevic. The allies' vacillation over the use of force accounted for the North Atlantic Council's placing the decision on January 30, 1999, "to authorize air strikes against targets on FRY territory" in the hands of the secretary general.[66]

Just a week after the confluence of NATO and UN views on the necessity for military action, the NATO allies made a last effort to bring the Serb leader into compliance with the UN and NATO demands. In the meeting co-chaired by the British and French foreign ministers under the auspices of the six-nation Contact Group, the parties convened at Rambouillet, a fourteenth-century French chateau on the outskirts of Paris, in early February 1999. U.S. officials were cautiously optimistic about the outcome. The conference produced familiar statements about Kosovo autonomy, the territorial integrity of Serbia, and an end of violence. A new constitution for Kosovo was included in an annex.[67]

The secretary of state's firm belief that there could be no settlement with Milosevic "without a very large stick forcing him to do so" won popularity in the White House and Defense Department. This was the critical moment. Even General Clark, who had worked closely with Holbrooke at Dayton, believed that Milosevic could not turn down a deal: "I can't believe that Milosevic won't sign, when the crunch comes. He always holds out. He has to be leaned on very hard. But he will come around."[68]

In this case they were mistaken. As Milosevic anticipated, disagreements among the NATO allies surfaced as France tried and failed to subordinate any NATO force in Kosovo to the Contact Group rather than to the NAC. While France failed in this instance, it did succeed in winning over most of the allies to the need for UN authorization before deploying force in the province. The United States opposed this proposal for fear of a precedent giving the UN Security Council the right to decide on the use of force against Serbia. A British compromise settled on UN endorsement for what would become KFOR, in place of an explicit NATO approval of UN authorization for war.[69]

In one sense this internal squabble hardly mattered since the Serbs had no intention of accepting a solution involving genuine autonomy for Kosovo or a foreign military presence in the province. Milosevic had sent low-level representatives to Rambouillet, unlike his mission to Dayton where he had been a central figure. He assumed that the proposals would be rejected by the Kosovars since they did not grant independence. He also assumed that dissension among NATO leaders over subordinating NATO to the UN would immobilize the allies. The difficulties over the "dual key" arrangements with UNPROFOR, the UN force in Bosnia, not only were expected to prevent NATO from sharing command responsibilities with the UN but would give Milosevic freedom to pursue his ethnic cleansing in Kosovo.[70]

Arguably, it was the Bosnian experience that was the major factor behind Milosevic's rejection of the Rambouillet agreement. The prospect of an IFOR replicated in Serbia soil was unacceptable to what remained of the Federal Republic of Yugoslavia. One more visit by Holbrooke to Belgrade on March 22, 1999, failed to win Milosevic's acceptance. Only force could be the next step, and by March it was facilitated by the U.S. decision to join the British and French in assigning troops to a future KFOR. The next step was accelerated by Milosevic's launching a new offensive against Kosovar civilians as well as against the KLA, reportedly with forces 50 percent larger than those dispatched in 1998.[71]

President Clinton, with the impeachment crisis behind him, noted on March 22, 1999, that forty thousand Serb security forces were poised for further attacks, in clear violation of the agreements Serbia had made in the cease-fire agreements in October 1998. The objective of military action in Kosovo was to stop the killing, return the refugees, and restore the self-government that "President Milosevic stripped away from them a decade ago." Clinton's hope was to achieve these goals by peaceful means. "If not, we have to be prepared to act."[72]

Two days later the president announced to the nation that "we and our 18 NATO allies agreed to do what we said we would do, what we must do to restore the peace." He still hoped that Milosevic would reverse his self-destructive course. If he should decide to honor the peace agreement and demilitarize Kosovo, then "our troops should take part" in a peace-keeping force. "Imagine what would happen if we and our allies instead decided to look the other way, as these people were massacred on NATO's doorstep. That would discredit NATO, the cornerstone on which our security has rested for 50 years now."[73]

The order to strike was given not by the United States or by the United Nations, but by NATO alone. It was Secretary General Solana, to whom the NATO ambassadors had given the authority for a phased air assault, who directed SACEUR General Clark to initiate military action. By granting Solana decision-making power, the allies were protecting themselves from domestic criticism.[74] In light of the positions of Russia and China, the UN Security Council was not involved. Yet, as noted above, the UN secretary-general was discomfited by yet understanding of NATO's decision. In his own way Annan had given his imprimatur to the action.

The NATO allies did their best to minimize the damage to UN's credibility as peacekeepers after the Russian Federation condemned the use of force against Serbia without the council's authorization. On March 24, 1999, the Russian delegate on the Security Council asserted that NATO air assault subverted the charter and international law, and Russia joined Belarus and India in a draft resolution demanding immediate cessation of force and a resumption of negotiations. The resolution was defeated on March 26 with only three in its favor as the United States claimed that council resolutions 1199 and 1203, whose mandates Serbia violated, justified NATO's actions. The council accepted the NATO position that day, with important support on humanitarian grounds from the Organization of the Islamic Conference Contact Group. The European Union gave its imprimatur to NATO's action by adding its voice to the condemnation of Serbia.[75]

The North Atlantic Council made a point of claiming that its military efforts did not signify any disregard for the United Nations. NATO supported "the political aims of the international community, which were reaffirmed in recent statements by the UN Secretary-General and the European Union." Once Belgrade withdrew its forces from Kosovo, the NATO allies would seek passage of a UN Security Council resolution encompassing both the demilitarization of Kosovo and the deployment of an international military force (KFOR) to protect the return of refugees. Granting the UN the primary responsibility for securing peace after the conflict ended appeased those NATO allies who had been uncomfortable with the absence of a specific Security Council mandate.[76] The UN did not authorize the war, but NATO nevertheless tried at every opportunity to assure the world of its conformity to UN principles.

At the same time NATO sought to prevent Russia from becoming permanently alienated from the allies despite its objections to the organization's unilateral actions. Even as Russia in April 1999 remained vehemently opposed to NATO's attack against Serbia, the ministers maintained that Russia had an important role to play in finding a solution for the Kosovo conflict. They wanted to work constructively with Russia, "in the spirit of the Founding Act of 1997." Their determination to include Russia ultimately bore results—and the results were remarkably similar to the end product in Bosnia. Before the conflict ended, Russia had agreed to participate in KFOR as it had in IFOR, with Russian troops under its own national command, though in a U.S. sector under the direction of the NAC. As in Bosnia, Russia reluctantly yielded on the key points of total Serb military withdrawal and acceptance of NATO at the core of the peacekeeping force.[77]

Russia had to yield to the power of the West, at least for the time being, but with resentments that had grown deeper since 1995 and that were expressed in its theatrical preemption of NATO occupation of the Pristina airport after Milosevic had yielded. Russia was not yet in a position to occupy what it felt to be its appropriate role on the world scene. But NATO's sensitivity to Russia's amour propre helped to secure that country's temporary abandonment of its traditional position as Serbia's patron. Russia's pressure on Milosevic played a positive role in the ending of the conflict.[78]

In the course of the seventy-eight-day war, NATO had to deal with problems within the alliance itself. The mistaken assumption that Milosevic would give in to NATO's might as he had in 1995 led to fissures within NATO, between General Clark and his superiors in Washington who distrusted the SACEUR's independent streak, and between the Anglo-Americans and those allies who opposed mobilization of ground troops. The air strikes as a show of NATO strength initially failed to move the Serb leader. But Milosevic overestimated his ability to divide the allies, and as the bombing intensified and began to strike vital Belgrade installations, Milosevic looked for an exit from the conflict.[79]

No matter how bitter the relations between Clark and the Pentagon and no matter how far apart the allies' thoughts on the conduct of the war, the efforts to link NATO to the UN never flagged. The humanitarian factor in the war proved to be an important bridge between the two organizations. In April 1999, Solana asked the UNHCR what measures NATO could take to assist the high commission in its increasing burden of assisting refugees in Albania and Macedonia; some 270,000 people fled to those countries in the first two weeks after the war began. Airlifting supplies was a necessity.[80]

When NATO aircraft bombed the Chinese embassy in Belgrade, the president of the UN Security Council expressed sorrow over loss of lives but did not rebuke the United States. In fact, he emphasized that NATO was investigating the circumstances.[81] The UN seemed eager to accept NATO's excuse that the bombing was accidental not purposeful. But when the Security Council deplored Serb violations of human rights in a resolution adopted by thirteen members, with China and Russia abstaining, Serbia complained that the council was too ready to condemn Serb behavior in Kosovo while ignoring the NATO campaign of terror against Serbs.[82] The Serbs and the Russians saw a double standard on display at the United Nations, with NATO as the beneficiary.

With NATO's blessing, the UN was closely connected to the peace process as the war began drawing to a close. The proposals emanating from the G-8 foreign ministers meeting in Bonn on May 6, 1999, resulted in a UN resolution with terms for ending the conflict and embodying a road map for a political solution. Serb compliance was aided by a combination of KLA successes on the ground, NATO's credible threat of a ground attack, increasing damage to critical installations in Belgrade, and warnings from its Russian ally. By the beginning of June the Serbs had accepted the G-8 principles after a presentation of the peace plan by the Russian president's personal envoy. On June 9, 1999, NATO suspended its air operations.[83]

A day later the UN Security Council adopted Resolution 1244(1999) by a vote of fourteen to zero, with only one abstention. Russia was on board and the objectives of the war were ratified under UN auspices. These included phased withdrawal of Serb forces, monitored by "the deployment of the international security presence." The Kosovo Liberation Army would also be demilitarized, and autonomy, but not independence, would be assured. Resolution 1244 also gave the secretary-general the task, "with the assistance of relevant international organizations, to provide a civil service that would be in charge of the interim administration of the province." Its charge was extensive, from supporting economic reconstruction to maintaining civil law and order, to promoting human rights.[84]

The UN Interim Administration Mission in Kosovo (UNMIK) appeared in UN documents as the major player in Kosovo, and the UN secretary-general's reports from June through December 1999 centered on the mission's activities. The reports revealed shortcomings as well as accomplishments in Kosovo, but aside from acknowledging cooperation with KFOR, they left no question about the chain of command, which began and ended with the UN, as symbolized by the requirement under Resolution 1244 that the NATO secretary general report to the UN Security Council on the activities of KFOR. No direct mention of NATO can be found in Resolution 1244. According to the resolution, it was the Security Council that "decides on the deployment in Kosovo, under United Nations auspices, of international civil and security presences."[85] In one sense Resolution 1244 marked the success of NATO in its efforts to legitimize its action without the Security Council's authorization. But the resolution also sanctioned the United Nations as the institution in charge of the return of peace to Kosovo, with NATO's KFOR as an auxiliary body in the service of the world organization.

NATO versus the UN in Kosovo

This was not the understanding that NATO leaders had in mind in collaborating with the UN. The forty-four thousand troops from seventeen NATO and non-NATO countries, including the Russian Federation, comprised the KFOR under NATO—not UN—command. Serbia's submission could not have been secured had its compliance been left to the UN, any more than it could have been in Bosnia four years before. NATO had won the war, and NATO was maintaining the peace through KFOR, achievements the UN only implicitly acknowledged. The disparity between the authority inherent in Chapter 7 of the UN Charter and the reality expressed in a defense organization's possession of the power to enforce the UN's mandates created discomfort in NATO circles and facilitated the illusion that it was the UN that punished Serbia for its repression in Kosovo. In Bosnia this issue was resolved by the United Nations' explicitly turning authority over to NATO. In Kosovo NATO acted independently of the UN yet sought to demonstrate the compatibility of its actions with the terms of the UN Charter.

An analogy may be made with the efforts of the North Atlantic Treaty's framers to give their organization legitimacy in 1949 by citing the one article of the UN Charter—the right of collective self-defense—that fit its needs and then liberally sprinkling the name of the United Nations among the treaty's articles. The purpose in 1949 was to obscure the reality that it was not a regional organization that would serve under the authority of the UN Security Council. Yet the U.S State Department wanted the aura of legitimacy that NATO's status as a regional organization would bestow.

It required semantic contortions to link NATO and the UN in 1949—and again in 1999. Defenders of NATO's "unilateral" intervention would admit, as Brookings Institution scholars Ivo Daalder and Michael O'Hanlon did, that "UN authorization for intervention is highly desirable, even if it is not required." Still, the subsequent decisive role of the UN after the conflict ended seemed to ease their discomfort sufficiently to say that "NATO's intervention in Kosovo did not weaken the UN's role in such situations; indeed, in some ways it strengthened that role."[86] Historian Alan Henrikson tried to resolve the question of legitimacy by envisioning NATO, with its military capabilities, as "the *enabler* of the participation of others, including the United Nations Organization. This surely is a basis of the legitimacy of the actions it took in Kosovo. NATO does not legitimize power. But it does give power to legitimacy."[87]

The foregoing analyses were just two of many efforts to harmonize the roles of NATO and the UN. The legality of NATO intervention was a major subject of the October 1999 issue of the *American Journal of International Law*. While the UN Charter clearly prohibits intervention by a single state, or even a combination of states, the horrendous situation in Kosovo, bordering on genocide, justified NATO action, according to Columbia Law School professor Louis Henkin, if the UN Security Council was not "available" because of the veto. In its absence the Security Council's Resolution 1244 that approved the Kosovo settlement on June 10, 1999, could also be cited as justification of the seventy-eight-day war.[88] The majority of the scholars represented in the journal accepted the argument that the urgency of the moment required encroachment on a state's sovereignty.

Yet Catherine Guicherd of the NATO Parliamentary Assembly recognized that the emerging consensus over the primacy of human rights had not crystallized into an unambiguous rule allowing humanitarian intervention. Reluctantly, she judged that NATO was unable to embed the Kosovo campaign into international law. At best, the allies could claim it as an exception. The solution would be to adjust international law to accommodate a Kosovo operation. Henkin agreed: "Kosovo demonstrates once again a compelling need to address the deficiencies in the UN charter."[89]

If the NATO allies were as concerned about conformity with the UN Charter as were the pundits and scholars in the wake of the war, the question arises: Why did they ignore the precedent of the Korean War in 1950 when the Uniting for Peace resolution bypassed the UN Security Council and the Soviet veto? Then the UN General Assembly assumed the power to make decisions that the charter had reserved to the council. Although the 1950 resolution had disappeared from international consciousness by 1999, it was still on the books. During the forty-year history of the Cold War after Korea, it never resurfaced as a NATO answer to deadlock on the Security Council. One obvious yet not wholly satisfactory response to this query is that the United States and its allies still distrusted that the General Assembly, with its anticolonial heritage, would act in their interests. From this perspective, it would be more dangerous to have the General Assembly sit in judgment of U.S. or NATO actions than the Security Council. Diego A. Ruiz Palmer of NATO's international staff had another explanation. He did not believe that the NATO secretary general or any of the NAC members "has any recollection of that resolution."[90]

A glance at reactions to the intervention in the UN Security Council would disclose vigorous dissent from Russia and its friends. The Belarus–India–Russian Federation resolution two days after the bombing began centered on the question of the council's authorization, as did the objections from Russia and Yugoslavia on the same day. Opposition in the UN General Assembly extended to more neutral observers. A communiqué from the Rio Group of Latin American nations on March 26, expressed the group's anxiety over the air strikes. It centered its argument on NATO's contravention of the provisions of Article 53 and 54, which denied any action by "regional agencies" without the authorization of the Security Council.[91] Devotion to the letter of the charter was an understandable reflex from smaller powers that benefited from UN mandates.

While this connection would have been sufficient to sound an alarm in NATO circles, it was still unlikely that the General Assembly would have stood in the way of NATO's intervention. The powerful Islamic bloc had made its position clear even before the aircraft struck. It viewed the Racak massacre as another of the

Serbian "crimes against humanity" that should be condemned by the UN Security Council. When the war began, the Organization of the Islamic Conference Contact Group on Bosnia granted that the Security Council should have been the organ to protect the Muslims of Kosovo. But it recognized the necessity for decisive international action.[92] Still, the putative support of a General Assembly majority might not have been a sufficient inducement for NATO to invoke the 1950 precedent.

While legal scholars debated the legitimacy of NATO's intervention, they did not judge the equally contentious issue of the UN's supremacy over NATO. The superiority of the world organization had been repeated over the years when Kofi Annan equated NATO with the EU and the OSCE as "regional organizations" reporting to the UN Security Council under the terms of Article 53. Security Council Resolution 1140 of June 10, 1999, passed just as the war ended, making the inferior position of NATO explicit. In outlining the future of Kosovo, the Security Council emphasized that it had "the primary responsibility . . . for the maintenance of international peace and security" in that province. In this capacity it was the Security Council that "authorized member states and relevant international organizations [NATO among them] to establish the international security presence in Kosovo." And it was the UN secretary-general's expression of concern over the humanitarian disaster, not that of any NATO official, that explains the need for military action. NATO seemed to agree with the UN interpretation of the relationship when on June 7 it welcomed "the unswerving determination of the new Special Representative of the Secretary General to continue UNMIK's efforts to implement UNSCR 1244."[93]

It is not surprising that Britain and France, with their permanent seats on the UN Security Council, would not be as upset with the text as was their U.S. counterpart. In the Security Council they carried more weight than they did as lesser partners to the United States in the North Atlantic Council. Removing UN authority in exceptional circumstances raised the danger of minimizing their roles in the Security Council.[94] When the relationship between the organizations did come into focus, the United States had sharp rejoinders. Secretary Albright worried in May 1998 that, in initiating the draft of Security Council Resolution 1160, Britain was suggesting that a Security Council mandate was needed before NATO could implement its demands. "If so," she observed, "we would have set a precedent that NATO required Security Council authorization before it could act."[95] The idea of UN authorization raised the issue that had lain dormant in the Bosnian crisis, namely, that NATO was a regional organization subject to UN authority under Article 53 of the UN Charter. The idea of Russia or China exercising a veto over NATO actions was as unacceptable in the 1990s as it had been during the Cold War. Neither Albright nor any other official in the Clinton administration would be as vehement as Holbrooke in disagreeing with "the decision to put Kosovo under the United Nations, to which I am totally opposed. I think it was a tremendous mistake. . . . The worst consequence of putting Kosovo's administration under the United Nations is still ahead of us: which is the final negotiations over Kosovo's final status, in which the United Nations will run those negotiations and they will be much harder to conduct than if they were done in the ad hoc, U.S.-led fashion that the Dayton talks were."[96]

The events of the first decade of the twenty-first century confirmed Holbrooke's forebodings about the solution of the Kosovo problem, even if the United Nations role was not solely to blame. In Bosnia the cession of authority by the UN to NATO was clear-cut, although it was intended to be temporary. The lack of clarity about the primacy of the UN over NATO in Kosovo and in the Middle East, however, helped to provoke crises in the next decade that are not yet resolved in 2009.

9

After 9/11
Afghanistan and Iraq

Change and Continuity, 1990s and 2000s

In many ways the direction of NATO-UN relations was only a deepening, both in friction and in collaboration, of a pattern that had been set in the 1990s. The abrupt end of the Cold War lessened the likelihood of vetoes on the part of the permanent members of the UN Security Council. It also fostered a partnership of sorts between NATO and the UN through crisis management in the Middle East and the Balkans.

There were limits, however, to the movement toward collaboration. Secretary-General Boutros Boutros-Ghali's surrender of authority to NATO in 1995 was demonstrably grudging. He was suspicious of U.S. motives behind NATO's demand for control of the Bosnian operation.[1] And four years later his successor, Kofi Annan, was discomfited, along with many members of the UN Security Council, by NATO initiatives against the Serbian president, Slobodan Milosevic, over atrocities in Kosovo. It was not only the Russian and Chinese members that stood in the way of NATO action; NATO partners had their doubts about the alliance acting without explicit authorization from the Security Council. As permanent members of the council, Britain and France could lose status if NATO poached on its territory.[2] Yet as leading members of NATO, frustrated with the behavior of Russia and China, they could welcome Secretary General Solana's assurance that the UN had already granted sufficient authority for them to strike without additional sanctions.[3]

The crises of the 1990s opened the way for closer connections between NATO and the UN. But intimacy did not necessarily breed comity. The UN Charter made it clear in Chapter 7 that the UN was the prime mover in seeking and securing global peace. NATO regarded these crises as opportunities to express its support and agreement, in principle, but added caveats that can be traced to the origins of the treaty in 1949. NATO officials were uncomfortable with the frequent identification of the organization as one of many regional organizations that could serve the United Nations. This category certainly fits the EU and the OSCE—and as NATO recognized, for practical purposes, it also fit NATO under Article 52 of the charter, engaging in regional actions consistent with the charter's principles. But the terms of the North Atlantic Treaty excluded Article 53, on the grounds that as a regional organization, NATO would be obligated to report its activities to the UN Security Council where the Soviet Union had a permanent seat. Soviet oversight of NATO deliberations in 1949 would have made a mockery of an organization designed to cope with Soviet aggression.

Irrespective of the Soviet adversary in the Cold War, NATO's relations with the UN, marginal as they were in those years, rested on its assumption that the alliance was an independent actor. Such was the position of the United States in the 1990s. What muddied the clarity of this position were the hesitations of the other partners—the two European allies on the UN Security Council as well as the doubts of the lesser powers—about a challenge to the authority of the world organization. The UN was accorded deference specifically in the preamble of the Washington treaty. Article 7 explicitly stated that "the Treaty does not affect . . . the primary responsibility of the Security Council for the maintenance of international peace and security." This emphasis reflected a faith in the ultimate success of the UN, found particularly in the views of Senator Vandenberg and U.S. adherents of the United Nations in 1949.

Fifty years later the American believers in the supremacy of the UN were confined to a few faithful. But this was not the sentiment of most of the European allies. With the end of the communist menace, the European partners now regarded reliance on the UN as a check on the influence of the American superpower in a unipolar world, given the attitudes toward NATO expressed by the administration of George W. Bush.[4] The new millennium coincided with the rise of U.S. unilateralism in the new administration as reflected in its rejection of the Kyoto Protocol and the International Criminal Court, as well as its abrogation of the Anti-Ballistic Missile Treaty. This flouting of the views of its allies evoked negative reactions within NATO, from France and Germany, especially, as well as from the traditional adversaries of the Cold War, a rejuvenated Russia and a rising China.

9/11 and Afghanistan

The enormity of the radical Islamic attack on September 11, 2001, that resulted in over three thousand deaths in the towers of the World Trade Center in New York, in the fields of Pennsylvania, and in the corridors of the Pentagon, momentarily bonded NATO with the UN, and Europe with America. The UN Security Council and the North Atlantic Council expressed their outrage over the terrorist action. NATO invoked the treaty's Article 5 on September 12, requiring the allies to consider the attack against the United States as "an attack against them all." On the same day the UN Security Council unanimously condemned the assaults and, two weeks later, labeled them "a threat to international peace."[5]

NATO Secretary General George Robertson, a former defense minister in Tony Blair's cabinet, was a strong supporter of the United States and an even stronger supporter of increased NATO defense budgets. It is noteworthy that he reported to his counterpart, Kofi Annan, at the UN on the meetings of the North Atlantic Council on September 11 and 12 when the NAC agreed to invoke the North Atlantic Treaty's Article 5, "consistent with article 51 of the United Nations Charter if it is determined that the attack was directed from abroad against the United States."[6] This language paid obeisance to the paramount principles of the UN Charter, if not quite to the superior authority of the UN Security Council.

That the UN recognized the right of the United States and its NATO allies to invoke Article 5 of their North Atlantic Treaty was never in question. More problematic was NATO's use of the article. NATO scholar Ryan Hendrickson noted that initially the United States hesitated to invoke the article, perhaps because it might complicate a U.S.-controlled military response.[7] But even in the heat of the moment, the ambiguous relationship between NATO and the UN came into play. Under the terms of the treaty's Article 5, the allies would exercise the right of individual or collective self-defense recognized by Article 51 of the UN Charter. The last paragraph of Article 5, however, specified that such measures taken to repel the attacks "shall immediately be reported to the Security Council." Eight measures, including the deployment of NATO AWACs to the United States were taken in response to the terrorist attacks. Those measures "shall be terminated," according to Article 5, when the Security Council assumes the responsibility for restoring and maintaining international peace and order.

But no such report was made in 2001. In fact, only at the October 2005 meeting of the North Atlantic Council did NATO submit a report to the UN Security Council. The delay may have been the result of other preoccupations at the time, though NATO analyst David Yost is skeptical about this explanation. He noted that, in subsequent reports relating to Article 5, the NATO secretary general made no reference to the UN Charter even though his letters of January 6, 2006, and April 17, 2007, referred to "full implementation of Resolution 1373," calling for action under Chapter 7 of the UN Charter.[8] The most likely explanation for the cavalier treatment of this feature of Article 5 was the taint of NATO subordination to the United Nations. The United States, if not all the NATO partners, continued to harbor fears that the UN might take control of operations in Afghanistan.[9]

The UN Security Council's response to the Al Qaeda attacks initially took the form of Resolution 1368, adopted unanimously on September 12, condemning terrorist attacks as threats to international peace and security and calling "on all States to work together to bring to justice the perpetrators, organizers, and sponsors." The EU's foreign ministers used similar language. Arguably, it was *Le Monde* of Paris that provided the most poignant moment, when its editorial director on the first page of the paper proclaimed "nous sommes tous Américains [We are all Americans]." He evoked the language of President Kennedy in Berlin, even though he mistakenly placed the occasion in 1962 instead of 1963.[10]

The new spirit of cooperation between the United States and the UN was in evidence two weeks later when the Security Council adopted, again unanimously, the U.S.-sponsored resolution obliging all member states to cooperate in the campaign against the terrorist organizers, including the use of force.[11] The Russian ambassador to the UN, Sergei Lavrov, was in full accord with the resolution, saying, "We are ready now." At the UN General Assembly, the Russian Federation stressed the need to move to concrete action and noted that the Commonwealth of Associated States, of which it was a key member, had set up an anti-terrorist center.[12] The United States and Britain's rejection of terrorists and those who support them was a reason for the United Arab Emirates to thank the president of the United States and the prime minister of the United Kingdom "for their statements rejecting the idea that terrorism and Islam are one and the same."[13]

To implement the resolutions, the Security Council created a counterterrorism committee to report within ninety days the members' compliance with the resolution. Reports from actions taken by member states in support of the resolution were received in November and December including one from the European Union. The General Assembly was quick to line up with the United States. Unlike the EU, its lack of any formal link to the UN made a NATO response conspicuous by its absence. But in its communiqué of December 6, 2001, the NAC did express its appreciation and support "of the efforts of the United Nations and its central role in this field, and undertake to fully implement the efforts of the UN Security Council Resolution 1373."[14]

The resolution contained gray areas, the most significant being the absence of any definition of who is a terrorist. Some states also expressed concern sotto voce about the Security Council's acting on an American initiative without a specific sanction from the UN. Sympathy for the United States notwithstanding, UN members remembered how disdainful the George W. Bush administration had been of the organization in the administration's first nine months of office.[15] Voices of caution were heard about an excessively strong reaction to the actions of Al Qaeda. Although Romano Prodi, president of the European Commission, declared on September 12 that the European Union would assist the United States "with every means at its disposal," the EU's communiqué on September 29 warned that retaliation for the terrorist attacks should be "proportional" to be legitimate under the authority of SC 1368. In fact, as early as September 13,

German defense minister Rudolf Scharping noted, "We do not face a war. We face the question of an appropriate response." And while the Bundestag passed a resolution on September 19 by a large margin, making military facilities available to the United States and NATO, Chancellor Gerhard Schroeder noted that there was no state of war with any particular country, and "we are not in a war against the Islamic world either."[16] Russia also gave out conflicting signals about the extent of Russian military cooperation. The defense minister, Sergei Ivanov, contradicted the foreign minister on September 15 in ruling out "even hypothetical assumptions" that Russia would participate in military action or in lending assets to U.S. forces. President Vladimir Putin seemed to side with the foreign minister on September 24 in allowing U.S. arms to be funneled to the rebel army and opening Russian air space to shipments of humanitarian aid.[17]

Retaliation in Afghanistan against the Taliban harboring Osama bin Laden and the Al Qaeda was primarily in the hands of the United States. NATO played a minor role in the military operation. By the end of September, President Bush spoke of the United States being in "hot pursuit" of the terrorists in Afghanistan. The CIA and U.S. special forces working with anti-Taliban opposition rapidly moved toward recapturing the country from the Taliban's hands. While the command of the operation was American, the NAC noted on December 6 that NATO is "helping to provide humanitarian assistance to the Afghan people, who have suffered under the Taliban regime." The NATO communiqué emphasized that the UN was not excluded: "Our fight, the fight of the international community, is against the terrorists, their networks and those who harbour them, as stated in Resolution 1368 of the UN Security Council."[18]

Long before 9/11, Afghanistan had been on the agenda of the UN Security Council. It had been a country in turmoil since the failed Soviet intervention of the 1980s, as Islamist forces under the Taliban fought with increasing effectiveness against regional warlords. In February 2001 under UN auspices the president of Afghanistan had sought negotiations with the Taliban.[19] Two days after the Al Qaeda attack, the secretary-general proposed, at Afghanistan's request, the convening of a special meeting of the Security Council to address the threat posed by "foreign military and armed personnel" to regional and international peace. In early October, the secretary-general informed the UN General Assembly and Security Council of his intention to appoint a veteran UN diplomat, Lakhdar Brahimi of Algeria, as his special representative in Afghanistan with overall authority in planning for the rehabilitation of the shattered country. The outcome of these activities was the creation of an international security assistance force (ISAF) to assist the Afghan Interim Authority under Hamid Karzai, chairman of the transitional administration, in the implementation of the UN mandate.[20]

The Northern Alliance of Afghan leaders with help from anti-Taliban forces in southern Afghanistan captured Kabul on November 13, 2001, necessitating early international initiatives to help stabilize the situation. The key international actor was the United States with its Operation Enduring Freedom, which augmented and supplied the Afghan enemies of the Taliban. The U.S. operation was independent of NATO's invocation of Article 5, since the Pentagon did not want to be obligated to the alliance. As Secretary of Defense Donald Rumsfeld put it, "the mission determines the coalition, and we don't want coalitions to determine the mission."[21]

The United Nations, however, facilitated the process through a UN-sponsored conference in Bonn in late November where provisional arrangements for an Afghan government were concluded on December 5, 2001.[22] The new ISAF would be the UN's instrument, headed by a British commander. Ironically, in light of the Iraq experience a year and a half later, the United States, according to the assistant secretary of defense for policy Douglas Feith, did not want to create a U.S.-controlled administration in Kabul. Nor did the Pentagon want the UN in its place. This sentiment helped to account for U.S. backing of the Bonn conference, which was intended to keep the Afghans responsible for their own governance. Feith noted Secretary Rumsfeld's good intentions but also his misplaced confidence in his laissez-faire assumptions concerning Iraq a year later.[23] Uneasy though the United States may have been with the UN involvement, it had to recognize that it was the Afghans at Bonn who had asked the UN to recruit an international force with full U.S. approval.

While the period is not sufficiently appreciated in NATO, the fall of 2001 was a high point of UN-U.S. relations—and, by extension, of NATO cooperation with the UN. By December 2001, U.S. forces, in close concert with the UN, were instrumental in completing the liberation of Afghanistan from the Taliban. With explicit endorsement and implicit authorization of military means, the UN was intimately involved every step of the way. Security Council Resolution 1386 authorized the establishment of the ISAF on December 20, 2001. On the next day the General Assembly asked the secretary-general to report periodically on "the progress of the UN and the efforts of his Special Representative to promote peace in Afghanistan."[24]

Although NATO itself was not a formal partner in any of these activities, the United States in essence spoke for the allies. The NATO communiqué stated, "We will continue our support to the United States for the U.S.-led operation against the terrorists until it has reached its objectives." The NAC also stressed "that military tools alone are not sufficient to combat terrorism effectively. The response must be multi-faceted and comprehensive. In that regard, we support the efforts of the United Nations and its *central* role in this field, and undertake to fully implement UN Security Council Resolution 1373."[25]

It was obvious that the allies viewed the Bush policies following 9/11 as being necessary to restore global stability. The disaster appeared to revive their reliance on U.S. leadership of NATO. They welcomed America's immediate dismissal of the idea of an American occupation of Afghanistan; the president claimed to have studied the history of countries that attempted to occupy that mountainous land and was "fully aware of the difficulties the Russians had in Afghanistan."[26] For the time being, the discord emanating from the unilateral challenges to the UN's and NATO's positions on vital international problems abated. The allies appreciated Washington's pressure on Pakistan to stop protecting Al Qaeda networks and applauded Bush's effort to uncouple the Al Qaeda from the larger Muslim world. The president made a special, if not eloquent, address to the American Muslim community on September 17, 2001, recognizing that such acts of terror were abhorrent to Moslems and violated the true faith of Islam. Bush was now perceived as reverting to the multilateral building of the kind of coalition against terrorists that had characterized his father's administration as well as the history of U.S. involvement in NATO.[27]

These notes of harmony between the U.S. and the UN, between NATO and the UN, and between the United States and its allies in NATO did not survive the year, however. The very success of the Afghanistan operation helped to reopen old wounds within the alliance and facilitated the display of those wounds once again in the UN arena. The removal of the Taliban was so rapid that U.S. political and military leaders were tempted to deprecate the military contributions of the allies. The campaign against Al Qaeda and its Taliban hosts was run from the MacDill Air Force Base in Tampa, Florida, with little concern for the views of the military at SHAPE or the civilian authorities in Brussels. General Tommy Franks, operating out of the Central Command in Florida, controlled the air war. Although there were problems of coordination with CIA operatives on the scene in Afghanistan as well as differences between General Franks and the Pentagon, the rifts that developed were not as debilitating as those the SACEUR had endured over Kosovo in 1999. The successes of the Northern Alliance of warlords and other anti-Taliban forces in taking control of most of the country in the first two weeks of November were due in large measure to a command-and-control arrangement overseen by the U.S. Central Command thousands of miles away.

The partners' willingness to do more than provide intelligence information and to root out terrorist cells met with mixed reactions in the United States. While invigorating the NATO alliance was heartening, European offers of military aid appeared to American skeptics as a devious way for them to exercise leverage over military operations in Afghanistan. The Pentagon feared that anything more than a token contribution would lead to interference with the U.S. conduct of the war. And these suspicions had some merit. European willingness to join the American campaign against the Taliban may have been motivated by more than the allies' acceptance of the obligations in Article 5. The European allies may well have hoped to ensure a multilateral response legitimized by the UN that would emphasize commitment to stabilization in Afghanistan over the hunt for Bin Laden.[28]

Nevertheless, overall, U.S. misgivings about European interference were unwarranted. Their contributions were too slight to permit the North Atlantic Council the power it was able to exercise in the Kosovo campaign. The allies did fill gaps in equipment and personnel, consistent with the spirit displayed in the dispatch of NATO AWACs to patrol the Atlantic coast of the United States. Not surprisingly, the more recent NATO allies felt a responsibility to demonstrate their fidelity to the nation that had so vigorously championed their admission to the alliance.

These modest additions to the U.S. arsenal in Afghanistan would fit comfortably into a vision of NATO projected by Pentagon planners under the leadership of Secretary of Defense Donald Rumsfeld and Deputy Secretary Paul Wolfowitz. They evinced a pattern of behavior as old as the North Atlantic Treaty itself. In the first strategic concept of January 1950, the United States would supply the strategic airpower while the European powers would perform the lesser role of supplying ground forces.[29] Although Secretary of State Colin Powell envisioned a more central role for the NATO allies in the common struggle against terrorism and the threats of mass destruction, the Bush administration influenced by Rumsfeld and Vice President Dick Cheney reverted to the unilateral spirit that had prevailed before 9/11.

Planning the Iraq Invasion

The temptation to dispense with allies, demonstrated in Afghanistan, was present from the beginning of the Bush administration with respect to Iraq. The behavior of Saddam Hussein in violating UN sanctions and in preparing weapons of mass destruction had been a problem for the Clinton administration that was not resolved by sporadic bombing of probable sites of illegal arms or of sanctions that were too easily flouted. If Al Qaeda in Afghanistan had to be the primary target after 9/11, this only meant deferment of the Iraq challenge. But not for long. British commentator Michael Binyon observed on September 12, 2001, that the anti-Western leaders of Syria, Libya, and Iraq who had been encouraging verbal or physical attacks might feel the wrath of an aroused America. While Syria and Libya professed to have renounced their terrorist past, "President Saddam Hussein of Iraq may be rejoicing in this mother of all catastrophes, basking in the acclaim of the militants now cheering the outrage in New York." Binyon suggested that "George W. Bush may not now wait for an excuse to complete his father's Gulf War business and bomb the man seen as responsible for backing America's enemies."[30]

This message resonated with the hawks and neoconservatives within the Bush administration. Pentagon official Douglas Feith made the case that even though Saddam Hussein had not "actually conspired in the 9/11 attack," his record suggested that "if left in power he would soon slip out from under the UN sanctions and eventually take aggressive action." Feith speculated that Saddam's long history of working with terrorists made it possible that he would align with Al Qaeda and exploit his weapons of mass destruction.[31]

The president's State of the Union Address of January 2002, in which he specifically linked Iraq with Iran and North Korea as the "axis of evil," should have given the allies an indication of just what direction the administration was taking. NATO was not mentioned in the speech. Deputy Secretary of Defense Wolfowitz amplified the president's message when he attended a Munich conference in early February 2002 to let the Europeans know that NATO was to be shoved aside. The treatment of the allies in the Afghanistan operation was a harbinger of future behavior. Wolfowitz repeated Rumsfeld's point that the mission would determine the coalition in any U.S. military operation. NATO and the UN were not serious partners in these proceedings.[32]

While it was not until the summer that the public language became more bellicose, behind the scenes the Pentagon had been drawing up war plans as early as the fall of 2001. In the spring these plans became more detailed as Secretary Rumsfeld worked with General Franks to develop invasion plans. As James Mann observed, "in the most general sense, the course for military intervention was charted in the spring of 2002, roughly a year before the start of the war." Investigative reporter Bob Woodward suggested that charting a course may have been too modest a description of the administration's activities. On May 19, 2002, General Franks informed the president that if he had a ninety-day time frame, the Central Command could generate an air and ground force invasion that could end the regime within twenty-five days. Franks already had two brigades in Kuwait, and within three weeks he could have a ground force of fifty thousand men. With a "running start," as Rumsfeld observed Franks's plans, there could be two more divisions dispatched to Kuwait within two or three weeks. Pre-positioning troops was "a very smart recommendation by Don and Tommy," as Woodward quoted the president. This was being done so quietly, it did not matter that they left options for war on the table without a final commitment.[33]

By late fall the stealth approach was working: some sixty thousand U.S. troops were in the region. As for funding, some would come from congressional supplemental appropriations for the Afghanistan War and the rest from unused old appropriations. Not only did the Pentagon fail to inform Congress it was reprogramming funds, but that body (ostensibly controlling the purse strings) had no knowledge of impending troop movements until the *Washington Post* and the *New York Times* carried front-page stories in late July 2002.[34]

Unaware of these plans, the European allies had a different perspective on Iraq. Without illusions about Saddam's behavior, they saw him as a secular tyrant without the baggage of an Islamist and certainly without the motives that governed the acts of the terrorists on 9/11. Saddam Hussein's actions in their judgment were confined to controlling Iraq and, as such, posed only a limited threat to the outside world. Unleashing weapons of mass destruction would be fatal for the survival of his regime. Given this mind-set, the Europeans believed he could be deterred by embargoes, no-fly zones, and periodic air strikes from resuming the poison gas attacks upon Iraqi Kurds. The risks of an American-led invasion were not worth the possible consequences. In desperation he might turn on his own people once again. Or a breakup of the country could lead to Turkey's annexing the Kurdish areas while Iran could seize the Shiite heartland of southern Iraq. At this juncture the Iraqis were still some years away from acquiring nuclear capability. UN-sponsored intrusive weapons inspections should contain Saddam Hussein for the time being. Such were the European rationalizations for avoiding a military option.[35]

American critics of the Bush administration, including those from the Republican establishment, shared these sentiments. Countering the utopian neoconservatives were those who claimed the realist mantle of Henry Kissinger. Among them were Brent Scowcroft, and retired generals Norman Schwartzkopf, the Gulf War commander, and Anthony Zinni, head of the Central Command in 2002. Zinni noted that many generals were reluctant to go to war with Iraq when "our relationships in the region are in major disrepair." He worried about the "deep chasm growing between that part of the world and our part of the world." In an indirect swipe at the president and vice president Zinni observed that, whereas the military men wanted to avoid war, "those who never fired a shot in anger" have no such qualms.[36]

General Brent Scowcroft, now seventy-seven years old, had no career to worry about. Speaking from his experience as President Ford's national security adviser, he aired his views on national television and published an impassioned letter in the *Wall Street Journal* on August 16, 2002, warning that an unscrupulous Saddam Hussein might attack Israel again if America went to war. Israel in turn might respond with nuclear weapons, "unleashing an Armageddon in the Middle East" and arousing the Arab street to overthrow America's friends in the Middle East. Rather than rush to war, he urged, the administration should first have the UN insist on returning weapons inspectors to Iraq. If Saddam Hussein "doesn't agree to it, that gives you the *casus belli* we really don't have right now."[37] Scowcroft was not alone in his forebodings. Veterans of the Cold War including a major figure of the older Bush's administration, James A. Baker, shared these concerns.

The reality was that Bush and Cheney, along with Rumsfeld and Wolfowitz, were not listening. Their minds had been made up long before the summer of

2002. Vice President Cheney, arguably the most influential figure in the Bush administration, spoke before the annual convention of the Veterans of Foreign Wars on August 26, 2002, and used the occasion to present the case for "preemptive action" against Iraq. The term was a misnomer; preemption usually means counteraction to forestall an imminent assault. A more accurate term would have been "preventive action," to move before a recognized potential threat could materialize. Before his speech ended, he had come to that conclusion. In essence he was asking for regime change, rather than getting inspectors back to Iraq to identify the weapons of mass destruction (WMDs) that had been prohibited by the UN. He was convinced Saddam Hussein already had them in the form of biological and chemical weapons programs. With nuclear weapons in the near future, Saddam "would then be expected to seek domination of the entire Middle East, take control of the world energy supplies, . . . and subject the United States or any other nation to nuclear blackmail. . . . Therefore the United States would have to take preventive action." Whatever distinction there may have been between "preemptive" and "preventive" war was irretrievably blurred.[38]

The theme of Cheney's address was translated into policy through the National Security Strategy document in September 2002. This paper spoke to the putative idealism of the neoconservative advisers by declaring in its introduction that "Today, humanity holds in its hands the opportunity to further freedom's triumph over all these foes." The paper addressed as well the conviction that the United States would use that opportunity to rid the world of the Iraqi menace: "The United States welcomes our responsibility to lead in this great mission, and we will not hesitate to act alone, if necessary, to exercise our self-defense by acting pre-emptively." This Bush Doctrine seemed to leave no room for the United Nations or for the NATO alliance.[39]

The possibility of a forceful overthrow of Saddam Hussein did not attract national and international attention until the summer of 2002. The administration failed to anticipate public discussion in August 2002, although the articles in the New York Times should have alerted politically astute advisers such as Karl Rove who believed that "nothing much could be accomplished before Labor Day because in August the president is sort of on vacation." White House Chief of Staff Andrew Card added that "from a marketing point of view, you don't introduce new products in August." But differences within the administration between the cautious secretary of state, Colin Powell, and the aggressive vice president, Dick Cheney, were leaked out to make what Powell recalled more "exciting an August" than he had expected. August was made all the more exciting by the contents of the hearings of the Senate Foreign Relations Committee in that month. Republicans joined the chorus of disapproval when Majority Leader Dick Armey felt "it was unbecoming of America's tradition to attack another country without provocation."[40]

What is surprising is that the barrage of broadsides from neoconservative advisers and the known biases of Rumsfeld and Cheney did not alert critics from inside and outside Washington to the direction of U.S. policy before the exposures in the summer of 2002. The two insiders had been linked for years, going back to the Ford administration when Cheney was the president's chief of staff and Rumsfeld was secretary of defense. Cheney had been secretary of defense during the Gulf War, an experience that may have colored his postwar judgments. Both men believed that the dangers from terrorism would not be terminated with the defeat of Saddam Hussein. They also believed that the president's powers were unduly restricted by the wave of reforms in the 1970s that reflected the abuse of power during the Johnson and Nixon presidencies. There should have been enough signals from them and from such neoconservative leaders as William Kristol of the *Weekly Standard* to warn the country that the United States had reverted to a unilateral approach to the world before the flurry of commentaries in July and August. Yet Richard Haas, leaving his post as head of the State Department's policy planning staff in March 2003, claimed that he had been in the dark about the war planning that had preceded July 2002.[41]

The UN Compromise, November 2002

Even though the allies had not been informed of the Bush administration's intentions on Iraq in the first half of 2002, there was enough unease stemming from U.S. unilateralism in Afghanistan and from the belligerence of the president's State of the Union Address to revive old resentments of the United States' behavior toward its NATO partners. As always in the past, France was quick to express its grievances. But in 2002 France was no longer isolated. After July 2002, French public opinion sensed the American appetite for war and was appalled by it. Polls revealed that opposition in France to U.S. and NATO military action rose from 65 in September 2002 to 77 percent in February 2003. Opposition in Russia rose from 79 percent in November 2002 to 87 percent in March 2003. In Britain public approval of Bush's handling of the Iraq issue fell from 30 percent in September 2002 to 19 percent in January 2003.[42]

These figures told just how Europeans felt about what they perceived to be the reckless foreign policies of the Bush administration, illustrating the gap between hard power and soft power, between Mars and Venus.[43] The figures were mirrored in the often contemptuous dismissal of Europeans by the American public. A comparison may be made with the European discontent concerning U.S. leadership a generation before with the projected deployment of medium-range missiles in Europe.

But the German reaction was of a different and more dangerous order than in 1979. Chancellor Gerhard Schroeder's resentment of America's dismissal of Germany's support of the war against Al Qaeda may have contributed to the zeal with which he waved the banner of anti-Americanism in his election campaign of September 2002. There may have been another dimension in his behavior also. It was not just that Schroeder appeared to be losing the election to his conservative challenger; he was trailing badly in the polls. Rather, he sensed an opportunity for Germany to declare its independence from American tutelage. Knowing the mood of the German—and European—public, he could challenge Bush with a statement that Germany would not participate in an Iraq invasion, or join a war even with the United Nations' blessing. Nor would Germany pick up any part of its cost as it had done in the Gulf War.[44]

If this distancing from America had come from a French rather than a German source, it would have elicited far less anger from the Bush administration or from Congress. President Jacques Chirac certainly agreed with Schroeder, when he condemned "attempts to legitimize the unilateral and preemptive use of force." Such sentiments were standard fare in Franco-American relations. But given the American steadfast support for Germany in the Cold War, including Germany's pivotal role in the unification process, it was greeted as a betrayal, all the more so when Bush felt he had a promise that Iraq would be kept out of the German election campaign.[45]

The new element in German behavior was the assertion of a special way—Sonderweg, a German way—of dealing with the world, not just with the United States. Schroeder and his defense minister, Franz Munterfering, were referring to a neutral approach between East and West. But the emotions the Sonderweg aroused inevitably reminded listeners abroad of the German way under the Nazis.[46] The justice minister herself invited unwelcome attention to a German way when she claimed that Bush and Hitler both resorted to aggression abroad in order to divert attention from domestic problems. This was an inflammatory message to send to the world, and particularly to the United States, which prided itself on its patronage of the fledgling German democracy.[47]

The feeling of personal betrayal led to a breach between the president and the chancellor that was only partially papered over when a victorious Schroeder toned down his rhetoric and professed his intentions to respect Germany's obligations to NATO and to the international community. These intentions were extensive, ranging from the U.S. use of German air space and bases to an impending co-command, with the Dutch, of the ISAF in Kabul. These gestures did not appease the Bush administration. Bush snubbed Schroeder the following year, as much for his putative betrayal of trust (unlike Bush's judgment of Russia's Vladimir Putin) as for his past anti-American posture.[48]

Germans now served as a surrogate for West Europeans in general and only confirmed the unilateral direction of the United States' Iraq policy. If the road to war was still not clearly apparent to the NATO allies, it was because of the intervention of Republican critics of Bush policies rather than guile on the part of war hawks to mask their intentions in the wake of the Cheney speech. Most important at this juncture was the role of Secretary of State Colin Powell. A prime mover in the Gulf War as chairman of the Joint Chiefs of Staff, he could not be classified as a dove. Generally in agreement with the administration's effort to oust Saddam Hussein, he opposed military action until all other options had been exhausted and until, in light of his Powell Doctrine, overwhelming military power was in place. He understood that a major element in preparation for invasion would be support from both the NATO allies and the UN Security Council. Key members of both organizations needed to be in harmony with the U.S.-led plan to deal with the Iraqi threat to peace.[49]

Ten days before Cheney's provocative speech, Powell thought he had won agreement to have the UN send weapons inspectors back to Iraq before any unilateral action took place. Powell had been urging this action publicly throughout the year. The president seemingly sided with the secretary when he addressed the UN General Assembly on September 12, 2002, proclaiming that "my nation will work with the U.N. Security Council to meet our common commitments." The one steadfast ally, Britain's prime minister Tony Blair, needed the president's assurance that, if war should follow, it would be to enforce UN resolutions. And the thrust of Bush's address appeared to the allies as being in conformity with their insistence on enhanced inspections to force the Iraqis to give up their WMDs. If so, the allies missed Bush's underlying message that if the Security Council resolutions continue to be violated, both new and old, then "the purposes of the United States should not be doubted. The Security Council resolutions will be enforced, the just demands of peace and security will be met, or action will be unavoidable. And a regime that has lost its legitimacy will also lose its power."[50]

The text of his talk should have been clear to Europe, namely, if this resolution fails to convince Saddam Hussein to change his ways, the United States will have to go to war on the strength of the many Security Council resolutions that Iraq has ignored. Rather than alarming the allies, the president's speech soothed their fears. The United States after all urged expanded inspections, not regime change.

But behind the scenes the Cheney faction was lobbying for more than tough inspections and for warnings that force might be used if Iraq once again evaded compliance. The Pentagon wanted assurance that member states could enforce the resolutions, in effect authorizing unilateral U.S. military intervention. Not surprisingly this approach was unacceptable to France, Russia, and China, countries that at most would tolerate more intrusive inspections. Regime change was obviously the U.S. goal, and the permanent members of the UN Security Council who asserted that Saddam Hussein's full compliance with UN resolutions would be the equivalent would not satisfy the war hawks.[51]

It required eight weeks of negotiations before a compromise resolution (SC 1441) could be produced. European opponents suspicious of U.S. intentions refused to accept anything that would authorize the U.S. use of force against Iraq. The acceptable language warned Iraq of "serious consequences" if they obstructed the inspectors. The United States and Britain for their part could interpret the resolution to mean that if inspections failed they could go to war. The terms of the resolution sounded tough. The document is characterized by phrases such as "final opportunity to comply," or "enhanced inspection regime," or "unimpeded, unconditional, and unrestricted access," but as in most compromises, this strong language obscured the continuing differences within both NATO and the UN Security Council. France led the dissenters in NATO, and they were joined by Russia and China in the UN. Such was the price for unanimous adoption of Resolution 1441 at the 4644th meeting of the Security Council, on November 8, 2002.[52]

The compromise held some promise of rapprochement between the United States and France, if not with Germany. French foreign minister Dominique de Villepin observed that "President Bush's speech is fully compatible with the French position." At a summit meeting in Prague later in November, NATO allies finessed the Iraq problem with elliptical language that enlarged the Atlantic alliance's territorial obligations to what had been out-of-area issues in the past. "Euro-Atlantic" implied more than the territory defined in 1949 as NATO invited seven new countries into the alliance and extended its range to the Baltic nations. In a separate statement on Iraq the heads of state pledged full support for the implementation of SC 1441. They called on Iraq to comply with this "and all relevant Security Council recommendations" or risk facing, as the resolution stated, "serious consequences as a result of its continued violation of its obligations."[53]

The allies' claim to "stand united in their commitment" rang hollow as fissures in the alliance quickly reappeared. The Iraqis helped to widen the gap by the twelve-thousand-page presentation of their weapons program within the required thirty days demanded in Resolution 1441. When the United States denounced this presentation as not just incomplete but another example of Iraq's duplicity, France protested that even if the information was false, this was not enough to justify force. Although the United States felt there was sufficient justification for war, it reluctantly agreed to seek a second resolution, partly to win as much international support as possible but also to appease Prime Minister Blair's critics in Britain.[54]

When the inspectors initially faulted Iraq for its halting cooperation, Iraq seemed to improve its cooperation in early February, enough to blunt U.S. demands. Or so it seemed. Later that month the United States along with Britain and Spain submitted a second resolution declaring that it was time to give meaning to the serious consequences promised under SC 1441. The resolution failed.[55] And given the halfhearted efforts made by the Bush administration on behalf of the resolution, failure was inevitable. It did not matter. The United States was ready to go ahead with war, irrespective of any resolution.

NATO Divided

The onset of war fully exposed the serious divisions within the alliance between France and Germany on one side and the United States and Britain on the other. The smaller allies were similarly divided, although public opinion was as hostile in Spain and Britain as it was in France and Germany. Most of the NATO allies nominally sided with the United States. The new members from central Europe were more articulate in their support than their Western counterparts. They recalled that the United States had been more vigorous than the older allies in bringing them into NATO. Recognition of a pro-American stance on the part of the Poles and Czechs evoked an ill-tempered riposte from President Chirac. He warned in February that their membership in the European Union may be in jeopardy. Chirac was not pleased either with older European partners, such as Denmark, Spain, and Italy for backing the U.S. approach to Iraq without informing France and Germany.[56] The divergent interpretations of SC 1441 grew deeper during the winter of 2003.

U.S. behavior was no less provocative. Trading insults took childish forms in the United States when French fries served in the congressional restaurant were renamed "freedom fries." But there was nothing childish about Schroeder's increasingly strident defiance of the United States. The chancellor made it clear that under no circumstances would Germany vote for any resolution in the UN that justified a resort to war. The French went farther. As a permanent member of the UN Security Council, France enlarged on the German position. On the assumption that Resolution 1441 authorized only more intensive inspections, Chirac not only threatened to veto any UN resolution that permitted military action but lobbied other council members to join the opposition. He succeeded. Traditionally friendly Latin American allies Mexico and Chile would not line up with the United States.[57]

The NATO atmosphere had become toxic as France and Germany in North Atlantic Council meetings celebrated the fortieth anniversary of the de Gaulle–Adenauer Elysée treaty of January 21, 1963, and emphasized its anti-American character. Nominally, it was Turkey's invoking Article 4 of the treaty that made NATO a war zone separating the United States and its friends in the East from the Franco-German entente, with Belgium frequently joining its neighbors. The issue presumably was how the allies would respond to an Iraqi attack against Turkey in the event of a war. This was essentially a bogus issue. Contingency planning was a constant preoccupation at SHAPE, and Turkey's exposed position neighboring both the Soviet Union and the volatile Middle East made it a major focus. Not that Turkey welcomed a war with Iraq. Its people were as opposed to U.S. intervention as was public opinion among the European allies. The Turkish government worried about the effect of war on its own restless Kurdish population. But the United States precipitated conflict with France and Germany by demanding formal NATO approval of defensive aid to Turkey. This was an occasion for France and Germany to oppose any aid, judging that it was just an excuse to rally NATO behind an American invasion.[58]

The result was increased acrimony in NATO, which spilled out into the public square. While the European street continued to oppose war plans with support from much of the international press, the Americans received strong backing not just from Britain's Blair but also from Secretary General George Robertson, who had been an aggressive lobbyist for the reluctant allies' improving their military capabilities. Initially, he did not press for NATO action on Turkey, recognizing the depth of Franco-German opposition, but once the United States formally placed Turkey on the agenda on January 17, 2003, he sided with the Americans. But Robertson failed to gain consensus within the NAC.[59]

It was at this point that Turkey used Article 4 to force the allies to give center stage to its requests for aid. The result was open confrontation in the NAC, with the United States rather than Turkey leading the charge. Turkey's reticence reflected ambivalence over an impending war. Robertson resolved the conflict by utilizing the Defense Planning Committee (DPC) as the venue for further discussion. Since France had not been a member of this committee since its departure from SHAPE in 1966, the secretary general and the United States managed to approve Turkey's requests under the rubric of Article 4, even though Belgium's protests and Turkey's uneasiness made NATO's position somewhat less than persuasive as an agent of the U.S. drive for war. It took six emergency meetings over an eleven-day period before NATO overcame the deadlock on February 19, 2003.[60]

How meaningful was this success in NATO? If the U.S. "victory" over France in the DPC had signified a clear NATO stance in favor of war, it might have made a difference in the UN Security Council. France remained determined to oppose war under any circumstance. The most that the United States could achieve in the UN was to isolate its adversarial ally for vetoing a second resolution specifically authorizing military action. Was mobilizing the majority of NATO allies against France worth the effort? Russia, after all, had no intention of accepting the resolution. For that matter, the United States itself only pressed for a resolution in order to satisfy Blair, whose position on the side of the Americans was unpopular with the British public and with the left wing of his own party. It should have been clear to all observers that a new resolution never stood a chance of passage. And from the American perspective, no resolution was necessary; SC 1441 was enough to justify the invasion of Iraq.

It was not NATO and the UN that were at loggerheads in 2003. The struggle was within NATO itself, and it was played out in the UN as France with the support of Germany and the publics of all the allies railed against war. Philip Gordon and Jeremy Shapiro pointed out that only Nelson Mandela had ever received the applause enjoyed by France's foreign minister, Dominique de Villepin, for his vehement antiwar statement before the Security Council on February 14, 2003.[61] Turkey seemed to join the antiwar consensus on March 1, when its parliament denied the United States permission to launch an attack on Iraq from Turkish soil. On March 5, France, joined by Germany and Russia, declared that it would not accept any UN resolution that authorized the use of force.[62] But the most provocative statement was supplied by President Chirac when he announced on television on March 10, 2003, that France would veto any automatic step toward war, "whatever the circumstances, because France believes this evening that there is no reason to make war to reach the objective we have given ourselves, the disarmament of Iraq." President Bush on television, following a meeting in the Azores with Blair and the Iberian foreign ministers, announced a forty-eight-hour ultimatum demanding that Saddam Hussein surrender or face an invasion.[63] The invasion began two days later, on March 19, 2003.

Rapprochement: NATO, UN, and the United States

The spring of 2003 was a season of triumph for the United States. Everything turned out just as the Pentagon, the neocons, and the president had anticipated. The Iraqis were quickly defeated without the Middle East bursting into flames, neither on the Arab street nor in the oilfields. The Turks did not occupy Kurdish Iraq and the Iranians did not push into southeastern Iraq. Unlike in the Gulf War, Saddam Hussein fired no missiles at Israel and Saudi Arabia. Victory was won with even fewer fatalities than were suffered in 1991. Small wonder that President Bush, in the full flight regalia of a navy pilot, flew onto the deck of the aircraft carrier *Abraham Lincoln* on May 1, 2003, where a banner proclaimed "mission accomplished."[64]

Only a few months later, this sense of easy victory justifying U.S. unilateralism had dissipated, however. Not only did the United States appear to be trapped into the kind of quagmire reminiscent of the Vietnam War but there was increasing recognition among critics on both sides of the Atlantic that the enemy was primarily in Afghanistan, where the Taliban had not been wholly defeated and Osama bin Laden remained free, across the border in Pakistan. These perceptions were underscored by the ultimate recognition that Saddam Hussein's weapons of mass destruction did not exist. Resistance from Sunni insurgents, increasing even after the capture of the Iraqi president, combined with the majority Shiites to oppose U.S. domination. "Liberation" by the summer of 2003 had turned into an occupation that led to increasing numbers of U.S. casualties as the contending parties in Iraq—Sunni, Shiite, and Kurd—failed to produce a stable regime. Ironically, Al Qaeda, which had not been a factor in prewar Iraq, became a magnet for radical Arabs in the region.

Predictably, European opponents of the war and of American unilateralism enjoyed some Schadenfreude over the deflating of U.S. triumphalism. And they certainly made their feelings known, with the full approval of their publics. But this reversal of fortune on the part of the United States did not drive America out of NATO or the UN. Nor did either of those organizations turn their backs on the United States and leave the country to stew in its own juices in Iraq. Too much was at stake. The United States may have blundered badly, but it was still the most important member of the UN and the most influential ally in NATO. Nor could either organization ignore the potential consequences of chaos in Iraq. The fears of an Armageddon, not realized in the spring of 2003, could become a reality in the following years. By the end of 2003 both organizations were cautiously engaged in supporting the United States in Iraq. Yet reconciliation was not easily achieved. Neither Germany nor France would send troops to Iraq or underwrite the cost of the war, as they had in 1991.[65]

What was surprising was neither the lingering transatlantic animosity over the U.S. intervention in Iraq without explicit UN authorization, nor the divisions within NATO that remained unresolved. Rather, it was the willingness of both organizations to be involved in the reconstruction of the country. In the UN, this process began only three weeks after Bush's victory celebration and before the guerrilla war that cast such a pall over the initial successes. On May 22, 2003, the Security Council adopted with only one abstention Resolution 1483, lifting the economic sanctions on Iraq that had been imposed in 1990. All prohibitions against trade with Iraq and provision of financial and economic resources were removed. Exports of petroleum and natural gas could be in the market once again. In short, the Security Council was using the removal of the Saddam Hussein regime to normalize relations with a reformed Iraq.[66]

In August 2003 the Security Council welcomed the formation of a broadly representative governing council as a step toward a fully representative government and established a UN Assistance Mission in Iraq (UNAMI) to support the secretary-general's implementation of the charges that had been identified in Resolution 1483.[67] As the security situation deteriorated in the fall of 2003, the Security Council's Resolution 1511 "*authorizes* a multinational force under a unified command" to contribute to the mission of the UNAMI. The resolution included military forces. This resolution also noted the convocation of an international donors' conference in Madrid on October 23–24, 2003, to pledge resources for the reconstruction of Iraq's economic infrastructure.[68]

Irrespective of the UN's opposition to the U.S. invasion, these were substantial measures of involvement in the future of postwar Iraq. The death of the senior UN administrator, Sergio Vieira de Mello, in a terrorist bombing on August 19, 2003, that killed seventeen and wounded more than one hundred at Baghdad's UN headquarters, resulted in the withdrawal of most UN personnel. Yet the incident did not terminate UN's support for the transitional government and, by implication, for the continued U.S. efforts to suppress both the Sunni insurgency and the pro-Iranian Shiite militias. While the UN mandates would be reviewed periodically, the Security Council extended its sponsorship of UNAMI in the following year.[69]

NATO was more reticent than the UN in identifying with the United States in Iraq. The divisions were too deep to have healed by the time of the June 2003 ministerial meeting of the NAC. The final communiqué did note that the alliance had ended its deployment of surveillance aircraft and missile systems to defend Turkey against any possible attack from Iraq. Given the speed and efficiency of the initial U.S.-led coalition, this could not have been a major issue for the allies. Still, they felt the need to say that the ministers "consulted regularly during the Iraq crisis, including in keeping with the Alliance's role under Article 4 of the Washington Treaty."[70] There was little enthusiasm in this announcement.

More significantly, the allies gave their blessing to Poland's request for support in the role it was playing in the stabilization of Iraq. NATO's military were working with Polish officials in meeting their requirements, and the NAC planned to review NATO's contribution to the stabilization efforts "on a regular basis." In a terse but significant paragraph, the allies welcomed the UN Security Council's adoption of Resolution 1483 normalizing relations with post-Saddam Iraq and were looking for ways to help implement it.[71]

But the Iraq issue, vital as it was to the alliance's future, was not the major concern of the communiqué. Much more space was given to NATO's role in the Balkans, in its struggle against terrorism, and in its increasingly close relations with the EU. Iraq was still too sensitive and the differences still too lively for NATO to take the modest steps toward involvement in Iraq as were taken by the United Nations. Some movement toward rapprochement between the United States and Britain on one side and France and Germany on the other was in progress, but it was limited.

NATO's tone was somewhat warmer a year later when the NAC at its summit meeting in Istanbul issued a special statement on Iraq endorsing "the formation of an interim Government of Iraq," authorized in Security Council Resolution 1546, as another important step in the rehabilitation of the country. That statement gave a backhanded approval of U.S. efforts in Iraq, awkwardly phrased, by its continued support of Poland's leadership of the multinational division in Iraq: "We also acknowledge the efforts of nations, including many NATO allies, in the Multinational Force for Iraq, which is present in Iraq at the request of the Iraqi government and in accordance with UNSCR 1546." NATO's role, unlike the UN presence, was only elliptically identified. Six months later, NAC's comment from Brussels was considerably stronger on behalf of Iraq's sovereignty: "Consistent with UNSC resolution 1546, all 26 Allies are contributing to the NATO mission to assist in training Iraqi security forces."[72]

NATO's continued advocacy of a stable Iraqi government was evident in the Defense Committee's communiqué in June 2006 but was always accompanied by the caveat that its welcome and support had to be consistent with UN Security Council resolutions. NATO's language hardly constituted a whole-hearted endorsement of the United States' war against dissidents or its management of Iraq's political and economic reconstruction. As the text noted, aid to Iraqi security forces would be arranged through training "in or out of the country." The reluctant Germans and French would not allow any of their military to be involved in training Iraqis inside Iraq.[73]

Had the war turned out differently, the United States might have been as dismissive and contemptuous of allied assistance as it had been in Afghanistan in 2001 or in Iraq prior to March 2003. As it was, the Bush administration backed off from its unilateral stance when the Iraqi operation required far more resources than the Americans had anticipated. The United States needed both allied support and the UN provenance. It received some measure from both organizations, more from the UN than from NATO, although NATO backing was the more important at this juncture. As early as July 2003 Senator Joseph R. Biden (D-DE) spoke in favor of a Senate resolution urging the Bush administration to seek help from NATO allies in order to reduce the U.S. military presence and its attending costs in Iraq.[74] This advice was heeded—with mixed feelings on all sides.

As the United States stepped up its efforts to internationalize the occupation of Iraq, it received by the end of July 2003 at least a commitment from twenty-eight countries to send soldiers and personnel to Iraq augmenting the 146,000 U.S. and 11,000 British troops in the country.[75] The United States wanted as much NATO involvement as it could get, but not to the extent of converting the Iraq venture into a NATO operation. The allies shared that position, at the same time as NATO wanted some check on U.S. unilateralism. Nor could the United States allow the NATO flag to fly under a UN umbrella, no matter how important this was for the legitimacy the UN could confer. Many of the allies would have preferred this arrangement. By the end of the Bush administration, the wounds within NATO were not yet healed. Neither Iraq nor Afghanistan was free of conflict, and in Iraq few soldiers from the allied powers remained in the country. In

2009, the burden of constructing a stable Iraqi democracy remains a challenge for the United States and the Iraqi government.

Into the Future

Despite the conflicts within NATO and between the United States and the United Nations over Iraq, in the twenty-first century new linkages have been fashioned among international organizations that embraced NATO, the UN, the EU, and the OSCE in Iraq and Afghanistan as well as in the Balkans. These organizations were all involved for the most part in positive relationships in the Kosovo province of Serbia over the past ten years. There the OSCE took the responsibility for supervising elections of the provisional government that had been established in 2001. The KFOR, the U.S.-led NATO force under a UN mandate that maintained peace following the removal of Serb military, increasingly shared responsibility with the EU in Kosovo, much as SFOR did in Bosnia.[76] All of these activities functioned under the guidance of the UN. That the UN remained the principal player was confirmed in October 2005 when the Security Council supported the secretary-general's intention to start the political process that would determine the future status of Kosovo "as foreseen in Council Resolution 1244 (1999)."[77] The end product, still challenged by Belgrade in 2009, was independence for Kosovo in 2008.

The UN took rightful pride in bringing together regional organizations in the service of its goals. The secretary-general always included NATO as a regional organization, even though NATO's reach in Afghanistan as well as in Iraq extended far beyond its original "region." NATO itself took over the command and control of ISAF in August 2003 under the continuing UN mandate.[78] Before this transfer of responsibility took place, the Security Council "took note that increased involvement of NATO would be within the context of the UN mandate of ISAF and that the alliance would operate according to current and future Security Council resolutions and in close consultation with the Afghan Interim Authority, as well as with the Special Representative of the Secretary-General."[79] This was a clear signal of the UN's ultimate authority, but it was also a signal of the UN's insecurity in the face of NATO's dominant military presence in that country.

There was good reason for doubts about the subordination of NATO (and particularly of its most powerful member) to the world organization. Although a letter from Jaap de Hoop Scheffer, Robertson's successor as NATO's secretary general, dutifully attached a quarterly report of ISAF's operations to the UN secretary-general for submission to the Security Council, this was only pro forma submission of NATO to the authority of the UN. More significant was the NATO's defense ministers' statement in 2006 that, while there would be "close coordination," the missions of ISAF and the U.S. Operation Enduring Freedom "will remain distinct."[80]

As a new president assumed office in the United States in 2009, Afghanistan was the most serious engagement in the U.S. and NATO war on the radical Islamic elements threatening the international community. Notwithstanding the diplomatic language of communiqués, with their promise of NATO's commitment "to continuing our close cooperation and coordination with the United Nations, the European Union, and other international institutions and the international community at large" in bringing peace and security to Afghanistan, too many of the familiar conflicts within NATO still plagued all its members.[81] The United Nations continued to assert its authority over both NATO and U.S. operations but was forced to recognize the limitations imposed by its lack of military power. By having to delegate to presumably inferior bodies, as the UN was compelled to do explicitly in 1993 and implicitly in too many instances, the world organization undercut its control over the regional organizations.

The most prominent challenge in 2009 is the resurgence of the Taliban in Afghanistan. The war there is being waged primarily in the south and along the Pakistan border, but despite the presence of German and French troops in the north and in the capital, their governments have confined their activities to non-combat functions. The burden of fighting and the consequent suffering of casualties has been borne primarily by the United States and Britain and to a lesser extent by Canada and the Netherlands. Inevitably, this has led to tensions that no amount of rhetoric can conceal. The Americans have been rebuffed repeatedly by their European allies. The most that Germany and France will offer are military trainers embedded with Afghan units as long as those units are not in combat areas. Both Canada and the Netherlands, which also have troops in the danger zones, are facing pressure to bring their troops home.[82]

When the U.S. commander of ISAF left his post in June 2008, he offered a sober assessment of the situation in Afghanistan. U.S. forces, augmented by Marine battalions, increased from thirty-six thousand in early 2007 to fifty-two thousand in 2008, but he deemed these numbers insufficient to cope with the increasing power of the Taliban. A dysfunctional government in Pakistan, unable or unwilling to cope with Taliban allies on its territory, was making the situation all the worse.[83] But the larger problem is that the solidarity of NATO is being threatened by the unequal burdens assumed by the major allies. As Paul Cornish of the Royal Institute of International Affairs put it in December 2007: "What you're seeing is some member states of NATO saying 'we're part of this mission, and we want the overall thing to achieve its goal but we won't take the risk that others are taking'; that is divisive and it's corrosive at the heart of NATO."[84] As NATO wrestled with these internal problems, the UN stood above the fray. In the mutually accepted table of organization, the UN remained the authority in charge of stabilizing Afghanistan. In reality, the UN appeared to be irrelevant in the war against the Taliban and in the resolution of intra-NATO problems.

Tensions within NATO were not confined to Afghanistan. The Franco-German caveats applied to Iraq as well, and even more openly in light of their opposition to the U.S. invasion. And while NATO applauded the efforts of the European Union to develop its military capability, there remains an underlying concern that the EU, centered on a Franco-German relationship, would both perform too many redundant tasks and in the long run challenge the authority of the older organization. The UN persists on playing the role, not always credibly, of senior partner, but the Security Council has two veto-wielding permanent members whose interests do not always converge with NATO's—and certainly not with those of the United States. Russia's endorsement of Serbia's rejection of an independent Kosovo in 2008 suggests that the alliance can expect further quarrels in the UN over the Balkans and other disputed areas in the future. Russia's conflict with Georgia in August 2008 was an example of challenges NATO will continue to face.

But on balance, the positive links between the UN and NATO could outweigh the negative, just as the common interests of the NATO allies should be able to bridge the internal gaps. Beyond Afghanistan the allies have displayed their ability to work together in Bosnia in a way projected as early as January 1994 when at its summit meeting in Brussels NATO agreed to endorse the concept of the Combined Joint Task Forces (CJTF) that would allocate NATO military assets to the emerging EU, for European problems that need not involve the NATO as an institution.[85] The spirit of CJTF resided in NATO's decision to conclude the SFOR operation in Bosnia in 2004 by turning over the responsibility of deploying "a new and distinct UN-mandated robust Chapter VII mission in the country" to both the European Union forces (EUFOR) and a NATO presence in Sarajevo. A letter from the chairman of the presidency of Bosnia Herzegovina on November 10, 2004, confirmed acceptance of the two complementary entities "as the legal successors of the NATO-SFOR mission and mandate." NATO had given its blessing to this linkage at its Istanbul summit in June 2004.[86]

The division of labor between NATO and EU was evident in NATO's assets employed in Operation Concordia in Macedonia from March to December 2003 and Operation Althea in Bosnia after December 2004. The range of cooperation extended beyond Europe to aiding the African Union in Darfur and the UN mission (UNAMA) in Afghanistan. Although the CJTF seemingly had failed in the 1990s, as France intended to use NATO assets without gaining approval from NATO headquarters, by 1993 the so-called Berlin-Plus arrangements, completed in 1993 between NATO and the EU, were in place. These arrangements permitted the EU to operate with NATO resources in Africa while NATO chose not to be involved.[87]

A negative prognosis for the future of both NATO and the UN as well as the relationship between them would be understandable. Whether NATO can properly be identified in the twenty-first century as a "regional" entity, given its current range of operations, is questionable. Stability has not been achieved either in Afghanistan or in Iraq in 2009. Nor has the terrorism associated with Al Qaeda been eradicated. Deep divisions within NATO remain unresolved, and the lines demarcating the respective authority of NATO and the UN are still blurred. The competition between NATO and the EU remains barely under the surface. But the destructive passions of the past ten years have cooled, and NATO has joined with the EU and the OSCE in seeking ways of working more effectively with the world organization. Ties are now more intimate—if not always more cordial— between NATO and the UN. A joint declaration of NATO-UN cooperation on the secretariat level in September 2008 suggests that there is more optimism about future relations between them than there was at the beginning of the millennium.[88] But given the sensitivity of the links between the UN and NATO, the UN secretariat urged NATO not to publicize the agreement. Even so, "the quiet signing" caused the Russian foreign minister to accuse Ban Ki-moon in October 2008 of acting without proper consultation with members of the UN Security Council. Objection notwithstanding, the document signaled to both organizations that "cooperation and coordination are desirable and necessary—something that has not always been clear in the past."[89]

10

Summation

The perceptive Dutch scholar Dick Leurdijk observed in 1994 that, "in the good old days of the Cold War," the UN and NATO co-existed but "lived apart," linked merely by mutual references in official texts. He judged that the "two organizations represented rather different worlds, political cultures and schools of thought."[1] Only after the end of the Cold War did problems of crisis management, notably in the former Yugoslavia, force the two organizations into a new and close relationship.

There is no disputing that the UN Security Council's intervention in the Balkans changed the connections after 1991. The UN needed NATO and European regional arrangements in order to implement the flurry of resolutions on the Balkan crises. But the mutual dependence in subsequent crises in Afghanistan and Iraq in the next dozen years revived and deepened rifts between NATO and the UN that went back to the origins of the Atlantic alliance. These rifts centered on the question of authority. Would NATO replace the United Nations as the guarantor of international peace and security in Europe? This question in turn devolved on the ambiguous role NATO was playing as a regional organization under the aegis of the UN.

This issue has plagued the alliance from its beginnings. How to bring NATO into harmony with the charter of the UN, its professed objective in Article 7 of the treaty, without subjecting it to the jurisdiction of the UN Security Council was a difficult task for the framers of the North Atlantic Treaty in 1949. The treaty's very purpose was to further the aims of the UN Charter without allowing the Soviet Union to have access to activities designed to deter communist aggression against the allies. Propelled by such supporters of the UN as Senator Vandenberg, NATO was required to conform to the UN's principles without compromising the defense of its members from one of the permanent members of the UN Security Council.

The elliptical language of Article 5 of the treaty illustrated the alliance's dilemma. It claimed the right of collective self-defense, based on Article 51 of the UN Charter, without mentioning Chapter 8, which placed the activities of regional agencies under the scrutiny of the Security Council. But a little-noticed second paragraph of the treaty's Article 5 pays homage to the Security Council's authority, by agreeing that "any such armed attack and all measures taken as a result thereof shall immediately be reported to the Security Council." The article also noted that NATO's "measures shall be terminated when the Security Council has taken the measures necessary to restore and maintain international peace and security." While these sentences reflect deference to the Security Council, they also invite a broad construction of just how effective Security Council measures would have to be before a report was issued. Very likely the treaty's framers expected that the final paragraph would be set aside as an afterthought. Certainly, the allies customarily behaved as if reporting to the Security Council was unnecessary, on the assumption that it would be unlikely to take the "necessary measures."

By contrast, the European Union had none of these obstacles to collaboration with the United Nations. It was clearly a regional organization, and it accepted the supremacy of the UN without the reservations, hesitations, and resentments projected by NATO. The EU enjoyed a status in the UN General Assembly that NATO never had—or wanted—in the past. Although NATO has sought links with the UN since the 1990s in non–Article 5 areas, it encountered suspicion from those members who have identified the alliance as a creature of the United States, whose military objectives were not aligned with those of the UN's Third World majority.[2]

Concern about the risk of excessive submission to the UN dictated caution in dealing with the world organization. Its military collaboration in the Bosnian crisis was a case in point. NATO would use its military assets on behalf of UN objectives on a case-by-case basis. Connections on the staff level encouraged NATO in the summer of 2005 to propose a memo of understanding that would create a framework for dialogue and cooperation. The proposal still had not won approval from the General Assembly by the time Kofi Annan left office. But his successor as secretary-general, the Korean diplomat Ban Ki-moon, signed a joint declaration on UN/NATO secretariat cooperation on September 23, 2008. Although he requested that the agreement be "kept low key," it opens the way for a new relationship between the two organizations.[3]

The two organizations complement each other in many ways. Basically, NATO has capabilities that the UN lacks, not only in its military capacities but also in its extensive experience with multilateral military operations. When the UN Charter was framed in 1944, it had included a military dimension in Article 47 that was intended to enforce collective security. But the nationalist propensities of the superpowers, arguably more than the outbreak of the Cold War, prevented implementation of this article. Yet the need for a military arm in the UN was demonstrated repeatedly as its resolutions failed to influence actions of aggressors.

For NATO the UN provides the legitimacy it had always felt it needed even as it evaded or opposed UN policies. This hunger for legitimacy is clearly reflected in many of the articles of the North Atlantic Treaty that tried to embed the pact in the body of the charter. While the two organizations seemed to have had separate existences, as Leurdijk noted, NATO was always aware of the UN's importance. Whenever possible NATO tried to use the UN—as it did, unsuccessfully, in the Soviet actions against Hungary in 1956 and, more successfully, in opposing the Soviet invasion of Afghanistan in 1979—as a vehicle for condemning the Soviets for violating the terms of the charter. In the post–Cold War 1990s the alliance was grateful for the UN's tacit approval of military action against Serbia over Kosovo. Although the U.S. invasion of Iraq in 2003 won no blessing from a divided UN, the world organization quickly made its presence felt in the reconstruction of Iraq—in fact, more quickly and in better spirit than was shown by many in the NATO alliance. The smooth transition of ISAF in Afghanistan in 2003 from a UN entity to a NATO operation was in marked contrast to the UN's grudging yielding of control of UNPROFOR to IFOR in Bosnia in 1995.

The NATO allies also valued the UN as an arena in which to thrash out internal problems. There was high drama in the UN when two leading NATO allies, Britain and France, were on the dock, condemned by both the United States and the Soviet Union for their failed campaign to reoccupy the Suez Canal in 1956. Four years later Belgium was the object of reprobation by the UN, prodded by the Soviets, for its interference in the affairs of the newly freed Congo. On this occasion, as over Suez, the allies were divided although the United States did its best to appease both the UN and its Belgian ally. In that same decade, it was the United States that was isolated both in the UN and in NATO as the Vietnam War expanded after 1965. The UN was no more able to offer successful mediation than were America's allies in NATO. In all these cases the UN was a factor in NATO councils even when it was not the final arbiter of the outcome of the conflicts.

While Kurt Waldheim and Kofi Annan were more submissive to U.S. and NATO assertiveness, Dag Hammarskjöld and Boutros Boutros-Ghali were less resigned to their limited powers over NATO. But even as the two organizations lived apart during the Cold War, the peacekeeping mechanisms that grew out of the Suez crisis were not only a measure of UN influence over NATO but also a service to the allies. Hammarskjöld's deft handling of the Suez crisis set a precedent that was useful in subsequent confrontations between the organizations, ranging from the Congo to Afghanistan. The United States and the Soviet Union were both beneficiaries of UN involvement in Cold War conflicts. Just as the United States was pleased to have the imprimatur of the UN bestowed on U.S.– North Vietnamese peace negotiations in 1973, Mikhail Gorbachev welcomed the introduction of UN observers in 1989 to help end the ill-fated Soviet intervention in Afghanistan.

The post–Cold War world of the past two decades reveals the mutual dependency of NATO and the UN without resolving the critical question of authority. In fact, the issue of supremacy flared more dramatically after the Cold War. Resentment of the advantages NATO's superior military strength had over the limited muscle of the UN was never more evident than in Boutros-Ghali's surrender of power to NATO in Bosnia in 1995. His animus was directed against the United States whose overbearing weight in NATO marginalized the UN's role in the Dayton agreements. To a lesser extent, in keeping with a very different temperament, Kofi Annan deplored NATO's behavior in the Kosovo campaign in 1999, even as he understood its motives.

There was a marked contrast between the roles that the NATO secretary general played during and after the Cold War. While the UN secretary-general could speak forcefully and often effectively for his organization, the NATO secretary general emerged simply as a chairman of an often divided North Atlantic Council dominated by the United States. He was not the equivalent of the UN secretary-general. Nor could the NATO secretary general, often a European civilian leader of a smaller member, compete on equal terms with the American supreme allied commander or with such dominating figures from the United States and France as Robert McNamara or Charles de Gaulle. When the Soviet empire collapsed and new challenges threatened the world's peace and security, NATO's leaders became more visible and more significant figures. The forceful interventions of Manfred Woerner and Willy Claes in the Bosnian conflicts of the mid-1990s and of Javier Solana in the Kosovo War in 1999 reflected their new status vis-à-vis the UN secretaries-general Boutros-Ghali and Kofi Annan as well as the enhanced power of NATO itself.[4]

The question as to how much deference NATO owes to the UN's supremacy as the primary guarantor of global peace and security remains open to debate today. Conceivably, the European Union, with its organic ties to the UN, might be a bridge between the two organizations. The numerous professions of solidarity with the EU that are present in abundance in NATO communiqués suggest the potential for successful mediation, whereby NATO could be an arm of the UN without sacrificing its own autonomy. Informally, NATO is serving in this capacity in Africa in 2009.

The EU may also be an obstacle to further curbing the UN's authority by virtue of the presence of NATO's leading European partners' possessing veto power in the UN Security Council. There has always been a strain of resentment against the dominant voice of the superpower on the North Atlantic Council. If NATO should be wholly free from the UN's supervision, France and Britain would continue to occupy an inferior place in the alliance. By supporting the Security Council's prerogatives, they would be able to elevate their own status as genuine equals of the United States, and even be able to challenge it on the world stage in company with the other permanent members, Russia and China.

The UN General Assembly imposed its own barrier to NATO integration. As David Yost has observed, the establishment of a Department of Peacekeeping Operations (DPO) in 2007 opened the possibility of freeing the UN from the military sustenance NATO had provided over the past decade.[5] The DPO, with ninety thousand troops, quickly developed into the largest UN agency. France could claim credit for proposing an operational level of commanding peacekeeping, modeled on the UN Interim Force that was adopted in the summer of 2006 in Lebanon. This new department could lessen UN dependence on NATO's military capabilities.

The torrent of negative commentary on the alliance, as NATO was riven with dissent over Iraq and bogged down in Afghanistan since 2004, has raised the prospect of a marginalized organization, dissolving through irrelevance if not through disintegration. One well-informed critic felt that NATO deserved the derision inspired by Lord Salisbury's judgment of Britain's policy on the Eastern question in 1877: "The commonest error in politics is sticking to the carcass of dead policies." Anticipation of NATO's imminent demise has a long history, exemplified by Ronald Steel's *End of the Alliance,* published in 1964. Yet the current French and German rapprochement with the United States as well as the East European members' continuing allegiance to the alliance attest to its continuing relevance.[6]

For service to the UN, NATO remains the one international organization that has experience in managing military forces. Notwithstanding the built-in conflict over NATO's autonomy within the UN, both sides recognize a space for what Alan Henrikson has called a "nonallergic" relationship. He saw positive connections after the Cold War: "Though not exactly Siamese twins, they have come to depend on each other symbiotically." While it is unlikely that NATO will morph comfortably into the subordinate regional role of the EU, a symbiotic relationship with the UN remains relevant, if not permanent, in the twenty-first century.[7]

APPENDIX A

UN Charter

Extracts from the Charter of the United Nations

San Francisco, 26th June, 1945

WE, the peoples of the United Nations, determined—
to save succeeding generations from the scourge of war, which twice in our lifetime has brought untold sorrow to mankind, and
to reaffirm faith in fundamental human rights, in the dignity and worth of the human person, in the equal rights of men and women and of nations large and small, and
to establish conditions under which justice and respect for the obligations arising from treaties and other sources of international law can be maintained, and
to promote social progress and better standards of life in larger freedom, and for these ends—
to practise tolerance and live together in peace with one another as good neighbours, and
to unite our strength to maintain international peace and security, and
to ensure, by the acceptance of principles and the institution of methods, that armed force shall not be used, save in the common interest, and
to employ international machinery for the promotion of the economic and social advancement of all peoples,
have resolved to combine our efforts to accomplish these aims.
Accordingly, our respective Governments, through representatives assembled in the city of San Francisco, who have exhibited their full powers found to be in good and due form, have agreed to the present Charter of the United Nations and do hereby establish an international organisation to be known as the United Nations.

Chapter 1.—Purposes and Principles

ARTICLE 1

The Purposes of the United Nations are: —

1. To maintain international peace and security, and to that end: to take effective collective measures for the prevention and removal of threats to the peace, and for the suppression of acts of aggression or other breaches of the peace, and to bring about by peaceful means, and in conformity with the principles of justice and international law, adjustment or settlement of international disputes or situations which might lead to a breach of the peace;

2. To develop friendly relations among nations based on respect for the principle of equal rights and self-determination of peoples, and to take other appropriate measures to strengthen universal peace;

3. To achieve international co-operation in solving international problems of an economic, social, cultural, or humanitarian character, and in promoting and encouraging respect for human rights and for fundamental freedoms for all without distinction as to race, sex, language, or religion; and

4. To be a centre for harmonising the actions of nations in the attainment of these common ends.

ARTICLE 2

The Organisation and its Members, in pursuit of the Purposes stated in Article 1, shall act in accordance with the following Principles: —

1. The Organisation is based on the principle of the sovereign equality of all its Members.

2. All Members, in order to ensure to all of them the rights and benefits resulting from membership, shall fulfil in good faith the obligations assumed by them in accordance with the present Charter.

3. In making recommendations under this Article the Security Council should also take into consideration that legal disputes should as a general rule be referred by the parties to the International Court of Justice in accordance with the provisions of the Statute of the Court.

ARTICLE 37

1. Should the parties to a dispute of the nature referred to in Article 33 fail to settle it by the means indicated in that Article, they shall refer it to the Security Council.

2. If the Security Council deems that the continuance of the dispute is in fact likely to endanger the maintenance of international peace and security, it shall

decide whether to take action under Article 36 or to recommend such terms of settlement as it may consider appropriate.

* * *

Chapter VII.—Action with Respect to Threats to the Peace,
Breaches of the Peace, and Acts of Aggression

ARTICLE 39

The Security Council shall determine the existence of any threat to the peace, breach of the peace, or act of aggression, and shall make recommendations, or decide what measures shall be taken in accordance with Articles 41 and 42 to maintain or restore international peace and security.

ARTICLE 40

In order to prevent an aggravation of the situation, the Security Council may, before making the recommendations or deciding upon the measures provided for in Article 39, call upon the parties concerned to comply with such provisional measures as it seems necessary or desirable. Such provisional measures shall be without prejudice to the rights, claims or position of the parties concerned. The Security Council shall duly take account of failure to comply with such provisional measures.

ARTICLE 41

The Security Council may decide what measures not involving the use of armed force are to be employed to give effect to its decisions, and it may call upon the Members of the United Nations to apply such measures. These may include complete or partial interruption of economic relations and of rail, sea, air, postal, telegraphic, radio and other means of communication, and the severance of diplomatic relations.

ARTICLE 42

Should the Security Council consider that measures provided for in Article 41 would be inadequate or have proved to be inadequate, it may take such action by air, sea or land forces as may be necessary to maintain or restore international peace and security. Such action may include demonstrations, blockade and other operations by air, sea or land forces of Members of the United Nations.

ARTICLE 43

1. All Members of the United Nations, in order to contribute to the maintenance of international peace and security, undertake to make available to the Security Council, on its call and in accordance with a special agreement or agreements, armed forces, assistance and facilities, including rights of passage, necessary for the purpose of maintaining international peace and security.

2. Such agreement or agreements shall govern the numbers and types of forces, their degree of readiness and general location, and the nature of the facilities and assistance to be provided.

3. The agreement or agreements shall be negotiated as soon as possible on the initiative of the Security Council. They shall be concluded between the Security Council and Members or between the Security Council and groups of Members and shall be subject to ratification by the signatory States in accordance with their respective constitutional processes.

ARTICLE 44

When the Security Council has decided to use force it shall, before calling upon a Member not represented on it to provide armed forces in fulfilment of the obligations assumed under Article 43, invite that Member, if the Member so desires, to participate in the decisions of the Security Council concerning the employment of contingents of that Member's armed forces.

ARTICLE 45

In order to enable the United Nations to take urgent military measures, Members shall hold immediately available national air force contingents for combined international enforcement action. The strength and degree of readiness of these contingents and plans for their combined action shall be determined, within the limits laid down in the special agreement or agreements referred to in Article 43, by the Security Council with the assistance of the Military Staff Committee.

ARTICLE 46

Plans for the application of armed force shall be made by the Security Council with the assistance of the Military Staff Committee.

ARTICLE 47

1. There shall be established a Military Staff Committee to advise and assist the Security Council on all questions relating to the Security Council's military

requirements for the maintenance of international peace and security, the employment and command of forces placed at its disposal, the regulation of armaments and possible disarmament.

2. The Military Staff Committee shall consist of the Chiefs of Staff of the permanent members of the Security Council or their representatives. Any Member of the United Nations not permanently represented on the Committee shall be invited by the Committee to be associated with it when the efficient discharge of the Committee's responsibilities requires the participation of that Member in its work.

3. The Military Staff Committee shall be responsible under the Security Council for the strategic direction of any armed forces placed at the disposal of the Security Council. Questions relating to the command of such forces shall be worked out subsequently.

4. The Military Staff Committee, with the authorisation of the Security Council and after consultation with appropriate regional agencies, may establish regional sub-committees.

ARTICLE 48

1. The action required to carry out the decisions of the Security Council for the maintenance of international peace and security shall be taken by all the Members of the United Nations or by some of them, as the Security Council may determine.

2. Such decisions shall be carried out by the Members of the United Nations directly and through their action in the appropriate international agencies of which they are members.

ARTICLE 49

The Members of the United Nations shall join in affording mutual assistance in carrying out the measures decided upon by the Security Council.

ARTICLE 50

If preventive or enforcement measures against any State are taken by the Security Council, any other State, whether a Member of the United Nations or not, which finds itself confronted with special economic problems arising from the carrying out of those measures shall have the right to consult the Security Council with regard to a solution of those problems.

ARTICLE 51

Nothing in the present Charter shall impair the inherent right of individual or collective self-defence if an armed attack occurs against a Member of the United Nations, until the Security Council has taken the measures necessary to maintain international peace and security. Measures taken by Members in the exercise of this right of self-defence shall be immediately reported to the Security Council and shall not in any way affect the authority and responsibility of the Security Council under the present Charter to take at any time such action as it deems necessary in order to maintain or restore international peace and security.

Chapter VIII.—Regional Arrangements

ARTICLE 52

1. Nothing in the present Charter precludes the existence of regional arrangements or agencies for dealing with such matters relating to the maintenance of international peace and security as are appropriate for regional action, provided that such arrangements or agencies and their activities are consistent with the Purposes and Principles of the United Nations.

2. The Members of the United Nations entering into such arrangements or constituting such agencies shall make every effort to achieve pacific settlement of local disputes through such regional arrangements or by such regional agencies before referring them to the Security Council.

3. The Security Council shall encourage the development of pacific settlement of local disputes through such regional arrangements or by such regional agencies either on the initiative of the States concerned or by reference from the Security Council.

4. This Article in no way impairs the application of Articles 34 and 35.

ARTICLE 53

1. The Security Council shall, where appropriate, utilise such regional arrangements or agencies for enforcement action under its authority. But no enforcement action shall be taken under regional arrangements or by regional agencies without the authorisation of the Security Council, with the exception of measures against any enemy State, as defined in paragraph 2 of this Article, provided for pursuant to Article 107 or in regional arrangements directed against renewal of aggressive policy on the part of any such State, until such time as the Organisation may, on request of the Governments concerned, be charged with the responsibility for preventing further aggression by such a State.

ARTICLE 54

The Security Council shall at all times be kept fully informed of activities undertaken or in contemplation under regional arrangements or by regional agencies for the maintenance of international peace and security.

This Article was taken over intact from the Dumbarton Oaks Proposals. It provides that the Security Council shall be kept informed, with regard to the activities undertaken or in contemplation under the regional arrangements or by regional agencies referred to in Article 52. It places a definite obligation upon Members and upon regional agencies. Such a provision would seem to be necessary to an effective control by the Security Council of the regional arrangements and agencies here referred to.

NATO Charter

North Atlantic Treaty

Washington, 4th April, 1949

Preamble

The Parties to this Treaty reaffirm their faith in the purposes and principles of the Charter of the United Nations and their desire to live in peace with all peoples and all Governments.

They are determined to safeguard the freedom, common heritage and civilisation of their peoples, founded on the principles of democracy, individual liberty and the rule of law.

They seek to promote stability and well-being in the North Atlantic area.

They are resolved to unite their efforts for collective defence for the preservation of peace and security.

They therefore agree to this North Atlantic Treaty.

Article 1

The Parties undertake, as set forth in the Charter of the United Nations, to settle any international disputes in which they may be involved by peaceful means in such a manner that international peace and security and justice are not endangered, and to refrain in their international relations from the threat or use of force in any manner inconsistent with the purposes of the United Nations.

Article 2

The Parties will contribute towards the further development of peaceful and friendly international relations by strengthening their free institutions, by bringing about a better understanding of the principles upon which these institutions are founded, and by promoting conditions of stability and well-being. They will seek to eliminate conflict in their international economic policies and will encourage economic collaboration between any or all of them.

Article 3

In order more effectively to achieve the objectives of this Treaty, the Parties, separately and jointly, by means of continuous and effective self-help and mutual aid, will maintain and develop their individual and collective capacity to resist armed attack.

Article 4

The Parties will consult together whenever, in the opinion of any of them, the territorial integrity, political independence or security of any of the Parties is threatened.

Article 5

The Parties agree that an armed attack against one or more of them in Europe or North America shall be considered an attack against them all and consequently they agree that, if such an armed attack occurs, each of them, in exercise of the right of individual or collective self-defence recognised by Article 51 of the Charter of the United Nations, will assist the Party or Parties so attacked by taking forthwith, individually and in concert with the other Parties, such action as it deems necessary, including the use of armed force, to restore and maintain the security of the North Atlantic area.

Any such armed attack and all measures taken as a result thereof shall immediately be reported to the Security Council. Such measures shall be terminated when the Security Council has taken the measures necessary to restore and maintain international peace and security.

Article 6

For the purpose of Article 5 an armed attack on one or more of the Parties is deemed to include an armed attack on the territory of any of the Parties in Europe or North America, on the Algerian Departments of France, on the occupation forces of any Party in Europe, on the islands under the jurisdiction of any Party in the North Atlantic area north of the Tropic of Cancer or on the vessels or aircraft in this area of any of the Parties.

Article 7

This Treaty does not affect, and shall not be interpreted as affecting, in any way the rights and obligations under the Charter of the Parties which are members of the United Nations, or the primary responsibility of the Security Council for the maintenance of international peace and security.

Article 8

Each Party declares that none of the international engagements now in force between it and any other of the Parties or any third State is in conflict with the provisions of this Treaty, and undertakes not to enter into any international engagement in conflict with this Treaty.

Article 9

The Parties hereby establish a Council, on which each of them shall be represented, to consider matters concerning the implementation of this Treaty. The Council shall be so organised as to be able to meet promptly at any time. The Council shall set up such subsidiary bodies as may be necessary; in particular it shall establish immediately a Defence Committee which shall recommend measures for the implementation of Articles 3 and 5.

Article 10

The Parties may, by unanimous agreement, invite any other European State in a position to further the principles of this Treaty and to contribute to the security of the North Atlantic area to accede to this Treaty. Any State so invited may become a Party to the Treaty by depositing its instrument of accession with the Government of the United States of America.

The Government of the United States of America will inform each of the Parties of the deposit of each such instrument of accession.

Article 11

This Treaty shall be ratified and its provisions carried out by the Parties in accordance with their respective constitutional processes. The instruments of ratification shall be deposited as soon as possible with the Government of the United States of America, which will notify all the other signatories of each deposit. The Treaty shall enter into force between the States which have ratified it as soon as the ratifications of the majority of the signatories, including the ratifications of Belgium, Canada, France, Luxembourg, the Netherlands, the United Kingdom and the United States, have been deposited and shall come into effect with respect to other States on the date of the deposit of their ratifications.

Article 12

After the Treaty has been in force for ten years, or at any time thereafter, the Parties shall, if any of them so requests, consult together for the purpose of reviewing the Treaty, having regard for the factors then affecting peace and security in the North Atlantic area, including the development of universal as well as regional arrangements under the Charter of the United Nations for the maintenance of international peace and security.

Article 13

After the Treaty has been in force for twenty years, any Party may cease to be a Party one year after its notice of denunciation has been given to the Government of the United States of America, which will inform the Governments of the other Parties of the deposit of each notice of denunciation.

Article 14

This Treaty, of which the English and French texts are equally authentic, shall be deposited in the archives of the Government of the United States of America. Duly certified copies thereof will be transmitted by that Government to the Governments of the other signatories.

In witness whereof, the undersigned Plenipotentiaries have signed this Treaty.

Done at Washington, the fourth day of April, 1949.

NOTES

Introduction

1. Lawrence S. Kaplan, "NATO and the UN: A Peculiar Relationship," *Contemporary European History* 7 (May 1998): 329–42.

2. Lawrence S. Kaplan, "The United States, NATO, and the Congo Crisis of 1969," *Review of Politics* 29 (April 1967): 239–56.

3. Lincoln Bloomfield, *The United Nations and U.S. Foreign Policy* (Baltimore: Johns Hopkins University, 1961); Francis O. Wilcox, "The Atlantic Community and the United Nations," *International Organization* 17 (Summer 1963): 683–708.

4. Conor Cruise O'Brien, *To Katanga and Back: A UN Case History* (New York: Grosset and Dunlap, 1966).

5. Important examples are Mats Berdal, "From Operation 'Maritime Monitor' to 'Allied Force': Reflections on Relations between NATO and the United Nations in the 1990s," in Gustav Schmidt, ed., *The History of NATO: The First Fifty Years,* 3 vols. (London: Palgrave, 2001), 1:57–69; Dick Leurdijk, *The United Nations and NATO in Former Yugoslavia, 1991–1996: Limits to Diplomacy and Force* (The Hague: Netherlands Institute of International Relations, "Clingendael," 1996); Mark A. Bucknam, "The Influence of UN and NATO Theater-Level Commanders on the Use of Airpower over Bosnia during Deny Flight, 1993–1995" (Ph.D. diss., King's College, London, 1999); Tim Ripley, *Operation Deliberate Force: The UN and NATO Campaign in Bosnia, 1996* (Lancaster, U.K.: CDISS, 1999).

6. Alan K. Henrikson, "NATO and the UN: Toward a Nonallergic Relationship," in S. Victor Papacosma and Mary Ann Heiss, eds., *NATO in the Post–Cold War Era: Does It Have a Future?* (New York: St. Martin's Press, 1995), 95–113; Alan K. Henrikson, "The Constraint of Legitimacy: The Legal and Institutional Framework of Euro-Atlantic Security," in Pierre Martin and Mark R. Brawley, eds., *Alliance Politics, Kosovo, and NATO's War: Allied Force or Forced Allies?* (New York: Palgrave, 2000), 41–55.

7. Gustav Schmidt, *The History of NATO: The First Fifty Years* (New York: Palgrave, 2001). The chapters in volume 1 are Hall Gardner, "NATO and the UN: The Contemporary Relevance of the North Atlantic Treaty," 1:39–55; and Jack Granatstein, "The United Nations and the North Atlantic Treaty," 1:29–37.

8. David S. Yost, "NATO and International Organizations," Forum Paper Series 3, NATO Defense College, ed. Cees M. Coops, Rome, September 2007.

Chapter 1

1. Jonathan Soffer, "All for One or All for All: The UN Military Staff Committee and the Contradictions with American Internationalism," *Diplomatic History* 21 (Winter 1997): 67.

2. See Theodore C. Achilles, "Fingerprints on History: The NATO Memoirs of Theodore C. Achilles," *Occasional Papers* 1, ed. L. S. Kaplan and Sidney R. Snyder (Kent, Ohio: Lyman L. Lemnitzer Center for NATO and European Community Studies, 1992).

3. National Security Council (NSC) 9, Report by the executive secretary of the National Security Council, April 13, 1948, subject: The position of the United States with respect to support for Western Union and other related free countries, in *Foreign Relations of the United States (FRUS) 1948*, 3:85–88.

4. George F. Kennan, *Memoirs, 1925–1950* (New York: Bantam Books, 1969), 428; Dean Acheson, *Sketches from Life of Men I Have Known* (New York: Harper and Brothers, 1959), 140.

5. Arthur H. Vandenberg, Jr., ed., *The Private Papers of Senator Vandenberg* (Boston: Houghton Mifflin, 1952), 404.

6. Memorandum of conversation with Senator Vandenberg by acting secretary of state, April 11, 1948, *FRUS 1948*, 3:82–84.

7. Vandenberg to Professor W. A. Young, April 15, 1949, roll 5, Arthur Vandenberg Papers, Bentley Historical Library, University of Michigan, Ann Arbor.

8. Senate Resolution 239, June 11, 1948, *FRUS 1948*, 3:135–36.

9. Achilles, "Fingerprints on History," 17.

10. The British Embassy to Department of State, undated, subject: Substance of a message from Mr. Bevin of May 14 on North Atlantic Security, *FRUS 1948*, 3:123.

11. Minutes of the fifth meeting of the Washington exploratory talks on security, July 9, 1948, ibid., 175, 178.

12. Memorandum by the participants in the Washington exploratory talks on security, September 9, 1948, ibid., 243.

13. Report of the international working group to the Ambassadors' Committee, December 24, 1948, ibid., 336.

14. Minutes of the sixteenth meeting of the Washington exploratory talks on security, March 7, 1949, *FRUS 1949*, 4:168–69.

15. Message to Congress transmitting the third annual report on U.S. participation in the United Nations, May 12, 1949, *Public Papers of the Presidents of the United States: Harry S. Truman, 1949* (Washington, D.C.: GPO, 1964), 251.

16. Acheson to the president, March 17, 1949, accompanying Truman's message.

17. *New York Times*, April 15, 1949.

18. Ibid., April 2, 1949; James Barros, *Trygve Lie and the Cold War: The UN Secretary General Pursues Peace, 1946–1953* (DeKalb: Northern Illinois University Press, 1989), 161; Trygve Lie, *In the Cause of Peace: Seven Years with the United Nations* (New York: Macmillan, 1954), 275–76.

19. "World Wide Security Found Only in World Wide Organization," Address before UN General Assembly, Lake Success, N.Y., April 5, 1949, *Vital Speeches of the Day* 15, no. 13 (April 15, 1949): 415–16.

20. Telegram, Chargé in the Soviet Union (Kohler) to secretary of state, January 29, 1949, *FRUS 1949*, 4:51–52, citing statement of Soviet minister of foreign affairs on the North Atlantic pact; memorandum of Soviet government on the North Atlantic Treaty, March 31, 1949, in Alvin Z. Rubinstein, ed., *The Foreign Policy of the Soviet Union* (New York: Random House, 1969), 268–69.

21. Ambassador of the Soviet Union (Panyshkin) to the secretary of state, March 31, 1969, *FRUS 1949*, 4:264.

22. Preliminary position paper prepared by the staff of the U.S. delegation to the General Assembly, March 30, 1949, ibid., 2:72.

23. Minutes of the sixth meeting of the U.S. delegation to the second part of the third session of the General Assembly, April 13, 1949, ibid., 2:77.

24. *Current Digest of the Soviet Press*, May 3, 1949, part 1, 14:35–39.

25. Chargé in the Soviet Union (Kohler) to secretary of state, April 6, 1949, *FRUS 1949*, 2:72–73.

26. A/AC.24/20, A/AC.24/33, in *Yearbook of the United Nations, 1948–1949*, 427–29. (The "A" refers to the General Assembly, followed by year, document number, and date. Major documents, particularly resolutions, are in the annual yearbooks, but I use primarily the *Index to Proceedings of the General Assembly* [New York: United Nations], which provides a paragraph explaining the contents of each document. Unless otherwise noted, there will be no further reference to the source.)

27. Ibid., 427.

28. A/AC.24/31, A/AC.24/33, ibid., 426–27.

29. UN General Assembly, 3rd sess., 2nd pt., 192nd plenary session, *Official Records*, April 13, 1949, 65–67.

30. Ibid., 193rd sess., April 14, 1949, 78.

31. Ibid., 192nd sess., April 13, 1949, 65.

32. Quoted in *New York Times*, April 14, 1949; Gladwyn Jebb, *Memoirs of Lord Gladwyn* (New York: Weybright and Talley, 1972), 232.

33. UN General Assembly, 3rd sess., 2nd pt., 193rd plenary session, *Official Records*, April 14, 1949, 80–81.

34. USSR draft resolution, April 14, 1949, in *UN Yearbook 1948–1949*, 429.

35. U.S. Senate, Committee on Foreign Relations, North Atlantic Treaty hearings, 81st Cong., 1st sess., 3 parts (Washington, D.C.: GPO, 1949), May 17, 1949, 3:1123.

36. Robert J. Donovan, *Tumultuous Years: The Presidency of Harry S. Truman, 1949–1953* (New York: W. W. Norton, 1982), 34.

37. Lawrence S. Kaplan, "NATO and the Language of Isolationism," *South Atlantic Quarterly* 57 (Spring 1958): 209–10; U.S. Senate, 81st Cong., 1st sess., *Congressional Record* 95, pt. 7 (July 5, 1949): 8819.

38. Radio address, March 18, 1948, "The Meaning of the North Atlantic Pact," *U.S. Department of State Bulletin*, no. 508 (March 27, 1948): 385.

39. U.S. Senate, Committee on Foreign Relations, 3 parts, hearings on the North Atlantic Treaty, May 12, 1949, 3:1007 (Washington, D.C.: GPO, 1949).

40. Ibid., April 28, 1949, 1:97.

41. Dean Acheson, *Present at the Creation: My Years in the State Department* (New York: W. W. Norton, 1969), 281.

42. U.S. Senate, Committee on Foreign Relations, hearings on the North Atlantic Treaty, April 27, 1949, 1:85.

43. Ibid., April 28, 1949, 1:136–37.

44. U.S. Senate, 81st Cong., 1st sess., *Congressional Record* 95, pt. 7 (July 11, 1949): 9208.

45. Ibid., 9209.

46. Ibid. (July 13, 1949): 9367–69.

47. House of Commons, *Parliamentary Debates,* 5th ser. (London: His Majesty's Stationery Office, 1949), vol. 464 (May 12, 1949): 2018.

48. *Keesing's Contemporary Archives: Weekly Diary of World Events* 7 (1948–1950): 10143.

49. Vincent Auriol, *Journal du Septennat, 1949,* July 21, 1949 (Paris: Librairie Armand Colin, 1974) 3:300.

Chapter 2

1. Evan Luard, *A History of the United Nations,* 2 vols. (New York: St. Martin's Press, 1982), 1:358–59.

2. Gary Ostrower, *The United Nations and the United States, 1945–1995* (New York: Twayne, 1998), 42.

3. "Hastings Lionel Ismay," *Oxford Dictionary of National Biography.*

4. Steven Z. Freiberger, *Dawn over Suez: The Rise of American Power in the Middle East, 1953–1957* (Chicago: Ivan R. Dee, 1992), 10–11.

5. Burton I. Kaufman, *The Arab Middle East and the United States: Inter-Arab Rivalry and Superpower Diplomacy* (New York: Twayne, 1996), 19.

6. Quoted in William Roger Louis, "Dulles, Suez, and the British," in Richard H. Immerman, ed., *John Foster Dulles and the Diplomacy of the Cold War* (Princeton, N.J.: Princeton University, 1990), 134.

7. Quoted in Richard H. Immerman, *John Foster Dulles: Piety, Pragmatism, and Power in U.S. Foreign Policy* (Wilmington, Del.: SR Books, 1999), 148.

8. Ibid., 149.

9. Barry Rubin, "America and the Egyptian Revolution, 1950–1957," *Political Science Quarterly* 97 (September 1982): 88.

10. Aleksandr Fursenko and Timothy Naftali, *Khrushchev's Cold War: The Inside Story of an American Adversary* (New York: W. W. Norton, 2006), 84–85.

11. Ibid., 86–88.

12. Robert R. Bowie, *Suez 1956* (New York: Oxford University Press, 1974), 19–22; Anthony Eden, *Memoirs: Full Circle* (Boston: Houghton Mifflin, 1960), 497.

13. Bowie, *Suez 1956,* 26.

14. Ibid., 26–28; *Débats parlementaires* 34, August 2, 4, 1956, 3847, 3868; House of Commons, *Parliamentary Debates,* 5th ser., vol. 558 (September 13, 1956): 999.

15. Freiberger, *Dawn over Suez,* 163–68.

16. Eden, *Full Circle,* 487.

17. Bowie, *Suez 1956,* 26–28; British Foreign Minister Selwyn Lloyd explained to

Parliament that if a resolution on a proposed conference had been brought before the UN Security Council, the Soviets would have vetoed it, and after weeks of delay, at a special meeting of the General Assembly, "at most, a recommendation might be won." See House of Commons, *Parliamentary Debates,* 5th ser., vol. 558 (September 13, 1956): 166.

18. Bowie, *Suez 1956,* 39.

19. Freiberger, *Dawn over Suez,* 166; Ostrower, *United Nations,* 82.

20. Freiberger, *Dawn over Suez,* 174–76.

21. Ibid., 175; presidential news conference, September 11, 1956, *Public Papers: Dwight D. Eisenhower, 1956,* 75.

22. House of Commons, *Parliamentary Debates,* 5th ser., vol. 558 (October 23, 1956): 491.

23. Andrew Cordier and Wilder Foote, eds., *Public Papers of the Secretaries-General of the United Nations: Dag Hammarskjöld,* 5 vols. (New York: Columbia University Press, 1972–1975; hereafter cited as the *Hammarskjöld Papers*), 3:297–98.

24. Evelyn Shuckburgh, *Descent to Suez: Diaries, 1951–1956* (London: Weidenfeld and Nicholson, 1986), 362.

25. *Hammarskjöld Papers,* 3:306.

26. S/1956/3710, October 30, 1956, *Hammarskjöld Papers,* 3:304. (The "S" refers to the UN Security Council, followed by the year, number, and date. The Security Council resolutions, reports, letters, and verbatim commentaries are all drawn from the *Index to Proceedings of the Security Council* [New York: United Nations]. Each entry includes a brief paragraph explaining the contents. Unless otherwise noted, there will be no further reference to the source.)

27. House of Commons, *Parliamentary Debates,* 5th ser., vol. 558 (October 30, 1956): 1377–78.

28. Eden, *Full Circle,* 588; Dwight D. Eisenhower, *Waging Peace, 1956–1961,* 2 vols. (Garden City, N.Y.: Doubleday, 1965), 77.

29. Harold Macmillan, *Riding the Storm, 1956–1959* (London: Macmillan, 1971), 158.

30. Memorandum of discussion at 302nd meeting of National Security Council, November 1, 1956, *FRUS 1955–1957,* 16:909–11, 915. The National Security Council (NSC) was created in 1947 to coordinate political, military, and intelligence activities of the U.S. government.

31. S/1956/3710, 3717, in *Hammarskjöld Papers,* 3:307–8.

32. Macmillan, *Riding the Storm,* 159; Dulles from Immerman, *Piety, Pragmatism, and Power,* 154.

33. *Hammarskjöld Papers,* October 31, 1956, 3:309–10.

34. A/3256, November 2, 1956, ibid., 314–15.

35. *Hammarskjöld Papers,* November 2, 1956, 3:318–19.

36. Ibid., 317–18.

37. John A. Munroe and A. I. Inglis, eds., *Mike: The Memoirs of Lester B. Pearson, 1948–1957,* 3 vols. (Toronto: University of Toronto Press, 1972), 2:246–47.

38. Freiberger, *Dawn over Suez,* 192.

39. *New York Times,* October 21, 1956, 1.

40. Fursenko and Naftali, *Khrushchev's Cold War,* 122–23; *Report of the Special Committee*

on the Problem of Hungary, UN General Assembly, supplement no. 18(A/3592), *Official Records,* 1–12.

41. Dixon from *New York Times,* October 28, 1956, 30.

42. Excerpts from debate in the UN Security Council on rebellion in Hungary, ibid., October 29, 1956, 10. See also *UN Yearbook 1956,* 67, 68; Nagy's telegram to diplomatic missions in Budapest declaring Hungary's neutrality, November 1, 1956, in Vojtech Mastny and Malcolm Byrne, eds., *A Cardboard Castle? An Inside History of the Warsaw Pact, 1955–1991* (Budapest/New York: Central European University Press, 2005), 83. Mastny and Byrne point out that the Soviets had decided on military intervention before Nagy's declaration of neutrality. Ibid., 8.

43. *UN Yearbook 1956,* 69.

44. *Hammarskjöld Papers,* 3:309, 313.

45. Ibid., 412–14.

46. Ibid., 413.

47. *Report of the Special Committee on the Problem of Hungary,* UN General Assembly, supplement no. 18(A/3592), *Official Records,* 1–12.

48. Immerman, *Piety, Pragmatism, and Power,* 152; memorandum of a conversation between the president and the secretary of state, August 30, 1956, *FRUS 1955–1957,* 16:334.

49. Fursenko and Naftali, *Khrushchev's Cold War,* 133–34.

50. House of Commons, *Parliamentary Debates,* 5th ser., vol. 560 (November 8, 1956): 365ff; *Times* (London), November 4, 1956, 4.

51. Anthony Nutting, *No End of a Lesson: The Story of Suez* (New York: Clarkson N. Potter, 1967), 96.

52. Diane B. Kunz, *Diplomacy of the Suez Crisis* (Chapel Hill: University of North Carolina Press, 1991), 131.

53. Ibid., 133; Fursenko and Naftali, *Khrushchev's Cold War,* 135–37.

54. *Hammarskjöld Papers,* November 2, 1956, 3:316–18.

55. General Assembly, 565th plenary session, first emergency special session, November 4, 1956, 88.

56. Ibid., 89; Document A/3290, 567th session, November 7, 1956, 112, 114.

57. Bowie, *Suez 1956,* 79–80; A/1956/563, November 3, 1956, 61.

58. Memorandum of conversation with the president: Dulles, Hoover, Goodpaster, December 15, 1956, *FRUS 1955–1957,* 16:1310.

59. Telegram from U.S. delegation at NAC ministerial meeting to State Department, no. 41, December 11, 1956, *FRUS 1955–1957,* 4:106–8. The Three Wise Men, also known as the Committee of Three, was appointed in May 1956 to advise the council on non-military cooperation in NATO.

60. Telegram, U.S. delegation to NAC ministerial meeting to State Department, no. 43, December 12, 1956, ibid., 116–22 (119–20); NAC ministerial meeting, December 11–14, 1956, at www.nato.inc/docu. NATO documents may be found in the annual published texts of communiqués, or in other publications of the NATO Information Service (most of the published versions from NATO's first generation in author's possession, including the North Atlantic Council, Defense, and other subordinate committees). All of these can be found online under *NATO Summits & Ministerial Meetings,* at the above Web address.

61. Paul-Henri Spaak, *The Continuing Battle: Memoirs of a European, 1936–1966* (Boston: Little, Brown, 1971), 128–31 (128, 130).

62. Lodge to Rep. Frances Bolton, June 18, 1957, *FRUS 1955–1957,* 11:501.

63. *Hammarskjöld Papers,* October 31, 1956, 3:309.

64. Radio and TV report to the American people on the developments in Eastern Europe and the Middle East, October 31, 1956, *Public Papers: Dwight D. Eisenhower, 1956,* 283.

65. Ismay, *NATO: The First Five Years* (Paris: NATO, 1954). There is only one passing reference to the Suez crisis in the Ismay Papers (Liddell Hart Centre for Military Archives, King's College, London), and this is in a letter to General Gruenther on March 31, 1957, in which Ismay lashed out at Nasser, saying, "we must either make Nasser behave himself . . . or knock him off his perch." But, he added, "I have *NOT* got in mind a repetition of last November's idiocy."

Chapter 3

1. *New York Times,* July 1, 1960, 1.

2. Ernest W. Lefever, *Uncertain Mandate: Politics of the UN Congo Operation* (Baltimore: Johns Hopkins University Press, 1967), 9.

3. Telegram from the president and prime minister of the Republic of the Congo to the secretary-general, July 12, 1960, *Hammarskjöld Papers,* 5:18–19.

4. Telegram from the president and prime minister of the Republic of the Congo, July 13, 1960, ibid., 19–20.

5. Ibid., 3.

6. Brian Urquhart, *Hammarskjöld* (New York: Knopf, 1972), 30.

7. S/1960/4387, July 14, 1960.

8. Paper prepared in the Bureau of International Organization Affairs, "The Fourteenth General Assembly and Future United Nations Prospects," May 1960, *FRUS 1948–50,* 2:240.

9. Lefever, *Uncertain Mandate,* 9.

10. Ibid., 10; Catherine Hoskins, *The Congo since Independence, January 1960–December 1961* (London: Oxford University Press, 1965), 114.

11. Telegram from the president and prime minister of the Republic of the Congo to the secretary-general, July 12, 1960, in *Hammarskjöld Papers,* 5:18–19.

12. Statement in the General Assembly on his reappointment for a second term, September 26, 1957, in *Hammarskjöld Papers,* 3:665.

13. Hoskins, *Congo since Independence,* 121.

14. Ibid., 131–32.

15. First report on assistance to the Republic of the Congo, July 18, 1960, *Hammarskjöld Papers,* 5:35.

16. S/1960/4400, dated July 20, 1960; S/1960/4389, dated July 19, 1960; opening statement in the UN Security Council, July 13, 1960, *Hammarskjöld Papers,* 5:13.

17. Opening statement in the UN Security Council, July 13, 1960, ibid., 22.

18. S/PV/873, July 13, 1960, ibid., 21–22, 26.

19. Ibid., 30.

20. S/1960/4387, July 18, 1960, ibid., 25–26.

21. S/1960/4402, July 13, 1960.

22. S/1960/4386, July 14, 1960.

23. S/1960/4387, July 14, 1960.

24. *New York Times,* July 16, 1960, 3; *Facts on File Yearbook, 1960,* September 11–21, 1960, 318.

25. Lefever, *Uncertain Mandate,* 103–4.

26. Ibid., 77–78.

27. James Dobbins et al., *The UN's Role in Nation-Building: From the Congo to Iraq* (Santa Monica, Calif.: RAND, 2005), 16–17.

28. Alan James, *Britain and the Congo Crisis, 1960–1963* (New York: St. Martin's Press, 1996), 131–35, 134. See also Rajeshwal Dayal, *Mission for Hammarskjöld: The Congo Crisis* (Princeton, N.J.: Princeton University Press, 1976).

29. House of Commons, *Parliamentary Debates,* 5th ser., vol. 626 (July 14, 1960): 1603; vol. 626 (July 11, 1960): 184; vol. 627 (July 20, 1960): 495.

30. Harold Macmillan, *At the End of the Day, 1961–1963* (New York: Harper and Row, 1994), 284–85.

31. Lefever, *Uncertain Mandate,* 114.

32. Eisenhower to de Gaulle, August 30, 1960, *FRUS 1958–60,* vol. 7, pt. 2, 416.

33. Hervé Alphand, *L'étonnement d'être: journal 1939–1973* (Paris: Fayard, 1977), 340.

34. Charles de Gaulle, *Memoirs of Hope: Renewal and Endeavor,* trans. Terence Kilmartin (New York: Simon and Schuster, 1976), 204–5.

35. James, *Britain and the Congo,* 86–87; telegram from the U.S. mission to the UN to the Department of State, January 31, 1961, no. 2059, *FRUS 1961–1963,* 20:35–37; FO 371 104941, JB1051/6, African Department, Congo, Foreign Office Minutes, January 30, 1961, The National Archives, Public Record Office (TNA/PRO), Kew, England.

36. S/1960/PV/873, July 13, 1960, 14–15.

37. FO 371 146696 JB 146696, JB 1073/1, no. 180, dated July 13, 1960; JB 1073/2, no. 182, dated July 14, 1960; JB 1073/3, no. 220, dated July 14, 1960; JB 1073/6, no. 231, dated July 20, 1960; JB 1073/12, no. 194, dated June 27, 1960, TNA/PRO, Kew, England.

38. S/1960/PV/888, August 20, 1960, 22.

39. Spaak, *Continuing Battle,* 358; Robert S. Jordan, with Michael W. Bloome, *Political Leadership in NATO: A Study in Multinational Diplomacy* (Boulder, Colo.: Westview Press, 1979), 100n151.

40. Pierre Wigny, "Belgium and the Congo," *International Affairs* 37 (July 1961): 278; V. Larock in Chambre des Représentants, *Annales parlementaires de Belgique,* July 5, 1960, 24.

41. Gaston Eyskens, press conference, *L'Avenir* (Namur), August 10, 1960.

42. M. Schot, *Annales parlementaires,* August 18, 1960; P. De Smet, *Compte rendu analytique,* July 19, 1960, 830.

43. M. Gillon, *Compte rendu analytique,* August 19, 1960, 873; *Le Courrier de l'Escaut* (Tournai), September 5, 1960.

44. *L'Avenir de Luxembourg* (Arlon), August 21, 1960 (quote); *La Nouvelle Gazette* (Brussels), August 30, 1960.

45. *Le Courrier de l'Escaut,* September 3, 1960.

46. Memorandum of conversation between the secretary and Prime Minister Lumumba of the Republic of the Congo, July 27, 1960, *FRUS 1958–60,* 14:364.

47. *La Libre Belgique* (Brussels), July 25, 1960; *New York Times,* July 23, 1960, 1.

48. Memo of conversation, July 27, 1960, *FRUS 1958–60,* 14:364; *New York Times,* July 23, 1960, 5.

49. *La Libre Belgique,* June 25, 1960; *La Nouvelle Gazette,* August 30, 1960.

50. Editorial note on 453rd meeting of the North Atlantic Council, July 25, 1960, *FRUS 1958–1960,* 14:354.

51. Ibid.

52. *Department of State Bulletin* 43, no. 1103, August 15, 1960, 245–46.

53. U.S. House of Representatives, 86th Cong., 2nd sess., *Congressional Record* 109, pt. 111 (June 30, 1960): 15277.

54. U.S. Senate, ibid., 106, pt. 12 (July 1, 1960): 15304.

55. Ibid., pt. 13 (August 28, 1960): 17427.

56. Ibid., 17413.

57. Ibid., pt. 12 (August 11, 1960): 16185; ibid., pt. 14 (August 30, 1960): 18270.

58. Quoted in Ostrower, *United Nations,* 94, 268n62.

59. Jordan, *Political Leadership,* 91–92; Spaak, *Continuing Battle,* 368, 360.

Chapter 4

1. *UN Yearbook 1973,* 163.

2. Bernard J. Firestone, *The United Nations under U Thant, 1961–1971* (Lanham, Md.: Scarecrow Press, 2001), xvii. For an evaluation of the impact of his Buddhist heritage, see Walter Doren, "U Thant: Buddhism in Action," in Kent J. Kille, ed., *The UN Secretary-General and Moral Authority: Ethics and Religion in International Leadership* (Washington, D.C.: Georgetown University Press, 2007), 154–55.

3. Kille, *UN Secretary-General,* xv, xvi.

4. Jordan, *Political Leadership,* 165–72.

5. Kille, *UN Secretary-General,* xviii, xix; statement on the role of religious convictions at the third international teach-in, Toronto, October 22, 1967, in Andrew W. Cordier and Max Harrelson, eds., *Public Papers of the Secretaries-General of the United Nations: U Thant, 1965–1967* (New York: Columbia University Press, 1976; hereafter cited as *U Thant Papers*), 7:601.

6. Lawrence S. Kaplan et al., *History of the Office of the Secretary of Defense: The McNamara Ascendancy* (Washington, D.C.: Office of the Secretary of Defense, 2006), 5:86.

7. Lyndon B. Johnson, *The Vantage Point: Perspectives of the Presidency, 1963–1969* (New York: Holt, Rinehart, and Winston, 1971), 118.

8. Transcript of his first press conference, December 1, 1961, *U Thant Papers,* 6:42; transcript of press conference, September 12, 1963, ibid., 6:442–43.

9. Firestone, *United Nations,* 768.

10. U Thant comments at press conference, January 16, 1967, *U Thant Papers,* 7:362–63.

11. Quoted in ibid., 7:4.

12. Lawrence S. Kaplan, "McNamara, Vietnam, and the Defense of Europe," in Vojtech Mastny et al., eds., *War Plans and Alliances in the Cold War: Threat Perceptions in the East and West* (London: Routledge, 2006), 291; Thomas W. Zeiler, *Dean Rusk: Defending the American Mission Abroad* (Wilmington, Del.: SR Books, 2000), 151.

13. Zeiler, *Dean Rusk,* 168.

14. Ibid., 152.

15. Thomas A. Schwartz, *Lyndon Johnson and Europe: In the Shadow of Vietnam* (Cambridge, Mass.: Harvard University Press, 2003), 83. See also George C. Herring, *America's Longest War: The United States and Vietnam, 1950–1975,* 2nd ed. (New York: Alfred A. Knopf, 1986), 168–69.

16. "Peace without Conquest," address at Johns Hopkins University, April 7, 1965, *Public Papers: Lyndon B. Johnson, 1965,* 396–97.

17. Ibid., 396; *Department of State Bulletin,* no. 1349 (May 3, 1965), 42:651.

18. Remarks at luncheon of UN Correspondents Association, April 15, 1965. *U Thant Papers,* 7:61–62, 65.

19. Telegram, American Embassy in Vietnam to State Department, February 15, 1965, *FRUS 1964–1968,* 2:270–71.

20. Address in San Francisco at the twentieth anniversary commemorative session of the UN, June 13, 1965, *Public Papers: Lyndon B. Johnson, 1965,* 704.

21. Quoted in Fredrik Logevall, "The American Effort to Draw European States into the War," in Christopher Goscha and Maurice Vaisse, eds., *La Guerre du Vietnam et l'Europe* (Brussels: Bruylant, 2003), 13.

22. Randall B. Woods, *Fulbright: A Biography* (New York: Cambridge University Press, 1955), 371, 372 (quotes).

23. Quoted in Schwartz, *Lyndon Johnson and Europe,* 84.

24. U.S. Senate, 88th Cong., 1st sess., *Congressional Record* 111, pt. 12 (July 8, 1965): 15966.

25. Lawrence S. Kaplan, "The Vietnam War and Europe: The View from NATO," in Goscha and Vaisse, *La Guerre du Vietnam et l'Europe,* 90–91.

26. Note by chairman of the expert working group, May 6, 1963, C-M(63)26, subject: The situation in the Far East (NATO Archives, Brussels), 8.

27. Ibid., 12.

28. Verbatim record of the meeting of the North Atlantic Council, The Hague, May 12, 1964 (NATO Archives, Brussels), 11:30 AM, C.VR(64)22, 10, and 3:30 PM, C.VR(64)23, 41.

29. Kaplan, *The McNamara Ascendancy,* 502; statement on French radio and television and exchange of toasts with President de Gaulle, April 30, 1966, in *U Thant Papers,* 7:224–25.

30. Verbatim record of the meeting of North Atlantic Council, Paris, December 15, 1964, 3:30 PM, C.VR(64)54 (NATO Archives, Brussels), 25.

31. Summary record of the meeting of North Atlantic Council, Paris, December 14, 1965, 10:15 AM, C.VR(65)50 (NATO Archives, Brussels), 9.

32. John M. Young, "British Governments and the Vietnam War," in Goscha and Vaisse, *La Guerre du Vietnam et l'Europe,* 122–23.

33. Summary record of the meeting of the North Atlantic Council, Paris, August 28, 1964, C.R(64)39 (NATO Archives, Brussels), 14, 11.

34. Address by Manlio Brosio to the NATO Parliamentary Conference, eleventh annual session, New York, October 4, 1965, 35:6, NATO Parliamentarians Conference (unbound volumes located in the Library of the Conference, now the North Atlantic Assembly, in the Petit Sablon, Brussels).

35. Ibid., October 8, 1965, E.14–E.15.

36. Fredrik Logevall, "The Western Powers and the Escalation of the War," in Andreas W. Daum et al., *America, the Vietnam War, and the World* (New York: Cambridge University Press, 2003), 183.

37. Summary record of the meeting of the North Atlantic Council, London, May 11, 1965, C.R(65)21 (NATO Archives, Brussels), 6.

38. Schwartz, *Lyndon Johnson and Europe*, 87, 88.

39. Logevall, "Western Powers and the Escalation of the War," 195; Schwartz, *Lyndon Johnson and Europe*, 86.

40. Transcript of remarks by Dean Rusk, at Ambassador Bohlen's residence, Paris, December 14, 1965, U.S. delegation to 36th ministerial meeting of North Atlantic Council, Conference files, 1964–1966, CF 2579–84, lot file 66D347 (NARA, College Park, Md.), 16.

41. Verbatim record of a meeting of the North Atlantic Council, Paris, December 14, 1965, C.R(65)51 (NATO Archives, Brussels), 5.

42. Ibid., 17–19.

43. Ibid., 32.

44. Minutes of the meeting of the Political Committee, Paris, May 18, 1965, PC(65)14 (NATO Parliamentarians Conference, Brussels), 32:4; meeting of joint meeting of Political Committee and Military Committee, Paris, May 11, 1966 PC(66)31/MC(66)6, ibid., 38:3.

45. Twelfth annual session, November 18, 1966, HN/PVI/(VE)66, ibid., 33–35.

46. Address by Manlio Brosio to the NATO Parliamentarians' Conference, 11th annual session, New York, October 4, 1965 (Brussels), 35:6.

47. Department of State Circular to all NATO Capitals, 1202, December 22, 1965, subject: Assessment of NATO ministerial meeting, December 14–16, CF 2570–84, lot file 66D347 (NARA, College Park, Md.).

48. Introduction to the 20th Annual Report, September 20, 1965, *U Thant Papers*, 7:161.

49. For statements of U.S. objectives in Vietnam, see *UN Yearbook 1965*, 187–88; *UN Yearbook 1966*, 146–47.

50. General Assembly, 20th session, plenary meetings, verbatim record, A/PV/1335, September 24, 1965, 3.

51. Ibid., 10.

52. Ibid., A/PV/1341, September 29, 1965, 11.

53. Ibid., A/PV/1397, December 16, 1965, 5.

54. Kent J. Kille, *From Manager to Visionary: The Secretary-General of the United Nations* (New York: Palgrave Macmillan, 2006), 143–44; James D. Ryan, *The United Nations under Kurt Waldheim, 1972–1981* (Lanham, Md.: Scarecrow Press, 2001), 34.

55. *UN Yearbook 1973,* 163.

56. Ryan C. Hendrickson, *Diplomacy and War at NATO: The Secretary General and Military Action after the Cold War* (Columbia: University of Missouri Press, 2006), 30–31.

Chapter 5

1. Nancy P. Newell and Richard S. Newell, *The Struggle for Afghanistan* (Ithaca, N.Y.: Cornell University Press, 1981), 109.

2. Henry S. Bradsher, *Afghan Communism and Soviet Intervention* (Oxford: Oxford University Press, 1999), 75–77; Cyrus Vance, *Hard Choices: Critical Years in America's Foreign Policy* (New York: Simon and Schuster, 1983), 384–86.

3. Newell and Newell, *Struggle for Afghanistan,* 108, 118.

4. Vance, *Hard Choices,* 387–89; Vladislav M. Zubok, *A Failed Empire: The Soviet Union in the Cold War from Stalin to Gorbachev* (Chapel Hill: University of North Carolina Press, 2007), 228.

5. Zbigniew Brzezinski, *Power and Principle: Memoirs of the National Security Adviser, 1977–1981* (New York: Farrar, Straus, Giroux, 1983), 353.

6. *UN Yearbook 1980,* 297–98.

7. Newell and Newell, *Struggle for Afghanistan,* 108, 118.

8. *New York Times,* January 1, 1980, 12.

9. S/1980/13717, December 31, 1980.

10. Letter dated February 11, 1980, from Pakistan transmitting resolutions and final communiqué of extraordinary session of Islamic Conference of Foreign Ministers, Islamabad, January 27–29, 1980, S/1980/13810 (A/35/109).

11. S/1980/13724, January 3, 1980; S/1980/13725, January 4, 1980.

12. S/13725, January 4, 1980.

13. *UN Yearbook 1980,* 297–98.

14. Ibid., 298.

15. Ibid., 298–99; S/RES/462 (1980), S/1980/13731, adopted by the UN Security Council on January 9, 1980.

16. General Assembly, 6th emergency session, plenary meeting, January 10–14, 1980, in *UN Yearbook 1980,* 306; Brian Urquhart, *A Life in Peace and War* (New York: Harper and Row, 1987), 190.

17. Linda Melvern, *The Ultimate Crime: Who Betrayed the UN and Why* (London: Allison and Busby, 1995), 162–63.

18. Ibid., 226; Shirley Hazzard, "The League of Frightened Men," *New Republic,* January 9, 1980, 17.

19. Seymour M. Finger and Arnold A. Saltzman, *Bending with the Winds: Kurt Waldheim and the United Nations* (Westport, Conn.: Praeger, 1990), x, xxi; Kille, *From Manager to Visionary,* 124–25.

20. Kille, *From Manager to Visionary,* 126–27; Urquhart, *In Peace and War,* 227.

21. *UN Yearbook 1980,* 299.

22. General Assembly, 6th emergency special session, plenary meeting, January 14, 1980, 106.

23. Resolution ES-6/2, as proposed by twenty-four powers, A/ES-6/L/1 and Add.1 adopted by Assembly on January 14, 1980, in *UN Yearbook 1980,* 307.

24. Ibid.

25. Speeches at special session, in ibid., 301.

26. Resolution 462, as proposed by two powers, S/1980/13731, January 9, 1980.

27. *New York Times,* January 10, 1980, 1.

28. Ibid., March 19, 1980, 3.

29. Ibid., January 24, 1980.

30. Ibid., January 31, 1980, 5; Jimmy Carter, *Keeping Faith: Memoirs of a President* (New York: Bantam Books, 1982), 479.

31. A/C.3/35/SR.18, October 10, 1989, 12.

32. *New York Times,* November 21, 1980, 6.

33. Resolution 35/37, as proposed by forty-two powers, A/35/L.12, adopted by UN General Assembly on November 20, 1980, in *UN Yearbook 1980,* 308–9 (italics added).

34. *New York Times,* November 21, 1980, 6.

35. Ostrower, *United Nations,* 169.

36. Letter dated February 11, 1980, from Pakistan transmitting resolutions and final communiqué of extraordinary session of Islamic Conference of Foreign Ministers, Islamabad, January 27–29, 1980, S/1980/13810; S/1980/13724, January 3, 1980; S/1980/13725, January 4, 1980.

37. Waldheim's report on his visit to Iran, January 1–3, 1980, in *UN Yearbook 1980,* 309.

38. *New York Times,* January 25, 1980, 6.

39. Brzezinski, *Power and Principle,* 426–27.

40. Carter, *Keeping Faith,* 473; Brzezinski, *Power and Principle,* 432.

41. Address to the Nation, January 4, 1980, *Public Papers: Jimmy Carter, 1980,* pt. 1, 23; State of the Union, annual address to the Congress, January 21, 1980, ibid., 163.

42. Carter, *Keeping Faith,* 476; Address to the Nation, January 4, 1980, *Public Papers: Jimmy Carter, 1980,* pt. 1, 23.

43. Carter, *Keeping Faith,* 481.

44. Vance, *Hard Choices,* 391; Brzezinski, *Power and Principle,* 433–34.

45. *New York Times,* January 25, 1980, 10; April 23, 1980, 3.

46. *New York Times,* June 2, 1980, 2.

47. U.S. Senate, Committee on Foreign Relations, hearing on 1980 Summer Olympics boycott, 96th Cong., 2nd sess., January 28, 1980, 2, 5.

48. *New York Times,* June 23, 1980, 1, 8.

49. Carter, *Keeping Faith,* 254–55.

50. Brzezinski, *Power and Principle,* 424–25.

51. State of the Union, annual message to the Congress, January 21, 1980, *Public Papers: Jimmy Carter, 1980,* 165; State of the Union Address, January 23, 1980, before a joint session of the Congress, ibid., 197.

52. Address at commencement exercises, Notre Dame University, May 22, 1977, *Public Papers: Jimmy Carter, 1977,* 985.

53. State of the Union, annual message, January 21, 1980, *Public Papers: Jimmy Carter, 1980,* 114, 167, 171–72.

54. Ibid., 165.

55. Ibid., 166–67.

56. *New York Times,* January 2, 1980, 2.

57. *UN Yearbook 1980,* 301.

58. General Assembly, 6th emergency special session, plenary meeting, January 14, 1980, 106.

59. Vance, *Hard Choices,* 383.

60. *New York Times,* May 21, 1980, 14.

61. Brzezinski, *Power and Principle,* 293, 463.

62. Helmut Schmidt, "The 1977 Alastair Buchan Memorial Lecture," *Survival* 20 (January–February 1978): 4.

63. *New York Times,* February 15, 1980, 12.

64. U.S. Senate, Committee on Foreign Relations, subcommittee on Near Eastern and South Asian affairs, hearings on U.S. security interests and policies in Southwest Asia, 96th Cong., 2nd sess., February 6, 1980, *Congressional Record* (Washington, D.C.: GPO, 1980), 21. Clifford repeated his complaints even more strongly before the Senate Foreign Relations Committee on March 18, 1980, see *Counsel to the President: A Memoir,* with Richard Holbrooke (New York: Random House, 1991), 641.

65. Vance, *Hard Choices,* 391.

66. Ibid., 392.

67. Defense Planning Committee, ministerial session, Brussels, May 13–14, 1980, at www.nato.int/docu.

68. Ibid., December 9–10, 1980, 149–50.

69. *New York Times,* June 18, 1980, 2; Hendrickson, *Diplomacy and War,* 32–33.

70. North Atlantic Council, ministerial session final communiqué, Ankara, June 25–26, 1980.

71. *New York Times,* February 17, 1980, 11.

72. North Atlantic Council, ministerial session final communiqué, Ankara, June 25–26, 1980.

73. Defense Planning Committee, ministerial session, Brussels, December 9–10, 1980, ibid., 150.

74. Ibid., May 14, 1980, 131.

75. Letter from EC presidents to UN secretary-general, January 17, 1980, S/1980/13760, January 23, 1980.

76. Letters from heads of state and foreign ministers to the UN Security Council, May 5, 1980, S/1980/13925, May 6, 1980, and June 16, 1980, S/1980/14003, June 17, 1980.

77. See James Goldsborough, "Europe Cashes In on Carter's Cold War," *New York Times,* April 27, 1980, 42.

78. Melvern, *Ultimate Crime,* 286.

Chapter 6

1. Soffer, "All for One or All for All," 52.

2. Ibid.

3. Ibid., 66.

4. NAC communiqué, London, July 5–6, 1990, at www.nato.int/docu.

5. President's news conference following NATO summit in London, July 6, 1990, *Public Papers: George Bush, 1990,* 968.

6. Eduard Shevardnadze, *The Future Belongs to Freedom* (New York: Free Press, 1991), 106–7.

7. Cited in Karen A. Mingst and Margaret P. Karns, *The United Nations in the Post–Cold War Era* (Boulder, Colo.: Westview Press, 1995), 43.

8. Quoted in James A. Baker, *The Politics of Diplomacy: Revolution, War, and Peace, 1989–1992* (New York: G. P. Putnam's Sons, 1995), 272. President Bush agreed with Baker that Glaspie was treated unfairly in the press. George Bush and Brent Scowcroft, *A World Transformed* (New York: Alfred A. Knopf, 1998), 310.

9. Baker, *Politics of Diplomacy,* 273.

10. U.S. Senate, S. Con Res 247, 101st Cong., 2nd sess., *Congressional Record* 138, pt. 19 (October 2, 1990): 26959, 26951–52.

11. U.S. Senate, Foreign Relations Committee, hearings on U.S. policy in the Persian Gulf, September 5, 1990, 101st Cong., 2nd sess., 113, 117.

12. Ibid., 106.

13. Bush and Scowcroft, *A World Transformed,* 425.

14. "The Cold War Is Over but 'Demons' Remain," *Christian Century* 107, no. 25 (September 5–12, 1990): 787.

15. Baker, *Politics of Diplomacy,* 337.

16. Stanley Meisler, *The United Nations: The First Fifty Years* (New York: Atlantic Monthly Press, 1995), 263.

17. S/RES/660, August 2, 1990; eleven subsequent resolutions listed, in *UN Yearbook 1990,* 192; exegesis in Ken Matthews, *The Gulf Conflict and International Relations* (London: Routledge, 1993), app. 4, 309–11.

18. S/1990/21472, August 3, 1990.

19. Shevardnadze, *Future Belongs to Freedom,* 101.

20. Bush and Scowcroft, *A World Transformed,* 326.

21. Baker, *Politics of Diplomacy,* 282.

22. Ibid., 283.

23. Mikhail Gorbachev, *My Country and the World* (New York: Columbia University Press, 2000), 204.

24. Bush and Scowcroft, *A World Transformed,* 338.

25. Baker, *Politics of Diplomacy,* 398–99.

26. General Debate, agenda item 9, A/45/PV.12, September 28, 1990, 51–52.

27. Baker, *Politics of Diplomacy,* 327.

28. Joseph Lepgold, "Britain in Desert Storm: The Most Enthusiastic Junior Partner," in Andrew Bennett et al., eds., *Friends in Need: Burden Sharing in the Persian Gulf War* (New York: St. Martin's Press, 1997), 69; Margaret Thatcher, *The Downing Street Years* (New York: HarperCollins, 1993), 816–17; *Times* (London), August 6, 1990, 1.

29. Lepgold, "Britain in Desert Storm," 75.

30. Matthews, *Gulf Conflict,* app. 5, 313; Norman Friedman, *Desert Victory: The War for Kuwait* (Annapolis, Md.: Naval Institute Press, 1991), 57.

31. Isabelle Grunberg, "Still a Reluctant Ally? France's Participation in the Gulf War Coalition," in Bennett et al., *Friends in Need,* 123.

32. Ibid.; *Le Monde,* August 3, 1990, 3.

33. Lawrence Freedman and Efraim Karsh, *The Gulf Conflict, 1990–1991: Diplomacy and War in the New World Order* (Princeton, N.J.: Princeton University Press, 1993), 167; Bush and Scowcroft, *A World Transformed,* 176.

34. Freedman and Karsh, *Gulf Conflict,* 167; Baker, *Politics of Diplomacy,* 314.

35. Freedman and Karsh, *Gulf Conflict,* 117–18.

36. Ibid., 119.

37. Ibid., 118.

38. Ibid., 353–54.

39. Baker, *Politics of Diplomacy,* 288–89.

40. Ibid., 374.

41. Freedman and Karsh, *Gulf Conflict,* 161–62.

42. Ibid., 102–7.

43. Matthews, *Gulf Conflict,* 313, 315.

44. Javier Perez du Cuellar, *Pilgrimage for Peace: A Secretary-General's Memoir* (New York: St. Martin's Press, 1997), 237.

45. Ibid.

46. Baker, *Politics of Diplomacy,* 278; Lepgold, "Britain in Desert Storm," 71.

47. Meisler, *United Nations,* 268; Mingst and Karns, *United Nations in the Post–Cold War Era,* 85.

48. Report of the Secretary-General, Perez de Cuellar, on the Work of the Organization to the General Assembly on September 13, 1991, in *UN Yearbook 1991,* 5; Bruce Russett and James S. Sutterlin, "The UN in a New World Order," *Foreign Affairs* 70, no. 2 (Spring 1991): 69.

49. Quoted from *The Independent,* August 31, 1990, in Freedman and Karsh, *Gulf Conflict,* 161.

50. *UN Yearbook 1991,* 168.

51. Perez de Cuellar, *Pilgrimage for Peace,* 252–53.

52. Melvern, *Ultimate Crime,* 299.

53. Ibid., 188–93.

54. Report of the Secretary-General, September 13, 1991, *UN Yearbook 1991,* 3.

55. "The President's Views: 'Very Clearly, Good vs. Evil,'" *U.S. News and World Report* 109 (December 31, 1990): 24.

56. Report of the Secretary-General, September 13, 1991, *UN Yearbook 1991,* 14.

57. Letter from president of the EC to the secretary-general, August 2, 1990, S/1990/21426 (A/45/368); letter, August 6, 1990, S/1990/21502 (A/45/409); letter, August 12, 1990, S/1990/21502 (A/45/409); letter, December 17, 1990, S/1990/22018 (A/4/888).

58. Letter, September 27, 1990, S/1990/21834 (A/45/558); letter from EC to UN secretary-general, December 17, 1990, S/1990/22018 (A/45/888).

59. Letter, August 22, 1990, the permanent mission of Italy to UN, transmitting text of declaration on situation of foreigners in Iraq and Kuwait issued by the EC at the extraordinary ministerial meeting of political cooperation, S/1990/21590.

60. Letter, August 22, 1990, permanent mission of France to UN transmitting WEU final communiqué at close of the ministerial session, Paris, S/1990/21603.

61. Matthews, *Gulf Conflict,* 61–62; Freedman and Karsh, *Gulf Conflict,* 152.

62. Defense Planning Committee and nuclear planning group, Brussels, December 6–7, 1990, at www.nato.inc/docu (italics added); NAC communiqué, Brussels, December 17–18, 1990, ibid.

63. Defense Planning Committee and nuclear planning group communiqué, Brussels, May 28–29, 1991, at www.nato.int/docu.

64. Quoted in letter from Diego A. Ruiz Palmer, head of the planning section, Operations, Division, International Staff, to author, December 9, 2008.

Chapter 7

1. Harry Kreisler, "Conversations with Sir Brian Urquhart," March 19, 1996, *The UN in the Post–Cold War World* (Berkeley: UC Institute of International Studies, 1992), 7–8.

2. Ibid., 8.

3. Perez de Cuellar, *Pilgrimage for Peace,* 495.

4. NATO press communiqué issued by heads of state and government in meeting of North Atlantic Council, Rome, November 8, 1991, par. 4, at www.nato.int/docu.

5. Ibid., 2.

6. Ibid., 3.

7. NATO press release S-1(98)88, "The Situation in Yugoslavia," statement issued by the heads of state and government participating in the meeting of the North Atlantic Council, Rome, November 1–8, 1991, 1, at www.nato.int/docu.

8. Quoted in Richard Holbrooke, *To End a War* (New York: Random House, 1998), 27; "our vital national interests were not at stake," Baker, *Politics of Diplomacy,* 636.

9. NATO press release S-l(98)88, 1–2, at www.nato.int/docu.

10. Warren Zimmermann, "The Last Ambassador: A Memoir of the Collapse of Yugoslavia," *Foreign Affairs* 74, no. 2 (March–April 1995): 3.

11. Ibid., 5–7, 9.

12. Quoted in Melvern, *Ultimate Crime,* 309.

13. Misha Glenny, *The Fall of Yugoslavia: The Third Balkan War* (New York: Penguin Books, 1994), 179; Holbrooke, *To End a War,* 30.

14. S/RES/713 (1991), September 25, 1991.

15. *UN Yearbook 1991,* 217–18.

16. S/RES/724 (1991), December 15, 1991.

17. Baker, *Politics of Diplomacy,* 639; Holbrooke, *To End a War,* 30; Carrington from Susan L. Woodward, "International Aspects of the Wars in Yugoslavia," in Jasminka Udovicki and James Ridgeway, eds., *Burn This House: The Making and Unmaking of Yugoslavia* (Durham, N.C.: Duke University Press, 1997), 225.

18. "The Members of the United Nations . . . shall make every effort to achieve pacific settlements of local disputes through . . . regional agencies before referring them to the United Nations." UN Charter, ch. 8, par. 2, in Leland M. Goodrich and Advard Hanbro, *Charter of the United Nations* (Boston: World Peace Foundation, 1948), 114.

19. Ejub Stitkovac, "Croatia: The First War," in Udovicki and Ridgeway, *Burn This House,* 166.

20. Meisler, *United Nations,* 314.

21. S/RES/743 (1992), accepted unanimously at 3055th meeting of UN Security Council, February 21, 1992.

22. S/RES/816 (1993), adopted 14-0-1, at 3191st meeting of Security Council, March 31, 1993.

23. A/47/121 (1992), December 18, 1992.

24. Meisler, *United Nations,* 319.

25. Christopher quoted in Ivo Daalder, *Getting to Dayton: The Making of America's Bosnia Policy* (Washington, D.C.: Brookings Institution, 2000), 36.

26. Holbrooke, *To End a War,* 31; Colin Powell, "U.S. Forces: Challenges Ahead," *Foreign Affairs* 71, no. 1 (Winter 1962–1963): 39; also David Owen, *Balkan Odyssey* (New York: Harcourt Brace, 1995), 101–2; Madeleine K. Albright, *Madame Secretary* (New York: Miramax Books, 2003), 181–82.

27. Randall B. Woods, "Clinton, Fulbright, and the Legacy of the Cold War," in Todd G. Shields et al., eds., *The Clinton Riddle: Perspectives on the Forty-Second President* (Fayetteville: University of Arkansas Press, 2004), 102.

28. William G. Hyland, *Clinton's World: Remaking American Foreign Policy* (Westport, Conn.: Praeger, 1992), 31.

29. Final communiqué, ministerial meeting of the North Atlantic Council in Oslo, June 4, 1992.

30. Final communiqué, ministerial meeting of the North Atlantic Council in Brussels, December 17, 1992, ibid., 48.

31. Ibid.; S/RES/781 (1992), adopted 14-0-1, 3122nd meeting, October 9, 1992; S/RES/786 (1992), adopted unanimously, 3133rd meeting, November 10, 1992.

32. Hendrickson, *Diplomacy and War,* 45–46.

33. Ibid., 52.

34. Ibid., 54; *Keesing's* (April 1993): 39426.

35. Meisler, *United Nations,* 280–82.

36. Albright, *Madame Secretary,* 207.

37. Boutros Boutros-Ghali, "Agenda for Peace," in Adam Roberts and Benedict Kingsbury, *United Nations, Divided World: The UN's Role in International Relations* (Oxford: Clarendon Press, 1994), 1; "An Agenda for Peace 1995," 2nd ed. (New York: United Nations, 1995), 11, 28–30 (29).

38. Meisler, *United Nations,* 290.

39. Owen, *Balkan Odyssey,* 164.

40. U.S. Senate, Committee on Foreign Relations, hearings, 103rd Cong., 3rd sess., May 11, 1995, 12.

41. John Kriendler, "NATO's Changing Role: Opportunities and Constraints," *NATO Review* 41, no. 4 (June 1993): 1; S/RES/816, adopted 14-0-1, 3191st meeting, March 31, 1993.

42. S/1993/836, June 4, 1993.

43. Bucknam, "UN and NATO Theater-Level Commanders," 54–56.

44. Bucknam speculated that the term "dual key," with its echoes of nuclear safeguards,

may have come into the UN-NATO lexicon at a NATO meeting on February 10, 1994, in order to soften the impact of the NAC ultimatum following the Sarajevo massacre. Ibid., 98. Daalder agrees with the date and calls it "an infamous" arrangement to satisfy British and French concern about air strikes. Daalder, *Getting to Dayton*, 22–23.

45. Kofi Annan, "UN Peacekeeping Operations and Cooperation with NATO," *NATO Review* 47, no. 5 (October 1993): 3–7.

46. Final communiqué, ministerial meeting of the North Atlantic Council, Istanbul, June 9, 1994, at www.nato.inc/docu.

47. Decisions taken at the meeting of the North Atlantic Council, August 9, 1993, at www.nato.inc/docu.

48. Owen, *Balkan Odyssey*, 365.

49. Hendrickson, *Diplomacy and War*, 62; Meisler, *United Nations*, 324.

50. Decisions taken at the meeting of the North Atlantic Council, February 9, 1994, at www.nato.inc/docu.

51. Decisions on the protection of safe areas taken at the meeting of the North Atlantic Council in permanent session, April 24, 1994, ibid., 21–23.

52. Report of the secretary-general, September 2, 1994, in *UN Yearbook 1994*, 85.

53. Quoted in Bucknam, "UN and NATO Theater-Level Commanders," 148.

54. Ibid.

55. U.S. Senate, Committee on Armed Services, hearing on "Situation in Bosnia," 103rd Cong., 2nd sess., December 1, 1994, 12.

56. Holbrooke, *To End a War*, 65.

57. Saadia Touval, *Mediation in the Yugoslav Wars: The Critical Years, 1990–1995* (London: Palgrave, 2002), 143.

58. Hendrickson, *Diplomacy and War*, 71–72.

59. Ibid., 72–73.

60. Ibid., 73; Holbrooke, *To End a War*, 99.

61. Hendrickson, *Diplomacy and War*, 88.

62. Excerpted from Noel Malcolm, *Los Angeles Times Book Review*, November 15, 1998, 11.

63. Jan Willem Honig and Norbert Both, *Srebrenica: Record of a War Crime* (London: Penguin Books, 1996).

64. Holbrooke, *To End a War*, 64–65; Bucknam, "UN and NATO Theater-Level Commanders," 160, 171; S/1995/444; *New York Times*, June 23, 1995, A7.

65. Joyce P. Kaufman, *NATO and the Former Yugoslavia: Crisis, Conflict, and the Atlantic Alliance* (Lanham, Md.: Rowman and Littlefield, 2002), 118; Holbrooke, *To End a War*, 67; Daalder, *Getting to Dayton*, 44–46; NATO press communiqué, Defence Planning Committee and Nuclear Planning Group, June 8, 1995, par. 5, at www.nato.int/docu.

66. Holbrooke, *To End a War*, 66–67; Daalder, *Getting to Dayton*, 57; NATO press communiqué, Defence Planning Committee and Nuclear Planning Group, June 8, 1995, par. 5, at www.nato.int/docu; *New York Times*, June 23, 1995, 6.

67. *New York Times*, June 25, 1995, A6; Daalder, *Getting to Dayton*, 61–64; U.S. Senate, *Congressional Record* 141, pt. 14 (July 26, 1995): 20442.

68. Holbrooke, *To End a War*, 71–72.

69. Report of the Secretary-General, September 2, 1994, in *UN Yearbook 1994*, 85;

Bucknam, "UN and NATO Theater-Level Commanders," 199; Wesley K. Clark, *Waging Modern War: Bosnia, Kosovo, and the Future of Combat* (New York: Public Affairs, 2001), 51.

70. Quoted in Holbrooke, *To End a War,* 73.

71. Bucknam, "UN and NATO Theater-Level Commanders," 167.

72. Daalder, *Getting to Dayton,* 119.

73. Holbrooke, *To End a War,* 99; Hendrickson, *Diplomacy and War,* 81.

Chapter 8

1. Holbrooke, *To End a War,* 106.

2. Owen, *Balkan Odyssey,* 365.

3. Kaufman, *NATO and the Former Yugoslavia,* 122.

4. Clark, *Waging Modern War,* 63.

5. Quoted in Holbrooke, *To End a War,* 102.

6. U.S. Senate, 104th Cong., 1st sess., *Congressional Record* 141, pt. 25 (December 13, 1995): 36905–8.

7. Holbrooke, *To End a War,* 143.

8. Ibid., 116.

9. Ibid., 318. It is worth noting that *Le Monde,* December 15, 1999, also omitted any reference to Dayton in its celebration of the treaty on pages 1 and 2.

10. Owen, *Balkan Odyssey,* 335.

11. Boris Yeltsin, *Midnight Diaries,* trans. Catherine A. Fitzpatrick (New York: Public Affairs, 2000), 256–57; Holbrooke, *To End a War,* 117.

12. Clark, *Waging Modern War,* 57.

13. Leurdijk, *The United Nations and NATO,* 105–6.

14. Holbrooke, *To End a War,* 322.

15. Ibid., 92.

16. Albright, *Madame Secretary,* 207, 209.

17. S/1996/936 (1996), November 13, 1996, letter from Egypt supporting Boutros-Ghali's reappointment as UN secretary-general; S/PV/3714, November 19, 1996, draft resolution on recommendation to the General Assembly for Boutros-Ghali's second term as secretary-general; Albright, *Madame Secretary,* 211.

18. Boutros Boutros-Ghali, *Unvanquished: A UN-U.S. Saga* (New York: Random House, 1999), 247.

19. Ibid., 245.

20. Report of the secretary-general to the UN General Assembly, October 17, 1995, in *UN Yearbook 1995,* 8–9 (italics added).

21. Boutros-Ghali, *Unvanquished,* 246.

22. Hendrickson, *Diplomacy and War,* 73.

23. Holbrooke, *To End a War,* 202.

24. NATO press communiqué M-NAC-2(95)18, ministerial meeting of North Atlantic Council, Brussels, December 5, 1995, par. 4, at www.nato.int/docu.

25. Ibid., par. 10.

26. NATO press communiqué, M-NAC-(1996) 63, ministerial meeting of the North Atlantic Council, Berlin, June 3, 1996, pars. 8, 10, at www.nato.int/docu.

27. Ibid., par. 8. The Dayton Peace Accords, initialed at Wright-Patterson Air Force Base on November 21, 1995, and signed in Paris on December 14, 1995, in U.S. Department of State, Bureau of Public Affairs, *Dispatch Supplement,* vol. 7, supplement 1.

28. Dayton Peace Accords, in U.S. Department of State, Bureau of Public Affairs, *Dispatch Supplement,* March 1996, vol. 7, supplement 1, 2.

29. S/RES/1031 (1995), December 15, 1995; Leurdijk, *The United Nations and NATO,* 102.

30. S/RES/1021 (1995), December 14, 1995.

31. Leurdijk, *The United Nations and NATO,* 149; Albright, *Madame Secretary,* 271.

32. John L. Cirafici, "SFOR in Bosnia 1997: A Watershed Year," *Parameters* 29 (Spring 1999): 80, 83.

33. Gerald Knaus and Marcus Cox, "Wither Bosnia? Five Years after Dayton," *NATO Review* 48 (Winter 2000–2001): 7.

34. Fouad Ajami, "Under Western Eyes: The Fate of Bosnia," *Survival* 41 (Summer 1999): 47, 49.

35. S/1996/49, January 23, 1996, letter from secretary-general transmitting second report to the Security Council on operations of IFOR; S/1996/460, report of secretary-general pursuant to S/RES/1045 (1995), June 21, 1996, concerning establishment of the UN Mission in Bosnia and Herzegovina (UNMIBH).

36. "Kofi Annan," *Columbia Encyclopedia* (New York: Columbia University Press, 2001–2007).

37. "Javier Solana," *NATO Who's Who: Secretaries General* (www.nato.int/cv/secgen/solana.htm); Hendrickson, *Diplomacy and War,* 90–91.

38. NATO press release M-NAC2(99)166, December 15, 1999, ministerial meeting of NAC, Brussels, pars. 10, 11, at www.nato.int/docu.

39. Judith Miller, *New York Times,* May 19, 1999, 11.

40. "Secretary-General Presents His Annual Report to General Assembly," UN press release SG/SM7136, GA/9596, September 20, 1999, quoted in Alberto R. Coll, "Kosovo and the Moral Burdens of Power," in Andrew J. Bacevich and Eliot A. Cohen, *War over Kosovo: Politics and Strategy in a Global Age* (New York: Columbia University Press, 2001), 138.

41. Hendrickson, *Diplomacy and War,* 95.

42. Ibid., 92–93.

43. Holbrooke, *To End a War,* 291–93.

44. Albright, *Madame Secretary,* 379; Ivo H. Daalder and Michael O'Hanlon, *Winning Ugly: NATO's War to Save Kosovo* (Washington, D.C.: Brookings Institution, 2000), 6, 10, 11.

45. Kaufman, *NATO and the Former Yugoslavia,* 151.

46. Daalder and O'Hanlon, *Winning Ugly,* 9–10.

47. Ibid., 14; Kaufman, *NATO and the Former Yugoslavia,* 155.

48. Kaufman, *NATO and the Former Yugoslavia,* 156; Clark, *Waging Modern War,* 108; Albright, *Madame Secretary,* 381.

49. Albright, *Madame Secretary,* 382; Daalder and O'Hanlon, *Winning Ugly,* 28–29.

50. Clark, *Waging Modern War,* 110.

51. Quoted in David S. Yost, *NATO Transformed: The Alliance's New Roles in International Security* (Washington, D.C.: United States Institute of Peace, 1998), 236.

52. S/RES/1160 (1998), March 31, 1998; Albright, *Madame Secretary,* 384.

53. S/RES/1199 (1998), September 23, 1998, adopted with one abstention, as with 1160; report of the secretary-general to the UN Security Council prepared pursuant to Resolutions 1160 and 1199, in *UN Yearbook 1998,* 379–80.

54. NATO press release M-NAC-1(98)61, May 28, 1998, statement on Kosovo issued at the NAC ministerial meeting in Luxembourg, pars. 1–3, 6, at www.nato.inc/docu.

55. Hendrickson, *Diplomacy and War,* 96–97.

56. Daalder and O'Hanlon, *Winning Ugly,* 42–43.

57. Ibid., 45; Hendrickson, *Diplomacy and War,* 97, 101.

58. S/1998/998, October 19, 1998, letter from Polish minister of foreign affairs as chairman of OSCE, transmitting agreement on the Kosovo Verification Mission of the OSCE to the UN secretary-general; Daalder and O'Hanlon, *Winning Ugly,* 47–48.

59. Remarks by Secretary-General Javier Solana, Belgrade, October 15, 1998, at www. nato.int/docu.

60. S/RES/1203, October 24, 1998; endorsement of Holbrooke-Milosevic agreement, in Daalder and O'Hanlon, *Winning Ugly,* 252, 255.

61. Clark-Naumann agreement with Serb and Yugoslav authorities, Record of NATO-Serbia(FRY) meeting in Belgrade, October 25, 1998, ibid., 256–58 (FRY is the Federal Republic of Yugoslavia); statement on Kosovo, issued at the ministerial meeting of the North Atlantic Council, Brussels, December 8, 1998, at www.nato.int/docu.

62. Statement by NATO secretary general on behalf of the NAC, Brussels, January 17, 1999, at www.nato.int/docu; Solana quoted in Kaufman, *NATO and the Former Yugoslavia,* 172.

63. Craig Whitney, *New York Times,* January 29, 1999, 12.

64. Statement by Kofi Annan, NATO HQ, Brussels, January 28, 1999, pars. 2–5, at www.nato.int/docu/speech/1999/s990128aa.

65. Kille, *From Manager to Visionary,* 206, 207.

66. NATO press release (9)12, January 30, 1999, statement by NAC on Kosovo, cited in Daalder and O'Hanlon, *Winning Ugly,* 77.

67. Kaufman, *NATO and the Former Yugoslavia,* 175, 176.

68. Daalder and O'Hanlon, *Winning Ugly,* 69; Clark, *Waging Modern War,* 170.

69. Daalder and O'Hanlon, *Winning Ugly,* 80; Sten Rynning, *NATO Renewed: The Power and Purpose of Transatlantic Cooperation* (New York: Palgrave Macmillan, 1995), 85–86.

70. Dag Henriksens, *NATO's Gamble: Combining Diplomacy and Airpower in the Kosovo Crisis, 1998–1999* (Annapolis, Md.: Naval Institute Press, 2007), 170.

71. Ibid., 174; Albright, *Madame Secretary,* 406.

72. Remarks on the situation in Kosovo, March 22, 1999, in *Public Papers: William J. Clinton, 1999,* vol. 1, 427.

73. Address to the nation on air strikes against Serbian targets in the Federal Republic of Yugoslavia (Serbia and Montenegro), March 24, 1999, ibid., 452. David Halberstam suggested that Clinton was "tiptoeing in the war, acutely aware of congressional

opposition at home and the fragility of the alliance overseas." This would explain his cautious statement: "I do not *intend* to put our troops in Kosovo to fight a war." David Halberstam, *War in Time of Peace: Bush, Clinton, and the Generals* (New York: Scribner's, 2001), 423 (italics added).

74. Hendrickson, *Diplomacy and War,* 104–6.

75. S/1999/328, March 24, 1999; S/PV/4989, March 26, 1999, Russian-sponsored draft resolution, not adopted after failing to obtain required majority (3–0), with twelve abstaining; S/1999/363, March 31, 1999, letter from Iran transmitting statement of the Organization of Islamic Conference Contact Group on March 26 expressing concern over Yugoslavia's failure to accept a political solution in Kosovo; S/1999/414, April 8, 1999, letter from Germany transmitting call by Special General Council of European Union for Milosevic to agree to stationing an international military peacekeeping force.

76. NATO press release S-1(1999)62, April 23, 1999, Washington, D.C., statement on Kosovo, issued by heads of state and government participating in NAC on April 23 and 24, 1999, pars. 2, 6, at www.nato.int/docu.

77. Ibid., par. 7; John Norris, *Collision Course: NATO, Russia, and Kosovo* (Westport, Conn.: Praeger, 2005), 178–79.

78. Norris, *Collision Course,* 307.

79. Clark, *Waging Modern War,* 240–41, 252–53; Daalder and O'Hanlon, *Winning Ugly,* 140–41.

80. S/1999/391, exchange of letters April 2 and 3, 1999, between Solana and UN High Commissioner for Refugees seeking assistance to refugees from Kosovo.

81. S/PRST/(1999)12, May 4, 1999, statement recalling president of the UN Security Council's "deep distress and concern" over the bombing of the Chinese Embassy.

82. S/1999/528, May 7, 1999, Yugoslavia's complaints of the UN Security Council's bias.

83. S/1999/516, May 6, 1999, letter transmitting statement of chairman of G-8 foreign ministers' meeting concerning principles for political solution to the Kosovo crisis; Kaufman, *NATO and the Former Yugoslavia,* 196–200.

84. S/RES/1244, June 10, 1999, app. C, in Daalder and O'Hanlon, *Winning Ugly,* 275–77, quotes from nos. 3, 6, 11.

85. No. 5, ibid., 275; no. 20, ibid., 278; S/1999/692, June 17, 1999, letter from secretary-general to the UN Security Council transmitting NATO secretary general's initial report on KFOR operations for period June 12–15, 1999; S/1999/1266, December 17, 1999, letter from secretary-general to Security Council, transmitting monthly report on the operations of KFOR for period October 17–November 23, 1999.

86. Daalder and O'Hanlon, *Winning Ugly,* 219.

87. Henrikson, "Constraint of Legitimacy," 53.

88. Louis Henkin, "Kosovo and the Law of 'Humanitarian Intervention,'" *American Journal of International Law* 93, no. 4 (October 1999): 825.

89. Catherine Guicherd, "International Law and the War in Kosovo," *Survival* 41, no. 2 (Summer 1999): 20; Henkin, "Kosovo and the Law of 'Humanitarian Intervention,'" 828.

90. Henrikson, "Constraint of Legitimacy," 46; Diego A. Ruiz Palmer letter to author, December 9, 2008.

91. S/1999/347 (A/53/884), March 26, 1999, from Mexico, transmitting communiqué by Rio Group to the UN Security Council.

92. S/1999/76, January 26, 1999, letter from Qatar transmitting statement on the situation in Kosovo, issued by the Islamic group at the UN, S/1999/363, March 31, 1999.

93. S/RES/1244, quoted in no. 20; press release M-NAC-D-1 (2001)88, June 7, 2001, NAC statement on the Balkans.

94. Rynning, *NATO Renewed*, 84.

95. Albright, *Madame Secretary*, 384.

96. Quoted in Norris, *Collision Course*, 297.

Chapter 9

1. Boutros-Ghali, *Unvanquished*, 247.

2. Yost, "NATO and International Organizations," 17.

3. Hendrickson, *Diplomacy and War*, 104–5.

4. Thomas S. Mowle and David H. Sacko, *The Unipolar World: An Unbalanced Future* (London: Palgrave Macmillan, 2007).

5. NATO communiqué PR/CP (2001) 124, statement by the North Atlantic Council, September 12, 2001; S/RES/1368 (2001), September 12, 2001; S/RES/1373 (2001), September 28, 2001.

6. S(2001)1943, September 12, 2001, letter from NATO secretary general to UN secretary-general, sent to permanent representatives in the UN Security Council, notifying them that "the [North Atlantic] Council agreed that if it is determined that this attack was directed from abroad against the United States, it shall be regarded as an action covered by Article 5 of the Washington Treaty."

7. Hendrickson, *Diplomacy and War*, 120.

8. SC(2006)0013, January 10, 2006, and SC (2007)0260, April 18, 2007, in Yost, "NATO and International Organizations," 56n78.

9. Ibid., 56.

10. S/RES/1368 (2001), September 12, 2001; *Le Monde*, September 12, 2001.

11. S/RES/1373 (2001), September 28, 2001.

12. *Keesing's* 47, no. 9, 44335; A/56/433, October 3, 2001.

13. A/56/463, October 11, 2001.

14. Examples include S/2001/1103, November 23, 2001, letter from France on participation of its military forces; S/2001/1287, letter from EU concerning its report to Counter-Terrorism Committee; press release M-NAC-2(2001)159, December 6, 2001, par. 9, on NATO's response to terrorism.

15. *New York Times*, September 29, 2001, B1, B4.

16. *Keesing's*, 44336.

17. Ibid., 44335.

18. *New York Times*, September 28, 2001, B1, B4; press release M-NAC-2(2001)159, December 6, 2001, par. 4.

19. See Chapter 5 for background of the failed Soviet invasion.

20. S/2001/870, September 13, 2001, identical letters addressed to secretary-general

and to president of UN Security Council; S/2001/934, October 3, 2001, identical letters from secretary-general to presidents of the UN Security Council and the General Assembly; S/RES/1386 (2001), December 20, 2001, authorizing establishment of an International Security Assistance Force (ISAF) in Afghanistan.

21. Rumsfeld statement on *Face the Nation,* September 23, 2001, quoted in Thomas S. Mowle, "Global NATO: An Alliance for a Unipolar World," in S. Victor Papacosma, ed., *NATO's Current and Future Challenges,* Occasional Papers 6 (Kent, Ohio: Lemnitzer Center for NATO and European Union Studies, 2008), 45.

22. S/2001/1154, letter from secretary-general to UN Security Council transmitting agreement on provisional arrangements in Afghanistan, signed in Bonn on December 5, 2001.

23. S/2001/1217, December 19, 2001, letter from United Kingdom informing secretary-general of its willingness "to become the initial lead nation" for ISAF; Douglas J. Feith, *War and Decision: At the Dawn of the War on Terrorism* (New York: Harper, 2008), 133–34, 149.

24. S/RES/1386 (2001), December 20, 2001, adopted unanimously, 4443rd meeting; A/56/220A, December 20, 2001, par. 13.

25. NATO press release M-NAC-2 (2001)159, December 6, 2001, pars. 3, 9 (italics added).

26. President's comments in *New York Times,* September 28, 2001, 1, B4.

27. Remarks at the Islamic Center of Washington, September 17, 2001, *Public Papers: George W. Bush, 2001,* 1121; Elizabeth Pond, "The Dynamics of the Feud over Iraq," in David M. Andrews, ed., *The Atlantic Alliance under Stress: U.S.-European Relations after Iraq* (Cambridge, England: Cambridge University Press, 2006), 32–33.

28. Jolyon Howarth and John T. S. Keeler, *The EU, NATO, and the Quest for European Autonomy* (London: Palgrave Macmillan, 2003), 4.

29. Steven L. Rearden, *History of the Office of the Secretary of Defense: The Formative Years, 1947–1950* (Washington, D.C.: Office of the Secretary of Defense, 1984), 481–82.

30. Michael Binyon, *Times* (London), September 12, 12, 2001.

31. Feith, *War and Decision,* 215.

32. Address before a joint session of Congress on the State of the Union, January 29, 2002, *Public Papers: George W. Bush, 2002,* 131; Pond, "Dynamics of the Feud over Iraq," 34.

33. James Mann, *Rise of the Vulcans: The History of Bush's War Cabinet* (New York: Viking, 2004), 334; Bob Woodward, *Plan of Attack* (New York: Simon and Schuster, 2004), 336–37.

34. See article by David E. Sanger and Thom Shanker on United States' exploring a Baghdad strike, in *New York Times,* July 29, 2002, 1.

35. Elizabeth Pond, *Friendly Fire: The Near-Death of the Transatlantic Alliance* (Washington, D.C.: Brookings Institution Press, 2004), 45–46.

36. Anthony C. Zinni, *The Battle for Peace: A Frontline Vision of America's Power and Purpose* (New York: Palgrave Macmillan, 2006), 46–47.

37. Quoted in Mann, *Rise of the Vulcans,* 337.

38. Vice President Speaks at VFW 103rd National Convention, August 26, 2002, at www.whitehouse.gov/news/releases/2002/08/2002/20826.

39. Quoted from introduction to the National Security Strategy document in Richard

E. Rupp, *NATO after 9/11: An Alliance in Continuing Decline* (New York: Palgrave Macmillan, 2006), 254n25; quote in Mats Berdal, "The UN Security Council: Ineffective but Indispensable," *Survival* 45, no. 2 (Summer 2003): 17–18.

40. All quotes from Ivo H. Daalder and James M. Lindsay, *America Unbound: The Bush Revolution in Foreign Policy* (Washington, D.C.: Brookings Institution, 2003), 136.

41. Pond, *Friendly Fire,* 50.

42. Philip H. Gordon and Jeremy Shapiro, *Allies at War: America, Europe, and the Crisis over Iraq* (New York: McGraw-Hill, 2004), 144.

43. The image of America as Mars and Europe as Venus is from Robert Kagan, *Of Policy and Power: America and Europe in the New World Order* (New York: Knopf, 2003).

44. Steven Szabo, *Parting Ways: The Crisis in German-American Relations* (Washington, D.C.: Brookings Institution, 2004), 9–13; Pond, *Friendly Fire,* 56–58.

45. Chirac quoted in Daalder and Lindsay, *America Unbound,* 138; Pond, *Friendly Fire,* 61.

46. Szabo, *Parting Ways,* 115–17.

47. Pond, "Dynamics of the Feud over Iraq," 37–38.

48. Ibid., 38.

49. Mann, *Rise of the Vulcans,* 340.

50. Daalder and Lindsay, *America Unbound,* 138–39; address to the UN General Assembly, September 12, 2002, *Public Papers: George W. Bush, 2002,* 1576.

51. Daalder and Lindsay, *America Unbound,* 140–41.

52. S/RES/1441 (2002), decision to set up an enhanced inspection regime in order to ensure Iraq's compliance of its disarmament obligations, 4644th meeting, November 8, 2002. See particularly pars. 5, 13.

53. Quoted in Rupp, *NATO after 9/11,* 129; press release (2002)127, November 21, 2002, Prague summit declaration issued by heads of state and government in NAC meeting; press release (2002)133, November 1, 2002, Prague Summit statement on Iraq.

54. Daalder and Lindsay, *America Unbound,* 141; Gordon and Shapiro, *Allies at War,* 146–47.

55. Daalder and Lindsay, *America Unbound,* 144.

56. Pond, "Dynamics of the Feud over Iraq," 42–45.

57. Ibid., 42, 44.

58. Rupp, *NATO after 9/11,* 134.

59. Hendrickson, *Diplomacy and War,* 122–23, 132.

60. Ibid., 134–35; Rupp, *NATO after 9/11,* 137–38; Hall Gardner, *NATO and the European Union: New World, New Europe, New Threats* (Burlington, Vt.: Ashgate, 2004), 290.

61. Gordon and Shapiro, *Allies at War,* 145; Gardner, *NATO and the European Union,* 290.

62. Gordon and Shapiro, *Allies at War,* 149–50; Pond, *Friendly Fire,* 73.

63. Quoted in Gordon and Shapiro, *Allies at War,* 152; Address to the Nation, *Public Papers: George W. Bush, 2003,* 277–80.

64. *New York Times,* May 2, 2003, A17.

65. Pond, "Dynamics of the Feud over Iraq," 52.

66. S/RES/1483 (2003), adopted unanimously, May 22, 2003, 4761st meeting.

67. S/RES/1500 (2003), adopted with one abstention, 4808th meeting, August 14, 2003.

68. S/RES/1511 (2003), adopted unanimously, 4844th meeting, October 16, 2003, par. 13 (original italics).

69. *New York Times,* August 20, 2003, 1, 8; S/RES/1557 (2004), adopted unanimously, 5020th meeting, August 12, 2004.

70. NATO press release (2003)059, June 3, 2003, final communiqué, NAC ministerial meeting in Madrid, par. 4, at www.nato.int/docu.

71. Ibid., par. 5.

72. S/RES/1546 (2004), formation of a sovereign interim government of Iraq, adopted unanimously, 4987th meeting, June 8, 2004; press release (2004)098, June 28, 2004, statement on Iraq, issued by heads of state and government in Istanbul, par. 5; press release (2005)022, February 22, 2005, statement issued by heads of state and government at a NAC meeting in Brussels, par. 3.

73. Press release (2006)064, June 8, 2006, final communiqué of meeting of defense ministers in Brussels, par. 6.

74. U.S. Senate, 108th Cong., 1st sess., *Congressional Record* 149, pt. 12 (June 27, 2003): 16855.

75. *Keesing's* 49, no. 7/8, 45534.

76. NATO press release (2006)064, June 8, 2006, final communiqué of meeting of defense ministers in Brussels, par. 4. Yost, "NATO and International Organizations," 74–76, makes a point of noting the increasing NATO-EU teamwork developing from principles of cooperation approved at the Washington summit in April 1999. These principles were known as "Berlin plus," building on agreements made in Berlin in 1996, and involved allied use of NATO assets for operations not involving the entire alliance.

77. S/PRST/51 (2005), October 24, 2005.

78. NATO press release (2003)059, June 3, 2003, par. 3.

79. S/2003/504, April 23, 2003, letter from president of UN Security Council, referring to UN secretary-general's letter of April 16, 2003, from NATO secretary general.

80. S/2004/222, March 17, 2004, letter from NATO secretary general with quarterly report of ISAF operations from November 12, 2003, to February 12, 2004; press release (2006)064, June 8, 2006; final communiqué of meeting of defense ministers in Brussels, par. 3.

81. NATO press release (2006)064, June 8, 2006; final communiqué of meeting of defense ministers in Brussels, par. 3.

82. Carolyn Wyatt, "Afghan Burden Tasks NATO Allies," December 12, 2007, BBC News, Noordwijk.

83. *Washington Post,* June 15, 2008, A16.

84. Quoted in Carolyn Wyatt, "Afghan Burden Tasks NATO Allies," December 12, 2007, BBC News, Noordwijk.

85. Declaration of the heads of state and government participating in the meeting of the North Atlantic Council, January 10–11, 1994, at www.nato.int/docu.

86. NATO press release (2004)096, June 28, 2004, Istanbul Summit communiqué, par. 8; S/2004/917, November 19, 2004, letter from presidency of Bosnia and Herzegovina on status of EUFOR and NATO; S/RES/1575 (2004), establishment of EUFOR, adopted unanimously, 5085th meeting, November 22, 2004.

87. Yost, "Enhancing NATO's Cooperation with International Organizations," *NATO Review* (Autumn 2007): 78.

88. Annex to DSG(2008)0714(INV), Jaap de Hoop Scheffer and Ban Ki-moon, September 23, 2008, subject: Joint Declaration on UN/NATO Cooperation, International Staff, Private Office of the NATO Secretary General, NATO Headquarters, Brussels.

89. Quoted in Michael F. Harsch and Johannes Varwick, "NATO and the UN," *Survival* 51, no. 2 (April–May 2009): 9–10.

Chapter 10

1. Dick. A. Leurdijk, *The United States and NATO in Former Yugoslavia: Partners in International Cooperation* (The Hague: Netherlands Institute of International Relations, "Clingendael," 1994), xiii, 1.

2. At a Wilton Park conference on "NATO at 60: Towards a New Strategic Concept," on January 15, 2009, held at Wiston House in West Sussex, England, Jamie Shea, director, Policy Planning, Private Office of the NATO Secretary General, noted NATO's frustration over the UN's rebuff of its current attempts to seek closer relations.

3. DSG(2008)0714 (INV), memo from NATO deputy secretary-general to permanent representatives (North Atlantic Council), September 23, 2008, subject: UN/NATO Declaration of Cooperation, International Staff, Private Office of the Secretary General, NATO Headquarters, Brussels.

4. Anna Locher and Christian Nuenlist, "Containing the French Malaise? The Role of NATO's Secretary General, 1958–1968," in Mary Ann Heiss and S. Victor Papacosma, eds., *NATO and the Warsaw Pact: Intrabloc Conflicts* (Kent, Ohio: Kent State University Press, 2008), 75–90.

5. Yost, "NATO and International Organizations," 68–69.

6. Stephen E. Meyer, "Carcass of Dead Policies: The Irrelevance of NATO," *Parameters* 33, no. 4 (Winter 2003–2004): 83; Ronald Steel, *End of the Alliance: America and the Future of Europe* (New York: Viking, 1964).

7. Alan K. Henrikson, "NATO and the United Nations: Toward a Nonallergic Relationship," in S. Victor Papacosma and Mary Ann Heiss, eds., *NATO in the Post–Cold War Era: Does It Have a Future?* (New York: St. Martin's Press, 1995), 107.

BIBLIOGRAPHY

The most pertinent sources are listed in the Introduction.

Archives

Bentley Historical Library, University of Michigan, Ann Arbor.
Liddell Hart Centre for Military Archives, King's College, London.
The National Archives (TNA), Kew.
National Archives and Records Administration (NARA), College Park, Md.
NATO Archives, Brussels.
NATO Parliamentary Conference (North Atlantic Assembly), Brussels.

Published Records

Chambre des Représentants. *Annales parlementaires de Belgique*. Brussels.
Cordier, Andrew W., and Wilder Foote, eds. *The Public Papers of the Secretaries-General of the United Nations: Dag Hammarskjöld*. 5 vols. New York: Columbia University Press, 1972–1975. Cited in the notes as *Hammarskjöld Papers*.
Cordier, Andrew W., and Max Harrelson, eds. *Public Papers of the Secretaries-General of the United Nations: U Thant, 1965–1967*. New York: Columbia University Press, 1976. Cited in the notes as *U Thant Papers*.
Foreign Relations of the United States (FRUS).
France, *Débats parlementaires*.
House of Commons. *Parliamentary Debates*. London: Her Majesty's Stationery Office, 1949–2008.
Mastny, Vojtech, and Malcolm Byrne, eds. *A Cardboard Castle? An Inside History of the Warsaw Pact, 1955–1991*. Budapest/New York: Central European University Press, 2005.

NATO. *Texts of Final Communiqués, 1949–2008.* Brussels: NATO Office of Information and Press, 1949–2008. All these NATO documents (including the North Atlantic Council, Defense, and other subordinate committees) may be found online under *NATO Summits & Ministerial Meetings,* at www. nato.int/docu.

Public Papers of the Presidents of the United States:

———. *Harry S. Truman, 1949.* Washington, D.C.: GPO, 1964.

———. *Dwight D. Eisenhower, 1956.* Washington, D.C.: GPO, 1956.

———. *Lyndon B. Johnson, 1965.* Washington, D.C.: GPO, 1966.

———. *Jimmy Carter, 1977, 1980.* Washington, D.C.: GPO, 1978, 1982.

———. *George Bush, 1990.* Washington, D.C.: GPO, 1991.

———. *William J. Clinton, 1999.* Washington, D.C.: GPO, 2001.

———. *George W. Bush, 2001.* Washington, D.C.: GPO, 2003.

U.S. Congress. U.S. Senate. Committee publications. Washington, D.C.: GPO, 1949–2008.

———. *Congressional Record.* Washington, D.C.: GPO, 1949–2008.

———. *Department of State Bulletin.*

United Nations. *Index to Proceedings of the General Assembly.* New York: United Nations, 1949–2008.

———. *Index to Proceedings of the Security Council.* New York: United Nations, 1949–2008.

———. *Yearbooks.* New York: United Nations, 1949–2008.

Newspapers and Journals

L'Avenir (Namur)

L'Avenir de Luxembourg (Arlon)

Le Courrier de l'Escaut (Tournai)

Current Digest of the Soviet Press

Facts on File Yearbook: Index of World Events, 1949–2009.

Keesing's Contemporary Archives: Weekly Diary of World Events, 1949–2009.

La Libre Belgique (Brussels)

Le Monde

NATO Review

New York Times

La Nouvelle Gazette (Brussels)

Parameters

Survival

Times (London)

Memoirs

Acheson, Dean. *Present at the Creation: My Years in the State Department.* New York: W. W. Norton, 1969.

Achilles, Theodore C. "'Fingerprints on History': The NATO Memoirs of Theodore C. Achilles." In *Occasional Papers* 1, ed. Lawrence S. Kaplan and Sidney R. Snyder. Kent, Ohio: Lyman L. Lemnitzer Center for NATO and European Community Studies, 1992.

Albright, Madeleine K. *Madame Secretary.* New York: Miramax Books, 2003.

Alphand, Hervé. *L'étonnement d'être: journal 1939–1973.* Paris: Fayard, 1977.

Auriol, Vincent. *Journal du Septennat, 1947–1954.* Vol. 3. Paris: Armand Colin, 1974.

Baker, James A. *The Politics of Diplomacy: Revolution, War, and Peace, 1989–1992.* New York: G. P. Putnam's Sons, 1995.

Boutros-Ghali, Boutros. *Unvanquished: A UN-U.S. Saga.* New York: Random House, 1999.

Brzezinski, Zbigniew. *Power and Principle: Memoirs of the National Security Adviser, 1977–1981.* New York: Farrar, Straus, Giroux, 1983.

Bush, George, and Brent Scowcroft. *A World Transformed.* New York: Alfred A. Knopf, 1998.

Carter, Jimmy. *Keeping Faith: Memoirs of a President.* New York: Bantam Books, 1982.

Clark, Wesley K. *Waging Modern War: Bosnia, Kosovo, and the Future of Combat.* New York: Public Affairs, 2001.

Eden, Anthony. *Memoirs: Full Circle.* Boston: Houghton Mifflin, 1960.

de Gaulle, Charles. *Memoirs of Hope: Renewal and Endeavor.* Translated by Terence Kilmartin. London: Weidenfeld and Nicolson, 1971.

Holbrooke, Richard. *To End a War.* New York: Random House, 1998.

Jebb, Gladwyn. *Memoirs of Lord Gladwyn.* New York: Weybridge and Talley, 1972.

Kennan, George F. *Memoirs, 1925–1950.* New York: Bantam Books, 1969.

Lie, Trygve. *In the Cause of Peace: Seven Years with the United Nations.* New York: Macmillan, 1954.

Macmillan, Harold. *Riding the Storm, 1956–1959.* London: Macmillan, 1971.

———. *At the End of the Day, 1961–1963.* New York: Harper and Row, 1994.

Munroe, John A., and A. J. Inglis, eds. *Mike: The Memoirs of Lester B. Pearson, 1948–1957.* 2 vols. Toronto: University of Toronto Press, 1972.

O'Brien, Conor Cruise. *To Katanga and Back: A UN Case History.* New York: Grosset and Dunlap, 1966.

Owen, David. *Balkan Odyssey.* New York: Harcourt Brace, 1995.

Perez du Cuellar, Javier. *Pilgrimage for Peace: A Secretary-General's Memoir.* New York: St. Martin's Press, 1997.

Shevardnadze, Eduard. *The Future Belongs to Freedom*. New York: Free Press, 1991.

Shuckburgh, Evelyn. *Descent to Suez: Diaries, 1951–1956*. London: Weidenfeld and Nicholson, 1986.

Spaak, Paul-Henri. *The Continuing Battle: Memoirs of a European, 1936–1966*. Translated by Henry Fox. Boston: Little, Brown, 1971.

Urquhart, Brian. *A Life in Peace and War*. New York: Harper and Row, 1987.

Vance, Cyrus. *Hard Choices: Critical Years in America's Foreign Policy*. New York: Simon and Schuster, 1983.

Vandenberg, Arthur H., Jr., ed. *The Private Papers of Senator Vandenberg*. Boston: Houghton Mifflin, 1952.

Yeltsin, Boris. *Midnight Diaries*. Translated by Catherine A. Fitzpatrick. New York: Public Affairs, 2000.

Zinni, Anthony. *The Battle for Peace: A Frontline Vision of America's Power and Purpose*. New York: Palgrave Macmillan, 2006.

Articles, Chapters, and Theses

Bucknam, Mark A. "The Influence of UN and NATO Theater-Level Commanders on the Use of Airpower over Bosnia during Deny Flight, 1993–1995." Ph.D. diss., King's College, London, 1999.

Henkin, Louis. "Kosovo and the Law of 'Humanitarian Intervention.'" *American Journal of International Law* 93, no. 4 (October 1999).

Henrikson, Alan K. "The Constraint of Legitimacy: The Legal and Institutional Framework of Euro-Atlantic Security." In *Alliance Politics, Kosovo and NATO's War: Allied Force or Forced Allies?* ed. Pierre Martin and Mark R. Brawley. New York: Palgrave, 2000.

Kaplan, Lawrence S. "McNamara, Vietnam, and the Defense of Europe." In *War Plans and Alliances in the Cold War: Threat Perceptions in the East and West*, ed. Vojtech Mastny et al. London: Routledge, 2006.

Lepgold, Joseph. "Britain in Desert Storm: The Most Enthusiastic Junior Partner." In *Friends in Need: Burden Sharing in the Persian Gulf War*, ed. Andrew Bennett et al. New York: St. Martin's Press, 1997.

Logevall, Fredrik. "The Western Powers and the Escalation of the War." In *America, the Vietnam War, and the World*, ed. Andreas W. Daum et al. New York: Cambridge University Press, 2003.

Pond, Elizabeth. "The Dynamics of the Feud over Iraq." In Andrews, *Atlantic Alliance under Stress*, 32–33.

Soffer, Jonathan. "All for One or All for All: The UN Military Staff Committee and the Contradictions with American Internationalism." *Diplomatic History* 21 (Winter 1997): 52–67.

Yost, David S. "NATO and International Organizations." Forum Paper Series, ed. Cees M. Coops. Rome, September 2007.

Monographs

Andrews, David M., ed. *The Atlantic Alliance under Stress: U.S.-European Relations after Iraq*. Cambridge, England: Cambridge University Press, 2006.

Bacevich, Andrew J., and Eliot A. Cohen. *War over Kosovo: Politics and Strategy in a Global Age*. New York: Columbia University Press, 2001.

Barros, James. *Trygve Lie and the Cold War: The UN Secretary General Pursues Peace, 1946–1953*. DeKalb: Northern Illinois University Press, 1989.

Bennett, Andrew, et al., eds. *Friends in Need: Burden Sharing in the Persian Gulf War*. New York: St. Martin's Press, 1997.

Bowie, Robert R. *Suez 1956*. New York: Oxford University Press, 1974.

Bradsher, Henry S. *Afghan Communism and Soviet Intervention*. Oxford: Oxford University Press, 1999.

Daalder, Ivo H. *Getting to Dayton: The Making of America's Bosnia Policy*. Washington, D.C.: Brookings Institution, 2000.

———, and Michael O'Hanlon. *Winning Ugly: NATO's War to Save Kosovo*. Washington, D.C.: Brookings Institution, 2000.

———, and James M. Lindsay. *America Unbound: The Bush Revolution in Foreign Policy*. Washington, D.C.: Brookings Institution, 2003.

Dayal, Rajeshwal. *Mission for Hammarskjöld: The Congo Crisis*. Princeton, N.J.: Princeton University Press, 1976.

Feith, Douglas J. *War and Decision: At the Dawn of the War on Terrorism*. New York: Harper, 2008.

Finger, Seymour M., and Arnold A. Saltzman. *Bending with the Winds: Kurt Waldheim and the United Nations*. Westport, Conn.: Praeger, 1990.

Firestone, Bernard J. *The United Nations under U Thant, 1961–1971*. Lanham, Md.: Scarecrow Press, 2001.

Freedman, Lawrence, and Efraim Karsh. *The Gulf Conflict, 1990–1991: Diplomacy and War in the New World Order*. Princeton, N.J.: Princeton University Press, 1993.

Freiberger, Steven Z. *Dawn over Suez: The Rise of American Power in the Middle East, 1953–1957*. Chicago: Ivan R. Dee, 1992.

Fursenko, Aleksandr, and Timothy Naftali. *Khrushchev's Cold War: The Inside Story of an American Adversary*. New York: W. W. Norton, 2006.

Gardner, Hall. *NATO and the European Union: New World, New Europe, New Threats*. Burlington, Vt.: Ashgate, 2004.

Glenny, Misha. *The Fall of Yugoslavia: The Third Balkan War.* New York: Penguin Books, 1994.

Gordon, Philip H., and Jeremy Shapiro. *Allies at War: America, Europe, and the Crisis over Iraq.* New York: McGraw-Hill, 2004.

Goscha, Christopher, and Maurice Vaisse, eds. *La Guerre du Vietnam et l'Europe.* Brussels: Bruylant, 2003.

Halberstam, David. *War in Time of Peace: Bush, Clinton, and the Generals.* New York: Scribner's, 2001.

Hendrickson, Ryan C. *Diplomacy and War at NATO: The Secretary General and Military Action after the Cold War.* Columbia: University of Missouri Press, 2006.

Henriksens, Dag. *NATO's Gamble: Combining Diplomacy and Airpower in the Kosovo Crisis, 1998–1999.* Annapolis, Md.: Naval Institute Press, 2007.

Herring, George C. *America's Longest War: The United States and Vietnam, 1950–1975.* 2nd ed. New York: Alfred A. Knopf, 1986.

Honig, Jan Willem, and Norbert Both. *Srebrenica: Record of a War Crime.* London: Penguin Books, 1996.

Hoskins, Catherine. *The Congo since Independence, January 1960–December 1961.* London: Oxford University Press, 1965.

Howarth, Jolyon, and John T. S. Keeler. *The EU, NATO, and the Quest for European Autonomy.* London: Palgrave Macmillan, 2003.

Immerman, Richard H., ed. *John Foster Dulles and the Diplomacy of the Cold War.* Princeton, N.J.: Princeton University Press, 1990.

Immerman, Richard H. *John Foster Dulles: Piety, Pragmatism, and Power in U.S. Foreign Policy.* Wilmington, Del.: SR Books, 1999.

James, Alan. *Britain and the Congo Crisis, 1960–1963.* New York: St. Martin's Press, 1996.

Jordan, Robert S., with Michael W. Bloome. *Political Leadership in NATO: A Study in Multinational Diplomacy.* Boulder, Colo.: Westview Press, 1979.

Kaplan, Lawrence S., et al. *History of the Office of the Secretary of Defense: The McNamara Ascendancy.* Vol. 5. Washington, D.C.: Office of the Secretary of Defense, 2006.

Kaufman, Burton I. *The Arab Middle East and the United States: Inter-Arab Rivalry and Superpower Diplomacy.* New York: Twayne, 1996.

Kaufman, Joyce P. *NATO and the Former Yugoslavia: Crisis, Conflict, and the Atlantic Alliance.* Lanham, Md.: Rowman and Littlefield, 2002.

Kille, Kent J. *From Manager to Visionary: The Secretary-General of the United Nations.* New York: Palgrave Macmillan, 2006.

———, ed. *The UN Secretary-General and Moral Authority: Ethics and Religion in International Leadership.* Washington, D.C.: Georgetown University Press, 2007.

Kunz, Diane B. *Diplomacy of the Suez Crisis.* Chapel Hill: University of North Carolina Press, 1991.

LeFever, Ernest. *Uncertain Mandate: Politics of the UN Congo Operation.* Baltimore: Johns Hopkins University Press, 1967.

Leurdijk, Dick A. *The United Nations and NATO in Former Yugoslavia, 1991–1996: Limits to Diplomacy and Force.* The Hague: Netherlands Institute of International Relations, "Clingendael," 1996.

Mann, James. *Rise of the Vulcans: The History of Bush's War Cabinet.* New York: Viking, 2004.

Matthews, Ken. *The Gulf Conflict and International Relations.* London: Routledge, 1993.

Meisler, Stanley. *The United Nations: The First Fifty Years.* New York: Atlantic Monthly Press, 1995.

Melvern, Linda. *The Ultimate Crime: Who Betrayed the UN and Why.* London: Allison and Busby, 1995.

Mingst, Karen A., and Margaret P. Karns. *The United Nations in the Post–Cold War Era.* Boulder, Colo.: Westview Press, 1995.

Newell, Nancy P., and Richard S. Newell. *The Struggle for Afghanistan.* Ithaca, N.Y.: Cornell University Press, 1981.

Norris, John. *Collision Course: NATO, Russia, and Kosovo.* Westport, Conn.: Praeger, 2005.

Ostrower, Gary B. *The United Nations and the United States, 1945–1995.* New York: Twayne, 1998.

Pond, Elizabeth. *Friendly Fire: The Near-Death of the Transatlantic Alliance.* Washington, D.C.: Brookings Institution, 2004.

Rupp, Richard E. *NATO after 9/11: An Alliance in Continuing Decline.* New York: Palgrave Macmillan, 2006.

Ryan, James D. *The United Nations under Kurt Waldheim, 1972–1981.* Lanham, Md.: Scarecrow Press, 2001.

Rynning, Sten. *NATO Renewed: The Power and Purpose of Transatlantic Cooperation.* New York: Palgrave Macmillan, 1995.

Schwartz, Thomas A. *Lyndon Johnson and Europe: In the Shadow of Vietnam.* Cambridge, Mass.: Harvard University Press, 2003.

Szabo, Steven. *Parting Ways: The Crisis in German-American Relations.* Washington, D.C.: Brookings Institution, 2004.

Udovicki, Jasminka, and James Ridgeway, eds. *Burn This House: The Making and Unmaking of Yugoslavia.* Durham, N.C.: Duke University Press, 2000.

Urquhart, Brian. *Hammarskjöld.* New York: Knopf, 1972.

Woods, Randall B. *Fulbright: A Biography.* New York: Cambridge University Press, 1995.

Yost, David S. *NATO Transformed: The Alliance's New Roles in International Security.* Washington, D.C.: United States Institute of Peace, 1998.

Zubok, Vladislav M. *A Failed Empire: The Soviet Union in the Cold War from Stalin to Gorbachev.* Chapel Hill: University of North Carolina Press, 2007.

INDEX

Acheson, Dean, 9, 11–13, 20–24
Achilles, Theodore A., 7, 10
Adenauer, Konrad, 63, 83
Afghan Interim Authority, 190, 207–8
Afghanistan, 207; Islamic fundamentalism
in, 93; motives for Soviet invasion of,
101–2, 108–9; responses to Soviet
invasion of, 93–96, 100–113, 101–5;
Soviet invasion of, 92, 98–99, 118;
Soviet withdrawal from, 113, 116, 213;
Soviets and, 92–93; supposed to be
outside boundaries of Cold War, 111;
Taliban in, 190–91, 208; UN after
Soviet invasion of, 95–98, 113; UN
missions in, 190, 208–9; UN-NATO
relations in, 1–2, 207–8, 211; U.S.
Operation Enduring Freedom in, 188,
190–93, 197, 203, 206
Africa, 41; colonialism in, 16, 46, 50;
NATO relations with, 45, 49, 57, 69,
85, 214; new nations in, 2–3, 53, 67;
Soviet relations with, 49, 52, 57, 68;
Soviet stance against colonialism in, 16,
58, 68; UN members from, 2–3, 47, 53;
U.S. relations with, 67. *See also* Congo
crisis; specific countries
African-Asian bloc in UN, 47, 49, 55, 61,
72
African Union, EU and NATO cooperation
with, 209
"Agenda for Peace" (Boutros-Ghali), 143–44
Akashi, Yasushi, 145–48, 151, 162–63
Al Qaeda, 192, 194, 198, 204, 210. *See also*
9/11 attacks on U.S.; terrorism
Albania, 98, 171, 173, 180
Albanians, in Kosovo, 170, 175, 180; ethnic
cleansing of, 169, 171–74, 176; KLA

actions by, 173, 181
Albright, Madeleine, 141, 164, 184;
Boutros-Ghali and, 143–44, 161–62; on
IFOR mission, 165–66; on legitimacy of
military intervention to defend human
rights, 169, 172
Algeria, 80; rebellion against France, 31, 37,
50; U Thant working on, 72–73
Alphand, Hervé, 60
Ambassadors' Committee, in NATO
formation, 11–12
Amin, Hafizullah, 92–94
Anderson, Robert B., 66
Anglo-Egyptian agreement (1954), 43
Anglo-Egyptian treaty (1936), 28
Anglo-French invasion. *See* Suez crisis
Anglo-Soviet Treaty of 1942, 18
Annan, Kofi, 190, 213; background of, 167;
on Balkans, 173, 176; good relations
with regional organizations, 176–77,
184; on NATO action against Serbs,
179, 186, 214; relations with NATO,
167, 184; on UN-NATO relationship,
146–47, 154, 161, 168–69
Anti-Ballistic Missile Treaty, U.S. abrogation
of, 187
Arab bloc, 97, 122, 124–25. *See also* Muslim
countries
Arab League, in Desert Storm coalition, 125
Argentina, 17, 103, 125
Armée Nationale Congolaise (ANC), 53, 67
Armey, Dick, 196
Arms: buildups, 105; Iraq's, 117, 122; sales,
63, 104, 122. *See also* nuclear weapons;
weapons of mass destruction
Arms embargo, against Balkans factions,
138, 140, 142–45, 152, 172–73

265

coalition, 122–23, 125–26, 129; on Egypt nationalizing Suez Canal, 31–33; hostility toward U.S., 160, 198, 201; influence in UN vs. NATO, 184, 186, 214–15; NATO and, 7, 81, 86, 201–3, 205, 209, 213; in Persian Gulf crisis, 130, 132; relations with Iraq, 122–23; relations with U.S., 37, 43, 45, 60–61, 122–23, 129, 187, 197; response to 9/11 attacks, 189; in Southeast Asia, 50, 75, 80–81; on Soviet invasion of Afghanistan, 106, 110; Soviets and, 7, 39–40, 42; in Suez Canal Users Association, 33–35; in Suez crisis, 27–31, 34–38, 42–46; UN and, 49, 55, 72, 151–52, 162, 213; Vietnam War and, 80–81, 85, 88; war against Iraq and, 199–204
Franco-Soviet Treaty of 1944, 18
Franks, Tommy, 192, 194
Frasure, Robert, 153
Freiberger, Steven, 28, 39
Freitas, Geoffrey de, 85
Fulbright, J. William, 79, 141

Gaitskell, Hugh, 59
Gandhi, Indira, 99–100
Gardner, Hall, 4
Gates, Thomas S., Jr., 66
General Assembly, UN, 68, 191; on Balkan Wars, 140, 183; establishing Department of Peacekeeping Operations, 215; lack of power to ensure compliance with directives, 41; NATO allies in, 86; new nations in, 72; protests against NATO actions in, 17–19, 49, 183; relation to Security Council, 16–17, 183; on Soviet invasion of Afghanistan, 96–101, 106, 111; Soviet isolation in, 2, 7, 16, 97; Soviet–U.S. relations in, 40–41; on Suez crisis, 36–37, 44; U.S. and, 97, 118, 183
General Framework Agreement for Peace in Bosnia and Herzegovina, 164–66
Geneva Accords (1954), 73, 86
Geneva Conference, 75–76, 87–88
German Democratic Republic, incorporated into Federal Republic, 115
Germany, 208–9; Balkan Wars and, 137–38, 152–53, 175; Desert Storm and, 123–26, 130; hostility toward U.S. in, 107–8, 198–99, 201; NATO and, 122, 124, 142, 168, 198; reunification of,

115, 122, 123, 130, 168; Soviets and, 7, 106–7, 112–13; in split among NATO allies, 201–3, 205; terrorism and, 189–90, 198; U.S. and, 83, 187, 198; war against Iraq and, 198, 201–4. See also East Germany
Gero, Erno, 39
Ghana, 52, 54–55
Gizenga, as pro-Soviet forces, 61
Glaspie, April, 116–17
Glenny, Misha, 137
Gomulka, Wladyslaw, 39
Gorbachev, Mikhail, 113–16, 120, 128
Gordon, Philip, 203
Granatstein, Jack, 4
Greece, 7, 28, 82, 125
Grenada, 98
Grimond, Jo, 59
Gromyko, Andrei, 17–18, 19, 87–88
Gruening, Ernest, 67
Guicherd, Catherine, 183
Guinea, 52, 54
Guiringaud, Louis de, 44
Gulf of Tonkin Resolution (1964), 74, 82, 117
Gulf War. See Desert Storm; Persian Gulf crisis
Guyana, 99

Haas, Richard, 197
Haekerrup, Per, 84
Hammarskjöld, Dag: in Congo crisis, 52–57, 62, 67–70; criticisms of, 53, 55, 57, 68–70, 72; other secretaries-general compared to, 26–27, 72, 91, 127; relations with U.S., 213; reputation of, 68, 72; as secretary-general, 26–27, 40; in Suez crisis, 27, 37–38, 43, 47
Hansen, Christian, 46
Hastings, Lord Ismay, 27, 48
Healey, Denis, 81–82
Helms, Jesse, 167
Hendrickson, Ryan C., 4–5, 110, 150, 163, 169, 188
Henkin, Louis, 182
Henrikson, Alan K., 4, 182, 215
Herter, Christian, 60, 66
Herzegovina, 142, 164–65
Hickerson, John D., 7, 10
History of NATO: The First Fifty Years (Schmidt), 4
Hitler, Adolf, 31–32

Suez crisis and, 33–35, 37; support for
Boutros-Ghali's second term in, 162;
on terrorism, 187–90; U.S.-Soviet
relations in, 114, 119; U.S. trying to get
resolution against Iraq from, 200–203;
U.S. war against Iraq and, 199–205; on
U.S. hostages taken in Iran, 101, 106;
Vietnam War and, 78, 86–87
Seguin, Philippe, 122
Senate, U.S.: defeat of League of Nations,
6, 9; Iraq war and, 206; isolationists
in, 8; NATO and, 7, 148–49; on
North Atlantic treaty, 12, 20–24, 26;
on Persian Gulf crisis, 117; UN and,
9–10, 162; on Vietnam War, 79. *See
also* Foreign Relations Committee, U.S.
Senate
Serbia, 139; calls for action against, 142,
183–84; cease-fire with Croatia, 139;
Kosovo as province of, 171, 176; NATO
air strikes against, 168–69, 179, 181;
NATO's willingness to strike against,
175–76; Russia as traditional protector
of, 160, 179; UN in, 142, 172; UN vs.
NATO in, 175, 182. *See also* Balkan
Wars; Milosevic
Serbs: aggressiveness of, 134, 146–47, 151;
atrocities by, 144–45, 148, 149, 155;
in Bosnia, 139; Bosnian, 151, 157–59,
170; calls for action against, 144–45,
150; on defensive, 153, 157; ethnic
cleansing by, 139–40, 169; flouting
UN authority, 138, 144–45, 148–49,
159; Milosevic and, 157, 170; Muslims
caught between Croats and, 166; NATO
action against, 144–45, 151, 180, 186;
NATO air strikes on, 146–47, 152, 157,
163; NATO and, 133–34, 153–54;
NATO vs. UN on, 148, 150, 186;
peace plans with, 158–59, 177, 181;
peacekeepers taken hostage by, 149,
151; territory for, 140, 153, 158; UN
sanctions against, 141–42, 144. *See also*
Balkan Wars
Shapiro, Jeremy, 203
Shevardnadze, Eduard, 115–16, 119–21
Shields, Mark, 118
Shuckburgh, Evelyn, 35
Singapore, 95
Sino-Soviet rift, 80
Slim, Mongi, 56–57, 72
Slovenia, 137, 138–39

Smith, Leighton, 154
Sobolev, Arkady, 40–41, 55
Society of Friends, opposition to NATO by,
16
Soffer, Jonathan, 115
Solana, Javier, 166, 179; background of,
167; on Kosovo, 173–74, 176, 180;
leadership of, 169, 214
Somalia, 95, 141
South East Asia, 74
South Vietnam, 83, 86; in domino theory,
80; effects of war on, 76; fall of, 90; U.S.
and, 73–74, 87; Vietcong as patriots in,
75. *See also* Vietnam War
Southeast Asia, 80–83
Soviet bloc. *See* Warsaw bloc
Soviet Union, 96–97; Afghanistan and,
92–93, 113; Africa and, 16, 49, 52,
57–58, 67–68; Arabs and, 91, 97;
boycotting of Moscow Olympics of,
103–4, 106–7; Carter and, 102, 104–5;
China and, 80, 95; colonialism and, 16,
29, 58, 98–99; Congo crisis and, 49–52,
55–57, 60–63, 67–68; containment of,
29, 42, 101, 105, 120; criticisms of UN
by, 68–69, 115; détente with, 110–13;
dissolution of, 1, 113–15, 124, 133,
138; Egypt and, 29–31, 42; Europe
and, 83, 115–16; European economic
ties to, 108, 112; Europeans' fear of, 7,
91–92; exploiting disagreements among
NATO partners, 3, 26, 37–38, 61,
71, 91; Hungary and, 26, 38–41, 46;
influence in Middle East, 42, 91, 101–2,
105, 120; invasion of Afghanistan by,
92, 106–13; Iraq and, 116, 119–21;
isolation in General Assembly, 2, 7, 16,
22; motives for invasion of Afghanistan
by, 95, 97–98, 101–2, 108–9; NATO
and, 1, 2, 49, 110–12, 187; NATO
conflicts with, 3, 26, 33, 213; NATO
formed in response to vetoes in Security
Council, 12–13, 15; nuclear weapons
of, 102, 122; opposition to North
Atlantic treaty, 14–15, 17–20, 26;
peace campaign by, 15–16; perestroika,
115–16; Persian Gulf crisis and, 119–21;
Poland and, 26, 39; pressure on Norway,
8, 14; relations with UN secretaries-
general, 27, 49, 55, 72, 96–97; relations
with U.S., 3, 16, 102, 115–16; relations
with West, 18–19; responses to invasion